Heart of Creation

Heart of Creation

The Mesoamerican World and the
Legacy of Linda Schele

Edited by
Andrea Stone

THE UNIVERSITY OF ALABAMA PRESS
Tuscaloosa and London

Copyright © 2002
The University of Alabama Press
Tuscaloosa, Alabama 35487-0380
All rights reserved
Manufactured in the United States of America

9 8 7 6 5 4 3 2 1
09 08 07 06 05 04 03 02 01

Typeface is AGaramond and Triplex

∞
The paper on which this book is printed meets the minimum requirements of American
National Standard for Information Science–Permanence of Paper for Printed Library
Materials, ANSI Z39.48–1984.

Library of Congress Cataloging-in-Publication Data

Heart of creation : the Mesoamerican world and the legacy of Linda Schele / edited by
Andrea Stone.
    p. cm.
Includes bibliographical references and index.
  ISBN 0-8173-1138-6
  1. Mayas. 2. Mayan languages—Writing. 3. Schele, Linda.   I. Stone, Andrea Joyce.
  F1435 .H4 2002
  972.81′016—dc21

                                                                                2001006525

British Library Cataloguing-in-Publication Data available

This book is dedicated to the memory of R. Benton (Ben) Leaf, by profession a Baltimore banker, by avocation a student of Maya epigraphy under Linda Schele. He followed her footsteps into the underworld on January 17, 1999.

Contents

Illustrations

Acknowledgments

Many individuals generously contributed their time and energy to this "labor of love" for a great Mayanist who left us all too soon at the height of her creative energy, intellectual powers, and leadership role in the arena of Maya studies. For assisting this tribute to Linda Schele, I would like to thank the director and staff of Pre-Columbian Studies at Dumbarton Oaks, which hosted me for a fellowship in 1998–99. The present volume was conceived and initially organized there, something that would have been impossible, or certainly much delayed, without the luxury of a Dumbarton Oaks fellowship. The cooperation of Linda's husband, David, was essential. He made her work available for reprinting and assisted in other small details. Simply put, without David's blessing, the project would have been scuttled. Alice Kehoe's comments on a draft of the introduction, as always, improved my writing. I extend thanks to two anonymous reviewers for their careful reading of the manuscript. They supplied more than the usual number of good suggestions for revision. Retired professor of Spanish at the University of Wisconsin-Milwaukee, Pierre Ullman kindly corrected the Spanish text and my translation of it. I am deeply grateful to all of the volume contributors; obviously without them this tribute would not have been possible. It is always a pleasure to work with friends, but especially so in this situation. I suspect that the spirit of the enterprise and their feelings for Linda made them a tad more cooperative than usual, much to my benefit. Tony Aveni was most helpful in locating the artwork that decorates the cover, a magnificent starry sky over the Pyramid of the Magicians at Uxmal created by Von Del Chamberlain, former director of the Hansen Planetarium in Salt Lake City. Von Del has generously allowed us to reproduce the photograph in honor of Linda to whom he showed the glories of the night sky in the planetarium theater in 1992. As might be expected, Linda was thrilled to see the Maya creation event writ large in the stars, and the experience of showing it to her was equally memorable for Von Del. I am indebted to Judy Knight of the University of Alabama Press for trying to make the editing process as painless as possible, even doing some of the "grunt" work herself when I could not meet her deadlines. She was quick acting and hands-on all the way through, rare qualities these days in a busy press editor. If it were not for her initial enthusiasm, this project would never have seen the light of day. The copy editor, Kathy Swain, showed patience and good humor as we sorted out endless details over the Internet.

This book is dedicated to Ben Leaf, who started out like hundreds of other avocational Mayanists, regularly attending the Texas hieroglyphic workshops where Linda Schele and the comradery of other like-minded folk drew him into serious glyph studies. Though maintaining his day job as a banker, Ben went on to be a fairly accomplished epigrapher. His most notable contribution is to the discovery of a future verbal form, **ut-om,** "it will happen." In a sense, Ben's is a textbook case of how the Texas workshops enriched the lives of nonacademics who not only benefited socially, emotionally, and intellectually from them but also reaped the rewards of making their own contributions to the field and eventually becoming glyph teachers themselves. The measure of Ben's affection for Linda, who got him into all of this, is evident in the fact that he flew to Guatemala to attend the service when her ashes were buried at Lake Atitlan. Unfortunately, he, like Linda, was taken away suddenly and prematurely, just a matter of months after her death. Although I cannot thank Ben now for letting me hitch a ride in his rented car to see archaeological sites in Yucatan some ten years ago, I can point out that he was the perfect layman-student of the ancient Maya under Linda Schele's tutelage.

I

Introduction

Andrea Stone

The last time I saw Linda Schele was in January of 1998. She had been battling pancreatic cancer since the previous summer, and her friends, gathering around her during this moment of crisis, held a symposium in her honor in Austin. The emotionally charged weekend culminated in a banquet, where I had the un-expected pleasure of sitting next to Linda. That evening we had a heart-to-heart talk, the most intimate I had ever had in the twenty years that I had known her. At its conclusion, I felt compelled to do something for my longtime mentor and blurted out that I would organize a session in her honor at the next meeting of the American Anthropological Association that was to be held in Philadelphia in December. Looking at me squarely in the eyes, she said: "I'll be there if I can."

Linda passed away a few months later, on April 18, 1998. On December 4 of that year the session was held, as promised. The speakers included Elin Danien, F. Kent Reilly III, Annabeth Headrick, Rex Koontz, Matthew Looper, Susan Milbrath, and Michael Coe, who served as discussant. The session was a cathar-tic experience for the covey of Linda admirers and curious onlookers who filled the hall that solemn winter evening. It began auspiciously, with the smell of copal incense filtering through the air, thanks, I later learned, to Duncan Earle, who was in the habit of doing this regardless of location or prevailing fire codes. Indeed, my thoughts turned to the smoke alarm system, which I was sure would go off at any moment and get us all thrown out of the room. Nevertheless, de-spite the steady stream of copal, the smoke alarm was silent, and the papers proceeded without a glitch. The first one was by Elin Danien, who spoke about Linda's role in the Maya hieroglyphic workshops. Precisely when she was talking about Linda, the microphone taped to the podium slipped and made a loud boom. Elin turned her eyes heavenward and said, "Sorry, Linda." The crowd let out a great roar, and I knew then that Linda had kept up her end of the bargain; she *was* there. By the time Michael Coe concluded with his moving eulogy, the emotional energy in the room reached a fever pitch. Taking all of this in among the crowd was Judith Knight from the University of Alabama Press, who encouraged me to turn the session into a volume.

Thus was born this tribute to Linda Schele, a collection of chapters both about and inspired by her contributions to the field of Mesoamerican studies. I wanted this book to be as much a statement about Linda's ebullient personality as her scholarly brilliance because the two were inseparable. To bring her personality to life, I envisioned a section of the book modeled after a much earlier one, *Morleyana* (Anderson 1950), a compendium of anecdotes about the great Mayanist Sylvanus G. Morley, whose passing left a similar sense of loss among his colleagues and vacuum in the field of Maya studies. Linda Schele deserves to be remembered in this way because she, like Morley, was one of the most colorful personalities ever to walk the earth as a Mayanist. To honor her in the spirit of Morley's tribute, I have included a section in the book called "Schele-ana." It offers remembrances from people who played significant, but quite different, roles in Linda's life: from her husband, David Schele, who recalls some of Linda's last hours; to one of her first students, Dorie Reents-Budet; to two of her most important collaborators, Mary Ellen Miller and David Freidel. Their charming stories not only capture Linda's indomitable spirit but also provide a valuable record of the personality of an age of Maya scholarship. There is something appropriate about honoring Linda in a Morleyesque fashion. She left us fifty years after the passing of Morley, who died in 1948. As Coe reminds us in his essay, Linda's role as the chief disseminator of knowledge to the general public about the ancient Maya parallels Morley, who held this role in the first half of the century. A comment made about Morley in one of his obituaries seems to have been written with Linda in mind: "It is hardly an exaggeration to say that he has done more to spread an intelligent interest in Maya civilization than anyone since Stephens, over a century ago" (Roys and Harrison 1949:215).

Included in this volume are three essays that directly address Linda's work. Anthony Aveni reflects on Linda's forays into Maya astronomy. Nikolai Grube and Federico Fahsen document the history of Linda's little-known but extremely important hieroglyphic workshops offered to the Maya of highland Guatemala and Yucatan, and Elin Danien discusses how the workshops held in Austin touched off a national craze.

The book also includes a collection of scholarly writings on Mesoamerican iconography, epigraphy, and astronomy, mostly by Linda's former students. To varying degrees, they owe a debt to her pathbreaking work and reveal how productive the insights in *Maya Cosmos* have been for the succeeding generation of

Mesoamericanists. Linda instilled in her students the notion that the Mesoamerican belief system materialized in the living world of art, architecture, and ritual performance. The chapters in this volume instantiate that maxim in case studies that span the Preclassic to the Colonial, from the Maya area to Central Mexico.

Linda would have been the first to admit that her own students helped forge the grand vision of *Maya Cosmos.* Among them, Matthew Looper observed that the glyphic spelling of "road" in a death phrase at Palenque refers to the Milky Way (Freidel et al. 1993:76). His discovery laid the groundwork for Linda's view of the Milky Way as a pathway—a river for celestial canoes and a road for the souls of the dead. In this volume, Looper decodes a masterpiece of Maya sculpture, Zoomorph P from Quirigua. As I realized in my 1983 dissertation on the Quirigua zoomorphs, this sculpture amalgamates imagery of world creation with a complexity unparalleled in the corpus of Maya art. Looper's intimate knowledge of the insights in *Maya Cosmos,* however, has allowed him to propose the first comprehensive explanation of all of the sculpture's mind-boggling details.

Linda's influence on Kathryn Reese-Taylor, who studied anthropology at Texas, is seen in Reese-Taylor's multidisciplinary approach to architectural analysis. Just as Linda sought to reunite Maya religion with the living reality of architecture, Reese-Taylor attempts to situate in the built environment the archetypal cosmic locations known from Classic inscriptions. She associates such locations as the Eight Partitions House and the Wits Mountain, discussed in *Maya Cosmos,* with specific buildings at Cerros, Uaxactun, and Tikal. Her chapter breathes life into the architectural space of Maya ruins by showing its relationship to the praxis of ritual processions.

The lessons of *Maya Cosmos* have made their mark on studies outside the Classic Maya realm proper. Their impact on the Mesoamerican Preclassic is illustrated in chapters by F. Kent Reilly III and Julia Guernsey Kappelman, both students of Linda. Reilly views the design of the Olmec site La Venta as a "landscape of creation . . . on which to enact the rituals of rulership," extending the *Maya Cosmos* vision of the charter of political legitimacy to the Olmec. He champions the idea that Classic Maya ideology and art can be used as a model for understanding basic themes of Olmec art. Most intriguing here is the notion that the mythic cycle of the death and resurrection of the Maize God, brilliantly elucidated in *Maya Cosmos,* is present in Olmec art. Kappelman's chapter echoes these ideas but in this case links Classic Maya Maize God imagery with Late Preclassic Izapan sculpture. The parallels are remarkably close, affirming connections between Izapan culture and early manifestations of lowland Maya culture.

Another Schele student, Rex Koontz, in analyzing Epiclassic El Tajin, benefits from a different set of revelations in *Maya Cosmos:* those concerning the iconography of warfare (Freidel et al. 1993:Ch. 7). Koontz identifies certain perforated sculptures at Tajin as the bases of war banners, just as *Maya Cosmos* showed the existence of stone banner supports at Maya sites and Teotihuacan. Koontz also invokes Coatepec, the mythic mountain associated with the birth of the Aztec's patron deity, as a model for understanding no less than the famous Pyramid of the Niches at El Tajin. His use of Coatepec symbolism forms a link with Linda's recent ideas, but here the influence flowed from student to teacher, as Linda graciously acknowledged in her book *The Code of Kings* (Schele and Mathews 1998:330, n. 18).

Annabeth Headrick similarly received her Ph.D. under Linda's aegis. Headrick's chapter concerns a nondescript, battered sculpture from Teotihuacan that, surprisingly, reveals insights into the kinds of ritual celebrations that may have been held there. This chapter was directly inspired by comments made to Headrick by Linda just before her death. The discussion of cosmic trees and pole-raising ceremonies echoes dominant themes in Linda's writing (e.g., Schele 1995a).

Constance Cortez received her M.A. degree under Linda Schele before heading to UCLA for a Ph.D. Her dissection of the imagery of the Xiu Family Tree, an illustration from a Colonial Yucatec chronicle, exploits an understanding of Classic Maya iconography gained from her days as a student of the Maya in Austin.

Neither Susan Milbrath nor Marc Zender formally studied with Linda Schele, but both authors delve into topics that Linda's work impacted. Milbrath's interests lie in Mesoamerican astronomy (Milbrath 1999); similarly, Maya astronomy was one of Linda's pet subjects. As Aveni's chapter suggests, through averments made in *Maya Cosmos* about the Milky Way and constellations, such as Scorpius and Orion, Linda advanced further than anyone before her the notion that Classic Maya imagery had astronomical correlates. She believed passionately that the Maya mapped their lore onto the shifting celestial patterns made by heavenly bodies. In the same spirit, Milbrath crafts an argument that the Maya viewed the serpent-footed God K as the planet Jupiter. Linda also had a long-standing interest in the meaning of God K.

Another of Linda's great contributions to Maya studies is her detailed reconstruction of Classic Maya dynastic history, epitomized by *A Forest of Kings* (Schele and Freidel 1990). Apart from this monumental work, throughout her long career Linda wrote ceaselessly on matters of Maya history in both formal publications and in the more informal Texas and Copán Notes series. Marc Zender's chapter adds to our knowledge of historical interaction along the Upper Usumacinta through an examination of local toponyms at three Maya sites. His chapter establishes the kind of nuts-and-bolts details of local history and site interaction that Linda absorbed like a sponge and used as building blocks in her masterful historical overviews. Indeed, one of her last major scholarly papers was on just this kind of material (Schele 1995b).

Among this collection of chapters that illustrate the depth and character of

Linda Schele's influence on Mesoamerican studies, I wanted to include a recent work by Linda herself. Rather than select something utterly new (made difficult by the fact that she did not leave many recent unpublished papers), I selected an article from the Texas Notes series that, though informally published, deserved a bit of polishing. Barbara MacLeod and I corrected and updated Linda's "Creation and the *Ritual of the Bacabs*" for the present volume. At first regretting that the article did not represent vintage Schele in that it does not focus on iconography, glyphs, or other aspects of material culture that she handled so deftly, I later realized that it signals other trends of her mature work. The article shows her increasing interest in drawing connections between the Classic Maya and those of much later periods, in this case the early Colonial period when the *Ritual of the Bacabs* was written. As Duncan Earle narrates so colorfully in his remembrance, Linda was gravitating ever more strongly toward the position that profound continuity exists between the Maya of old and those of the present. The article also reveals the depth of her knowledge about Maya ideology and imagery as she makes sense of the recondite allusions in the *Ritual of the Bacabs* by relating them to Classic Maya creation mythology and the astronomy that undergirded that mythology. As I read Linda's interpretations of the *Ritual of the Bacabs,* I felt as though I were listening to the musings of a high priest expounding on the intricacies of some arcane lore. Through an accumulation of knowledge over nearly three decades of brilliant research, Linda had achieved a kind of wisdom about the ancient Maya that transcended her time and place. Finally, the article illustrates Linda's abiding belief in the importance of the creation event as the legitimizing context of Maya religious and political expression. She herself stated, "Creation mythology, especially, provided the framework for political charter and historical causality" (Schele 1996:413). In the passages dissected in the *Ritual of the Bacabs,* the creation event is even shown by Linda to empower the curing process. The title of this book is taken from the incantation for "traveler seizure" in the *Ritual of the Bacabs,* analyzed in Linda's article. *Uy ol ch'ab',* "the heart of creation" in Yucatec Maya, captures the spirit of a line of inquiry about Maya religion central to her outlook. The title also alludes to Linda as a center of exceptional creativity within the universe of Mesoamerican scholars.

Linda Schele's Early Work

The story of Linda Schele's odyssey from Nashville, Tennessee, where she was born on October 30, 1942, to the ruins of Palenque in 1970 reads like a tale of personal discovery guided by the hand of destiny.[1] It almost seems that Linda Schele's fate was to spend her life as a Mayanist, even though her academic training was not the usual one for such a career. Linda earned undergraduate degrees in fine arts and education from the University of Cincinnati in 1964, settling on an M.F.A. degree from Cincinnati in 1968. When she first encountered the ancient Maya world in 1970, she was a professional painter, gainfully employed as an assistant professor in the Art Department of the University of South Alabama in Mobile. Yet she never looked back from her newfound vocation as a Mayanist once that fateful encounter was made.

Fate looked most kindly on Linda in guiding her to Palenque, a place where she could meet a circle of Mayanists who would nurture her through her early years and, without malice or jealousy, nudge her along the path to success. Academics are not always so accepting of those lacking the right credentials or Ivy League polish. Linda's bombastic, earthy manner, with all its color and warmth, did not even remotely match the stereotype of a serious scholar. In other circumstances Linda could have been ignored or treated with disdain.[2] The kind of reception she received during her first few years as a Mayanist, working in the "Palenque Circle," is evident in the reminiscences told at the end of this book by Merle Greene Robertson, Elizabeth Benson, David Kelley, and Gillett Griffin. The encouragement offered by these individuals, plus others such as the late Floyd Lounsbury, must have figured into her decision to plunge head-on into academia and leave the life of a practicing artist behind. It also is no accident that the hieroglyphic workshops that she instituted years later at the University of Texas at Austin fostered the same kind of uncritical acceptance of newcomers from which she had benefited.

Linda landed not only in the right spot among the right people but also at the right moment: when the state of knowledge of Maya hieroglyphic writing had reached a critical mass and was about to explode at the First Mesa Redonda de Palenque meeting in 1973. She was a major player in the intellectual advances made at that meeting. The breakthroughs concerning the historical reconstruction of the Palenque dynasty were of such magnitude that Linda was catapulted into the limelight and was to remain there for the rest of her career. Her rise in the Maya field was immediate. It is remarkable to think that she gazed upon her first Maya ruin in 1970 and by the mid-1970s was already widely influential.

The elements of Linda's unique brand of genius that continued throughout her long career can be detected in her earliest work. She wrote her first paper on Palenque in 1972,[3] began to give papers as a professional Mayanist in 1973, and published her first paper in 1974. Even as a neophyte Mayanist, she wrote in a strong, authoritative voice, exuding confidence and a sense of expertise on complex subjects. How could anyone so new to a field do this? First, she wrote only about what she knew intimately, subjects she had mastered, usually from firsthand experience. Part of her genius lay in her ability to excel at virtually whatever she attempted, in skills that went well beyond her training in the arts, a testimony to her native brilliance. Her strategy of "total conquest" over a subject meant that her work remained relatively focused, at least in the first decade of her career. This was not the case with most other scholars of Maya art, who often worked from published sources and handily jumped from site to site.

In those early years, Linda concentrated on the art and epigraphy of Palenque. She published articles in 1974, 1976, and 1977 dealing specifically with the Cross Group and Sarcophogus Lid. At this time she also produced a major study, which was never published, of the iconography of the Sarcophogus sides, work conducted with Floyd Lounsbury, Peter Mathews, and David Kelley at a Dumbarton Oaks mini-conference. In 1979 she published "Genealogical Documentation on the Tri-Figure Panels of Palenque" and, with Peter Mathews, a catalogue of the Palenque *bodega*. During the mid-1970s Linda was also compiling a glyph-by-glyph commentary on the Cross Group and Temple of the Inscriptions Tablets. These commentaries became the basis of the first notebooks for the Texas workshops on Maya hieroglyphic writing. The herculean work she did at the Texas workshops on the Palenque inscriptions beginning in 1978—these workshops focused exclusively on Palenque for about ten years and forced Linda to codify annually the changing state of knowledge—worked perfectly with her instincts to hammer away at complex material. By returning to the same material over and over, Linda was able to refine, update, and advance her ideas so that they assumed tremendous authority and matured rapidly into evermore sophisticated and all-encompassing paradigms. Her ideas were influential in shaping the general direction of the field.

Thus, Linda dominated her subject by means of a rigorous focus; her exceptional natural abilities; the sheer intensity of her attack on a problem; and the boldly creative, sometimes unorthodox, approaches she took to finding solutions. Her responses were not the conventional ones inculcated by academic training. She worked intuitively, engaging her subjects with a unique freshness that was constantly reinventing itself. Whatever it took, she did it, whether it was devising an experiment, making her own maps and architectural drawings, or conferring with specialists. She also relished coauthoring before it became de rigueur in hieroglyphic studies by the late 1980s. Linda coauthored more than one hundred books, articles, workshop notebooks, and notes with twenty different individuals, an impressive number of collaborative publications for someone in the humanities. Coauthoring added strength to her intellectual stance and reflected a deep commitment to the interdisciplinarity of Maya studies. She begins her article "The Palenque Triad: A Visual and Glyphic Approach," written in 1976, with the following: "This paper on methodology evolved from conversations between Mayanists with linguistic, glyphic, and iconographic specialties on the kinds of data that each specialty could and should provide to the other." Her belief in the necessity of interdisciplinary dialogue and her reliance on intellectual cross-fertilization was at a conscious level of her thinking.

In "Palenque: The House of the Dying Sun," published in 1977, Linda recounts an experiment she conducted with David Joralamon in which they watched the setting winter solstice sun illuminate the God L Panel in the Temple of the Cross and, as seen from the Tower, descend behind the Temple of the Inscriptions. Here, Linda wears the hat of a field scientist collecting empirical data. These direct observations of celestial events powerfully reinforce her interpretation of the Palenque emblem glyph, making her arguments seem as unassailable as those put forth by Pakal in mortar and stone to assert his own divinity. As an impressionable student sitting in her class, I recall her describing these astronomical revelations with such drama that I went to Palenque myself to take my own pictures of the winter solstice hierophany.

That is not to say Linda did not emulate the older generation of Mayanists. Indeed, her first solo article published in 1974, "Observations on the Cross Motif," shows particularly strong influences from the establishment, something that is not surprising to see, even for someone as creative as Linda, in such an early effort. This paper closely follows the ideas of previously published sources on the Cross Group, mainly those of George Kubler, Heinrich Berlin, and David Kelley. Kubler's name crops up repeatedly in the article. As the consummate art historian, certainly the most preeminent in Precolumbian art of his day, Kubler's pronouncements on things visual carried great weight. His monograph *Studies in Classic Maya Iconography* (1969) returns repeatedly to the art historical notion of themes. For instance, Kubler (1969:2) laid out a Panofskian framework for iconographic analysis using Panofsky's categories of natural subject matter, themes, and intrinsic subject matter. He spoke of "thematic recognition" (3) and said that the murals of Bonampak were a "narrative expansion of the principal themes of Classic Maya iconography" (13). In "Observations on the Cross Motif," Linda's invocation of "thematic correspondences" between the Cross Group and the Temple of the Inscriptions reveals Kubler's influence. Kubler's systematic approach to Maya iconography was the most sophisticated thing around in Maya studies when Linda leapt onto the stage, and, having just been published, *Studies in Classic Maya Iconography* was state of the art. No wonder she was drawn to it in early attempts at finding her own voice.

Linda's second solo article, "Accession Iconography of Chan Bahlum" (1976), has the more assertive quality that we have come to expect. She speaks in her distinct idiom of an engaged scholar using the observations of colleagues as a stimulus for exciting new ideas. She openly narrates her own learning processes, correcting former assumptions, as though the reader has become privy to her personal revelations. This compelling narrative style later reaches its dramatic peak in *Maya Cosmos* (and, as Aveni notes, it was not universally embraced). The ideas in "Accession Iconography" seem more strongly influenced by Floyd

Lounsbury than those in "Observations on the Cross Motif," and now there is discussion of the *Popol Vuh* and astronomy: shades of *Maya Cosmos*. The article also uses dictionary entries; for instance, it discusses Kelley's discovery not only that Landa's *le* glyph could be translated as "leaf" but also that it had secondary meanings associated with lineage. To prove this point, Linda lists the relevant dictionary entries in Yucatec and also discusses dictionary work she had conducted with Jeffrey Miller. "Accession Iconography" first reveals a methodology carried through Linda's later work: identifying the linguistic correlates of iconographic/glyphic elements. Few Mayanists of the time, let alone art historians, did this as competently as she nor understood the ramifications of their findings so well. Thus, "Accession Iconography of Chan Bahlum" contains the latest understanding of Palenque's dynastic history, treats the iconography of the Cross Group with a kind of sophistication worthy of George Kubler, and includes new drawings. The measure of its influence can be seen in the number of articles in the Third Mesa Redonda de Palenque volumes, published in 1979 and 1980, that cite "Accession Iconography" as well as Linda's earlier Mesa Redonda papers: nearly every one.

By her own admission in "The Palenque Triad: A Visual and Glyphic Approach," Linda considered herself foremost a specialist in Maya art more than a specialist in Maya writing. With her background as a practicing artist, her greatest confidence lay in her visual skills, such that she conveyed a sense of understanding the mindset that produced the extraordinarily complex Classic Maya imagery. She attempted to analyze Maya art from an emic perspective and framed her language in terms of what the Maya "chose" to do visually. She stressed the logic and systematic nature of Maya iconography. In "The Palenque Triad," she shows how each member of the triad was depicted in three-dimensional sculpture, based on her original drawings of the Palenque bodega sculpture, and then how the three-dimensional forms translated into two-dimensional representations. What appeared to be oddly distorted abstractions were actually logical projections of a three-dimensional object onto a two-dimensional plane. No Mayanist before her had dealt with the transmogrifications of forms rotating in space in such a convincing way. Although Spinden had talked about frontal and profile representations in *A Study of Maya Art* as early as 1913, he did not bring it to Linda's level of specificity.

To put Linda's manner of thinking about forms in space in perspective, I might contrast it with that of George Kubler, whose depth of scholarship in art history made him such a towering figure on visual issues. Kubler's approach to spatial analysis tended to be spectator oriented. He would typically re-create the viewer's subjective experience observing art works, say, walking through the rooms housing the Bonampak murals. The approach was more etic in that it established how space and form would strike any observer. On the other hand, Linda's spatial analyses often emphasized a kind of culturally embedded internal logic that had to be discovered.

For example, in *Studies in Classic Maya Iconography* in regard to the Tablet of the Foliated Cross, Kubler comments that the leaf that the "short figure" (Pakal) stands on "could not bear the man's weight" (6–7). He also notes that the scale of the figure in the shell would not correspond to the same visual order of the principal figures; he then points out that Kan B'alam stands on a zoomorphic head of yet another scale. These observations make a case for the conceptual nature of spatial relationships in the Tablet of the Foliated Cross but at the same time project a sense of the Maya's inconsistency, perhaps even confusion, in combining figures of different scales. By contrast, Linda would often rationalize apparent inconsistencies; we might be looking at a scene from the inside out or from heaven to earth. In all cases, the artistic choices fit into a coherent visual system that requires work to be understood, but once understood may be seen as brilliant. In "The Palenque Triad" Linda asserts, "The precision of Maya two-dimensional drawings suggests a strong tradition and training for accurate observation and skilled reproduction in flat contour patterns of observed three-dimensional phenomena" (Schele 1979a:409). Linda's belief in the logical integrity of the ancient Maya's representational system is an underlying assumption in her writing.

By 1979 her article "The Puleston Hypothesis: The Water Lily Complex in Classic Maya Art and Writing," a major paper that, unfortunately, was never published, shows another stage in the evolution of her work of the 1980s, when she was permanently settled in her role as professor of art history at the University of Texas at Austin. Her concern is not Palenque but a broadly conceived iconographic analysis, in classic Schele fashion stimulated by conversations with a colleague, this time Dennis Puleston, regarding the ecosystem of raised fields and their implications for Maya iconography. As with most of Linda's work, the paper is highly interdisciplinary, meshing dirt archaeology, linguistics, and iconography. The reading of the *imix* glyph as *naab'*, "water-lily" and "a body of still water," as opposed to Thompson's idea of "abundance," is a revelation in this paper that eventually led to the identification of the *imix* glyph as water and the plazas in the architectural space of Mesoamerican ceremonial centers as symbolic oceans (Schele and Grube 1990). The fact that the Puleston paper uses a glyphic decipherment as a touchstone is characteristic of Linda's work of the 1980s, such as "Human Sacrifice among the Classic Maya" (1984b), with its *nawah* reading, and her *"Balan-Ahau"* paper (1985). Linda also considers the water-lily complex through time, particularly in Olmec and Izapan cultures. Much of this is a departure from her work of the 1970s, which was tightly focused on Maya topics, and it clearly points to her growing interest in showing the pan-Mesoamerican basis, particularly the Olmec roots, of Maya iconography. Indeed, Linda's work of the 1990s explores great mythic paradigms in Mesoamerican ideology and art. She saw widespread patterns in the symbolism of the world tree, the world mountain, and the act of world creation (Freidel et al. 1993:132; Schele 1996). Her latest work incorporates Central Mexican material concerning the legendary Tollan and Coatepec into a theoretical model of pan-Mesoamerican founding myths (Schele and Kappelman 2001; Schele and Mathews 1998:37–40). She was moving ineluctably toward a new, all-encompassing vision of Mesoamerican culture history that, had she lived, might have been the subject of her next book.

Linda seemed to derive her phenomenal energy and enthusiasm from the fact that she was part of an enterprise to transform radically our understanding of the ancient Maya. She wrote in 1976, "I believe that the study of the Maya is on the threshold of major breakthroughs" (Schele 1976:10).[4] She never stopped repeating this message. It was a drumbeat of her role as a teacher, for she energized her own students by making them believe that they were on the same mission. It was also a dictum in her own research that strove to break barriers and transform thinking in a radical way. By the 1990s she seemed at home with the notion of rapidly discarding her own outmoded paradigms. New evidence, particularly hieroglyphic evidence, was constantly altering the factual basis of our understanding of the ancient Maya. Linda was unapologetic about offering up new interpretations in fairly rapid succession. This could be seen as a source of criticism of her work, but it fits the reality of Maya studies as in a perennial state of revision.

Linda's determination to make ancient Maya history and religion come alive, reaching out in an unprecedented way to popular audiences, represents the culmination of a tradition of humanistic thought that shaped Mesoamerican studies in the late nineteenth and early twentieth centuries (Willey and Sabloff 1993:73). At the turn of the century a cadre of humanists and antiquarians, dominated by Europeans, particularly Germans such as Eduard Seler, Hermann Beyer, and Ernst Förstemann, were highly influential and published prolifically on ancient writing, language, religion, astronomy, ethnohistory, and ethnology, all of which were fodder for reconstructing the ideological motivations of the ancient Maya and explaining their culture and religion in fairly vivid terms. Fortunately, even after the overhaul of Maya archaeology, beginning in 1929 when Kidder replaced Morley at the Carnegie Institution and introduced "a 'pan-scientific' methodology to produce a cultural synthesis of the Maya" (Givens 1992:142), the thread of humanistic studies continued, largely through research on the Maya writing system, whose importance was never lost. A resurgence of research on Maya writing after World War II, stimulated by the discoveries by Yuri Knorosov on phoneticism and Tatiana Proskouriakoff and Heinrich Berlin on the historical basis of Maya texts, swept up Linda in the 1970s. She not only rode the crest of that wave but also fulfilled the humanistic promise of Mesoamerican studies. In this regard she has established the model among Mesoamericanists for transforming complex, narrowly focused research into books that are compelling and paint a broad picture of ancient cultures that can be comprehended by any interested reader.

If imitation is the sincerest form of flattery, then I could not have flattered Linda more myself. As a student of hers in the late 1970s and early 1980s, I copied everything she did. I used the same kind of pen (a Pilot, razor sharp, usually red); adopted the same kind of filing system, the evidence of which I still see in the hanging files in my study; used the same kinds of techniques for making illustrations and slides and from her learned to use Kodalith and LPD-4 film; and copied her in other innumerable ways. She was simply so good at everything she did, from the intellectual to the technical. Fortunately, she has had such a lasting impact on her students and colleagues, which the remaining chapters in this volume will demonstrate, that her approach to the enterprise of understanding ancient Mesoamerican culture will live on in their work and the work of their students.

Notes

1. Details of Linda Schele's personal life and career are documented in Coe (1992:201–203) as well as a series of obituaries, including Freidel (1998); Grube (1998); Reilly and Henderson (1998); Coe (2000); Palaima et al. (2000); and Kelley (2000). Tremendous personal insights can be gleaned from the film *Edgewalker: A Conversation with Linda Schele.*

2. Coe (1992:201) minces no words as to how the Carnegie crowd would have reacted to Linda.

3. Linda cites this paper, "Observations on the Palace at Palenque," as a work written in 1972 in another early paper, "The Attribution of Monumental Architecture to Specific Palenque Rulers," which she gave at the Forty-first International Congress of Americanists in 1974. Neither of these papers was published. She also lists "Observations of the Palaces at Palenque," probably the same paper, as a work of 1973 (Schele 1974).

4. This comment appears in the manuscript version of the paper but was omitted from the published version.

Reaching for the Stars

Linda Schele's Contributions to Maya Astronomy

Anthony Aveni

Of the moral effect of the monuments themselves, standing as they do in the depths of the tropical forest, silent and solemn, strange in design, excellent in sculpture, rich in ornament, different from the works of any other people, their uses and purposes, their whole history so entirely unknown, with hieroglyphics explaining all but perfectly unintelligible, I shall not pretend to convey any idea. . . . No Champollion has yet brought to them the energies of his inquiring mind. Who shall read them?

—John Lloyd Stephens (1841:158–160)

Nineteenth-century explorer John Lloyd Stephens wrote that statement when he first stood agog amid Copan's stelae. He would move on to Uxmal, Chichen Itza, Palenque—all the great sites we know so well. Linda and I came to Palenque, too. We arrived separately in the same year, 1970, for our first awe-inspiring encounters with Mesoamerica's monuments. She came to draw the carvings, I to measure the orientations of the buildings they adorned. Though we would become fast friends and colleagues, the real meeting of our minds would not take place for two decades.

For Förstemann, Morley, and even Thompson it can fairly be said that "reading hieroglyphic texts" was all in the numbers. Tales of the indefatigable Vay Morley donned in pith helmet and spats clambering over vines in search of a decipherable Long Count are legion. And who can forget Thompson's famous description of Maya astronomer priests strutting about Copan's equivalent of the Athenian Agora, their minds preoccupied with otherworldly thoughts? "So far as this general outlook on life is concerned, the great men of Athens would not have felt out of place in a gathering of Maya priests and rulers, but had the conversation turned on the subject of the philosophical aspects of time, the Athenians— or, for that matter, representations of any of the great civilizations of history— would have been at sea" (Thompson 1954:162).

This was the paradigm on the Maya inscriptions that ruled the first half of the twentieth century: glyphs were all about the gods depicted on the stelae— gods who roamed the sky executing their pristine periodicities. To know their own fate the Maya became obsessed with tracking down these cosmic denizens and expressing their wanderings numerologically, like their Old World counterparts, the Babylonians, whose astronomical cuneiform texts were in the midst of a decipherment heyday. Halfway through our century, however, Tatiana Proskouriakoff, with the help of Heinrich Berlin and others, changed all that. The view of the Maya they proffered revealed the content of the engravings that so mystified Stephens to be more human than transcendent. The characters enveloped in the numbers and glyphs became representations of very real, royal people. Moreover, the events so precisely meted out had more to do with birth, death, and local place rather than eclipse, conjunction, and lunation.

Still, thoughts about Maya astronomy were not extinguished; they were only relegated to the back burners of scholarship. David Kelley, Floyd Lounsbury, and later Victoria and Harvey Bricker, John Justeson, and others continued their studies of numeration and astronomy, though much of it was concentrated on the codices, where cosmological interests linked with divinatory matters made good sense.

Meanwhile, in the wake of Great Britain's Stonehenge controversy of the 1960s, the interdisciplinary field of archaeoastronomy, which occupied my interest and that of my colleague, Horst Hartung, along with a number of others, began inquiries into the role of sacred landscapes in the expression of astronomical concepts in the unwritten record. Pity that we archaeoastronomers paid too little attention to the glyphs.

By the mid-1970s Linda, with one Mesa Redonda de Palenque under her belt, was already beginning to be established as one of the major respondents to Stephens's question cited in my epigraph. I first experienced the absolute magnitude of Linda's luminosity (to put it in astronomical terms) on the occasion of the Second International Archaeoastronomy Conference held at Colgate in the fall of 1975. I had invited her to present an exploratory paper on Palenque hierophanies and their link to emblem and skull variant glyphs (Schele 1977). Following a long rainy first day of papers we were all rollicking in the stuffy, colonially appointed dining room of the Colgate Inn at the obligatory banquet. Over in one corner I spotted Dave Kelley and Linda (still clad in their raincoats) preoccupied in deep, animated discussion. They were drawing glyphs on napkins, and when they exhausted that medium, they moved on to the larger domain of the tablecloth. Meanwhile, the meal coursed from appetizer to soup, through the main course, each plate being presented and taken away to the oblivion of most absorbed participants. As the desserts were wheeled out, Linda's brain suddenly landed back on planet earth. She abandoned her eye-to-eye contact with the elfin Kelley and blurted out "Hey, where's my (expletive deleted) peas? Somebody took away my peas! I wasn't finished!" Linda's newfound reputation as an eccentric epigrapher received a significant boost that night. She got her peas!

I think Linda took the first steps toward integrating the Maya historical and astronomical paradigms that occupied the first two-thirds of our century when she worked on *The Blood of Kings* (1986) with Mary Ellen Miller. A gloriously rich text not just for the images that appear in it, *The Blood of Kings* is also a book about cosmology and the role of sacred space in the formulation of arguments about the developed ideologies of the Maya ruling class. Here I first truly appreciated the temple as the gateway to the maw of the underworld, and I began to discern how the iconography associated with the buildings often lent support to all those astronomical alignments Hartung and I had been measuring and analyzing. After a discussion of a new kind of iconography that was introduced circa 50 B.C.E. in Structure 5C-2nd at Cerros involving the sun and Venus, Schele and Miller explain: "For the Maya, the purpose of state art was to construct symbolic arrays and thus to define models of social reality whose purpose was generating social cohesion. The Maya solution to social crisis was not to manipulate economics or intensify agricultural technology; instead, they adjusted ideology" (1983:106). The case may be overstated, but the implication is clear: Politics and astronomy, dynastic history and the cosmos are not strange bedfellows after all.

If *The Blood of Kings* hints, *A Forest of Kings* (1990), with David Freidel, flatly proclaims that what happened in the sky played a major role in legitimizing Maya rulership on terra firma. Developing an idea first discussed by Virginia Miller (1989) and Ellen Baird (1989), Linda traces the Tlaloc-Star-War symbolism deep into Maya dynastic history by naming names and tying them to specific sky events. The sheer force of the number of detailed decipherments in *A Forest of Kings* stands as a significant contribution to Maya studies, but this was not enough to overcome critical reaction to the style of the prose. Some scholarly readers were put off by Linda and David's novelistic narrative, for example their portrayal of the capture of Uaxactun's ruler by the Lord of Tikal:

In spite of all their efforts, Smoking-Frog and his company swirled around
the base of the king's pyramid, killing and capturing the valiant warriors
of the Uaxactun royal clan. The king and his men fought to the last. At
the moment of his capture, the king of Uaxactun reached furiously for
Smoking-Frog's throat. Laughing, the Tikal lord jerked him to his knees by
his long bound hair. The defeated king glared up at the arrogant Smoking-
Frog, costumed in the regalia of the new, barbarous warfare—the round
helmet, the spearthrower, and the obsidian club. He cursed him as his captor's minions stripped him bare and tied his elbows behind his back with
rough sisal rope. (1990:153)

My problem with *A Forest of Kings,* however, was that much of the astronomical analysis suffered from inaccuracy. Being a nitpicker I remember questioning
the content of the three-page-long footnote 47 of chapter 4 in which Linda lists
all the sky phenomena she correlates with dynastic events carved on the stelae. I
observed that many of the events Linda chose to fit with dates of civic or religious significance just did not happen when she said they did. And without statistical analysis and the inclusion of information about ranges of visibility of
given phenomena, it became difficult for the reader to determine the degree of
arbitrariness involved in her association of actual celestial events with key points
in dynastic history. Nonetheless, I was struck by the way real-time astronomy
crept into the analysis. I ended up writing a thirty-three-page paper in which I
conducted my own analysis beginning with the proposed sky events in that footnote (along with additional ones in *Maya Glyphs: The Verbs* [1982] [Aveni and
Hotaling 1994]).
     One problem in linking Long Count dates with astronomical events is that
there are so many of the latter from which to choose. In addition, sky phenomena
such as "Venus at maximum elongation (from the sun)" are difficult to pin down
to an accuracy of less than several days, so how do we know whether the implied
connections are real or fortuitous? (Milbrath also addresses this question in chapter 8 of this volume.) Our study explored the nature of Maya exact science
through a statistical consideration of culturally tagged astronomical date sets in
the monumental inscriptions, arranged by category of sky observation rather
than (as it is usually done) by that of site provenance. Having dealt with all the
probabilities, we concluded that Maya astronomers did indeed make some deliberate correlations between chronology recorded on the monuments and astronomical phenomena reckoned in real time. Although scholars will continue to
debate whether the inscriptions in the codices are tied directly to Maya secular
history and whether the astronomical portions of the inscriptions indicate mean
timings or precisely recorded ones or forecast astronomical phenomena, we
found that certain monuments more likely were intended to mark staged celebra-

tory events that required the proper astronomical backdrop: Venus high in the sky, morning star returning, Jupiter in retrograde, and so on.

Venus events were especially significant in the monumental inscriptions, a result we might well have expected given the ethnohistoric evidence. Contrary to what we find in the Venus Table in the *Dresden Codex,* the first evening rather than the first morning appearance is more significant. This result we attributed to the fact that evening appearances were more accessible to the viewer in the spatiotemporal setting of the Maya Classic, the morning view often having been obscured by proximity to the sun and the angle from the horizon. This makes sense if you want the most impressive cosmic backdrop to grace the ritual stage. Also, it raises the possibility that the Maya may have observed different aspects of the planet at different times in their history. That the Maya paid considerable attention to Venus when it strayed farthest from the sun was very clear from the analysis. Finally, we discovered that the Maya employed like-in-kind observations; thus they watched departures from the second stationary point of the superior planets, particularly Jupiter, and related those to the perceptible descent of Venus from maximum altitude toward the sun.

Although our study of astronomy in the monumental inscriptions provides an accurate and relatively complete listing of astronomical dates in the monumental inscriptions accompanied by statistical analysis of those dates, it would not have been accomplished without Linda's bold and original assertions. Bottom line: but for the detail Linda was correct! The Maya rulers *were* charting out seminal events in their lives by employing timed celestial phenomena as benchmarks. With *A Forest of Kings* the synthesis of natural and dynastic histories in the monumental inscriptions was well under way.

I was there at the Eighth Mesa Redonda de Palenque in 1993—there in the "steam room" disco made over into a lecture hall on the outskirts of town that replaced the old *palapa* at Moises Morales's La Cañada—to witness one of Linda's most magnificent tours de force. There she formally presented the concept of the Milky Way as a cosmic tree, the one writ large in that celebrated chapter 2 of her *Maya Cosmos* (Freidel et al. 1993; see also Schele and Villela 1996). Seated in the front now, I was positioned within Schelean "Ik range" as she passionately plucked transparency after transparency off the overhead and cast each at our collective feet with the virtuoso moves of a Leonard Bernstein—Brava! What a performance! Earlier she had greeted me with that archetypal ursine abrazo that anyone who has been hugged by Linda knows so well: "You're right, Tony! Venus was really it for the Maya!"

I remember having mixed feelings about *Maya Cosmos* when I reviewed it in *American Anthropologist* in 1996. I dubbed it "a curious combination of reasoned scholarship and emotional revelation" (Aveni 1996:97). Maybe I am just a stuffy academic, but I thought the authors too often characterized themselves as "stunned," "breathless," and "beside themselves" when making discoveries. One disclosure was termed "mind-blowing," another "like a lightning bolt in my mind." Although Linda and David may have employed this tactic to affect a popular audience, I worried that they risked putting off too many of their professional colleagues and that consequently their arguments would lose efficacy.

Creation as revealed in the sky was the subject of that controversial second chapter. These "eureka" pages, I thought, were among the most boldly creative in the entire text, even though I had not been completely sold on all the findings. My critique of this chapter deserves some elaboration because it raises the issue of how we might understand the kind of astronomy the ancient Maya actually practiced. The basic idea was that many of the major images from Maya cosmic symbolism are actually maps of the sky. The foundation of this hypothesis, elaborated in detail in chapter 3 of this volume, is rooted in the concept of the Milky Way as world axis standing in the middle of the cosmos. This pale white streak so distinctly visible in the dark skies over Mesoamerica aligns north-south on dates that commemorate the day of creation in monumental inscriptions. The well-known Classic ceramic identified as the Blow Gunner Pot loomed as a major key to the decipherment puzzle. It shows one of the hero twins of the *Popol Vuh* (the K'iche' Maya version of the myth of creation) shooting down an impostor sunbird, emblematic of a previous creation, who is perched in a treetop. A scorpion is positioned to the right of the base of the tree—just the way the celestial scorpion (generally, if not unanimously, regarded to be the same as that of the Western zodiac) lies astride the Milky Way. This schema becomes the takeoff point for the identification of additional real sky elements in the cosmic myth.

Crossing the Milky Way at the overhead point at the putative moment of Maya creation is the zodiac snake, the identity of its component constellations having been gleaned from images on ceramics, in the codices, and via linguistic analysis. For example, the three stones of creation mentioned in the *Popol Vuh* are identified as being located in Orion, while our Gemini, the Twins, becomes the copulating peccaries found in the murals of Bonampak. The latter marks one of the intersection points of the Milky Way and the zodiac.

Although many of Linda's constellation identifications make sense, as does the notion that the sky is a kind of blackboard for sketching out stories relating supernatural and human affairs, some of her arguments could be disputed on the grounds that not much symbolism linking trees and the Milky Way has emerged in the Maya ethnographic literature and that alternative identifications of some of the constellations are possible. See, for example, the work of Harvey Bricker and Victoria Bricker (1993) on the Maya zodiac. At a deeper conceptual level I questioned the concept of mapping in general. When Linda and David generated their map of the sky on the night of a creation ritual dated C.E. 690 in the inscriptions of Palenque, they discovered that *it works:* their sky map fits their interpretation of a pattern on the Blow Gunner Pot or on the famous Sarcophagus Lid in the Temple of Inscriptions, which shows the deceased ruler plummeting down the tree of life toward the jaws of the underworld and ultimate apotheosis. Yet the map or template that informs *what works* in the creation ritual, according to David and Linda's interpretation, functions too much like a map in Western culture. However, there is little indication in the Mesoamerican record (or anywhere else outside the West for that matter) that indigenous representational devices really exist that consist of two-dimensional surfaces depicting scalar projection of the relative position of selected features in a topography—the true definition of a map.

Even if the iconographic texts that Linda interpreted as maps do more or less *work,* there are other questions. First, does the south-to-north axis of the Milky Way really transform into an upright tree? This depends on whether "north" is the same as "up" in Maya directional symbolism, a case for which has been made in the literature. Second, the Maya were astute astronomers who watched the sky as a way of comprehending the many cycles that unfolded above as well as around them. Still, which cycles were they concerned with in these cosmographic texts? They could have been expressing seasonal rather than epochal cycles, for Linda's sky mapping scheme works just as well in this regard. Such alternative interpretations need some attention.

When Andrea Stone asked me to write about Linda's contribution to Maya astronomy for this volume, I went back to *Maya Cosmos* for a brief reread. I must confess it looks better to me now than it did then, especially since McGee and Reilly (1997) have now documented many of Linda's identifications in contemporary Lacandon cosmology. I am still not sure the Milky Way is the world tree. Nevertheless, even if the birth date of the universe turns out not to have been singled out in the particular iconographies to which Linda refers, clearly she has made her point: the Maya were reflecting in their ritual behavior in microcosmic time the actions they believed were exhibited by their ancestors, the gods, in the cycles that make up the web of time in the macrocosm.

Maya Cosmos will not be the last word on the Maya expression of cosmic belief. Nonetheless, this vast storehouse of information laced with provocative ideas, which dares to cross the uncrossable chasm of cultural continuity by attempting to link Maya past and present, will stimulate the meeting of the minds of Mayanists for years to come. Thus the integration of cosmos and history continues thanks to Linda's originality, not to mention her chutzpah!

What fresh furrows of the Mesoamerican cosmic mentality might Linda have plowed had she stayed with us? *The Code of Kings* (with Peter Mathews 1998), fresh out on the eve of her demise, is fast becoming the great synthetic overview of sacred space and dynastic rulership. It reveals the myriad ways in which cosmological ideas are expressed in a variety of urban settings. I already have in mind several astronomical problems I will need to work on as a result of reading it. And what of those voluminous Copán and Texas Notes to which we Linda aficionados subscribed via Kinko's? I can see the potential for integrating the contents of many of the astronomical ideas expressed in the notes with those related in her last great work. Here alone she has left a rich legacy for future students of Maya astronomy.

Beneath Linda's genius, her showboat personality, her fearless will to undertake boldly so many next steps, lay an incredibly infectious enthusiasm. This is what I think sparked her desire to popularize—the workshops, the tours, the wish to go to any length to please. Her charisma aroused displeasure and I think, even envy among some of her colleagues. Linda's was an unorthodox sort of behavior for the scholar (especially the epigrapher), who is generally stereotyped to live a lonely life among the stacks with laptop in tow. I believe this ineradicable capacity to reach out is one hallmark of the truly great teacher. For me it reached a crescendo in a correspondence I had with Linda back in 1988. I was writing *Empires of Time* (1989), and I wanted to trace Linda's characterization of the merging of legendary and "real" history delineated in the inscriptions of the Tablet of the Cross at Palenque. I thought it useful to include as a figure in my book Linda's exquisite drawing of Pakal handing over the instruments of office to Kan B'alam, so I wrote her for permission to reproduce it. The reply I received is like no other in my thirty-five years of publishing. It went like this: "Dear Tony, Of course you may have permission to reproduce any of my drawings for publication anytime and anywhere. Sincerely, Linda." Sincerely, Tony.

3

Creation and the *Ritual* of *the Bacabs*

Linda Schele (edited by Barbara MacLeod and Andrea Stone)[1]

The *Ritual of the Bacabs* is a collection of curing chants for the treatment of disease. Since the publication of its translation by Roys (1965), the *Ritual of the Bacabs* has received sporadic attention from scholars studying Classic Maya cultural traditions (Freidel and Schele 1988a), perhaps because the reference system in the *Bacabs* is so obscure as to appear unintelligible to a person not raised in the tradition. This state began to change when David Freidel and I were preparing our study of the creation myths of the Classic Maya period for *Maya Cosmos* (Freidel et al. 1993). In a study of the Milky Way in Maya myth by Peter Dunham (1980), we came across a passage in the *Ritual of the Bacabs* that referred to the Pleiades. In reading this passage, we realized that it described not only the Pleiades but also the entire area of the sky the ancient Maya saw as one of the two celestial nexus of creation. Eventually we were forced to remove that section of information from our book for editorial reasons, but the importance of the passage stayed with me waiting for a moment in which I could focus on the problem.

In preparing this paper, I enlisted the help of Barbara MacLeod to aid me in generating a new translation. I am not an expert in Yucatec, especially of metaphorical conventions so important to the *Ritual of the Bacabs,* but I believe that the Classic Maya story of creation informs our understanding of the *Ritual of the Bacabs* in ways that were previously unexpected. Any translator faces the problem of choosing one of many meanings to translate into the second language. Roys's knowledge of Yucatec ethnohistorical sources was encyclopedic, but he did not have the Classic period texts to help him in his work. In this study, I will present alternatives, based heavily on his translations, but choosing meanings that make sense in light of the Classic period texts.

In my view, the chants in *Ritual of the Bacabs* attack disease within the context of Maya creation. The version of creation in the *Bacabs* is close, if not identical, to the versions recorded in Classic period texts and perhaps earlier. Most passages begin with a description of the moment of creation that establishes time and place. Thereafter, the text recounts the genealogy, place, and context of the birth of the disease. By knowing the parentage and origin of the disease, the *h-men* gained control over it.

This paper offers translations of a few particularly relevant sections and suggests ways in which they reflect the Classic period version of creation.

Manuscript Pages 4–5 (Roys 1965:3–4): The Incantation for Jaguar-Macaw Seizure

Hun ahaw[2]	*hunuk*	*kan ahaw*
One Ahaw	now and forever	4 Ahaw
One Ahaw, the everlasting (recurring) 4 Ahaw		

Roys suggested that Hun Ahaw was a god of death known to the Yucatecs, but according to the Tablet of the Cross at Palenque, Hun Ahaw was the day on which the Hun Ye Nal, the First Father (also the Maize God), was born. *Hunuk* means "perpetual and the only." Roys translated it as "unique"; but the purpose is to mark this 4 Ahaw as the day of creation—4 Ahaw 8 Kumk'u.

kan ahaw	*b'in*	*ch'ab'*
4 Ahaw	it is said, was	creation
4 Ahaw was the creation		

kan ahaw	*b'in*	*ak'ab'*
4 Ahaw	it is said, was	darkness
4 Ahaw was the darkness		

This section is a formulaic couplet identifying 4 Ahaw as the day of creation and darkness. Classic period scenes of creation show the 4 Ahaw 8 Kumk'u event against a black background because the sky was not raised to give room for the light to appear until 542 days after 4 Ahaw.

ka	*sih*	*ech*
when	born	you
When you were born		

mak	*ech*	*tah*	*ch'ab'*
who	you	lord	creation

Who was the lord of your creation?

mak	*ech*	*tah*	*ak'ab'*
who	you	lord	darkness

Who was the lord of your darkness?

u ch'ab' ech	*k'in chak ahaw*	*kolop u wich k'in*
he created you	sun great lord	snatcher of the eye of the sun[3]

The Great Sun Lord, Snatcher of the Eye of the Sun, created you

This passage has the first question about the conditions of birth for the disease. The *h-men* begins by establishing the being who created the disease; here the Creator is identified as the Sun God. Next the *h-men* begins his enquiry about the genealogy of the disease.

ka	*sih*	*ech*
when	born	you

When you were born

max	*a*	*na'*
who	your	mother

Who was your mother?

max	*a*	*koob'*	*kit*
who	your	genital	father[4]

Who was your genital father?

ka	*ch'abtab'*	*ech*
when	was created	you

When you were created?

chakal ix chel
Red Ix Chel

sakal ix chel
White Ix Chel

ix	*hun*	*ye*	*ta*
lady	one	its point	lancet

Lady Universal[5] Point of the Lancet

ix	*hun*	*ye*	*ton*
lady	one	its point	penis[6]

Lady Universal Point of the Penis

la	*a*	*na'*
this	your	mother

This is your mother

la	*a*	*kob'*	*a*	*kit*
this	your	genital	your	father

This is your genital father

The mother and father of the disease are named. Hun Ye Ta and Hun Ye Ton seem to be forms that are directly equivalent in structure to Hun Ye Nal, the Classic period name of the First Father. Notice that both names have the *ix*-prefix that usually marks female names. Here, however, the last two lines clearly indicate that both the mother and father have been named. The *ix*- may be a diminutive in this context, rather than a female marker. I also suspect that the Hun Ye Ta/Hun Ye Ton pair may refer to bloodletting as one of the parents. Bloodletting and the resulting vision rites were couched in metaphors of birth during the Classic period.

kan ki	*tu*	*pach-e*
(who) ascended	at its	back

Ascended behind it

kan ki	*tu*	*pach*	*che'*
(who) ascended	at its	back	tree

Ascended behind the tree

maxkal	*sih*	*kech*
steam bath	born	you

The steam bath bore you

u	*kol*	*ch'ab'e*
its	frenzy[7]	creation

The frenzy of creation

u	*kol*	*ak'ab'e*
its	frenzy	darkness

The frenzy of darkness

Here the place of creation for the disease is given as a place called *maxkal*. Roys took the *maxkal* to be a tree. However, David Bolles (n.d.) cites evidence from many Yucatec sources that *maxkal* is a Mayanization of the Aztec word *temazcalli:*

> maxca*l* 1) db) steam bath house, sauna. Called temazcal in Spanish, from temazcalli = bath house in Nahuatl (tema = bath and calli = house). From the archeological evidence in Yucatan and from the present-day existence of temazcallis in the highlands of Mexico it seems that maxcals were mostly either in-ground structures with a wickiup type roof or occasionally below-ground structures. In the "Ritual of the Bacabs" Roys translates maxcal as being a plant (see second entry for maxcal), but maxcal is often paired with the word acantun, which might be an alternative spelling for actun = cave, and in two instances with dzulb'al = arbor, which Roys (see Roys/Bac 5/below) believes to be a ceremonial hut. Further, acantun and dzulb'al are often paired in the Bacab manuscript without maxcal. It would thus seem that Arzápalo is correct in his translation of maxcal as temazcal.

This idea fits the creation story at Palenque because Houston (1996) has identified the sanctuaries inside the temple of the Group of the Cross as effigy steam baths. They are called *pib'-na* in the texts of the Cross Group.

Manuscript Pages 15–16: The Incantation for Traveler Seizure

The incantation for the traveler's sickness is one of the most revealing of the passages in the *Ritual of the Bacabs*. It begins in the standard way—by setting the time and place of creation.

Kan Ahaw	*b'in*	*ch'ab'*
4 Ahaw	it is said, was	creation

4 Ahaw was the creation

kan Ahaw	*b'in*	*ak'ab'*
4 Ahaw	it is said, was	darkness

4 Ahaw was the darkness

ka   sihi   ki
when   was   born
When it was born

uy   ol   ch'ab'
its   heart (hole)   creation
The heart of creation

uy   ol   ak'ab'e
its   heart (hole)   darkness
The heart of darkness

The crack in the back of the Turtle in Orion is named glyphically as the *ol* in several Classic period texts. "The heart of creation, the heart of darkness" mentioned very likely refers to this part of the sky.

Tal   tu   ho   tas   ka'an
came   from its   five   level   sky
He came from the fifth level of the sky

The creation text of Quirigua says that the jaguar stone of the first three stones of creation was set up at *Na Ho Chan*, "House (or First or Female) Five Sky" (MacLeod 1991). The gods who painted the images of the creation places on the sky are called *Na Ho Chan Itz'at*, "First Five Sky Sages (or Artists)" (MacLeod 1992).

yalix   ti   tzab'
and then it was thrown   into/from   Snake-Rattles
And then it was thrown into/from the Snake Rattles (Pleiades[8])

yalix   ho   ti munyal
and then it was thrown   five   into/from the clouds
And then it was thrown five into/from the clouds

The Snake-Rattle is widely accepted as the Yucatec name for the Pleiades. They are in the constellation of Taurus very near the Gemini-Orion nexus named by *Na Ho Chan*. "Five in the Clouds" may refer to the same general area.

tan   ch'uch'   wah   b'atan   tankase[9]   ok
they are   suckling   each   other   seizure   foot
They are suckling each other Traveler Seizure

Barbara MacLeod pointed out to me that *tamakas* is a Yucatec name for the Milky Way as well as the word for "seizure." Because the Milky Way crosses the ecliptic at this point in the sky, the double reference may be intended.

Manuscript Page 17

makx	u	*na'*
who	his	mother

Who is his mother?

yal	*b'in*	*ix k'ak'*	*tan*	*chel*
her child	they say	Lady Fire	in the center	Rainbow

They say he was the child of Lady Fire in the center of the Rainbow

yal	*b'in*	*ix k'ak'*	*te*	*ka'an*
her child	they say	Lady Fire	in	Sky

They say he was the child of Lady Fire in the Sky

yal	*b'in*	*ix k'ak'*	*te*	*munyal*
her child	they say	lady fire	in it	clouds

They say he was the child of Lady Fire in the Clouds

Here the parentage is given, again as a place in the sky: the child of a woman who is named Fire in the Rainbow, Fire in the Sky, and Fire in the Clouds.

Manuscript Page 19

u	*lub'ul*	*b'in*
he	falls	they say

They say he falls

tu	*kan*	*b'e*
at its	four	roads

At the four crossroads

tu	*kan*	*lub'*
at its	four	resting places

At the four resting places

I think the four roads and four resting places are symbolized by the *k'an*-cross with its perpendicular crossings and its four marked corners. The *k'an*-cross is at

the base of the foliated cross on the Tablet of the Foliated Cross, which symbolizes the reborn Maize God. It is also at the point of the crack on the Orion
turtle's carapace. The four roads are made by the crossing of the Sak Be (the
Milky Way) and the ecliptic.

yiknal		*ix*	*ho*	*kan*	*b'e*
in the company of		lady	five[10]	four	roads

In the company of Lady Five Four Roads

yiknal		*kit*	*ho*	*kan*	*lub'*
in the company of		father	five[11]	four	resting places

In the company of Father Five Four Resting Places

Here personalities of this place are named as Lady Five Four Roads and Father
Five Four Resting Places. The number five must refer to the *Na Ho Chan* references discussed above. Apparently the parents of this disease, like the sky artists
of creation, carry the number of this sky location in their names.

ten	*k lub'* ...	*a ch'u*	*tankase*
I	fall ...	your ??	seizure

I curse you, seizure (following Roys 1965:7)

ki b'in	*yalab'*	*tumenel*	*ix ho kan b'e*	*ix ho kan lub'*
it will	said	by	lady five four roads	lady five four resting places

It will be said by Lady Five Four Roads, Lady Five Four Resting Places

Now Lady Five Four Roads and Lady Five Four Resting Places is named as
the agent of the defeat of Traveler's Seizure.

Manuscript Pages 150–151: The Incantation for Fire Biting on Wood

The incantation for fire also relates to the sky and the first fire of creation.

Hun	*kan*	*ahaw*
One	4	Ahaw

The Everlasting 4 Ahaw

This establishes the time frame as that of creation.

tunx	*b'akin*	*oki*	*tu*	*wayasb'a*	*a*	*k'ak'*
where	how	enter	in its	sign[12]	your	fire

Where and how did it enter into the sign of your fire?

kech	*yax*	*winik*	*che'*
you	first	human	wood [tree]

You the first wooden human

The incantation begins asking the first wooden man how the sign *(wayasb'a)* of the fire enters into the world.

u	*kum*	*ix*	*b'olon*	*puk*
her	pot	lady	nine	hills

The pot of Lady Nine Hills

la	*oki*	*tu*	*wayasb'a*	*u*	*k'ob'enil*[13]	*a k'ak'*
that	entered	into its	sign	its	hearth stone	your fire

That one entered into the sign of the hearth stones of your fire

kech	*yax*	*winikil*	*che'*
you	first	human	wood

You the first wooden human

This passage establishes that the pot of Lady Nine Hills entered into the hearthstones of the fire. Lady Nine Hills *(B'olon Puk)* in Yucatec is *B'olon Witz* in the Classic system. Although *B'olon Witz* is not yet associated directly with creation, it does occur in ritualistic contexts at Copan. The sign of the hearthstone is a triangle of stars in Orion—Alnitak, Saiph, and Rigel. According to the modern K'iche', the Orion nebula is the flame in the hearth. According to the Aztecs, the belt of Orion was the fire drill for making first fire (Aveni 1980:35–36).

u	*chakb'akel*	*ix*	*hun*	*itzamna*
its	thigh	lady	one	itzamna

The thigh of Lady Everlasting Itzamna

la	*oki*	*tu*	*wayasb'a*
that one	entered	into its	sign

That one entered its sign

This reference is very obscure, but I (Freidel et al. 1993) have evidence that Itzamna was both a paddler of the Milky Way canoe and a rider of peccaries. The constellation of Gemini was *ak ek'*. *Ak* is "peccary," "turtle," and "dwarf." Thus, Itzamna as the peccary rider and the canoe paddler is associated with Gemini, and Gemini lies adjacent to the Orion hearth. This passage, too, may be describing the sky.

u nach		*cheil*	*a k'ak'*
it takes into its teeth		wood	your fire

Your fire biting on wood

kech	*yax*	*winikil*	*che'*
you	first	human	wood

You the first wooden human

Oxlahun	*munyal*
thirteen	cloud

Thirteen Cloud

tunx tun	*b'akin*	*oki*	*tu*	*wayasb'a*	*u b'utz'il*	*ak'ak'*
where/then	how	entered	into its	sign	its smoke	your fire

Where and how did it enter into the sign of the smoke of your fire?

kech	*yax*	*winikil*	*che'*
you	first	human	wood

You the first wooden human

oxlahun	*ka'an*
thirteen	sky

Thirteen Sky

tunx	*b'akin*	*la*	*oki*	*tu*	*wayasb'a*	*yelel*	*a k'ak*
where	how	that one	entered	into its	sign	its flame	your fire

Where and how did that one enter into the sign of the flame of your fire?

kech	*yax*	*winikil*	*che'*
you	first	human	wood

You the first wooden human

u tunichil	tun	b'akin	sayab'	oki	tu	wayasb'a	u chukil
its stones	then	how	spring	entered	into its	sign	its soot

a k'ak'

your fire

Then the stones of the spring how entered into the sign of the soot of your fire

kech	yax	winikil	che'
you	first	human	wood

You first wooden human

ox	nikib'	sus	tunx	b'akin	oki	tu	wayasb'a	u tanil
3	small piles	sand	where	how	entered	into its	sign	its ashes

a k'ak'

your fire

3 small piles where, how entered into the sign of the ashes of your fire

kech	yax	winikil	che'
you	first	human	wood

You the first wooden human

This last long passage is less transparent, but it seems to relate a series of things—thirteen cloud, thirteen sky, stones from a spring, and three small piles of sand—to the various parts of the fire.

Manuscript Page 161: The Incantation for the Scorpion, When It Stings

Finally, there is an incantation for a scorpion bite that seems to describe the constellation of Scorpio against the background of the Milky Way. It is a counter for a scorpion bite.

pichint[14]	ech	tan	k'ula
poured out	you	in the center of	the k'ula

Pour you out into the center of the k'ula (holy water?)

ti	b'in	a ch'ah	u yamulil	a pachi
there	they say	you took	its undulations	your back

There, they say, you got the undulations in your back

I am not sure what the *k'ula* was, but it could be either the ocean or the deep waters of a cenote.

pichint	*ech*	*b'in*	*tan*	*yol*	*che'*
pour out	you	they say	in the center	its heart	tree

Pour you out, they say, in the center of the heart of the tree

The reference was obscure to Roys, but it is clear to me. *Sinaan,* the scorpion, was poured into the center of a tree that can only be the Milky Way in its north-south orientation. The Classic period Maya called this the *Wak Chan Ahaw* (Standing Sky Lord) and understood it to be the tree at the center of the cosmos.

ti	*b'in*	*ta ch'ah*	*u yax cheil*	*a pachi*
there	they say	you took	the first tree	your back

There, they say, you took the First Tree (the World Tree) of your back

a	*yax*	*cheil*	*nak'i*	*kech*
your	first	tree	belly	you

Your First Tree as your belly

Here the tree is clearly identified as the *Yax Che',* the First Tree, or ceiba that many sources identify as the Yucatec version of the tree at the center of the world. The passage says that the *Yax Che'* is at the back and the belly of *Sinaan,* and so it is. Scorpio's head lies outside the Milky Way, but its curving body is surrounded at the belly and back by the crystalline beauty of the *Xibalba Be.*

Conclusions

There are many other passages that can be directly mapped onto the sky and associated directly with Classic period creation mythology. The assortment of references that have so confounded interested students now make growing sense as a strategy of combating disease by knowing the origin and genealogy of the disease at the time of creation. The descriptions of creation and the portions of the sky related to it in the *Ritual of the Bacabs* matches closely and in detail the cosmology of the Classic period as it was associated with the sky.

Notes

1. Editors' Note: This chapter was originally distributed as Texas Notes on Precolumbian Art, Writing, and Culture No. 57 (1993). Translations of the Yucatec text have been corrected and updated.

2. Editors' Note: The Yucatec transcription uses the orthography for Mayan languages approved by the Guatemalan Academy (López Raquec 1989). Citations from Roys's publication retain the Colonial Yucatec orthography.

3. Roys translated this name as "snatcher-of-the-eye-of-the-sun," but Barrera Vásquez (1980:334) translates *kolop* as *"lágrimas."*

4. "Genital father" seems to have the same meaning as "birth father" in modern English. The *h-men* does not want to know who raised or nurtured the disease, but rather who fathered it.

5. Barrera Vásquez (1980:246) glosses *hun* as *"cosa general y universal."*

6. *Ton* is usually taken to mean "testicles," but Barrera Vásquez (1980:807) has it as *miembro viril.*

7. Roys (1965:4) translated *cool* as "lust," but Barrera Vásquez (1980:332) has it as *"excitación."*

8. Roys (1965:7) made this connection. This places the location in the Taurus-Pleiades region.

9. Barbara MacLeod (personal communication 1993) pointed out to me that Barrera Vásquez (1980:768) lists *tamakas* as *"locura, frenesí,"* the word used here as "seizure." He also glossed *tamakas* and *tamkas* as *"Vía Láctea."* She suggested there may have been a play on words. I agree, especially since there are references to snake-rattles in the same passage. Editors' Note: *tamakas* could be the origin of the word "tommy-goff" used in Belize to refer to a fer-de-lance.

10. Roys (1965:148) transcribes this name as *Ix Hol Kan B'e,* "Lady Opening at the Four Roads."

11. Following Roys's translation of the name in the previous phrase, this name may be Father Opening at the Four Resting Places.

12. Barrera Vásquez (1980:917) glosses *wayasb'a* as *"figura o parábola, señal, adivinar por sueños o signos."*

13. Editors' Note: Barbara MacLeod has recently suggested *k'ob',* "hearth," as a new decipherment of the object "changed" at the 13.0.0.0.0 4 Ahaw 8 Kumk'u creation event.

14. Barrera Vásquez (1980:652) glosses *pich* both as *"echar de alguna vasija"* and *"sacar espina o sangrar tumor con espina." Pich* can mean poured out, as Roys translated it, or it can mean perforated.

4

The Landscape of Creation

Architecture, Tomb, and Monument Placement
at the Olmec Site of La Venta

F. Kent Reilly III

I discovered my fascination for the art and symbols of Olmec culture, as well as the archaeological site of La Venta, by attending Linda Schele's Maya and Meso-american seminars at the University of Texas. Through Linda's lectures and stimulating class discussions, I quickly became aware that the origin of much of the Classic period Maya elite imagery could be traced to the earlier Olmec. It was in these seminars that I first proposed a hypothesis that sought the origin of Maya conceptions of architecture as sacred space in the architectural and sculptural assemblages of such Olmec archaeological sites as La Venta. I further suggested that my hypothesis had a strong chance of being provable because I could go from the "known"—the many sites where Maya architecture functioned as a cosmological model—to the "unknown" and could ask the question: did Olmec architecture have a cosmological function?

Linda was encouraging, suggesting a multidisciplinary approach that employed the research methods of archaeology, ethnography, and art history. This approach has consistently proved fruitful in that it provides a framework for testing hypotheses with a series of methodologies. Using Linda's multidisciplinary method has led me beyond the general sacred-space identification of specific Olmec architectural configurations and toward a search for the identity of the ceremonies conducted within such spaces.

The specificity of the multidisciplinary approach takes into account the burials, caches, sculptural forms, and groupings into which sculpture was arranged. This methodology of "total inclusion" has led me to the recognition that at Olmec sites caches, burials, and sculptural arrangements were extensions of the ritual activity that took place within certain ceremonial spaces and that such spaces were extensions of the narrative quality of Olmec ritual activity.

In this chapter I will argue that the purposes of such rituals and the sacred space or cosmological "stages" on which they were enacted were twofold: Olmec architecture and monuments were constructed in order to provide a mythic and cosmological backdrop for the public validation of rulership. Olmec ritual, in effect, comprised the rites through which elite ancestors provided supernatural sanction for the ceremonial and political activities of their elite descendants. To demonstrate this hypothesis I will discuss the several categories of Olmec sculpture as well as certain caches and burials and the mythic meaning demonstrated through their placement.

The Cosmological Function of Maya Architecture

As just stated, it is my contention that Olmec architectural layout is the source of many aspects of Maya cosmological modeling. With this thought in mind, it would be appropriate, before discussing the Olmec site of La Venta, to review briefly some of the current thinking regarding the cosmological function of Maya architecture. As cosmological models, Maya architectural complexes served as conduits of supernatural power as well as the stages on which the rituals of rulership validation were enacted (Ashmore 1992; Freidel et al. 1993; Looper 1995a; Newsome 1991; Schele and Freidel 1990). In Maya architecture directional positioning has been identified clearly with specific aspects of cosmological layouts and with access to supernatural power. For example, the layout of the Twin Pyramid Complexes at Tikal embodies just such a pattern (Ashmore 1992). Within these groups, east and west represent the trajectory of the solar journey. The direction north signals "up" or a celestial location, the sky is also the source of ancestral power, and south marks the direction of the underworld and perhaps the access point to the Lords of the Night (Ashmore 1992).

It has also been demonstrated (Freidel et al. 1993; Schele and Freidel 1990) that architectural complexes at Classic Maya sites were backdrops for performances during which ritually costumed Maya rulers danced as the deities responsible for the present creation. Schele and others repeatedly argued that the rituals depicting creation events were reflections of the creation events in the *Popol Vuh* (Tedlock 1982). She further suggested (Freidel et al. 1993:59–75; Schele and Mathews 1998:44) that the triadic grouping of structures that is a familiar arrangement in so many Maya sites was an attempt, by their builders, to identify such ritual spaces as the cosmologically significant "Three Stone Place" where the foundations of the present creation were laid.

Recent research further demonstrates that the *Popol Vuh* creation story was closely akin to those of all Mesoamerican peoples, and its source can be traced to the Gulf Coast Olmec (Freidel et al. 1993; Kappelman 1997; Reilly 1994a; Schele and Mathews 1998). These hypotheses have been supported through the investigations of building layouts, plaza spaces, and stela and monument placement at the sites of El Mirador, Copan, Palenque, and Quirigua (Looper 1995a; Matheny 1989; Newsome 1991; Schele and Mathews 1998). With the cosmological functions of Maya architecture firmly established, I will now attempt to demonstrate that these patterns existed at the Olmec site of La Venta as well.

The Archaeological Site of La Venta

The archaeological site of La Venta lies near the border between the contemporary Mexican Gulf Coast states of Tabasco and Veracruz. The site was constructed atop a salt dome, whose gradual uplift over time has formed an island now rising above the swampy environment of the Tonala River basin and thus provides one of the largest areas of constantly dry land along this stretch of the Gulf Coast. The swampy terrain that surrounds La Venta today, however, has changed considerably since the site's construction. Modern satellite imagery reveals the ghostly outlines of the ancient river systems that once surrounded La Venta's island. In fact, the gradual uplift of the island primarily has caused these ancient streams to disappear (Rust 1992). The banks of these streams undoubtedly served as home to the bulk of La Venta's population, as well as providing the richest agricultural land, which supported the critical surplus to ensure the power of La Venta's elite.

Excavations in the 1940s, 1950s, and 1960s (Drucker 1952; Drucker et al. 1959; Heizer et al. 1968) revealed that La Venta reached its apogee circa 900–500 B.C.E. These same archaeological investigations identified the heart of La Venta in several architectural complexes, primarily composed of earthen mound structures. A plethora of large-scale stone monuments augmented each of these complexes, which were complemented by smaller scale sculptures and the remarkable caches of greenstone that have made the site famous. Early on in the history of the site's investigation, La Venta's earthen architecture was recognized as running along a central axis aligned eight degrees west of true north. This axial division defines a bilateral symmetry that functioned both in the architecture and in the layout of La Venta's greenstone caches.

Despite this knowledge, the first detailed map of La Venta was not produced until the late 1980s by the Proyecto Arqueológico La Venta directed by Rebecca González Lauck. Besides this critically important site map, González Lauck's investigations reveal that La Venta was occupied sometime before 1150 B.C.E. and that its inhabitants actively exploited the resources of the surrounding riverine and estuarine environment, primarily for food sources (González Lauck 1988; Rust 1992). The enormous artifact assemblage that Proyecto La Venta recovered illustrates that social organization at the site was stratified, with religious specialists, fishermen, farmers, and artisans supporting an elite class (González Lauck 1988, 1994, 1996; Rust 1992).

An examination of González Lauck's site map reveals that La Venta was organized into a north (Complex A) and south (Complex D) architectural grouping (Figure 4.1). A large central plaza and its surrounding structures—the La Venta Pyramid, the Stirling Acropolis, and Complex B—linked or delineated these groupings (González Lauck 1988, 1994, 1996; Reilly 1994a, 1999; Tate 1999). The southern architectural complex seems to lack the exclusivity and formal arrangement of the northern group. The monument distribution at La Venta also reflects this "ritual-use" separation between north and south: the central plaza and Complex A contain many more monuments than Complex D (Grove 1996, 1999). This pattern, however, may be merely an accident of current archaeological knowledge. An examination of the site map certainly reveals a plaza within Complex D and a passage, between the earthen mounds, into the great central plaza. Recent research has identified this path or road as a processional way (Grove 1996).

Archaeological investigations have closely scrutinized the northernmost of La Venta's architectural complexes. The enclosed court of Complex A contains two great greenstone masks and numerous caches of greenstone celts, as well as the famous La Venta Offering 4. Excavated at the foot of the Northeast Platform Mound, Offering 4 depicts a ritual tableau comprised of fifteen greenstone figures and a single sandstone one arrayed before a row of six greenstone celts (Drucker et al. 1959:152–161) (Figure 4.2). Recent studies reveal that these celts, when placed in an erect posture, are in fact miniature versions of stelae (Porter 1996). This revelation allows an interpretation of Offering 4 as a miniature tableau that depicts a stela ritual. Offering 4 was positioned in front of the Northeast Platform Mound, which is one of three mounds within the enclosed court. The placement of these three mounds in a single architectural grouping within La Venta's north court is highly suggestive of the previously discussed triadic arrangement of Late Formative and Classic period Maya pyramids and may in fact be ancestral to it.

The Northeast Platform Mound also holds a significant number of caches that are laid out in a pattern that forms a rough triangle. The contents of these caches have been identified as costume elements (Joyce 1987; Reilly 1999). These caches may ultimately prove to have been burials in which the skeletal material has disintegrated. Certain jade objects contained within these caches almost certainly are Middle Formative period examples of the Maya Jester God headdress

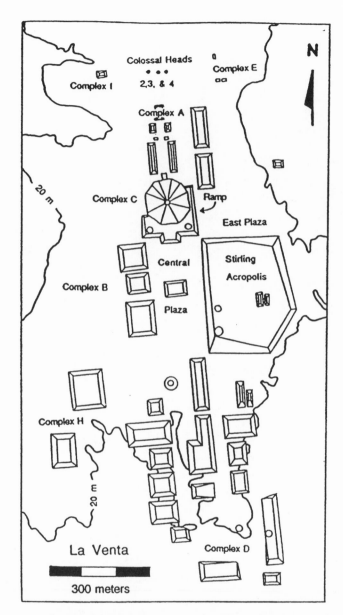

Figure 4.1. La Venta. The site map of La Venta reveals that it was organized into north and south architectural groupings. The center point of the site consists of a central plaza that is bordered on the north by the La Venta pyramid (redrawn by Barbara MacLeod from González Lauck 1994:Figure 6.6).

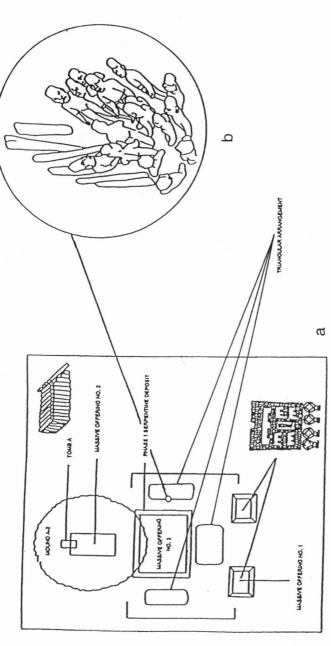

Figure 4.2. (*a*) La Venta, enclosed court, Complex A. The enclosed court (188 feet × 135 feet) consists of a patio surrounded by a basalt column "fence" set in an adobe brick wall. The interior of this court is dominated by three low platform mounds. The arrangement of these mounds is highly reminiscent of the triadic arrangement of buildings in Maya architectural complexes (drawing by Kent Reilly); (*b*) La Venta Offering 4. This offering of stone figures and greenstone celts was buried on the west side of the Northeast Platform of La Venta's enclosed court (drawing by Kent Reilly).

(Reilly 1999), underscoring its origin in the Formative period (Fields 1989, 1990). The location of these caches within the enclosed court of Complex A, along with the presence of at least two significant burials, strongly links this northern area of the site with rulership, elite ritual activities, and, ultimately, ancestors (Reilly 1994a, 1999).

The Categories of Sculpture at La Venta

The monuments of La Venta, dispersed over so much of the site's architectural spaces, can be organized into several categories, by form as well as by size: colossal heads, altars, stelae, bas-reliefs, three-dimensional representations of humans and zoomorphic supernaturals, and monument fragments (Figure 4.3). Though the term "colossal" is applied to much Olmec sculpture, many of these monuments—particularly human representations—are, in reality, life size. Thus, they were moved easily without enormous labor, unlike the truly colossal pieces, a fact pertinent to determining the ritual function of Olmec monuments.

La Venta's monuments also can be organized into stylistic categories. Although the stylistic development of Olmec sculpture has been repeatedly discussed (Coe 1965b; de la Fuente 1981; Milbrath 1979), few have attempted to organize temporally the sculptural corpus of a single site. Certainly, La Venta's four colossal heads, its several altars, and other sculptures conform to the Formative period Olmec style that was being created by 1000 B.C.E. at the site of San Lorenzo (Coe 1965b; Coe and Diehl 1980; Cyphers Guillén 1992, 1997, 1999). The style of several other monuments, however, strongly differs from the earlier San Lorenzo group and may very well be better classified as distinctive products of a La Venta Olmec style.

Other than the splendid murals at Bonampak, Chiapas, the cave paintings of Naj Tunich, Guatemala, and the ritual scenes recorded on Maya painted vases, our only record of Maya ritual enactments are carved monuments, often augmented by hieroglyphic inscriptions. These monuments depict gods and elite human actors, in static positions, performing their ritual actions, literally frozen in stone (Stuart 1996:160). For the Maya, the accompanying hieroglyphic inscription carries the narrative as a written description of ritual action.

Did, as I have previously suggested, Olmec sculpture, like Maya monuments with hieroglyphic inscriptions, in some way carry a narrative of ritual action? The question then arises, because the Olmec of La Venta apparently lacked hieroglyphic writing, how were action and narrative conveyed within their artistic corpus? This is an important question and one that is critical to our current and future understanding of Olmec monuments and the rituals that were conducted around them.

On the basis of Ann Cyphers Guillén's new discoveries at the archaeological site of San Lorenzo (Cyphers Guillén 1992, 1997), it can be demonstrated that the Olmec achieved a method of conveying the narrative of ritual action through the placement or grouping of monuments. In order to support this argument, however, we must examine the categories of La Venta's monuments in light of Cyphers Guillén's recent interpretations.

The best-known Olmec sculptural category—in fact, a hallmark of Olmec art—is the colossal heads (see Figure 4.3). Currently, seventeen examples of this

Figure 4.3. Examples of categories of Olmec sculpture. *(a)* Colossal head: La Venta Monument 4 (redrawn by Jack Johnson after a photograph by Kent Reilly); *(b)* Altar: La Venta Altar 5 (redrawn by Jack Johnson after a photograph by Kent Reilly); *(c)* Stela: La Venta Stela 3 (redrawn by Jack Johnson after a photograph by Kent Reilly); *(d)* Bas-relief: La Venta Monument 19 (redrawn by Jack Johnson after a photograph by Kent Reilly); *(e)* Three-dimensional: La Venta Monument 8 (redrawn by Jack Johnson after a photograph by Kent Reilly).

sculpture genre are known, and other examples almost certainly will be excavated. In his crucial study of the execution of these colossal heads, James Porter
(1989) has demonstrated that in some instances the colossal heads were recarved
from previously existing throne/altars. This discovery suggests that, for their
creators, such monuments were inherently transformational. It may be that at
some fundamental level, the colossal heads were interpreted by the Olmec as
visualizations of an inherent concept of supernatural transformation that was a
quality inherent in their elites (Coe 1972; Furst 1968; Reilly 1989). Certainly,
colossal heads, with their striking realism, dramatically present the charisma that
was part of an ideology with a human-centered dimension (de la Fuente 1981),
making it clear that the portraits are individualized (Clewlow 1974; Coe 1972;
Cyphers Guillén 1996; de la Fuente 1996; Grove 1981).

Grove (1981) has proposed that the specific headdresses unique to each colossal head convey the name of the elite individual that the head depicts. The headdress, however, could also identify the clan or lineage house to which the individuals belong (Gillespie 1999). Still, these distinctive headdresses may well be
ritual specific (Kappelman and Reilly 2001), conveying the identity of the supernatural entity or role that the individual was portraying.

Olmec thrones comprise another crucial monument category in the argument
for the narrative function of monument placement (see Figure 4.3). Characterized by overhanging ledges, these large sculptures were originally called "altars"
because of their shape. Grove (1973) has since identified them as elite benches or
thrones and thus "seats of power." Many of these altars/thrones are sculpted with
images of elites emerging from niches, holding infants in their arms. This motif
has been interpreted as emergence from the earth or otherworld (Grove 1973).
Other aspects of throne iconography may represent the access to celestially based
supernatural power, shamanism, and the shamanic journey or flight (Furst 1968;
Grove 1973; Kappelman and Reilly 2001; Reilly 1995).

The altars/thrones also may function as accession monuments for Olmec rulers (Freidel and Reilly 1998). This feature would link Olmec altars/thrones to the
ritual scaffolding on which Maya rulers are depicted during their accession rites.
For the Maya ruler, climbing such scaffolding meant ascending to the sky. In
Maya architecture, the roof-combs of temples—by depicting the ruler's accession
scaffolding in plaster images of the seated figure—commemorated this scaffolding rite (Freidel and Schuler 1999). An examination of an altar/throne from San
Lorenzo, Monument 20 (Coe and Diehl 1980:330–331), further supports this interpretation, as well-executed steps were cut into the back of this mutilated
altar/throne (Figure 4.4). By these steps the Olmec ruler ascended the altar/
throne, elevating himself into the sky realm (Freidel and Reilly 1998).

In a recent article Gillespie (1999) has argued convincingly that thrones func-

Figure 4.4. San Lorenzo Monument 20, front and back views. The slotted steps in the back of this altar functioned as a ladder by which the throne's occupant could climb to the top (redrawn by Jack Johnson from Coe and Diehl 1980:1:Figure 451).

tioned as visual validations of the Olmec elite's ability to access ancestral power. In Gillespie's view, such objects not only portrayed the power of ancestors but also embodied the prestige and economic power of elite lineage houses. Gillespie (1999:246) correctly warns that the reading of altar/throne iconography as text has been emphasized unduly without taking into account the social and archaeological contexts of these monuments. Nevertheless, it ultimately may prove that the Mesoamerican scholar's ability to read such "iconographic texts" does, indeed, provide key evidence for understanding the cultural function of the altar/throne monuments.

Gillespie (1999:240–241) interprets Olmec altars/thrones as important foci of ritual activity and suggests they are prototypes for the tabletop altars of the mod-

ern indigenous peoples of Mexico and Central America (Gillespie 1999:237). She
also links them to the modern K'iche' Maya belief that certain stone boxes *(warab
alha)* are where ancestors rest or sleep (Gillespie 1999:237; Tedlock 1982:17), a
theme previously explored by Freidel et al. (1993:185–193). Expanding on the concept of altars/thrones as the sleeping place of ancestors, Gillespie (1999:238–240)
links altars/thrones, the K'iche' *warab alha,* and certain categories of bench or
boxlike sarcophagi that the Olmec and the Classic period Maya both produced.
Gillespie's analysis demonstrates that the functions of Olmec monuments were
ideologically and socially multivalent and that their creators viewed them as
shamanic transformation mechanisms as well as elite status objects.

Stelae are one of the most important categories of Mesoamerican sculpture.
Although Maya stelae are best known, their origin and their accompanying cere-
monialism should be sought among the Olmec and at La Venta in particular. In
the monument corpus of San Lorenzo, two stelae fragments (Monuments 41 and
42) stylistically appear to have a very early date (Figure 4.5a). Once interpreted
as columns, these fragments may be the earliest evidence for the stela cult in
Mesoamerica (Coe and Diehl 1980:350–353; Reilly 1999). Though this may be
uncertain at San Lorenzo, the presence of stelae at La Venta is inarguable. With
the recognition that La Venta Monuments 25/26 are actually fragments of the
now-restored Stela 4, and with the recently excavated Stela 5 (González Lauck
1988, 1994) (Figure 4.2c), the corpus of stelae at La Venta continues to grow,
leaving little doubt as to their importance in the ritual life of this Olmec heartland site.

James Porter's (1996) identification of greenstone celts as the prototypes for
large stelae has advanced Olmec stelae studies dramatically. By comparing the
shape of many Middle Formative period stelae to the basic celt form, Porter has
demonstrated a relationship between the two (Figure 4.5b). In comparing the
Maize God images incised on celts with the nearly identical imagery carved on
certain stelae, Porter (1996:68–69) has further bolstered his compelling argument.

Several scholars have proposed that greenstone celts substituted for maize ears
in Olmec ritual (Joralemon 1971; Taube 1996). In an expansion of this argument,
Karl Taube (1996) has linked maize ears, celts, and celtiform stelae. Such approaches have correctly identified Maize God imagery on some stelae, and close
analysis of the costumes some Olmec elites wear on stelae (La Venta Stela 2)
clearly underscores the importance of maize and Maize God imagery to the
Olmec in elite ritual costuming (Fields 1990; Reilly 1994a; Taube 1996). Within
the context of monument placement at La Venta, however, do the stelae function
multivalently as altars/thrones do? In other words, are stelae more than just billboards to display iconographic information? Moreover, if so, what are these ritual
and ideological functions?

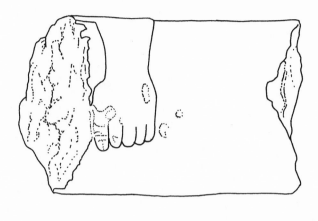

Figure 4.5. (a) San Lorenzo Monuments 41 and 42. These columnar fragments bearing sculpted images may be some of the earliest stelae fragments in Mesoamerica (redrawn by Jack Johnson from Coe and Diehl 1980:1:Figures 478–479).

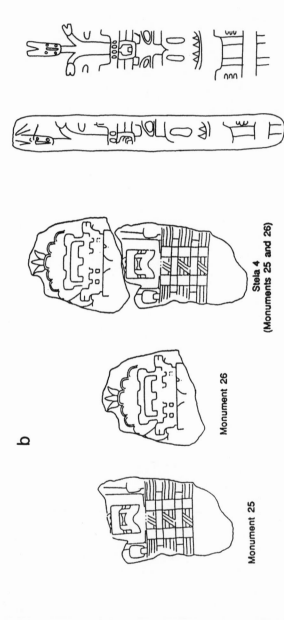

Figure 4.5. (b) La Venta Monuments 25 and 26 and a celt from La Venta Offering 4. James Porter's comparison of stelae and celts demonstrates that the stela form is derived from celts (drawings by Kent Reilly based on González Lauck 1994 and from a photograph by Kent Reilly).

The Function of Stelae among the Classic Period Maya

Because much of Classic Maya ideological symbolism and architectural layout are generally acknowledged to derive from Olmec sources, let us examine the better-understood function of Classic Maya stelae in elite ritual behavior. For the Maya, stelae served as surfaces or billboards on which to display hieroglyphic inscriptions that recorded specific dates, such as period-endings, and the images of rulers and gods. At a fundamental level, as David Stuart (1996:167–168) suggests, these stone columns comprise a "subclass of ceremonial stones employed in calendric reckoning, specifically in the count of 360-day 'years' and larger time units composed of these units." Stuart (1996:165–167) further interprets the presence of deity and royal imagery on these stelae as efforts to identify those gods and kings as the masters of time itself.

In closely analyzing the ritual function of Maya stelae, Stuart (1996:154–158) argues that they were bound or enclosed in bands of cloth during rituals that marked the conclusion of 360-day periods of time. Stuart (1996:157) further identifies the binding of stelae as a specifically royal ritual and links it with royal accession, noting that the act of tying or binding on the kingly Jester God headdress corresponds to the binding of stelae. In Stuart's (1996:158–165) view, the images of rulers and gods depicted performing these rituals on the carved surface of stelae functioned both to extend the royal person and to define stelae rituals as eternal, never-ending events.

Iconographic Similarities between Classic Maya and Olmec Stelae Rituals

Certainly, one may draw specific analogies between Stuart's interpretations of Maya stelae rituals and the ideology that generated Olmec monument imagery. Carving ritual imagery in stone ensured that the efficacy of the specific ritual enacted was rendered permanent and ongoing: the very medium of stone endowed the ritual depicted with the quality of an eternal present (Reilly 1994a). This concept also overlaps with the idea, discussed below, that Olmec monuments were often grouped in relation to each other so as to convey significant social and ideological messages to the viewer (Cyphers Guillén 1997, 1999).

Unfortunately, though many Late Formative monuments bear calendar dates and other hieroglyphic inscriptions, no strong evidence currently exists for such a writing or numerical system at Middle Formative La Venta. As yet, there is no way to determine whether the La Venta Olmec were numerically registering temporal cycles. Olmec sculptural and iconographic evidence strongly suggests, however, that the heartland Olmec and other peoples of the Middle Formative

Figure 4.6. San Lorenzo Monument 15 and Laguna de los Cerros Monument 9. Examples of bound or enclosed Olmec monuments from Olmec heartland sites (drawing by Jack Johnson after photographs by Kent Reilly).

horizon, neither Olmec politically nor ethnically, practiced the ritual of stelae bundling and the bundling of other monuments as well.

Depictions of bound or enclosed monuments from heartland Olmec art include San Lorenzo Monument 15 and Laguna de los Cerros Monument 9, which depict bound square stone objects (Figure 4.6). On these mutilated monuments, the battered remains of seated individuals can be distinguished (Coe and Diehl 1980:322). These monuments are almost certainly depictions of Olmec thrones, given their shape and the seated postures of the now-damaged figures that sit atop them (Freidel and Reilly 1998). Another category of bound objects includes certain colossal heads. The headdresses of two colossal heads from San Lorenzo (Monuments 3 and 4) are comprised of knots, ropes, and bindings (Kappelman and Reilly 2001) (Figure 4.7). The presence of so many bound monuments in the Olmec sculptural corpus certainly suggests that the stelae binding rituals Stuart identified may well be traced to the San Lorenzo phase of the heartland Olmec.

During the Middle Formative period, explicit depictions of bound or bundled objects appear at later sites outside the Olmec heartland. The carved bas-relief from Xoc, Chiapas, depicts a standing figure costumed in the Olmec style holding a large bundle in the crook of his left arm (Reilly 1994a:173–175). The Chalcatzingo Vase, now in the Art Museum at Princeton University, bears the incised image of an open bundle (Reilly 1994a, 1996). The middle of the three knots securing the bundle has been untied to reveal an object, which is either a mask (Reilly 1994a:175–179, 1996) or a carved celt (David Freidel, personal communication 1996) (Figure 4.8a and 4.8b).

Monument 21, also from Chalcatzingo, Morelos, contains one of the most striking examples of Middle Formative monument binding or bundling. Originally erected on the front of Terrace 15 during the Cantera phase (700–500 B.C.E.), this carved stela depicts a female with both her hands positioned against a rectangular, standing slab (Cyphers Guillén 1984; Grove 1984, 1989:128–139). Though the top part of Monument 21 is missing, enough remains to identify the standing slab as a stela with carved imagery on its surface, perhaps representing the dedication of Monument 21 itself. Certainly the protagonist's position, with her hands against the stela, strongly suggests that she is in the act of erecting a monument, perhaps this very one. Both the stela and the actor depicted on Monument 21 rest on a ground line in the form of an earth-monster mask (Grove 1989:137).

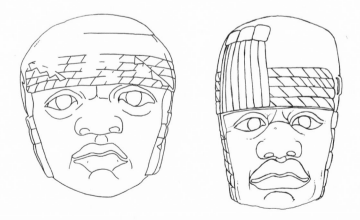

Figure 4.7. San Lorenzo Monuments 3 and 4. The headdresses of these two colossal heads are comprised of ropes and knots (redrawn by Jack Johnson from Coe and Diehl 1980:1:Figures 426 and 427).

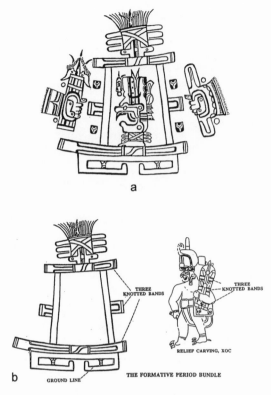

Figure 4.8. *(a, b)* A comparison between the now-destroyed bas-relief from Xoc, Chiapas, and the carved imagery on the Chalcatzingo vase (drawings by Kent Reilly).

A closer look at Monument 21 shows that two bands bind the depicted stela, each of them marked with a cleft motif (Figure 4.9a). This cleft motif also appears in the trefoil headdress of the four, inverted-T shaped monoliths that surmount the walls of the enclosed court at Teopantecuanitlan, Guerrero (Grove 1989:144–145). Likewise, elite Olmec personages wear this trefoil headdress that, derived from maize iconography, ritually functioned as a royal crown (Figure 4.9b). In these instances, this headdress functions just as the trefoil, Jester God headdress does for Maya kings in the Classic period (Fields 1990). The cleft motif surely echoes the small celts that are bound on the bodies of Olmec rulers and in their trefoil headdresses (Taube 1996:50–54). These bindings on the stela depicted on Chalcatzingo Monument 21 seem to confirm Stuart's assertion that the binding of a stela and the binding of a Maya king with the royal headdress were most strongly related. On Monument 21, then, the interaction of the protagonist with the bound stela further supports the argument that ritual binding began at least by the Formative period among the Olmec, prefiguring the Classic Maya usage of binding or enclosing stelae at calendrically significant dates.

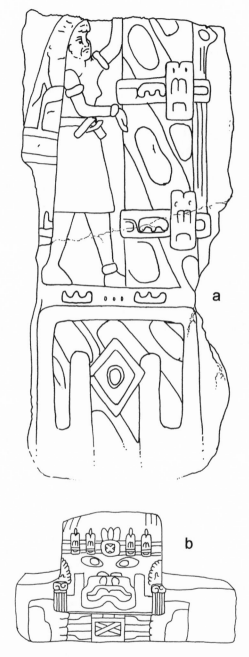

Figure 4.9. *(a, b)* Chalcatzingo Monument 21 and Monolith 1 from Teopantecuanitlan. Monument 21 is bound by two knotted bands. Each knot takes the form of a cleft element, perhaps a stylized maize seed. This same motif can be seen in the headdress of Monolith 1 from the Guerrero site of Teopantecuanitlan (drawings by Jack Johnson after photographs by Kent Reilly).

Ideology and Monument Placement at San Lorenzo Tenochtitlan

Through her ongoing archaeological investigation, Ann Cyphers Guillén has uncovered compelling evidence for a conscious program of monument placement at San Lorenzo (Cyphers Guillén 1992, 1997, 1999). In her words:

Olmec sculptures provided the individual strands of a conceptual framework about the earth and cosmos; yet when the sculptures are organized into visual displays, the symbols and concepts they evoke can be arranged and re-arranged to achieve a variety of messages and effects. Stone monuments, arranged in groupings, thus constitute statements about ideology, statements that permitted considerable variation in symbols and concepts (Cyphers Guillén 1999:156).

At San Lorenzo Group E and at the outlying site of Loma del Zapote, dramatic archaeological evidence supports Cyphers Guillén's hypothesis. Particularly in Group E, Cyphers Guillén can demonstrate an intentional positional relationship between an altar/throne (Monument 14), a colossal head (Monument 61), an aqueduct drain-line, and several other monuments and monument fragments. The archaeological evidence also suggests that these monuments were placed within an architectural frame that leads Cyphers Guillén to deduce ritual contexts indicating dedication, termination, and perhaps accession and enthronement (Cyphers Guillén 1999:162–165).

Three kilometers south of the San Lorenzo acropolis, the site of Loma del Zapote also provides Cyphers Guillén with two exceptional examples of intentional monument placement. Loma del Zapote Monument 11—a torso fragment of a life-size statue, lacking its head—seems to depict a costumed human being wearing a "spoon" pectoral in a unique sculptural posture: an extended right arm, a raised left arm, and the left leg crossed underneath the right leg, which dangles straight down (Figure 4.10a). The sculpture's posture is identical to that of the seated individual wearing an avian costume in Oxtotitlan Mural 1 (Figure 4.10b) (Cyphers Guillén 1999:168–170; Grove 1970). In the case of Oxtotitlan Mural 1, the figure sits on a zoomorphic mask, which is almost certainly a throne (Grove 1970; Reilly 1994a). The fact that Loma del Zapote Monument 11 is carved in this posture and is life-sized indicates that it was to be viewed as seen on a pedestal, surely a throne (Cyphers Guillén 1997, 1999:168). The fact that this *statue* of an elite individual or ruler could substitute for the ruler himself atop his seat of power also underscores Stuart's (1996:158–165) suggestion that depictions of Maya rulers in stone were "extensions of the Royal Self" and my contention that, lacking writing, the narrative action of Olmec ritual was conveyed through the arrangement and rearrangement of sculptural groupings.

a

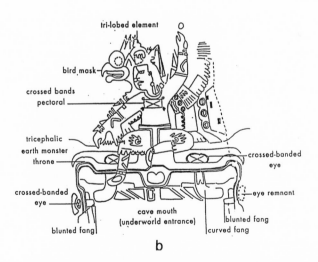

tri-lobed element

bird mask

crossed bands
pectoral

tricephalic
earth monster
throne

crossed-banded
eye

crossed-banded
eye

eye remnant

cave mouth
(underworld entrance)

blunted fang

blunted fang

curved fang

b

Figure 4.10. *(a, b)* Torso fragment from Loma del Zapote and avian-costumed figure from Oxtotitlan Mural 1. The human actors represented by a sculptural fragment and a mural painting are posed identically (drawings by Jack Johnson after photographs by Kent Reilly).

An even more powerful example of the interactive and multivocal nature of sculptural placement from the San Lorenzo area is the Rancho Azuzul sculptural grouping (León and Sánchez 1991–1996; Cyphers Guillén 1999). Cyphers Guillén (1999:170–174) describes the Azuzul figural group as consisting of four sculptures, two figures in each of two groups (Figure 4.11). These sculptures were originally positioned on top of a platform, which also supported a large earthen mound. There is no doubt that the statues are so positioned as to form a mythic or ritual scene.

In this monument grouping each figure wears an identical costume, holds an identical ceremonial staff or bar, and is the same size. The eyes of both figures are narrowed as in a trance. These human figures face the second sculptural pair, which are jaguars. Although these jaguars share many physical features they—unlike their twin human counterparts—are different sizes. Unlike the kneeling twins, both jaguars show evidence of reworking and most certainly are recarved monuments (Cyphers Guillén 1999:172).

Commenting on the unique arrangement of the Azuzul sculptures, Cyphers Guillén (1999:172) compares them to the later twin-centered myths of the Classic Maya and highland Mexican Mesoamerican cultures. She further suggests that the recarving of the jaguar figures points to the transformational nature of some Olmec sculpture and supports the view that shamanism formed a core ide-

Figure 4.11. Sculptural grouping or tableau from Rancho Azulul (drawing by Jack Johnson from photograph by Kent Reilly).

ology in Olmec religion (Furst 1968; Kappelman 1997; Reilly 1989, 1994a). Finally, Cyphers Guillén (1999:174) comments that "ritual reenactments of mythical or historical dramas using sculpture and architecture permitted the Olmec successfully to combine ceremony, rulership and cosmology."

The Ideology Underlying the Placement of Monuments at La Venta

As Cyphers Guillén has demonstrated, the pattern of monument arrangement at San Lorenzo implies a critical urgency in presenting the narrative of Olmec ideology and rituals in a tableau. Such deliberate monument arrangement, in a presumably nonliterate society, represented the rituals explaining the cosmic order to the viewer and further identified the elite actors as participating in the mythic fabric that bound the social order together. How, then, may we recover tenets of Olmec belief and political validation from such explicit sculptural arrangements, burial patterns, and other iconography?

As Linda Schele often stated, "When you are in doubt about a specific Mesoamerican ideological question, return to the cosmogenic myths contained in the *Popol Vuh* of the K'iche' Maya." Drawing ideological interpretations of Olmec iconography and monument placement from the texts and art of Classic and Postclassic Maya culture is closely akin to ethnographic analogy, also termed upstreaming or the direct historical approach. In the past, the direct historical approach in Mesoamerican studies has been severely criticized (Kubler 1967, 1984). More recent studies applied to Maya/Olmec ideological relationships, however, have unequivocally demonstrated that the direct historical approach continually yields fruitful results (Fields 1989, 1990; Freidel et al. 1993; Gillespie 1999; Reilly 1994a; Taube 1995, 1996).

Over the last few decades, the epic of the *Popol Vuh* has become central to any understanding of Classic Maya ideology (Coe 1973; Tedlock 1985:23–65). In the introduction to his translation of the *Popol Vuh*, Dennis Tedlock (1985) posits three major subdivisions in the narrative: the creation of the world, the tale of two sets of supernatural hero twins, and the creation of the present human population, emphasizing the origin of the royal K'iche' Maya lineage. Within these mythic subdivisions, certain episodes appear more frequently in the art of the Classic Maya and, as we shall see, in that of the La Venta Olmec. These include the gods laying the foundations of the world as a "three-stone place"; the Lords of Death decapitating the Maize God in the watery otherworld; and the Maize God's sons resurrecting him either from the cleft in a turtle's back or in the otherworld ballcourt. This turtle shell is also linked to the three-stone place of creation. Finally, in a recurrent, crucial scene, the gods create the current order of human beings at the First True Mountain of Maize (Freidel et al. 1993:59–122).

Over time a series of hieroglyphic and iconographic investigations have demonstrated that the Maize God is the critical actor in the *Popol Vuh* creation epic. *Popol Vuh* episodes focusing on this deity trace the life cycle of maize, the most important of Mesoamerican agricultural products. Certainly, the Lords of Death's decapitation of the Maize God in the underworld ballcourt draws a direct analogy to the act of harvesting maize, in which the ears of maize are torn or snapped from the stalk. When his sons, the "Hero Twins," resurrect the Maize God, the action mirrors the planting, sprouting, and developing growth of maize. Maize God iconography also played a critical role in the visualization of Mesoamerican elite power. In fact, maize iconography gives rise to the trefoil crown that Classic Maya and Olmec rulers wear (Fields 1989, 1990). By wearing this trefoil headdress, the ruler identified himself both as the Maize God and as the axis-mundi of the earthly realm, thereby connecting the different levels of the cosmos (Reilly 1994a:179–182). For the Classic Maya as well as for the Olmec, the ritual reenactment of the Maize God myth and the depiction of the great creation epic on monuments and other works of art made elite ideology materially visible while validating their authority (Coe 1973; Freidel et al. 1993; Schele and Freidel 1990).

Recently, many of these iconographic motifs and themes from the *Popol Vuh* epic have been identified in Olmec-style art (Fields 1989; Reilly 1991, 1994a, 1995, 1996, 1999; Taube 1996). On the basis of the models discussed, it has been proposed (Reilly 1994a, 1995, 1996, 1999) that the groupings of monuments and tombs at La Venta are purposeful and were meant to be understood as episodes from the Olmec creation myth, aspects of which the Classic Maya and the Colonial period *Popol Vuh* seem to share. In particular, the *Popol Vuh* creation episodes are analogous to evidence in the art, monument groupings, tombs, and caches of La Venta. Closely examining the site and its monuments suggests that architecture and monument arrangement may revolve around two fundamental ideological constructs: first, the sacred geography or landscape of creation and, second, the supernatural actors who mythically transformed this primordial landscape into the present earthly realm.

The La Venta Pyramid

Like their Maya inheritors, the builders of La Venta laid out the architecture as the landscape of creation to provide a sacred stage on which to enact the rituals of rulership (Reilly 1994b, 1999). At La Venta, this stage centers on a thirty-two-meter-tall pyramid (Group C) and on the large plaza aligned on its southern side (see Figure 4.1). Because of its size, this plaza surely was intended for more public ritual events (Reilly 1994b, 1999:18). To the north of the pyramid, however, the ritual spaces between two range mounds and within a large enclosed court were found to contain numerous greenstone caches and tombs (Group A) and thus were likely reserved for more exclusive rituals (Reilly 1999:18).

The La Venta pyramid (ca. 1000 B.C.E.), one of the first, large-scale, and man-made sacred mountains erected in Mesoamerica (Bernal-García 1988; Reilly 1999), would have appeared even more towering to an audience standing in the central plaza because this enormous earthen structure was constructed atop a large platform. At least six stelae, two altars, and several other monuments were recovered on this platform (González-Lauck 1996:76).

As previously noted, James Porter (1996) has argued convincingly that the celtiform shape of Olmec stelae derives from the greenstone celts that figure so prominently in caches, such as those in Complex A. Joralemon (cited in Coe 1977), discussing the celtiform shape, has suggested that the celts were ritually substituted for maize ears. Four of these La Venta stelae not only are carved from greenstone (Monuments 25/26, 27, 88, and 89) but also bear carved images of the Olmec Maize God (Taube 1996).

Karl Taube (1996:68–69, Figure 24) interprets these specific stelae as representations of the Maize God in the form of a monumentalized, handheld, ritual maize fetish. The bindings on the lower third of the four Maize God images further support Taube's argument (see Figure 4.5a). As integral parts of fetishes, such bindings tie the feathers and vegetation, which comprise the fetishes, together (Taube 1996:Figure 24). These same bindings, however, strikingly recall those used ritually to bundle stelae in the contexts previously mentioned. This evidence suggests that ritually binding and enclosing stelae is a very ancient practice. The pattern of stela bundling itself may be linked to the construction and setting of the monument. The binding may involve encasing the whole monument as a part of practically transporting (and protecting) the piece. It may also have an analogy in the life cycle of maize, however. The binding and covering that shrouds the monument, like the shucking of a maize ear, is removed on ceremonial occasions to reveal the ritual "kernel" of the event depicted. Such an iconographic complex undoubtedly represents the binding practice observed on Chalcatzingo Monument 21 as well as on the La Venta celtiform stelae. Interestingly, this monument bundle complex can be traced to smaller, handheld ritual objects, which may date to the period of the earliest ritual behaviors in Mesoamerica.

The placement of these four stelae as a monument grouping directly south of the La Venta pyramid epitomizes Ann Cyphers Guillén's (1999) proposal that myths, such as cosmological modeling, were ritually reenacted through the use of sculpture. In the case of La Venta Monuments 25/26, 27, 88, and 89, such stelae served as billboards proclaiming the pyramid's sacred geographical identity as an earthly manifestation of the First True Mountain of Maize. The fact that the supporting platform was also constructed in the form of the maize-derived trefoil further reinforces this identification (Heizer et al. 1968:129–130).

Although the central plaza in front of the pyramid was invested with a number of important monuments, the majority, unfortunately, are so fragmented that they resist meaningful iconographic interpretation. The most prominent exceptions are La Venta Colossal Head 1 and Stela 2 (Figure 4.12a and 4.12b). Returning to the Olmec colossal heads, David Grove (1981) has argued that placing La Venta Stela 2 next to Monument (i.e., colossal head) 1 was the conscious act of a later La Venta ruler. By erecting his stelae near the earlier monument and by wearing a towering headdress that incorporates elements from the headdress on Monument 1, Grove continues, this later ruler was relating himself to the earlier ruler depicted as the colossal head.

The headdress element that both monuments conspicuously share is the Maize God trefoil. On Colossal Head 1, the trefoil turns down, whereas on Stela 2 the trefoil appears in both upturned and downturned configurations on the carving of the elaborately costumed ruler. As discussed, the trefoil in a headdress identifies the elite wearer with the Maize God and with a specific cosmic function as the axis-mundi. Although separated stylistically and temporally, the tre-

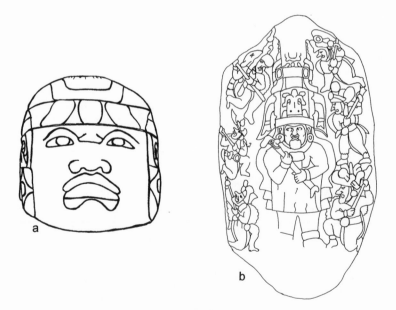

Figure 4.12. *(a, b)* La Venta Colossal Head 1 and Stela 2. Though stylistically distinct, each figure has the trefoil motif incorporated into its headdress (drawings by Jack Johnson after photographs by Kent Reilly).

foil element in the costume imagery of these two La Venta monuments suggests that both rulers are dressed as the Olmec Maize God.

Because the trefoil in the headdress identifies the Maize God, why were these two monuments, of different types, erected so near each other? Agreeing with Grove that the intentional placement relates to an expression of ancestral power, I believe the ancestral association derives from the supernatural identity signaled in the trefoil headdress, as well as suggesting a kin reference or even a relationship for propaganda purposes.

Cyphers Guillén's contention that Olmec monuments express transformation, both through their reworking and their grouping, is relevant here. La Venta Colossal Head 1 unquestionably depicts an Olmec ruler in the form of a colossal head. Likewise, La Venta Stela 2 fits Porter's celtiform category, as stelae relate to smaller greenstone celts that ritually signify ears of maize. The human figure carved on Stela 2 not only wears in its headdress the downturned trefoil that Colossal Head 1 also wears in its towering headdress but also wears in his costume the more traditional, upturned trefoil, which originates from a "bar-and-four-dots motif" strongly associated with the axis-mundi (Reilly 1994a:179–182). Undoubtedly, the elite individual on La Venta Stela 2 should be understood as representing the ruler as divinity, in this case the Maize God.

How does the ruler as Maize God image on Stela 2 relate to the elite figure wearing a downturned trefoil on Colossal Head 1? The answer to this question requires understanding a possible function for the colossal head as a sculptural form. Gillespie (1999:243) has suggested that Olmec colossal heads "have no formal equivalent in later Mesoamerican artworks." One possible exception to Gillespie's observation is the large carved monument depicting the severed head of the Aztec goddess Coyolxauhqui, which is now displayed in the Museo Nacional de Antropología e Historia in Mexico City. Although no direct relationship between these two temporally and culturally distinct monuments is demonstrable, a thematic connection between them may prove that they both represent severed heads.

Undoubtedly, the Coyolxauhqui monument represents a decapitated head. Because La Venta Colossal Head 1 wears the Maize God's trefoil headdress, the colossal head as a monument category may best be understood as depicting the Olmec ruler as the severed or decapitated head of the Maize God himself. If this interpretation can be documented further, then Olmec colossal heads, as a category, indeed may be understood as termination monuments. Porter's demonstration that in several cases Olmec colossal heads are, in fact, recarved altars/thrones seems to bolster this view. As suggested, altars/thrones may well function as accession monuments. If this is truly the case, it is reasonable that they would be recarved as termination monuments of deceased rulers. In fact, a given ruler's accession monument (altar/throne) might well be recarved—or transformed—

into his own termination monument (colossal portrait head). In line with this argument, Grove (1981), when examining monument destruction at San Lorenzo, La Venta, and Chalcatzingo, has proposed that the death of an Olmec ruler occasioned the decapitation of his portrait statuary and the mutilation of his other monuments.

If further research supports my hypothesis that La Venta Colossal Head 1 depicts a dead ruler as the severed head of the Maize God, then the same investigations may reveal that Stela 2 portrays a later ruler costumed as the resurrected Maize God. Certainly in Late Classic Maya art, the decapitated head of the Maize God is strongly associated with the resurrected Maize God. For example, on a Late Classic Maya plate (Freidel et al. 1993:68, Figure 2.4) the Hero Twins are shown resurrecting the Maize God; in fact, one twin is actually watering his "sprouting" father (Figure 4.13a)! The resurrected Maize God emerges from a

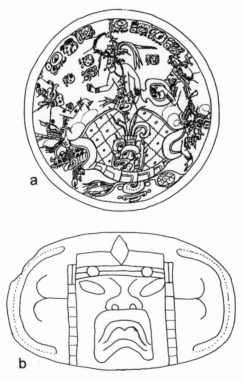

Figure 4.13. *(a)* Late Classic Maya plate. On this plate the Maya Maize God emerges from a cleft in a turtle shell (drawing by Linda Schele, © David Schele, in Freidel et al. 1993:Figure 2:4); *(b)* Olmec-style jade pectoral from La Encrucijada. This Olmec carved jade depicts the head of the Maize God on the underside of a turtle shell (redrawn by Kent Reilly from Taube 1996:Figure 22c).

cleft in the back of a turtle shell, a metaphor for the earth. In Maya art, turtle imagery repeatedly evokes the sacred landscape of creation. A turtle shell not only functions metaphorically as the earth from which the Maize God sprouts but also is depicted carrying the three stones of creation (Freidel et al. 1993:79–83).

Also on this Late Classic Maya plate, directly below the image of the sprouting Maize God, the artist has painted the Maize God's severed head. In this instance, the head serves metaphorically as the seed from which the Maize God has grown. The theme is strongly transformational, depicting that which is dead transforming into that which is alive and, more important, life-giving to others. This linking of severed heads with sprouting maize in a transformational theme is also inscribed on an Olmec-style jade pectoral from La Encrucijada, Tabasco (Figure 4.13b) (Taube 1996:62, Figure 22). This Formative period pectoral is a prototype for the Classic Maya resurrection scene discussed above. Here, vegetation sprouts from the cleft in the Maize God's head, which is positioned on the underside of a turtle shell. This pectoral is one of the most striking examples of the ideological and thematic continuity between Olmec and Maya art, underscoring the fact that although much of Mesoamerican art is stylistically vigorous, it is thematically conservative in many respects (Reilly 1998).

Returning to the function of the sculptural grouping composed of Colossal Head 1 and Stela 2 in the main plaza at La Venta, we should remember that an argument could be made that the pyramid, which dominates the plaza, ritually functioned as a critical location in a constructed geography of creation—"the first true mountain of maize." The archaeological context of Colossal Head 1 and Stela 2, combined with a close analysis of their iconography in conjunction with their placement in a public location in front of the pyramid, reveals a distinct ideological message. This message appears to associate one protagonist—fictive or actual—with a later descendant by means of their mutual supernatural identity as the Maize God. The placement of such sculptural groupings within the largest public plaza at La Venta identifies it as the space for ritual performances associated with the reenactments of such creation epics as the decapitation and resurrection of the Olmec Maize God. Such rituals undoubtedly functioned to validate a system of rulership whose claim to supernatural sanction drew from this great creation epic.

La Venta, Tomb C

The last aspect of Olmec monument placement I will discuss concerns elite tombs. The conservatism of certain themes in Mesoamerican art and ritual is nowhere better illustrated than in the organization of La Venta Tomb C. Constructed in a less accessible area than La Venta's public plaza, Tomb C was positioned between the range mounds in the northern half of Complex A (Wedel in

Drucker 1952:65–76, plate 14). Placed within Mound A-3, the construction of Tomb C may very well constitute the terminal event in the ritual life of the area of Complex A that Mounds A-3 and A-4 define (Reilly 1999:20–21) (Figure 4.14).

Called a "cyst tomb" by the excavators, Tomb C is an extremely large coffin or benchlike construction measuring 5.2 meters east to west, 1.8 meters north to south, and 1.2 meters in depth (Drucker 1952:68). The overall shape of Tomb C, with its construction from sandstone slabs, relates to the possible links between Olmec altars/thrones and bench or boxlike sarcophagi, recalling the K'iche' Maya concept of such structures as the sleeping or dreaming place of ancestors (Gillespie 1999:238–240).

Not only was Tomb C walled and roofed with sandstone slabs but also its floor was constructed from nine neatly dressed sandstone slabs, none of which was of identical proportions (Wedel in Drucker 1952:68). Perhaps for the builders of Tomb C, the nine flooring slabs represented the nine levels of the underworld. The evidence for such an analogy is problematic, however, because ritual structures such as Tomb C are rare in the Olmec heartland; the only other one at La Venta is the famous basalt Column Tomb in Mound A-2, and its floor is paved with only eight stones (Drucker 1952:22–33).

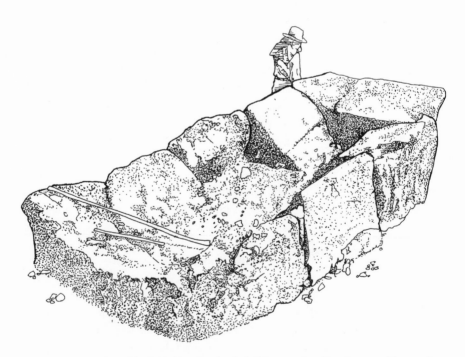

Figure 4.14. La Venta Tomb C (drawing by Jack Johnson after Drucker 1952:Plate 14a).

Although no human remains were recovered from Tomb C, beneath a thick bed of what is apparently brilliant red cinnabar, the position of jade costume elements suggests mortuary offerings or costume details attached to a burial (Wedel in Drucker 1952:68–71). Along the edges of the tomb floor were thirty-seven greenstone celts, twenty-four of which were paired (Wedel in Drucker 1952:69–70). Three coarse buff-ware vessels were scattered among these celts, and one was decorated with a snarling, fanged zoomorphic face (Wedel in Drucker 1952:69–70). The overall design of this face recalls the features carved on Chalcatzingo Monument 9 (Drucker 1952:Figure 18b).

In the excavators' opinion, the burial, or set of burial offerings, in Tomb C was covered in a shroud to which "scores of tiny jade beads, pendants, spangles, and other objects" had been sewn (Wedel in Drucker 1952:70). Had a corpse actually been deposited in Tomb C, the burial offerings show that the body would have been laid out with its head toward the east and its feet toward the west. Underneath this disintegrated shroud, earspools or earflares with dangles were in place on either side of where the head of the corpse may have once been. Above these earflares, the excavators recovered a jade tube that may have formed part of a headdress or headband. Lower down, running north to south, is what appears to be a belt constructed from large jade beads. Among the belt beads, a standing greenstone figure, a jade perforator, and a magnificently carved, obsidian core incised with the image of a raptorial avian were recovered. These three objects were so close to each other and to the jade belt that they may very well have been in a bag—now disintegrated—that hung from the belt.

Among the more striking burial offerings is a pair of earspools with corresponding jade counterweights or dangles. Beautifully incised, double-headed snakelike supernaturals bracket the central hole of each jade earspool. The bottom part of this "doubleheaded serpent bar" consists of a classic Olmec-style, downturned "were-jaguar" face. Above the central hole, two curling elements emerge from an incised, dotted oval, which closely resembles a sprouting seed. The dangles or pendants that hung from these earflares were carved in the shape of jaws (Figure 4.15a). The incised imagery is strikingly similar to the overall thematic design of the Sarcophagus Lid at the Classic Maya site of Palenque as well as to the costume details that the eighth-century ruler of Copan, Waxaklajun Ub'ah K'awil, wears on Copan Stelae B and F (Schele and Mathews 1998:133–174) (Figure 4.15b). The overall configuration of these earflares is that of the vision serpent's jaws bracketing a maize seed. Certainly this iconographic configuration represents a major theme on the Palenque Sarcophagus Lid, where the jaws of a vision serpent bracket the ruler Janab' Pakal II, dressed as the young Maize God (Schele and Freidel 1990; Schele and Mathews 1998:95–132; Schele and Miller 1986). In the carved images of Waxaklajun Ub'ah K'awil, a ritual shell object brackets the ruler's mouth; its overall shape and position on the Copanec

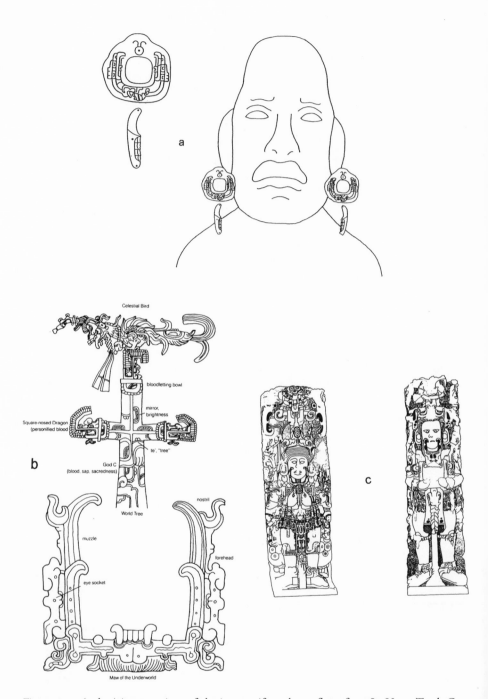

Figure 4.15. *(a, b, c)* A comparison of the jaw motif on the earflares from La Venta Tomb C, the Palenque Sarcophagus Lid, and Copan Stelae B and F (drawing by Kent Reilly after Drucker 1952:Figure 46; drawing by Linda Schele, © David Schele, in Freidel et al. 1993:Figure 2:12; and drawing by Linda Schele, © David Schele, in Schele and Mathews 1998:Figures 4.29 and 4.17).

ruler's face strongly recalls the earflare configuration and placement in La Venta Tomb C. Because of their positioning, these earflares also would have bracketed the face of the wearer. That the bracket-and-serpent motif used in La Venta Tomb C also appears in the Tomb of Janab' Pakal II again underscores the thematic conservatism of Mesoamerican art and vividly attests to its thematic origins in the culture of the heartland Olmec.

Considering the placement of Tomb C within the triangle that the three greenstone mosaic masks form (David Freidel, personal communication 1994)— a three-stone place—and then relating that placement to the resurrection iconography of the later Classic Maya, the iconographic and ideological similarities between the two cultures appear even more closely related. Tomb C itself is the benchlike dreaming or resting place of the ancestors, which Gillespie so elegantly describes. The tomb's placement among the three masks, however, as well as the resurrection and emergence imagery within the burial offerings, suggests that this benchlike tomb also served as a metaphorical equivalent to the turtle images, from whence the Maize God sprouts anew.

The layout of Tomb C conveyed the same thematic message as the imagery painted on the Classic Maya plate discussed previously. The brilliance of La Venta's builders comes arrestingly into focus when one takes into account the placement and construction of Tomb C, the intentional grouping of Colossal Head 1 and Stela 2, and the disposition of the celtiform stelae in front of the pyramid. The evidence of La Venta's layout, tombs, monuments, and iconography strongly supports an interpretation that its overall site plan re-creates the landscape of primordial creation. On this ritual stage, the rites of world renewal and elite validation were reenacted within the supernatural landscape and by the geography of the creation event.

The rulers of this heartland site were encoding and manipulating the symbolic messages contained in an epic legend to breathtaking effect. In other words, the architecture, monuments, caches, and tombs of La Venta physically remanifested the supernatural power released into the world at creation and were revalidated with each ritual representation. La Venta's art, architecture, and site layout magnificently proclaimed that this supernatural power could be accessed through the rituals performed at La Venta by its divine rulers who in themselves manifested the gods who had created this world.

5

Carved in Stone

The Cosmological Narratives of Late Preclassic Izapan-Style Monuments from the Pacific Slope

Julia Guernsey Kappelman

This chapter focuses on the themes of rulership and creation that were featured on Late Preclassic (300 B.C.E.–C.E. 200) Izapan-style monuments from the Pacific slope region, specifically from the sites of Izapa in Chiapas, Mexico, and Abaj Takalik, Guatemala. The monuments from these sites share a vocabulary of forms, a stylistic sensibility, and a variety of themes that were manipulated by the ruling elite to accommodate their claims to power in both this world and the supernatural sphere. Of greatest interest are those monuments whose imagery and messages are echoed in the sculptural corpus of both sites. The shared narratives of the monuments evidence active participation in a Late Preclassic communication sphere through which basic principles of rulership and worldview were articulated.

The term *Izapan style* takes its name from the site of Izapa, but it also applies to contemporaneous stone carvings from sites located throughout a broad geographic region extending from Chiapas to the valleys of central Veracruz and down into the highlands and coastal piedmont of Guatemala.[1] Typically, Izapan-style monuments are characterized by the fluid contours of their bas-reliefs and the complexity of details within their compositions (Coe 1965b). Izapan-style monuments also share a vocabulary of iconographic forms that, although distinct, links them to the art of the Middle Formative Olmec and Classic Maya.[2] In fact, their intermediary nature—stylistic, iconographic, and temporal—between the art of the Olmec and Maya has been emphasized in the literature since the earliest publications by Stirling (1943). Nevertheless, the messages encoded into these Late Preclassic Izapan-style monuments represent a mature expression of civilization. Not mere iconographic or stylistic intermediaries, Izapan-style monuments are testaments—carved in stone—to a sophisticated and dynamic Late Preclassic political ideology and worldview that was shared across a broad geographic region.

Both Izapa and Abaj Takalik occupied strategic locations along communication routes between the Pacific coast and interior regions of modern Mexico and Guatemala. Izapa, located in the Soconusco region of Chiapas, is approximately fifty kilometers northwest of the hill-terrace site of Abaj Takalik in the Guatemalan Pacific piedmont. This region represented a critically important crossroads of communication during the Late Preclassic between Mayan-speaking peoples to the east and Mixe-Zoquean–speaking peoples to the west. The Izapans probably spoke a Mixe-Zoquean language as the site is located at the southeasternmost extension of what has been defined as the Mixe-Zoquean language region.[3] Glyphlike forms that appear on several of the Izapa monuments also compare closely to hieroglyphs from the epi-Olmec script on La Mojarra Stela 1 (ca. C.E. 157), from Veracruz, whose language was ancestral to modern Zoquean languages (Justeson and Kaufman 1993). In contrast, the site of Abaj Takalik appears to have been ethnically Maya by at least the Late Preclassic period, as evidenced by the hieroglyphic inscription on Abaj Takalik Stela 5, which dates to circa C.E. 126 and bears the title *ajaw* spelled in Mayan with the phonetic complement *-wa* (John Justeson, personal communication 1997). Accordingly, the symbol systems and thematic programs shared by monuments from Izapa and Abaj Takalik appear to have transcended linguistic boundaries and ethnic divisions and become the lingua franca of a cross-cultural, Late Preclassic interaction sphere.

Examination of cosmologically—and politically—charged narratives found within the sculptural corpus at both sites provides important insight into the types of messages that were being communicated during the Late Preclassic. One recurrent theme concerns the birth and resurrection of the Maize God, featured in the monumental programs of Izapa, on Stelae 22 (Figure 5.1) and 67 (Figure 5.2), and Abaj Takalik, on Stela 4 (Figure 5.3).[4] Similar motifs were used to convey this creation narrative at both sites and appear to have been part of a standard, Late Preclassic iconography. For instance, all three stelae contain combinations of emergent figures, portals, twisting conduits, and a watery basal band that is bound on both ends by a zoomorphic mask. Although each is presented in a unique manner, the theme of all three appears to be the transportation, sacrifice, and rebirth of the Maize God from a watery realm that was marked by a cosmic portal. Featured as a part of this cosmological narrative during the Late Preclassic was the appearance of a cosmic conduit, depicted as either a twisted cord or as the undulating body of a serpent.

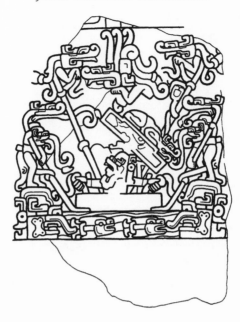

Figure 5.1. Izapa Stela 22 (drawing by Ayax Moreno; courtesy of the New World Archaeological Foundation).

Figure 5.2. Izapa Stela 67 (drawing by Ayax Moreno; courtesy of the New World Archaeological Foundation).

Figure 5.3. Abaj Takalik Stela 4 (drawing by the author after John Graham in Orrego 1990:Lámina No. 24).

The Maize God Narrative at Izapa

Izapa Stela 67 (Figure 5.2) depicts an individual, with arms outstretched and hands clasping scepters, being transported in a rectilinear, lidded device that floats above a watery band bound on either side by a zoomorphic head. Framing the figure is a scalloped cartouche or portal. Wrapping around the base of the rectilinear device and extending upward on either side is a long rope or cord. Visible in the upper-right corner of the stela is a partially effaced figure who appears to grasp and pull the cord upward; the remnants of a similar figure in the upper-left corner can also be discerned.

The posture of the figure on Izapa Stela 67 closely parallels Classic period renditions of the Maize God being reborn from a watery underworld location, often conceived of as a turtle carapace or piscine creature (Freidel et al. 1993; Quenon and Le Fort 1997; Taube 1985, 1996). For instance, a Maya Classic period codex-style vase (Figure 5.4) depicts the Maize God emerging from a turtle shell with arms outstretched in a manner similar to that of the figure on Izapa Stela 67. The position of the Hero Twins who flank the Maize God and grasp his hands on the Classic period vessel recalls the positioning of the small figures that pulled the cords on either side of the central figure on Stela 67.

This narrative of the birth of the Maize God, recorded through imagery and text on numerous Classic period ceramics and monuments, was one part of a

Figure 5.4. Codex-style vessel depicting the birth of the Maize God from a turtle shell (drawing by the author after Kerr 1994:No. 4681).

great Maya creation epic.[5] As Freidel et al. (1993) and Quenon and Le Fort (1997) observed, the Classic period narrative of the Maize God's rebirth consisted of four primary episodes: his birth, costuming, transportation in a canoe, and ultimate emergence/resurrection. These episodes could be presented independently or conflated into composite scenes that embraced several different events simultaneously. For instance, a vessel from the Popol Vuh Museum (Figure 5.5) depicts the birth of the Maize God from a piscine creature at the lower right, his costuming by two nude women at the left, and his transportation in a canoe at the top right (Freidel et al. 1993:92; Quenon and Le Fort 1997:885–886). Other objects, such as a series of incised bones from Tikal Burial 116, focus on the theme of the Maize God's transportation in a canoe.[6] While two of the bones depict the sinking of the Maize God's canoe as a metaphorical representation of his descent into the watery underworld, another features his successful passage to the location where he would be resurrected.

This transportation of the Maize God in a canoe is paralleled in the Izapan composition by the rectilinear device that floats in a watery basal band. In fact, the shape of the device on Stela 67 (Figure 5.2) compares closely to the canoe depicted on the vase from the Popol Vuh Museum (Figure 5.5). The Izapa composition also resembles an Early Classic covered bowl from Rio Hondo that likewise narrates events from the Maize God's rebirth (Quenon and Le Fort 1997:Figure 17). The watery bands of the Rio Hondo vessel emerge from per-

Figure 5.5. Popol Vuh Museum vase MS0740 (drawing by Linda Schele, © David Schele).

sonified water lily heads whose zoomorphic profiles recall those on Stela 67. Quenon and Le Fort (1997:890–891) observed that the Rio Hondo bowl depicts a watery environment that bears the souls of the dead in conch shells, while above, each of four fish-snakes burps forth the head of a Maize God. This life-death opposition parallels the descent of the Maize God as depicted on the Tikal bones and alludes to his eventual resurrection from the watery underworld.

In contrast to these Classic period examples, which portray the Maize God performing various scenes from the creation narrative, the protagonist on Stela 67 appears to be an Izapa ruler acting in the guise and role of the maize deity rather than the Maize God himself. On Stela 67, the central figure wears a buccal mask and beard, costume paraphernalia often worn by Late Preclassic elite ritual practitioners within the context of a performance.[7] Furthermore, the figure not only wears these costume components but also clasps scepters of rulership in his hands in a gesture of supreme authority.[8] A Late Preclassic image of deity imper-sonation, such as Izapa Stela 67, accords with the many Classic period images of rulers performing in the guise of the Maize God and reenacting passages from the creation narrative as, for instance, on El Peru Stela 34 and Copan Stela H (Freidel et al. 1993:277; Quenon and Le Fort 1997).

Izapa Stela 67, then, features an Izapa ruler reenacting the events of creation in the persona of the Maize God. The imagery of Stela 67 appears to reference more than one episode from the Maize God story, however. Although it depicts the transportation of the ruler/Maize God in a canoe through a watery realm, it also portrays him rising up from the canoe and framed by an enormous car-touche with scalloped edges. This cartouche on Stela 67 represents the Izapa version of a portal and appears on other monuments at the site within the context of emergence or rebirth. For instance, a similar portal with scalloped edges and centrally infixed crossed bands decorates the top of Izapa Throne 1 (Figure 5.6a). When seated on Throne 1, an Izapa ruler literally entered a portal or a liminal space in which he could communicate with the supernatural realm. Confirmation of this exists on Izapa Stela 8 (Figure 5.6b), which depicts a ruler seated on a throne—whose profile exactly matches that of Throne 1—within a quatrefoil cartouche that marks the back of an enormous zoomorph, itself a metaphor for a portal or opening into another realm (Norman 1976:105; Taube 1998). Above the quatrefoil on Stela 8 is a crenellated cartouche that corresponds to the portal on Throne 1. In other words, the Stela 8 composition suggests that the quatrefoil borne on the back of the zoomorphic beast is equivalent to the scalloped portal above which matches the decoration on the seat of Throne 1 and that both metaphorically alluded to the cosmic journey of the ruler. Accordingly, Stela 8 visually records the actions performed by an Izapa ruler as he sat on Throne 1, passed through the cosmic portal, and conjured the powers of the universe.

Of note, Izapa Throne 1 compares closely to an altar from El Peru (Figure 5.7a), which also depicts a ruler enthroned within a cartouche that is carried on the back of a zoomorphic beast (Freidel et al. 1993:215). The text on the El Peru

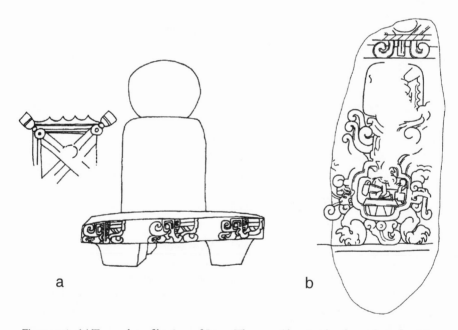

a

b

Figure 5.6. (a) Top and profile view of Izapa Throne 1 (drawing by the author after Norman 1973:Plate 63); (b) Izapa Stela 8 (after Norman 1976:Figure 3.8; courtesy of the New World Archaeological Foundation).

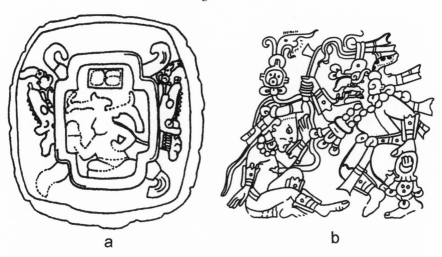

a   b

Figure 5.7. *(a)* El Peru Altar (drawing by Linda Schele, © David Schele, in Freidel et al. 1993:Figure 4:27); *(b)* Detail of *Dresden Codex,* page 42c (drawing by Matthew Looper).

altar describes the cartouche as *tu yol ak,* "at the heart of the turtle" or "in the portal of the turtle" (Linda Schele, personal communication 1997). Because the Maize God also emerges from a turtle, the enthroned ruler on the El Peru altar is placed directly within the context of the Maize God's rebirth. By analogy, Izapa Stela 67, Stela 8, and Throne 1 take on even greater cosmological significance when they too are understood against the backdrop of creation: the scalloped cartouches into which the Izapa rulers passed were not only metaphorical representations of cosmic portals but also powerful references to the creation narrative of the Maize God's rebirth. The Izapa rulers on Stelae 67 and 8 were analogous to the Maize God. Furthermore, the lidded, canoelike device on Stela 67 subtly alludes to this creation narrative. When the "top" of the canoe is closed over the lower portion, a *k'an*-cross shape is formed that compares closely with the *k'an*-cross motif on the El Peru altar. Clearly, during both the Late Preclassic and Classic periods, the *k'an*-cross motif marked a place of emergence and specifically the birthplace of the Maize God (Freidel et al. 1993:94).

This same narrative, with important variations, was also featured on Izapa Stela 22 (Figure 5.1). Stela 22, however, provides a counterpoint to the narrative of the Maize God's rebirth featured on Stela 67 by referencing instead the sacrificial death of the Maize God, an act necessary for his eventual resurrection. As on Stela 67, the figure on Stela 22 is transported in a canoe through a watery realm marked by swimming fish. Of note, however, the two zoomorphic heads that bound the waters on Stela 22 possess skeletal jaws, in marked contrast to the fleshy jaws of the zoomorphs on Stela 67. In addition, the Maize God on Stela 22 does not wield the scepters of rulership as he had on Stela 67, nor is he framed by the scalloped portal that symbolized his rebirth.

The subtle references to sacrifice on Stela 22 presage Classic period Maize God imagery that also references the death of the Maize God. For example, Taube (1985:176) noted the disembodied heads of the Maize God found at the center of Late Classic plates and discussed them as symbols of the harvested maize cut from the stalk. The imagery of Stela 22 also relates closely to that of the Tikal Bones that depict the sinking of the Maize God's canoe into the watery realm of the underworld or his requisite passage into death that preceded his resurrection and rebirth. Like these Classic period examples, Izapa Stela 22 appears to reference the sacrificial overtones of the creation narrative yet conflates this message with that of the Maize God's transportation to the place of resurrection.

When the pair is considered as a conceptual whole, Izapa Stelae 22 and 67 encompass both the sacrifice and the rebirth of the Maize God and embody the reciprocal relationship between death and creation that was predicated on the life cycle of maize and given narrative form through the myth of the Maize God (Taube 1985). Together they carry the same message of life-death opposition as seen on the Rio Hondo bowl, which likewise paired souls of the dead with emergent heads of the Maize God. Stelae 67 also provides valuable insight into the kinds of performances that must have characterized Late Preclassic rulership in which a ruler enacted passages from the creation story.[9] By equating his actions to those of the Maize God, a ruler was able to define himself as the guarantor of world order and continued agricultural prosperity.

Unfortunately, although the primary context of Stelae 22 and 67 is not known, their original locations must have been carefully woven into the complex sculptural program of Izapa.[10] With their aquatic emphasis, it is tempting to think that perhaps they were originally erected in association with the dams and aqueducts that channeled water through the ceremonial center to the Rio Izapa, which formed the eastern boundary of the site (Lowe et al. 1982:166–173). A reservoir and drainage system was also in place during the Late Preclassic around the base of Mound 60, the largest pyramidal structure, which was located at the heart of the central precinct at Izapa. These waters must certainly have functioned as a symbolic primordial sea, referencing the fertile, first waters of creation. At their center, Mound 60 rose, replicating the landscape of creation that had been built by Mesoamerican peoples at least since the time of the Olmec and that included the mountain of sustenance, where maize was created, rising from the waters of the primordial sea (Kappelman 2001).[11] An original, albeit speculative, location for Stelae 22 and 67 at the center of Izapa and adjacent to the waters that flowed through the site and around Mound 60, the mountain of sustenance, would have placed the monuments within this human-made landscape of creation. This position would have invoked a striking harmony between the rituals recorded on the monuments, their references to the creation narrative, and their context within the sacred landscape. Such an architectural and sculptural environment would also have provided an appropriate theater in which rulership and its cosmic foundations—the very themes of the monuments themselves—could have been dramatized (cf. Wheatley 1971).

Cosmic Umbilici at Izapa

Prominently featured within the compositions of Stelae 22 and 67, and intimately connected to their themes of rulership and cosmic order, was the manifestation of a twisted cord. On Stela 67, this cord emerges from under the canoe, pulled upward by the fragmentary remains of small figures on either side of the central figure. These cords are much more prominently depicted on Stela 22 (Figure 5.1): one set of serpentine cords emerges from beneath the canoe as on Stela 67, a second set is grasped by the Maize God, and a third rises up behind him in a V-shaped configuration. The cords then spiral upward, pulled by various anthropomorphic and zoomorphic creatures that congregate at the sides and top of the composition.

The manifestation of the twisted cord within these Izapa images carries significance on a number of different levels. As Miller (1974) originally demonstrated, twisted cords are synonymous with intertwined serpents and umbilici as symbols of cosmic communication and birth throughout the corpus of Precolumbian art. He further cited a belief among the Yucatec Maya, recorded by Tozzer (1907:153–154), of a celestial umbilicus that appeared during the first epoch of creation. This umbilicus was called the *kuxan sum,* and it connected the ancient rulers to deities in the celestial sphere.

The imagery of Stelae 22 and 67 indicates that, during the Late Preclassic, the emergence of twisted cords was critical to defining the generative act of the Maize God's death, transportation, and ultimate rebirth. Like the cords in the Yucatec Maya myth, the twisted or serpentine cords on Stelae 22 and 67 appear to have forged a path of communication between the natural world and the supernatural realm. This Late Preclassic imagery is in accordance with images from later periods that also detail the appearance of cords from the body of the Maize God at the moment of creation.[12] For instance, page 19 of the *Paris Codex* depicts the Maize God, eyes closed in death, suspended from a cord that emerges from his stomach during the creation of the universe (Freidel et al. 1993:99–100, Figure 2:32). This same imagery also appears at Chichen Itza. As Schele and Mathews (1998:249–251, Figure 6.49) observed, the west column in the inner doorway of the North Temple depicts two supine maize deities, each of whom supports a serpent that emerges from their torsos as a metaphor for both the umbilicus and the viscera of intestine sacrifice. Such imagery encapsulates both the sacrificial and generative symbolism of the Maize God narrative and recalls the same duality that characterized the imagery of Izapa Stelae 22 and 67 (Looper and Kappelman 2000).

Likewise, the *Dresden Codex* contains a passage that corresponds directly to this creation story. On page 42c (Figure 5.7b), Chaak strikes with his axe a fallen figure that is named in the accompanying text as the Maize God (Schele and Grube 1997:232). In Classic period vessel imagery, it is Chaak who cracks open the turtle shell from which the Maize God is reborn. As Chaak strikes the Maize God in the Dresden version of the story, a flowering cord—marked with an *ajaw* face and curling tendrils—emerges from the Maize God's torso (Stone 1995b). This *ajaw* face logograph carries the value *nik,* "flower," and was incorporated into Classic and Postclassic iconography as a symbol of vital life forces that was typically represented as a "white flower" or *sak nik*.[13] Accordingly, in the *Dresden Codex,* the rebirth of the Maize God from the turtle shell is substituted with an image of the emergence of a cord—depicted as a flowering vine imbued with a vital life force—from the torso of the Maize God. This flowery cord, metaphorically associated with both umbilici and intestines, embodied the sacrificial and procreative nature of the maize deity.

Twisted cord and umbilical imagery also carried powerful astronomical significance. As Freidel et al. (1993:99–107) explained, the Maize God's umbilicus was echoed in the night sky in the form of the ecliptic, or path of the sun. For example, an offering vessel from Tikal shows the Maize God at the center of the composition, holding a bicephalic serpent from whose open maws emerge the Paddler Gods. Freidel et al. (1993:79, Figure 2:9) described this image as that moment at creation when the Maize God stretched out the path of the sun and planets—or the ecliptic, represented as a double-headed serpent—across the sky. The *Paris Codex* image of the Maize God and umbilicus is seen as a representation of the laying out of the ecliptic at the moment of creation, metaphorically embracing references to sacrifice, birth, and the astronomy of the night sky.[14]

The plethora of twisted cords on Izapa Stelae 22 and 67 can thus be understood as powerful symbols of the generative act of the Maize God, whose death and rebirth ushered in the present creation and resulted in the manifestation of the ecliptic, which was itself perceived as a conduit, or cosmic umbilicus. The anthropomorphic and zoomorphic figures that facilitate the emergence of the cords on the Izapan stelae are probably analogous to the many "helper" figures included in Classic period imagery. As Quenon and Le Fort (1997:894) noted with respect to this, the Maize God was rarely depicted alone at his resurrection but was typically accompanied by the Hero Twins or various Chaak figures who split open the turtle carapace with their stone axes.[15]

The complex imagery of Stelae 22 and 67 anticipates the equally rich cosmological imagery of many Classic period monuments and vessels. It contains vivid references to passages from the creation story that featured the sacrificial and generative acts of the Maize God and the emergence of a cosmic conduit that connected this world to the supernatural realm. Even more important for an understanding of Late Preclassic Izapan-style monuments such as these, the imagery neatly wove the office of rulership into this paradigm by depicting a ruler in the role of the Maize God. The ruler on Stela 67—performing key events from the Maize God narrative—clasps in his hands the scepters of rulership while also manifesting the cosmic umbilicus or metaphorical ecliptic. In so doing, he defined himself as a conduit through which communication was established between the natural world and the supernatural sphere. He also defined himself as the guarantor of world order, who continued to make manifest the path of the sun and constellations, as had the Maize God at the moment of creation.[16]

The Creation Narrative at Abaj Takalik

This same message, with poetic variations, was also featured at the site of Abaj Takalik on Stela 4 (Figure 5.3) that, with its dense imagery and convoluted forms, exemplifies the Izapan style.[17] At the center of the image, a serpent ascends upward from a medallion-marked portal with a centrally infixed U that rests in the middle of a watery band. The serpent's body entwines around a flower-marked cartouche at the center of the composition and is marked by several curling projections, each of which bears a set of tubular beads. Emerging out of the toothy upper jaw of the serpent is the head of an individual who wears a jade bead at the end of his nose. The watery band at the base of the composition is enframed by zoomorphs whose open maws spew forth the water and whose position and appearance recall the zoomorphic heads that bound the watery bands on Izapa Stelae 22 and 67. They wear elaborate earflares and nose beads and possess U-infixed eyebrows and tall foreheads that terminate in trilobed, floral motifs.

The nose of the ascending serpent on Abaj Takalik Stela 4 is marked by a motif that consists of a curling, inverted U shape with central tab, flanking volutes, and emanating scrolls (Figure 5.8a). This motif frequently decorates the noses of serpents in Late Preclassic compositions and symbolizes a flower (Kappelman 1997). For example, the nose of the dangling serpent on Kaminaljuyu Altar 10 (Figure 5.8b) bears a flower rendered in the same manner as that of the Abaj Takalik serpent. Likewise, the noses of the serpents on Abaj Takalik Stela 1 and Altar 13 (Figures 5.8c and 5.8d) are marked with a similar floral form that consists of a central tab and flanking volutes. This Late Preclassic flower form is antecedent to Classic Maya examples of the *sak nik*, "white flower," that symbolized vital life forces and referenced the mythic origins of fertility and life. By bearing this floral emblem, the serpent on Abaj Takalik Stela 4 is marked specifi-

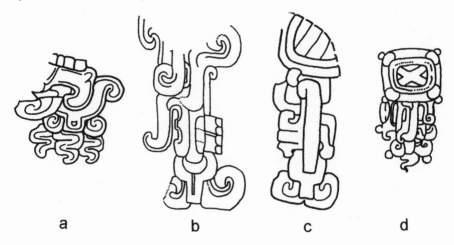

Figure 5.8. *(a)* Abaj Takalik Stela 4, detail (drawing by the author); *(b)* Kaminaljuyu Altar 10, detail (drawing by the author); *(c)* Abaj Takalik Stela 1, detail (drawing by the author); *(d)* Abaj Takalik Altar 13, detail (drawing by the author).

cally as a *sak nik* serpent, or bearer of a vital essence, and is analogous to Classic period representations of snakes that also bore the *sak nik* form and were understood as cosmic conduits, umbilici, or ecliptical representations.

The imagery of Stela 4 also compares closely to Classic period vessel imagery that depicts the birth of the Maize God from a piscine serpent (see Quenon and Le Fort 1997:Figures 5–7). In these images, only the face of the Maize God or his upper torso are visible emerging from the maw of the serpentine creature, much as in the Abaj Takalik version, where only the head of the individual is visible. As Quenon and Le Fort (1997:886–887) discussed, such scenes of birth from a watery underworld are well known and appear to represent one episode in the narrative of the Maize God's birth and resurrection. In another Classic period variation on this theme, the Maize God is carried, in a birth position, above a zoomorphic split skull whose forehead is marked with a "capped *ajaw*" version of the *nik* glyph (Figure 5.9). As Quenon and Le Fort (1997) and Looper (1995a) observed, this "capped *ajaw*" version of the *nik* sign is the same glyph that appears in "child of father" birth expressions. Accordingly, the Maize God's birth from the watery realm is marked with this *nik* floral emblem that connoted vital life essences and functioned as a metaphor for birth.

The scene on Abaj Takalik Stela 4 also recalls even more explicit Classic period descriptions of birth, as from the inscription on the Palenque Palace Tablet. There the text states that the "white flower soul," *sak-nik-nal,* of K'an Joy Chitam was born through a vision serpent that emerged from the "heart of the center of the Primordial Sea," *yol tan k'ak'-nab'* (Freidel et al. 1993:218–219, 440

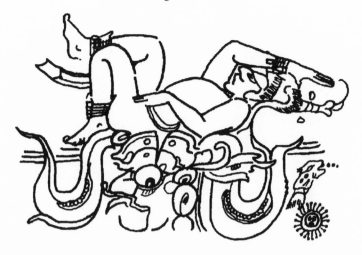

Figure 5.9. Scene of Maize God's rebirth (drawing by the author after Kerr 1990:No. 2723).

n. 16). This vivid description of a birthplace, identified as a portal in the middle of the primordial sea, exactly matches the imagery of Stela 4, which depicts the *sak nik* serpent ascending upward from the U-infixed portal at the center of the watery basal band.

The scene on Abaj Takalik Stela 4 thus depicts a highly metaphorical representation of the Maize God's birth from the watery realm of the primordial sea in much the same way as the two Izapan stelae do. The imagery of Stela 4, however, makes no reference to the episode in which the Maize God was transported in the canoe; instead, it focuses on a symbolic representation of birth that is phrased as a journey through the cosmic conduit of the *sak nik* serpent, which emerged from a portal in the middle of the distant primordial sea. Of note, the *sak nik* serpent conduit also functions as the analog to the twisted cords of Izapa Stelae 22 and 67. It is manifested at the moment of the Maize God's birth in much the same way as the twisted cords or cosmic umbilici of the Maize God were manifested at the moment of creation, as on the Late Preclassic Izapa stelae and in the Postclassic codical examples. Second, the *sak nik* serpent on Stela 4 carries subtle references to its astronomical function as an analog to the ecliptic. As Linda Schele (personal communication 1997) observed, the body of the serpent is marked by a *k'in,* or sun, glyph along its left side. The position of the *k'in* glyph in the contours of the *sak nik* serpent, as if being transported by it, alludes to the function of the serpent as a metaphorical ecliptic.[18]

The dense imagery of Stela 4, then, can be understood as a highly conceptual representation of the events of creation, which included the birth of the Maize

God from a watery location, the manifestation of a serpent conduit that connected the natural world to the supernatural sphere, and the laying out of the ecliptic, which was the analog in the night sky for the cosmic umbilicus of the Maize God. Although the imagery and narrative of Abaj Takalik Stela 4 is conceptually equivalent to that of Izapa Stelae 22 and 67, different metaphors are invoked and emphasized to create a unique presentation of this powerful passage from the creation story.

Conclusions

The narrative of the Maize God's death, transportation, and rebirth that appears on Izapa Stelae 22 and 67 and Abaj Takalik Stela 4 anticipates that of later Classic period monuments and ceramics and Postclassic codices that detail this passage from the creation story. The imagery of these three stelae, rendered in a fluid Izapan style, also incorporates many of the same formal and iconographic devices that would be featured in later Classic and Postclassic compositions and demonstrates that—already during the Late Preclassic—a standard repertoire of forms and narrative devices was consistently employed to recount specific mythological passages. Perhaps even more important, these three stelae evidence that these myths and their associated iconography were shared across linguistic and ethnic boundaries during the Late Preclassic period. In fact, it appears that this narrative of the Maize God's sacrifice and rebirth was central to the display and legitimization of power in both Mayan- and Mixe-Zoquean–speaking regions during the Late Preclassic. This is particularly well illustrated on Izapa Stela 67, which substitutes the image of the ruler for that of the Maize God, thus equating the performance and power of the Late Preclassic ruler to that of the maize deity whose actions ushered in the present creation. Seamlessly woven into this highly charged political and cosmological schema was the manifestation of cosmic conduits, whose presence marked a path of communication between this world and the supernatural sphere that was controlled by the ruler, acting in the persona of the Maize God. In effect, the imagery of Abaj Takalik Stela 4 and Izapa Stelae 22 and 67 evidences the mature expression of powerful political and cosmological messages that were monumentalized—and literally carved in stone—within the sculptural programs of Late Preclassic Pacific slope sites.

Notes

1. See Smith (1984) and Prater (1989) for a discussion of the problematic nature of the term *Izapan style*.

2. Numerous scholars have discussed the relationships among Olmec, Izapan-

style, and Classic Maya art. See Quirarte (1973), Norman (1976), and Parsons (1986) for the history of these arguments.

3. See Campbell and Kaufman (1976) and Lowe et al. (1982:9–10). At the time of the conquest, Ciudad Real (1952) recorded that Tapachultec, a Mixe tongue, was spoken in the Izapa region near the modern-day town of Tapachula.

4. Taube (1996:62) likewise suggested that Izapa Stelae 22 and 67 depict episodes from the myth of the Maize God.

5. See Freidel et al. (1993) for a thorough discussion of the Maya creation story and its associated astronomical symbolism.

6. See Freidel et al. (1993:89–91, Figures 2:25 and 2:26) and Quenon and Le Fort (1997:891) for a discussion of these incised bones from Burial 116 under Temple 1 at Tikal.

7. See, for example, the beards worn by the individuals depicted on Izapa Stela 11, Kaminaljuyu Stelae 10 and 19, and Monument J-41 from Building J at Monte Alban (Kappelman 1997:143). As Taube (1996:62) observed, Izapa Stela 11 may portray a variation on the theme of the Maize God's rebirth, as the bearded protagonist emerges—with arms outstretched in a position much like that of the figures on Stelae 22 and 67—from a toadlike beast.

8. Very similar stone scepters were recovered archaeologically in a Hato phase (50 B.C.E.–C.E. 100) urn burial from Izapa (Lowe et al. 1982:70, Figure 4.11) and in an urn burial of the same date at the site of El Sitio, Guatemala (Shook 1965:Figure 1d).

9. This is well documented during the Classic period as, for instance, on Copan Stela H, where the ruler 18-Rabbit is depicted in the jade skirt of the Maize God (Freidel et al. 1993:277–278).

10. Two fragments of Stela 22 were found during construction of a local highway (Norman 1976:127). A third, separately catalogued fragment was recognized as part of Stela 22 by Ayax Moreno, who incorporated it into his recent drawing of the monument (Figure 5-1). Stela 67 was reused as a building stone in the north playing wall of the later ballcourt in Group F (Lowe et al. 1982:226).

11. For a discussion of the nature and evolution of this archetypal landscape of creation, see Freidel et al. (1993:123–172), Reilly (1994b:192–233), and Schele and Mathews (1998:36–40).

12. Closely related to this thematic complex is a black-background cylindrical vessel that depicts the appearance of twisted serpentine cords at a place called *Na Ho Chan Witz Xaman,* a creation location associated with birth, sacrifice, and the appearance of the Maize God's umbilicus (Grube in Freidel et al. 1993:99–107, Figure 2:31; Schele and Mathews 1998:218).

13. Grube (in Schele 1992) identified the value for the *ajaw* face (T533) logograph and "capped *ajaw*" (T535) allograph as *nik,* "flower," and Stuart (1992) demonstrated

that the *ajaw* face outside of its cartouche functions iconographically as "flower." The concept of the *sak nik,* "white flower," appears in Maya texts, where it functions as a metaphor for living breath or soul force. See Freidel et al. (1993:183) for the history of this argument and Looper (1995a), Kappelman (2001), and Looper and Kappelman (2000) for discussions of the etymology and symbolism of the *sak nik* form.

14. In a paper presented at the 1999 Annual Conference of the College Art Association, Elizabeth Pope identified page 19 of the *Madrid Codex* as another version of this story in which the laying out of the ecliptic is directly tied to the narrative of the Maize God's rebirth. As she noted, the twisted cord on page 19 bears a *k'in* glyph, marking it as the ecliptic, and emerges from a blue temple that bears a turtle—a reference to the place of the Maize God's rebirth—on its roof.

15. The facilitating figures on Izapa Stelae 22 and 67 may also be related to the dwarves who often appear in Classic period vessel images within the context of the Maize God story.

16. This same iconographic repertoire would be repeated throughout the corpus of Classic period art as well. On the front of Copan Stela H, 18-Rabbit stands in the costume of the Maize God, while on either side of the stela a twisted snake cord that symbolizes the cosmic umbilicus twists upward (Freidel et al. 1993:278). Tiny Maize Gods peer out from behind the twisted serpent body, and a *sak nik,* "white flower," sign marks the nose of the serpent, referencing its identification as a flowery vine or cosmic umbilicus, much as it would mark the umbilicus of the Maize God in the *Dresden Codex.*

17. Stela 4 was first reported by Gustav Bruhl during his 1888 visit and was recovered from the finca San Isidro Piedra Parada, one of the two modern fincas that comprise the site of Abaj Takalik (see Orrego Corzo 1990:90).

18. Such imagery also provides a Late Preclassic antecedent for imagery such as that on page 19 of the *Madrid Codex* in which a *k'in* glyph is transported by a twisted cord umbilicus (see note 14 above).

6

Gardening with the Great Goddess at Teotihuacan

Annabeth Headrick

In the January of Linda Schele's last year of life, many of her students and colleagues came again to Austin, Texas, for an impromptu conference to celebrate Linda as a teacher, scholar, and friend. During a dinner at this event, Linda called me aside and spoke of an idea she had about the city of Teotihuacan. Her eyes told me that she did not have enough time to research and develop her idea fully, so she was giving it to me and asking me to see it into publication. It was a gift of a teacher, the kind she often bestowed on me and other students during discussions in her office, but this was a different type of contract. In this chapter, I seek to fulfill that contract and harvest the idea that Linda planted.

The discussion I had with Linda concerned a certain monument found at Teotihuacan (Figure 6.1). Perhaps the ugliest and shabbiest excuse for a sculpture, this battered and mutilated boulder now sits in the Plaza of the Moon, to the side of the plaza's altar. Rather than appearing as an important sculpture of the city, it looks today much more like a giant piece of rubble that was too difficult for archaeologists to move. Thus, it sits there at the heart of Teotihuacan largely ignored, but this was the sculpture that captured Linda's eye, something that perhaps many of us had thought too damaged to provide much useful information.

What Linda urged me to do was to return home and look more closely at this massive sculpture. She believed that the Teotihuacanos used this sculpture in the ritual raising of a world tree. She mentioned the rituals of the Aztecs as confirmation that such ritual tree erections were important Mesoamerican festivals, and, in typical Schele style, she raced through a litany of associations, connections, and conceptual implications that ensued from this revelation. As I walked

Figure 6.1. Damaged sculpture of the Great Goddess, Plaza of the Moon, Teotihuacan (photograph by the author).

away my mind was reeling because I knew that this was a profound idea with incredible ramifications, but I could not quite grasp all the subtleties compressed within her animated words. I had experienced a common event of Schele students. So often we would emerge after a session with her, dazed by the revolutionary ideas and sent off to mull them over till we could fully comprehend their implications.

When I returned home, I plowed through my slides and was, frankly, surprised that I had bothered to take a picture of this rock. The homely nature of its smashed surfaces surely did not send an obvious message of once-grand rituals around its base, and though there were traces of sculpted areas remaining, I did not recall spending much time studying the piece. In spite of the fact that the sculpture itself seemed to provide little support for Linda's idea, I proceeded to test the notion. Although I began with a healthy dose of skepticism, I came to find these tree-raising rituals ubiquitous in Mesoamerica and began to see that Linda's seed would indeed gestate into new insight on a Teotihuacan ritual.

The Great Goddess Sculptures

Although the battered condition of the sculpture makes iconographic identification difficult, the identity of the figure can, nevertheless, be assigned with a good deal of confidence. As Esther Pasztory (1997:99) has argued, the monument most likely represents one of the primary deities of the city, the Great Goddess.[1] Pasztory makes this argument by comparing it with another enormous sculpture that was also found in the Plaza of the Moon but near the southwest corner of the Moon Pyramid. It now stands in the Museo Nacional de Antropología in Mexico City (Figure 6.2). This second basalt figure exhibits the typical Teotihuacan carving style of a massive, square silhouette with rather large, abstracted features. On this undamaged sculpture we can see several traits that are characteristic of the Great Goddess. Most obvious is her colossal size. Standing at almost four meters, the sculpture is enormous, blocky, and commanding. On the top of the sculpture is a square, flat area formed by the broad, horizontal headdress she wears. The feminine identification stems from the short skirt and the capelike huipil. In addition, she pulls her hands into her chest where there is a large hole drilled. Most likely, this hole held either a reflective mirror of some sort or a piece of greenstone. The former is possible because both the eighteenth-century writers Gemelli Carreri (1995 [1700]) and Clavigero (1979 [1787]) reported that a gold disk originally filled the hole found in the chest of a sculpture on the Sun Pyramid. These observations must be viewed with some degree of skepticism, however, because neither of these men actually saw the gold disk, and they recorded only what they had heard the Spanish conquistadors had seen. Furthermore, gold is not a characteristic of Classic period assemblages, although

Figure 6.2. Great Goddess sculpture found in front of the Moon Pyramid, Teotihuacan (photograph by Dorie Reents-Budet).

metal could have been left by Aztec pilgrims, or the conquistadors might have mistook another shiny substance for metal. More convincing evidence comes from the fact that pieces of reflective mica were commonly used on Teotihuacan mirrors and incensarios, and from the Olmec culture on, Mesoamerican figurines frequently had disks of mica or obsidian. With this in mind, the hole in the Great Goddess's chest would function quite adequately as a tenon for such a mirror. Alternatively, the hole could have held a piece of greenstone like several of the Aztec stone sculptures found on the stairs of the Templo Mayor (Beyer 1965 [1920]:423). Above the hole the goddess wears a heavy beaded necklace that frames the strong protrusion of the jaw and head. The eyes and mouth are indicated by diagnostic simple ovals carved in a shallow fashion.

Returning to the damaged boulder (Figure 6.1), we can make a compelling comparison because there are enough similar elements. The boulder, though somewhat smaller at a height of 169 centimeters, has the same massive size and analogous treatment of the arms. The figure has its arms tucked into the chest, and a similar drilled hole appears between them. Remnants of the heavy beaded necklace still survive, as does the suggestion of the protruding head with its shallow, flat eyes. Such visual congruencies led Pasztory (1997:99) to wonder whether these two goddesses once formed a sort of matched pair serving as a gateway to the Moon Pyramid; however, the earliest information recorded about the location of these sculptures may offer another possibility.

In Gemelli Carreri's (1995 [1700]) comments about the Moon and Sun Pyramids, he relates that each of the temples had a large stone sculpture covered in gold. The sculpture in the temple of the Sun Pyramid was the one that he said had the gold disk in its breast. He continues by relating that the Spaniards took the gold disk and destroyed both of the sculptures by orders of Juan de Zumárraga, the first bishop of Mexico. He concludes by stating that the large remnants of each sculpture could still be found at the foot of the two pyramids. When Brantz Mayer (1844:221–227) visited Teotihuacan in the mid-1800s, he used Clavigero's (1979 [1787]) book as a guide and surmised that a massive stone in the Plaza of the Moon was the remains of the shattered sculpture from the Sun Pyramid. To the west of this, closer to the Moon Pyramid, he found the second sculpture, and although he published an image of the sculpture upside down, it is clearly the colossal goddess in the Mexico City museum (Mayer 1844:224; von Winning 1987:I:136–138). Viewing the map Mayer produced following his trip to the site (Figure 6.3), we can at least document the location of the two sculptures under discussion to 1840. On his map, he marked the damaged sculpture as "B" and the Museo Nacional's sculpture as "C." It should be noted that the battered sculpture lies a significant distance from the Sun Pyramid, and it is doubtful that the Spaniards, even in their zeal to destroy a heathen idol, would have exerted the necessary effort to roll the stone such a great distance. Thus, Pasztory (1997:99) may be correct in her assumption that both sculptures were closer to the Moon Pyramid, leaving many questions about the remains of a possible sculpture on the Sun Pyramid. Nevertheless, if the eighteenth-century accounts have a grain of truth, they might explain why the sculpture now in the Plaza of the Moon is so heavily damaged. In sum, I would suggest that the original location of the damaged sculpture was the Plaza of the Moon and that the damage came from means other than the Spaniards rolling it down the Sun Pyramid. Because of these early accounts of a large sculpture on the Sun Pyramid, however, we can never wholly dismiss the possibility that this sculpture was once associated with this temple.

Tree-Raising Rituals in Mesoamerica

I will momentarily set aside these sculptures as the assertion that the battered boulder might have served in a tree-raising ritual requires a discussion of such

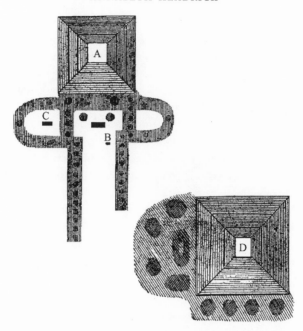

Figure 6.3. 1842 map of Teotihuacan by Brantz Mayer. *(a)* Moon Pyramid; *(b)* damaged boulder; *(c)* Great Goddess from the Museo Nacional; *(d)* Sun Pyramid (adapted from Mayer 1844).

rituals. Because we currently have no elaborate textual accounts from Teotihuacan itself, information from throughout Mesoamerica proves helpful. Perhaps the most famous tree ritual of current times is the *palo volador,* or flying pole dance, of Veracruz and the highlands of Puebla (Toor 1947:317–323). Most people are familiar with the *palo volador* through its many reenactments for tourists visiting the archaeological sites of both El Tajin and Teotihuacan. From the tourist's perspective it is an amazing experience to watch the five men climb a tall pole. Next, one of the men dances on the tiny platform of the summit and plays a drum and flute while the other four dramatically fall headfirst from the pole, spinning around in circles by means of the ropes attached to their feet. This feat of bravery must have been equally inspiring in Precolumbian times, but even in these tourist-driven versions, there is evidence that highly ritual aspects of the performance still survive. For instance, the *voladores* orbit the pole thirteen times, and because there are four of them, the total of circumambulations equals fifty-two, the number of years in the sacred calendar round (Durán 1994 [1581]:143, n. 1). The Aztecs conceived of the end of the fifty-two-year cycle as a commemoration of the world's creation and would celebrate it by ritually destroying their household items and extinguishing their fires. The rekindling of the new fire symbolized the creation of the sun and the beginning of time (Sahagún 1950–1982:7:25–32). Thus, the *voladores* memorialize the ancient tradition of celebrating the fifty-two-year cycle each time they circle the pole. This calendrical association of the *palo volador* suggests that the central pole carries deep significance, most likely functioning as a central world tree.

In versions of the *palo voladores* away from the tourists, the events surrounding the acquisition and erection of the pole provide further evidence of the deeply religious content embedded in the *voladores* performance. When the men find the tree, they ask its forgiveness for cutting it and pour *tepache,* a fermented beverage, on the tree to lessen the pain of cutting off the branches. While they fell the tree, the men sing, dance, and play around the tree. After the felling, they carry the tree back with great care. Along the way, whenever the men need to rest, they pour more alcohol on the ground when they must set the tree down. This act reinforces the respect that the men clearly offer to the tree. When the men enter the town with the tree there is a great celebration including fireworks and the ringing of church bells (Toor 1947:321). It is as though the town greets the tree as a sacred entity and welcomes it as it enters the civic space. Just before the tree is erected, offerings of a live chicken, liquor, and food are commonly placed into the hole (Durán 1971 [1574–1579]:163, n. 2; Toor 1947:319–320). Given such circumstances, the carnival-like atmosphere of the *palo voladores* conducted in the parking lots of archaeological parks belie the profound sacred underpinnings of the event.

In his account of the Aztecs, the sixteenth-century Dominican friar Diego Durán wrote about two different tree-raising rituals. One of these concerned a tree put up during rituals Durán calls the Feast of the Waters (Figure 6.4). In this tree raising, ritualists did not climb the tree; instead, the tree served a more visual, symbolic purpose. According to Durán (1971 [1574–1579]:160–167), on Tlaloc's feast day, men of all ages set up an elaborate artificial landscape in the main plaza in front of the Templo Mayor. The most important feature of this imitation forest was a central, perfect tree and four smaller trees, one at each of the four corners. The central tree was called Tota, or Our Father. The men found this tree by going to the Hill of the Star, the same hill where they drilled the new fire every fifty-two years, further confirming the calendrical nature of the event. On that hill they chose the largest and most perfect tree, especially favoring a tree with lush, verdant branches. As they cut the tree, they used a series of ropes to keep it from ever touching the ground, which continued as they carried it back to the ceremonial center. Once in town, the celebrants raised the tree in the main plaza of Tenochtitlan. In his illustration and text, Durán (1971 [1574–1579]:160–165) explained that ropes connected the central Tota tree to the other

Figure 6.4. Aztec Tota festival (drawing by Mareike Sattler after Durán 1971:Plate 14).

four trees. Thus, symbolically, the central world tree was connected by cords to the four cardinal directions. Underneath the trees, the people of Tenochtitlan were said to have held a festival, including song, dance, and games.

The event culminated when the men took down the tree, bound its branches, and placed it on a raft in Lake Texcoco. Simultaneously, the priests and lords carried a sacrificial young girl in a litter to the lake's edge where they boarded canoes and took the girl and the tree to a place in the middle of the lake called Pantitlan. Because a great whirlpool often formed there, they spoke of Pantitlan as the drain for the lake. In the final acts of the Tota celebration, the Aztecs plunged the tree into the "drain" and unbound the branches so that it was full once again. They next slit the girl's throat, let her blood flow into the water, and then threw the girl and offerings of stone and jewelry into the lake (Durán 1971 [1574–1579]:163–165).

The second tree ceremony mentioned by Durán (1971 [1574–1579]:203–209, 444–446) was part of the Small Feast of the Dead and the Great Feast of the Dead, during which the Aztecs remembered their deceased children and adults. For this ceremony, the people placed a bird made of amaranth dough atop a tall tree called *xocotl*, "precious pine" (Sahagún 1997 [1558]:60, n. 26). As with the *voladores* pole, they cut all the branches off the tree and smoothed the surface to perfection. Once again there was dancing and feasting, although this time Durán specified that the dancers were young boys and girls. On the final day of the feast, the dancing ceased just before sunset when the youths threw off their dance costumes of feathers and had a contest to see which one of them could climb to the top first and capture the amaranth dough bird. Later, they cut the pole down, and the people of Tenochtitlan ran to take away a memento of the tree, so sacred was the object.

In the *Florentine Codex*, Sahagún (1950–1982:2:111–117) offers another description of the *xocotl* rituals. Although there is no illustration of the event in the *Florentine Codex*, Sahagún did include two illustrations and a brief description in his *Primeros Memoriales* (Sahagún 1993 [1558]:Fol. 251r–251v, 1997 [1558]:60–62). Here, one illustration shows the same themes seen in the previous accounts (Figure 6.5a). The men enter from the left, carrying the tree. As in the *volador* ritual, the tree seems to be greeted with great ceremony because an individual carrying a shield and torch stands before it, and in the text Sahagún noted that an impersonator of Teteoinnan, a female terrestrial deity, came to greet the tree. In the image, participants use ropes to carry and erect the tree, mirroring the ropes of the Tota and *xocotl* rituals that Durán mentioned.

The following illustration in the *Primeros Memoriales* (Sahagún 1993) is in accordance with Durán's *xocotl* event because men climb the tree trying to capture the image on top (Figure 6.5b). Sahagún (1950–1982:2:111–117) similarly remarks on the rich rewards given to the quick man who reached the top first, but he suggests a more military meaning for the event. The youth who got the amaranth dough figure was referred to as the captor of the *xocotl* image, and throughout the festivities, men who had taken a captive in war dressed in butterfly backracks and carried shields. The martial aspect of the butterfly stems from the Aztec belief that butterflies were the souls of dead warriors (Sahagún 1950–1982:3:49). The importance of warfare in the *xocotl* rituals is further attested to in dances that captors performed with their captives, which ended when the captors took hanks of hair from their captives as trophies and threw the captives into a great fire to roast before being extracted from the fire and having their hearts removed. In Sahagún's illustration (Figure 6.5b), dancers and the dough figure on the tree carry shields while a sacrificial captive lies in a fire pit to the right.

Building on Sahagún's clear inclusion of military activities, Betty Brown (1988) has pointed out that the *xocotl* ritual was intimately tied to the celebration of an important Aztec military victory. Both she and Franke Neumann (1988) suggest that the dough figure on top of the pole represents Otontecuhtli, the patron deity of the Otomí. Thus, when the Aztec warrior captured and dismembered the dough figure, he symbolically reenacted the Aztec capturing of Otontecuhtli's people. In this interpretation, the Aztecs of Tenochtitlan seemingly historicized the event by shaping it to celebrate their victory over the Otomí.

a.

b.

Figure 6.5. Xocotl rituals. *(a)* Bringing in and erecting the tree; *(b)* Climbing the tree (drawings by Mareike Sattler after Sahagún 1993:Folio 251r-125v).

Viewed in this light, the paper ornaments worn in Sahagún's illustration seem appropriate (Figure 6.5b). Toward the bottom of the image, one of the dancers wears a paper headdress decorated with notched extensions. Likewise, the amaranth dough figure of Otontecuhtli on top of the *xocotl* tree also has the same headdress. As corroboration of the importance of the notched paper ornaments in this ritual, the *xocotl* tree pictured in the *Codex Magliabecchiano* has a figure

Figure 6.6. Pole ceremony from the *Codex Magliabecchiano* (drawing by Mareike Sattler after Nuttall 1903:38).

wearing the same headdress (Figure 6.6). This figure perches on the top of the pole and carries a warrior's shield and banner while three men hold the ropes so characteristic in Mesoamerican tree rituals. The notched forms in these headdresses are butterfly ornaments that, as stated before, symbolize the souls of dead warriors (Neumann 1988:282). These ornaments tap into the belief that warriors who died on the battlefield accompanied the sun for four years and then were transformed into butterflies to live a pleasurable afterlife (Sahagún 1950–1982:3:49). The butterfly provides a link between the Durán and Sahagún versions of the *xocotl* rituals. Durán explained that the Aztecs erected the *xocotl* tree during the Feast of the Dead, and Sahagún emphasized the importance of celebrating heroic, dead warriors. Thus, in both cases the theme orbits around ancestor commemoration that is also an aspect of butterfly symbolism, specifically ancestral warriors.

In summary, a set of themes emerges from these tree-raising rituals. Great reverence for the tree as it is cut and carried seems to be a constant in the acquisition of the tree. Upon the transition from wilderness to human-inhabited space, the town greets the tree joyously as it reaches the community. Diligence and offerings commonly mark the erection of the tree, just as ropes are a frequent aspect of the festivities. Finally, warfare, the remembrance of the dead, especially dead warriors, and a great deal of festive dancing and games all seem to be constants of Aztec tree-raising rituals.

Teotihuacan Tree Raising

Having painted a picture of Postclassic and Postcontact pole rituals, our gaze can return to the Teotihuacan monument and question whether it served as a base for a ceremonial tree. Because these pole ceremonies seem so prevalent in Mesoamerican ritual, particularly central Mexican traditions, it could be possible that the Teotihuacanos also had a tree-raising festival, but this assertion poses a critical problem. In all of these rituals the tree celebrants reportedly placed the tree directly in the ground, devoid of any sculpture. To be sure, Dúran (1971 [1574–1579]:162) states that "a deep hole had been dug" for Tota, and Sahagún (1950–1982:2:113) pointedly remarks that the Aztecs secured the *xocotl* in the earth with small stones and dirt filling the hole. This information aside, a certain image indicates that Teotihuacan was different, that the Teotihuacanos did indeed erect their tree on a sculpture.

In the apartment compound of Tepantitla are the well-known murals referred to as the Tlalocan murals. In the upper portion of the decorated walls an image of the Great Goddess faces the viewer frontally (Figure 6.7). Her arms stretch out as water drips from her hands, and her lower body consists of a cavelike womb from which the waters of the world flow. On top of her head the branches of a lush tree spread, with each branch ending in flowers about which birds flitter. This mural, I would contend, offers an image of the now-damaged boulder when it was being used at Teotihuacan as the base for a ritual tree.

The Tlalocan murals cover all four sides of a rectangular patio. Each of the painted walls has an upper and lower register corresponding to the characteristic talud-tablero architecture of Teotihuacan. Though not all of the walls have survived equally intact, the frontal image of the Great Goddess seems to have decorated all of the tablero, or upper walls; however, the lower, talud walls depict scenes of numerous small people, and in each lower wall the individuals seem to be engaged in a different activity. The variation in the talud spaces led Pasztory (1976) to standardize the names of the various walls based on thematic elements. Thus, the walls carry such names as the Water Talud, the Ballgame Talud, and the Medicine Talud.

The Tepantitla murals have been the subject of much debate over the years. Caso (1942) set the tenor for much of the discussion when he argued that the central figure of the upper mural (Figure 6.7) represents Tlaloc with two priests approaching him (Pasztory 1976:Figure 27). As for the lower murals, Caso focused only on one wall, the Water Talud (Figure 6.8). This wall includes a myriad

Figure 6.7. Great Goddess from the upper wall, Tepantitla, Teotihuacan (drawing by Linda Schele).

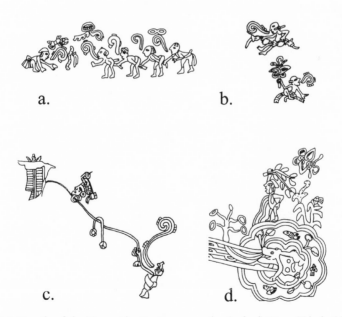

Figure 6.8. Details of the Tepantitla, Portico 2 murals. *(a, b, d)* Water Talud; *(c)* Ballgame Talud (adapted from Pasztory 1976:Figures 36, 39).

of frolicking people that Caso interpreted as happy souls in Tlalocan, the paradise of those who die from water-related causes. The figures include men dancing
with flowers and branches (Figure 6.8b), people playing the ballgame as well as
other games, and a charming dance of men grasping one another's hands through
their legs, which Taube (personal communication 1999) identifies as a centipede
dance (Figure 6.8a).

Many later commentators accepted Caso's basic premise, but Pasztory (1974,
1988, 1997) agreed with Furst (1974) that the central figure in the upper wall
depicted a female entity, eventually dubbed the Great Goddess. In addition,
Pasztory (1976:146–156) argued that the goddess took the form of a tree and
correctly identified that tree as the world tree emerging from the cosmic mountain at the center of the universe. With great insight, she moved the Tepantitla
image into the realm of the living by recognizing that the upper mural depicted
two priests before a decorated idol, that is, a scene that could have taken place
in the city of Teotihuacan itself (Pasztory 1974:179). The decorated idol that
Pasztory suggested, I would argue, was the damaged sculpture in the Moon
Plaza. In a similar vein, Pasztory (1974:180–226) viewed the scenes in the different lower murals as representations of ritual events that occurred regularly at
Teotihuacan instead of placing them in the supernatural realm.

In my own work (Headrick 1995), I have argued that the branches of the tree
emerging from the goddess's head carried an important civic message (Figure
6.7). The tree consists of two distinct branches that entwine in a curvilinear
fashion. Furthermore, each branch has a separate iconographic association because one branch has butterflies decorating it whereas the other branch has spiders. Comparing this to Aztec beliefs, I have suggested that the tree symbolized
the ideal gender roles of proper Teotihuacan citizens. The butterfly represented
the male population and encouraged them to risk their lives on the battlefield. If
they died in that pursuit, they would live in the paradise of the sun and eventually change into butterflies, resulting in a life of pleasure.

In turn, the spider was an important symbol of female endeavors in Mesoamerica. For instance, the spider is a prominent attribute of the Maya goddess
of spinning and weaving, and in the Aztec, Mixtec, and Maya pantheons, the
female goddess of weaving also functions as the goddess of childbirth (McCafferty and McCafferty 1993; Pasztory 1976:160–161; Taube 1992:99–105; Thompson 1970:247). Thus, Mesoamerican deity associations tend to clump the female
tasks of spinning, weaving, and childbirth under a deity who includes the spider
conspicuously in her imagery.

Aztec beliefs recorded by Sahagún indicate that the gender roles symbolized
by the butterfly and spider had an additional linkage that makes a direct correspondence between male and female roles. Sahagún (1950–1982:6:161–167) wrote
that women giving birth were metaphorically likened to male warriors because

the women similarly struggled and took a captive, but in this case the captive was the newly born child. As with men, women risked their lives in the battlefield of labor pains, and if they died in this effort, they also entered the warrior's paradise of the sun (Berlo 1983:92–93; Headrick 1995; Klein 1988). I would propose that the Teotihuacanos held similar beliefs as the later Aztec and that encoded within the symbolism of the Tepantitla Great Goddess are the parallel roles of men and women couched in militaristic terms. That is, the role of a warrior was a fundamental one for both men and women, but gender determined whether you fought that war on a battlefield or in childbed. When viewed in this light, the Tepantitla mural becomes a statement of proper gender roles for men and women but is carefully phrased in the iconography of war. In short, the mural may be a blueprint for proper social behavior, emphasizing that warfare and childbirth were the most important civic roles of men and women. Sahagún's image of the *xocotl* tree may suggest that the later Aztecs incorporated similar iconography of gender roles in their tree rituals. In the sacrificial scene from the *Primeros Memoriales* (Figure 6.5b), a male warrior carries his shield while a female figure in the upper-right corner not only carries a shield but also wears a spindle in her hair, certainly associating her with weaving but perhaps also with the female battle of childbirth. In fact, this woman may be the impersonator of Teteoinnan, the goddess of terrestrial fertility. Because Aztec beliefs so strongly connect weaving and childbirth, the simple inclusion of the spindle may have been sufficient to indicate the fundamental gender roles of women.

Within this framework, how can we then interpret the Tepantitla mural as an image of a tree-raising ceremony? First, remember that the damaged sculpture very likely depicts the Great Goddess because the remaining sculpted areas are consistent with the goddess housed in the Museo Nacional. Second, even though the top of this sculpture is heavily damaged, its similarity to the Museo Nacional sculpture may indicate that it too originally had a square, flat headdress above the head, providing an area to place the symbolic tree. Due to the damage, however, there is no extant evidence of such a flat area, yet the Teotihuacanos could have attached the tree by other means. Given the vinelike appearance of the Tepantitla tree (Figure 6.7), the Teotihuacan tree does not seem to have had the singular, massive trunk of the Aztec trees. Instead, it may have consisted only of decorative branches that would have been logistically easier to attach to a large sculpture. Thus, the Teotihuacan tree would not have been climbed as in many of the Aztec rituals. Without the climbing ritual it probably functioned more like Tota, the symbolic world tree that Durán described. Third, the decoration of sculpted deity images is well documented in Mesoamerican rituals. Throughout his description of Aztec ceremonies, Durán (1971 [1574–1579]) wrote that the images of gods were dressed in clothing, decorated with paper, and painted with blood. Fourth, the sculpture seems to be cut off at the waist and has no legs, and this feature may offer some insight into the symbolism of the goddess as she appears in both the mural and the damaged boulder.

Because the sculpture is so heavily damaged, it is possible that part of the sculpture is missing. Perhaps the lower section simply broke off, leaving only a partial sculpture. Careful examination of the bottom, however, reveals prominent bulges on either side that could be interpreted as a pair of legs bent into a squatting position. As pointed out by William Fowler (personal communication 1998), such a squatting position appears on Aztec female figures shown in childbirth, particularly the earth goddess, Tlazolteotl, who squats with her knees bent to her chest as she strains to give birth to a child (see Townsend 1992:Figures 84–86). If the damaged Teotihuacan sculpture does indeed depict a squatting figure, then it could, similarly, depict the goddess in a childbirth position.

This would be thematically in harmony with the Great Goddess in the Tepantitla mural. In her painted version, the goddess (Figure 6.7) also has an abbreviated lower body, and in this case the legs are entirely absent. The base of the Tepantitla goddess depicts her vaginal opening with the plentiful birth waters flowing out onto the land. Her hands drip more liquid on the ground, and her head sprouts the verdant tree, all of which indicate the role of the goddess as a female life giver. Furthermore, the spiders on the tree also support the association of the Tepantitla goddess with childbirth because of its strong connection with this female role throughout Mesoamerica. Taken as a whole, the iconographic elements of the Tepantitla goddess seemingly highlight her association with childbirth.

Although discussions of the Great Goddess often stress the similarities between the many depictions of her, iconographic elements do differ within the depictions, and thus the artists may have shown the goddess in different guises (Berlo 1992). Mesoamerican gods often have many aspects, each of which can be stressed for certain purposes. Perhaps the damaged boulder and the depiction of the ritual involving the boulder in the Tepantitla murals indicate that this sculpture celebrated the goddess's association with childbirth, life, and sustenance whereas other goddesses, such as the Museo Nacional sculpture that stands erect on its legs, emphasized a different aspect of the goddess.

A fifth feature of the Tepantitla mural that might indicate that the boulder was a base for a tree-raising ritual concerns the notable ropelike character of the branches of the tree (Figure 6.7). As mentioned, in so many Aztec tree-raising festivals, participants used ropes to carry, erect, and climb the tree. In addition, in the Tota rituals, cords symbolically connected the central tree to the four smaller trees in the cardinal directions. In one of the lower murals at Tepantitla, a figure holds a long cord to a tall object that seems to have some foliage on top (Figure 6.8c). Unfortunately, this portion of the mural is heavily damaged, and the remaining fragment of the "tree" significantly differs from the goddess tree above; however, the rope and the foliage may indicate that the artist provided a second view of the tree ritual. In regard to the upper mural again, profile priests approach the Great Goddess from each direction and sprinkle offerings on the ground as they near the tree (Pasztory 1974:Figure 27). This action markedly resembles the Postclassic and contemporary accounts of trees being greeted by priests and sprinkled with sacred alcoholic beverages when the men enter town with the tree.

Another clue comes from the evidence for sacrificial rites in the lower murals of Tepantitla. In a convincing argument, Pasztory (1974:196–199) suggested that figures with tears or painted in blue were likely images of sacrificial victims in the festivities. In particular, a standing figure in the Water Talud has the blue and red streams of water and blood pouring from his chest into the rounded shape of a lake (Figure 6.8d). This image of heart sacrifice has a striking resemblance to the girl whose blood was offered to Lake Texcoco in the Aztec Tota ceremonies. Such similarities suggest that a Teotihuacan version of tree-raising rituals may have mirrored the Aztec version by featuring human sacrifice at a lake.

Finally, the butterfly imagery in the tree fits with the Spanish accounts that tree rituals were tied to warfare and the souls of the dead. In the Water Talud a number of butterflies fly among the many figures engaged in games and dance, and one figure even carries a stick with a butterfly attached to the top (Figures 6.8b and 6.8d). Instead of seeing this as Caso's (1942) land of the dead, I would follow Pasztory (1974) in asserting that the scene most assuredly shows a living Teotihuacan; however, I would stress that the butterflies indicate that the dead are present. The butterflies, to Teotihuacanos, might have been viewed as the actual souls of dead warriors, whether from childbirth or the battlefield. The figure with the butterfly staff could hold it like a ceremonial banner, possibly indicating that he was a ritual participant actively engaged in remembering his ancestors who died in such a way. Under this interpretation the butterflies are present because they are the souls of the dead who visit the living because they have been recalled during this festival, much like the dead are still called into the land of the living during the Days of the Dead. The figures in the lower mural, then, become the people of Teotihuacan, the people who dance, celebrate, sacrifice certain individuals, and generally have a fiesta when the tree is raised. In this light, the mural seems to fit precisely with the Spanish ethnographic accounts that tree ceremonies were important festivals for the dead, particularly war dead.

In sum, the battered sculpture, though humble now, may have been the focus of one of the most important festivals in the annual Teotihuacan ritual cycle. The Teotihuacanos may have used the sculpture to raise the world tree symbolically as they scattered offerings at its base. Indeed, there is no definitive proof that this particular sculpture was the sculpture that the Teotihuacanos used in their tree-raising ritual, and the Museo Nacional sculpture or possibly a now-missing sculpture could have been the one painted in the Tepantitla mural. Nevertheless, the Tepantitla mural offers tantalizing evidence that the people of this city did have a tree ritual, and this ritual had many thematic similarities to those of the later Aztecs. The Tepantitla mural suggests that the rituals celebrated both military might and the death of ancestors, including butterfly souls of warriors. As the mural indicates, it was a grand party, where all of Teotihuacan sang, danced, and offered the precious gift of life when they sacrificed certain people.

Furthermore, the Tepantitla mural can be seen in an ever more human light. Instead of forcing it into the supernatural realm, we may now recognize that it seems to show less the supernatural and distant than the human and immediate. In other words, rather than viewing it as an image of the afterlife, the mural may depict an event that annually took place at Teotihuacan, a civic event that reinforced the fundamental social roles of men and women. Even the Great Goddess in the upper mural appears not so much as herself but as a depiction of a sculpture of the goddess, the human construct of the goddess's image. In this light, we see that Teotihuacan art may be more focused than previously thought on the human need to record history in a very narrative fashion; the Teotihuacanos featured themselves while the gods served as props on an elaborate, human stage.

Acknowledgments

This chapter sprang from Linda Schele's gift of an idea, and it was given life by Andrea Stone when she organized this volume. My heartfelt thanks to Andrea for her editing, patience, and suggestions.

Note

1. For more information on the identification and naming of the Great Goddess see Berlo (1992), Pasztory (1972), and von Winning (1987).

7

Terminal Classic Sacred Place
and Factional Politics at
El Tajin, Veracruz

Rex Koontz

The most exciting times of my professional life were spent in Linda's seminars on Mesoamerican art, epigraphy, and civilization. Here the exchange of ideas was intense, the level of debate was never modulated to suit others' levels (much to the chagrin of the entering graduate students), and the respect for the complexity and beauty of the achievements of Mesoamerican civilization was a constant. That said, when I first proposed the germ of the ideas presented in this chapter to her assembled seminar on Mesoamerican iconography, Linda was not entirely pleased. The argument seemed to her to smack of up-streaming with Aztec material while ignoring the now voluminous Maya material on sacred space and urban planning. Although this was not my intention (see the conclusions reached in this chapter), the point was well taken, and the debate was on. We both dug in our heels, and a protracted argument over the validity of the Coatepec paradigm took place over the next year. Linda was fierce in these sorts of debates, and the strength of my argument benefited enormously from our discussions. It was only later that I realized that it was in these discussions that I glimpsed, in some detail, what it was to be a serious, committed scholar—perhaps the chief gift of Linda to her students.

El Tajin in Space and Time

The site of El Tajin has long been recognized as the premier Classic period site in northern Veracruz. Recent archaeological work has refined the chronology, placing the site more firmly in the Epiclassic, with its apogee C.E. 800–1000 (Brüggemann 1992:29–31; Lira López 1998). In this new scenario, El Tajin was a small, unimportant site before its rapid Epiclassic rise. The swift rise of the site, evidenced by the large amount of monumental art and architecture built at the site's core in the short span of two centuries, raises two interrelated questions: What language of power was deployed to legitimate this sudden rise to Meso-american prominence? How did this language relate to other known languages of Mesoamerican legitimacy, if at all? Although these questions are framed in linguistic terms, the analysis cannot rely on traditional texts as evidence for the language of power and legitimacy at El Tajin. We have no master texts explaining to us the foundations of power at the site. We do have, however, the archaeologi-cal residue of the practice of power in the material culture and symbolism used in social discourse. A major locus of this discourse was the central area of El Tajin, where architecture, sculpture, and space were structured to announce the legitimacy of the Tajin elite. Through an analysis of the meaning of the central ceremonial plaza of the site, this chapter examines key public proclamations used to announce the site's identity and to legitimate its power during the polity's swift rise to prominence in this crucial transitional period in Mesoamerican history.

The most important and widely accessible program of narrative sculpture at the site is grouped around the Pyramid of the Niches and its adjoining central plaza (Figure 7.1). Because of the concentration of sculpture and its location at the heart of the site, the central plaza may be considered the primary statement of Tajin identity and legitimacy. The Pyramid of the Niches (Figure 7.2) has been the defining architectural feature of the central plaza from the time it was first published in the late eighteenth century (Gaceta de México 1785). Attempts to explain the pyramid's function and symbolism have treated both its architec-tural form and the iconography of the sculpture of the ruined sanctuary on top of the structure (García Payón 1951). This chapter explores the meaning of the building from a different angle, literally: I will examine the sculpture found at the foot of the pyramid as a clue to the meaning of the pyramid itself. I propose that the Pyramid of the Niches is analogous to Coatepec, the central sacred mountain of the Mexica and their prototype of sacred space. Furthermore, I will show that the rituals performed in this space were analogous to the Mexica ritu-als around the Templo Mayor in the center of Tenochtitlan, a pyramid that re-created the central sacred mountain of the Coatepec narratives.

The main facade of the Pyramid of the Niches borders the clearly delineated space of the central plaza (Figure 7.1). The plaza is defined on the north and south sides by Structures 4 and 2, respectively, and it is closed on the east by a side of Structure 3. Each of the two buildings flanking the Pyramid of the Niches in the central plaza (Structures 2 and 4) contained one piece of narrative sculpture.[1] Together, these two sculptures define the rituals enacted in and around the central plaza. Pascual Soto (1990:173) has shown that Structure 2 contained

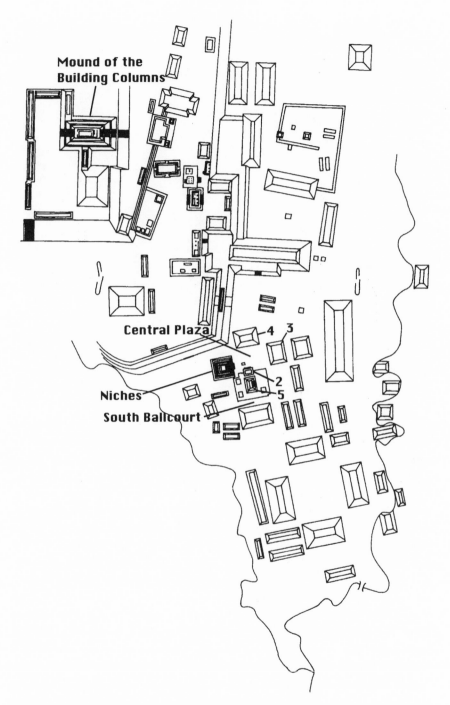

Figure 7.1. Map of El Tajin (modified after Kampen 1972:Figure 2).

Figure 7.2. Pyramid of the Niches, El Tajin (photograph by the author).

the trapezoidal panel formerly designated Pyramid of the Niches Sculpture 7 (Figure 7.3a).[2] Structure 4 contained an elaborately carved panel that probably came from its superstructure (Figure 7.4a), although it was found on the north flank of the pyramid (García Payón 1973). No other narrative panels may be connected directly with the central plaza space.[3]

Iconography of the Central Plaza Program

The Structure 2 panel is a trapezoidal sculpture with severe damage in the upper portion of the composition (Figure 7.3a). The central scene depicts two persons flanking a now missing central figure. The personage on the right wears full ballgame gear that includes a yoke and palma set around his waist. He holds a sacrificial knife in his right hand, and a ball with a skull inscribed in its center rests at his feet. Only the lower portion of the personage on the left remains, revealing the same ballplayer skirt and train seen on the knife-wielding figure. A central figure may be reconstructed from analogous compositions, as we will see below.

The three central actors are flanked on the left by a rabbit-headed anthropomorphic figure seated on an architectural motif and on the right by a human seated on a mirror image of the same building type. These buildings form a profile view of a typical Tajin ballcourt. Similar figures and ballcourt structures

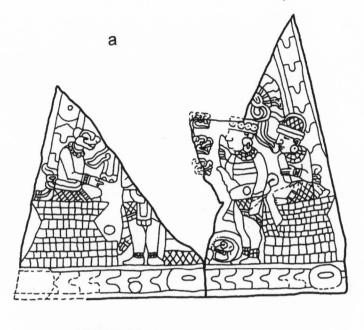

Figure 7.3. *(a)* Structure 2 panel, El Tajin (drawing by Daniela Medieros Epstein; courtesy of the artist); *(b)* Central figures, Great Ballcourt panel, Chichen Itza (drawing by the author).

appear in a panel from the major (south) ballcourt at Tajin, suggesting that the Structure 2 panel scene takes place in this nearby court, as Kampen (1972:38) and Wilkerson (1984:122–123) have suggested. Structure 2 makes the transition from the central plaza space to the platform of Structure 5, which in turn becomes the northernmost wall of the main ballcourt (Figure 7.1). Thus the placement of ballcourt iconography on this side of the central plaza connects the rituals held at the ballcourt with the central plaza.

A comparison of the central figures in the Structure 2 panel at Tajin with the central figures of the ballcourt bench panels from the contemporary Maya site

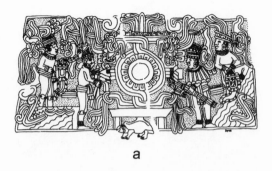

a

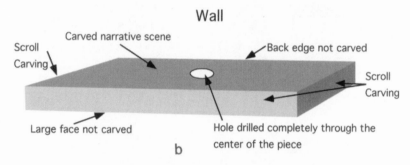

b

Figure 7.4. *(a)* Structure 4 panel, El Tajín (drawing by Daniela Medieros Epstein; courtesy of the artist); *(b)* Schematic of hypothesized placement of Structure 4 panel (drawing by the author).

of Chichen Itza (Figure 7.3b) allows us, hypothetically, to reconstruct the Tajín composition (Kampen 1972:66; Wilkerson 1984:124). Elements such as the ballgame gear, the sacrificial knife, and the skull/ball motif are analogous in the two compositions. The serpent heads that face the knife-wielding ballplayer in the Tajín panel may be compared with those that spring from the body of the decapitated sacrificial victim shown in the Chichen example, suggesting that the missing central figure in the Tajín example was seated with serpents emerging from the figure's neck. The detached head is indicated by the skull ball at the feet of the ballplayer, analogous to the skull ball in the center of the Chichen composition. Thus, the missing figure in the Tajín composition may be seen as a victim of ballcourt decapitation sacrifice, which is the theme of this panel.[4]

The only other narrative panel connected with the central plaza was found on the opposite side of the plaza in Structure 4 (Figure 7.4a) (García Payón 1973). The panel measures approximately 1 × 2 meters and has a thickness of 20 centimeters. An elaborate scene covers the top surface, and scroll carvings line three of the sides. The large surface on the face opposite the figurative image was left

Figure 7.5. *(a)* Mound of the Building Columns Sculpture 3, detail of figures with back mirrors (drawing by the author); *(b)* Altar figure, central plaza, El Tajin (drawing by the author).

blank, as was the thin side at the top. A hole was drilled through the center and neatly incorporated into the iconography, shown here in the center of the composition, surrounded by a raised circular rim and petaled motif. This hole passes through both large faces and has a consistent diameter and careful finish throughout the width of the panel. Given the placement of the carving, the panel must have been set horizontally against a wall, with the figurative scene facing upward and the scroll carving on three of the sides facing outward, as seen in Figure 7.4b.

The symmetrical composition consists of two pairs of figures facing a motif that covers the entire central portion of the image. The central motif is the key to this scene. It consists of a pole that grows from the back of a turtle and pierces an elevated panel. Above the panel, the tails of intertwined serpents surround the

pole and then divide, enframing the circular motif in the center of the composition. This circular motif consists of a petaled fringe surrounding the circle,
which we have seen is an actual hole that passes through the width of the stone.
The necks of the serpents intertwine above the hole, ending in a serpent head on
either side of the composition. A group of bunched feathers surmounts the entire
motif.

The same petaled circular motif that surrounds the central hole in the panel
appears on the backs of warriors, ballplayers, and other celebrants at Tajin (Figure 7.5a). To the later Mexica these back devices were known as *tezcacuitlapilli,*
a back mirror that was intimately associated with the warrior groups of the
Mexica (Taube 1983:165).[5] The circular object supported by the pole and enclosed
by serpents is, then, the depiction of a mirror.

García Payón (1973) identified the entire central motif (including the pole
support) of the Structure 4 panel as part of the "ballcourt marker" group, often
referred to in the literature by its Nahuatl name, *techmalacatl.* Freidel et al.
(1993:296–304), however, have convincingly argued that these devices are not
ballcourt markers but war banners. The authors have identified depictions of the
devices in scenes of warfare, such as the Late Classic Maya murals of Bonampak,
as well as in what are warfare-related ballgame ceremonies. In Bonampak Room
2, the battle scene is introduced by three participants holding banners of different colors and designs as the troops descend into battle (see Miller 1986:96–97,
Plate 2). These same devices appear in ballgame ceremonies, such as the one
illustrated by Coe (1982:34–35), where two ballplayers are engaged in the game
while a war banner stands behind them, probably as some sort of marker and/or
trophy.

Both descriptions and illustrations of these banners indicate that most were
made of perishable materials, with an emphasis on elaborate featherwork. Hundreds of banners, shields, mantles, headdresses, and other examples of featherwork were sent to Europe at the time of the conquest, but problems of conser-
vation and centuries of neglect have reduced their number to fewer than ten
(Pasztory 1983:278–280). Only one example of a featherwork banner, now in the
Museum für Völkerkunde in Vienna, has survived. Standing over a meter high,
it is constructed of feathers glued to maguey leaves and then attached to a bamboo framework.[6] The feathers form a fringe around a central hole, just as the petaled rim encircles the depiction of the banner at Tajin. Apart from this example,
several commemorative stone war banners survive from the Classic period. A
well-known example from the La Ventilla compound of Teotihuacan retains the
same basic form as the Tajin example (Aveleyra de Anda 1963). The feather or
petal fringe again encircles a central hole, which, given the analogy with the
tezcacuitlapilli device cited above, may form a mirror, here occupied by two

intertwined scroll motifs. The mirror must have been an important aspect of war banners throughout Mesoamerican history, for Sahagún's (1950–1982:2:146) informants described two of the most sacred banners of the Mexica as "devices for seeing."

Another example of a commemorative stone banner was recently excavated at Tikal. We know from the inscription carved into the lower portion of this banner that it was placed in a hole so that it could be raised upright (Freidel et al. 1993:299, 470). I propose that the Structure 4 panel at Tajin served as a base for such a banner. This would explain several aspects of this otherwise anomalous sculpture: the horizontal positioning, the size, and the hole drilled through the middle of the stone, wide enough (17 centimeters), if elevated, to serve as a steady base for a pole. The image on the main face of the Structure 4 panel illustrates just such a base, seen above the representation of the turtle near the bottom of the composition (Figure 7.4a). The war banner represented in the center of the composition rises through this base, just as the actual banner would rise through the central hole carved into the Structure 4 panel itself. Both the function and iconography of the Structure 4 panel, then, concern the raising of banners.

Only two sculptures at Tajin have deliberate breaks running down the center of their compositions. Pascual Soto (1990:110) noted that the Pyramid of the Niches Panel 1 was defaced in Precolumbian times in this manner. Although he does not mention the Structure 4 panel discussed here, it exhibits the same kind of break, which runs through the center in a way that suggests deliberate mutilation. Schele and Grube (1994a), in their discussion of the Classic Maya practice of ritual destruction following warfare, suggest that the bases of important items, such as palanquins, were broken after defeat. I make the argument above that the Structure 4 panel is just such a base for holding the central war banner of El Tajin. The deliberate break in the monument may be the result of its ritual destruction during an unknown defeat of El Tajin, pointing to its importance as a central ritual object.

A bundle of darts traverses the mirror at the center of the Structure 4 panel, amplifying the war associations of the banner. A related motif appears in the central plaza on the small altar directly in front of the Pyramid of the Niches (Figure 7.5b). Inscribed in the center of an anthropomorphic figure is the same mirror motif and dart combination seen in the Structure 4 panel, but here the darts are intertwined. This altar figure may then be seen as a personification of the central mirror of the Tajin banner, relating it to the warfare and banner iconography of the Structure 4 panel and marking the space of the central plaza as the space of banner raising.[7] In summary, warfare, with its ritual concerns of banner raising and ballcourt decapitation sacrifice, forms the fundamental set of themes of the three sculptures associated with the central plaza.

Coatepec Narratives

The same themes already described for the central plaza iconography—warfare, banner raising, and ballcourt decapitation sacrifice—are mirrored in Mexica narratives and images concerning Coatepec (Snake Mountain). The Coatepec episode, and the closely related sojourn at Tollan, is contained in the migration story of the Mexica, an account of their peregrinations throughout northern Mesoamerica and the eventual founding of their capital, Tenochtitlan. These accounts have been variously considered by researchers as histories, myths, or a manipulative combination of the two (Boone 1991:139–140). My concern is not with the mythic or historical nature of the content but with the description of the architectural spaces they create at one of the early stops. Durán (1994:26) refers to Coatepec as a "model" for the later capital of Tenochtitlan.[8] By this he means that the Mexica building types received their meaning through the Coatepec story, which I will summarize below.

On arriving at Coatepec, the Mexica built a temple for their patron deity, Huitzilopochtli. The god himself was given credit for building the adjacent ballcourt and skull rack. Huitzilopochtli then created a hole in the center of the ballcourt, called the *itzompan,* or place of the skull: "[Huitzilopochtli made] a hole in the middle, larger than a ball with which they now play the game, that is called *itzompan,* and then they filled it up halfway, leaving a triangle in the middle of the hole, which is called the well of water" (Tezozómoc 1878:2:228–229; translation cited in Leyenaar 1988:101).[9] From this *itzompan* hole, water flows to the crops that sustain the Mexica, who now settled in to farm and enjoy the fruits of their patron deity's creation of an agriculturally productive landscape.

A group of Mexica called the 400 Southerners (Centzon Huitznahua) began to sow discord when they announced that Coatepec was the true ceremonial center and the final destination for the Mexica. Huitzilopochtli, angered at the hubris of this group, descended from Coatepec and sacrificed the 400 Southerners in the first war: "And Uitzilopochtli just then was born. Then he had his array with him—his shield, *teueueli;* and his darts and his blue dart thrower, called *xiuatlatl;* and in diagonal stripes was his face painted. . . . Then he pierced Coyolxauhqui, and then quickly struck off her head. It stopped there at the edge of Coatepetl. And her body came falling below; it fell breaking to pieces; in various places her arms, her legs, her body each fell" (Sahagún 1950–1982:3:4).

Tezozómoc located the sacrifice of Coyolxauhqui not on Coatepec itself but in the *itzompan* ballcourt below: "And he [Huitzilopochtli] killed her in the ballcourt, and he decapitated her and ate her heart" (Tezozómoc 1992:35, author's translation).[10] The well of the *itzompan* then dries up, leaving the Mexica without food. Huitzilopochtli's victory was the first war of the Mexica and was treated as the paradigm for successful battle, just as Coatepec was the paradigmatic ceremonial center.

The key moment in this drama was the descent of Huitzilopochtli, which the Mexica conceived of as a hierophany, the birth of the physical body *(ixiptla)* of their patron deity (Boone 1991:134). The illustration of this event from the *Codex Azcatitlan* (Figure 7.6a) shows a war banner raised at the foot of Coatepec as Huitzilopochtli descends. The banner, which resembles banners carried by the Mexica war captains in the *Codex Mendoza* (Figure 7.6b), emerges from the back of the *xiuhcoatl*. Although the raising of the war banner itself is not mentioned in the texts, it is clear from this illustration and from the rituals surrounding this narrative that it was a crucial part of the story.

The Mexica festival called the Raising of the Banners, or Panquetzaliztli, held yearly in the central ceremonial precinct of Tenochtitlan, re-created this paradigmatic war (León-Portilla 1987). The descent of Huitzilopochtli from Coatepec was reenacted complete with ballcourt sacrifice and the raising of the banners. It ended in the sacrifice of imitators of the 400 Southerners. Most important, during this ceremony the central pyramid of Tenochtitlan became a re-creation of Coatepec, legitimating the ritual actions performed there (León-Portilla 1987:50–61).

In both ritual and myth the Mexica defined the foot of their sacred mountain, and its replica in stone, as the place of ballcourt sacrifice, banner raising, and war. We have already seen these same themes in the central plaza of El Tajin. If one accepts this analogy between the symbolic function of the foot of Coatepec and the meaning of the central plaza at El Tajin, then the Pyramid of the Niches may be identified as the Tajin Coatepec, the central sacred mountain of the site.

Drainage Systems and the *Itzompan* at El Tajin

The other primary characteristic of the Mexica Coatepec is its relation to the *itzompan* ballcourt. Due to the well in its center, the *itzompan* ballcourt was the source of water and the cause of abundance for the entire polity. If the Pyramid of the Niches is the Tajin Coatepec, then the two major ballcourts that frame the structure should include themes of water and abundance. In this sketch map of the Precolumbian drainage system of Tajin (Figure 7.7), the north ballcourt has a small ceremonial canal that connects it to the Pyramid of the Niches and on to one of the *arroyos* that define the center of the site, mirroring the description of the Coatepec ballcourt as a source of water. No ceremonial drainage system has been discovered in the other major ballcourt that frames the Pyramid of the

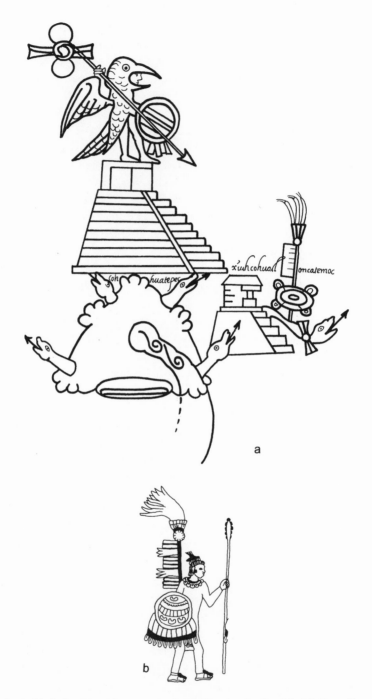

a

b

Figure 7.6 *(a) Codex Azcatitlan,* page 11, detail (drawing by Daniela Medieros Epstein; courtesy of the artist); *(b) Codex Mendoza,* page 67, detail (drawing by Daniela Medieros Epstein; courtesy of the artist).

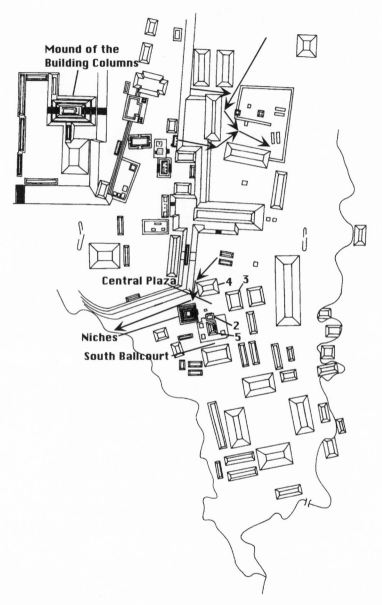

El Tajín, Precolumbian Drainage Systems

Mound of the
Building Columns

Central Plaza

Niches

South Ballcourt

4 3

2
5

Figure 7.7. Sketch map of the drainage system at El Tajín (redrawn and modified after Kampen 1972:Figure 2).

Figure 7.8. South Ballcourt, corner panel, detail, El Tajin (drawing by the author).

Niches. All four corner-panels of this ballcourt, however, contain framing images of skeletal beings, depicted mainly as skulls, rising from water (Figure 7.8). These images are always located toward the center of the court, where the Mexica describe the place of the skull and the well.[11]

Finally, the association of the foot of Coatepec as the place where banners are raised also explains the numerous large rectangular stones with holes bored in their middle (with diameters from approximately 21 to 25 centimeters) that stand in front of the Pyramid of the Niches on the central plaza side (Figure 7.9). These holes are comparable in depth and diameter to the hole puncturing the center of the Structure 4 panel, which, as we have seen, serves as the base for the raising of a war banner. I propose that the bases aligned at the foot of the Pyramid of the Niches served the same function, as places for the enactment of the elaborate banner ritual alluded to on the Structure 4 panel (Figure 7.4a). Thus the major banner-raising ceremony at Tajin occurred at the foot of the Pyramid of the Niches, just as the analogous ritual at Tenochtitlan occurred at the foot of the image of Coatepec, the Templo Mayor, again suggesting that the Pyramid of

Figure 7.9. Banner bases at the foot of the stairway, Pyramid of the Niches, El Tajin (drawing by the author).

the Niches at Tajin served a closely related symbolic function to the Mexica Templo Mayor/Coatepec.

Recent archaeological work on the Pyramid of the Niches has revealed a vertical shaft leading from the sanctuary on the summit into the interior (Wilkerson 1990:161). The shaft contains stone fill and a false stairway described only by a molding on the wall. At the bottom of the shaft, excavators found traces of cinnabar, a common substance found in Mesoamerican burials. No further evidence of a burial was found, however (Brüggemann 1992:77).

The shaft at the heart of the Pyramid of the Niches may be seen as symbolizing the cave at the heart of the Mesoamerican sacred mountain (Stone 1995a:32–34), specifically the Tajin Coatepec. A similar shaft is found at the contemporary site of Chichen Itza, where the High Priest's Grave contains a shaft running down the center of the building to a modified cave below, which Headrick (1991) associates with the cave of emergence described in Central Mexican narratives and images. Heyden (1981) has also discussed the shaft and modified cave underneath the Temple of the Sun at Teotihuacan as an early example of a cave of emergence. It is tempting to see the Tajin shaft as an example of the emergence theme, but both the above authors and others have pointed out the rich manipulation of the cave theme in Mesoamerican history (see especially Stone 1995a:21–44). Given the presence of cinnabar and the false stairway, it would seem that the architects were also alluding to the idea of burial and, if Brüggemann is correct, only the idea. Until a published report documenting the archaeological evidence appears, however, interpretations of the shaft will have to be considered preliminary.

Conclusions

In this study, I have argued that the Pyramid of the Niches at El Tajin is defined by symbolism analogous to the Mexica conception of Coatepec. This symbolic theme provided the basic language of identity and legitimacy at the heart of the site. At both Tajin and Tenochtitlan, the Coatepec theme was embodied in ritual narratives that recalled primordial mythic events that included banner raising and ballcourt sacrifice. That said, there are important differences in the elements of the theme that may only be touched on here, such as ballcourt number and configuration (Tajin has thirteen courts in its central area, whereas accounts of Tenochtitlan's central precinct mention only two) and patron deities (the Mexica patron deity Huitzilopochtli does not appear at Tajin, where a version of Tlaloc seems to fill the role of patron deity). Thus it is not the purpose of this chapter to suggest a direct historical connection between Tajin and the later Mexica but rather to point out an embedded set of Mesoamerican narrative elements, based around the configuration the Mexica called Coatepec and the related image of Tollan, and to suggest that these elements were functioning in a recognizable configuration during the Epiclassic period at Tajin. The connections identified in this chapter suggest that further research into the Early Postclassic version of the Coatepec paradigm, as well as its roots in earlier Mesoamerican programs, would be highly productive. Placing this charter of political legitimacy earlier than its Late Postclassic permutation raises the question of its antiquity in Mesoamerica and its mode of transmission and transformation.

Notes

1. Defining just what pieces were actually found in the plaza, however, is not without problems because of the irregular recording practices of the early archaeologists. The reconstruction that follows is based on recent detective work by Arturo Pascual Soto (1990) in the archives of the Instituto Nacional de Antropología e Historia and on my own observations in these archives.

2. Brüggemann (1992:21) also places this panel in Structure 2.

3. Narrative panels are associated with the superstructure of the Pyramid of the Niches (Kampen 1972:4–9) that may at first glance be associated with the central plaza. I would argue, however, that these panels define the symbolism and ritual associated with the summit of the structure and do not figure directly into the symbolism of the plaza below, which is the specific subject of this chapter.

4. See also the four panels from Aparicio, Veracruz, south of Tajin, for analogous depictions of sacrificed ballplayers (García Payón 1949). These panels, which were set into the four corners of a structure, repeat the ballcourt sacrifice iconography on each panel, and are said to come from a ballcourt at the site.

5. Recently, Karl Taube (1992:172–177) has shown the importance and ubiquity of back mirrors in Teotihuacan iconography and ceremonial dress, extending the antiquity of this important ritual item to the Classic period. In addition to examples from Teotihuacan, the author points out that these mirrors may be found in the iconography and burial furniture of Esperanza phase Kaminaljuyu and the contemporary lowland Maya. Other forms and uses of mirrors as ritual devices have been identified in earlier Olmec assemblages and iconography (Carlson 1981a). Seler (1990–1998:89) long ago identified the back mirror as an important Epiclassic/Early Postclassic prestige item at Chichen Itza. Beginning in the Epiclassic or Early Postclassic, these mirrors contained a pyrite surface with turquoise rim. Earlier mirrors were pyrite or other reflective material, sometimes with an elaborately carved stone backing.

6. Pasztory (1983:280) identified this object as a fan. At approximately 1.2 meters, however, the banner matches the scale of the banners portrayed in the Mound of the Building Columns at Tajin (see Kampen 1972) and at Tikal (Fialko 1988).

7. Ellen Spinden (1933:234) remarked on the similarity of this motif to the roof ornaments on the Upper Temple of the Jaguars, Chichen Itza, which in its painted interior has extensive warfare iconography that specifically highlights the role of war banners (Freidel et al. 1993:325–326).

8. "The Aztecs were so contented here [at Coatepec], although it was no more than a model, no more than a pattern, of the promised land" (Durán 1994:26).

9. "Y agujero enmedio, del grandor de más de una bola, con que juegan ahora a la bola, que llaman Itzompan, y luego la atajan por medio, quedando un triángulo enmedio del agujero, que llaman el pozo de agua, que en cayendo allí la pelota de batel [batey] (Tezozómoc 1878:227–229).

10. "Allá en Teotlachco [Huitzilopochtli] cómese . . . á la llamada Coyolxauh[qui] . . . la mató en Teotlachco, y la degolló y se le comió el corazón" (Tezozómoc 1992:35).

11. Spinden (1933:247) tentatively connected these images with Coatepec, although she did not consider the *itzompan* to be a place in the center of the court.

8

The Planet of Kings

Jupiter in Maya Cosmology

Susan Milbrath

In a 1986 symposium at the Kimbell Art Museum, host to the *Blood of Kings* exhibition, Linda Schele (1986) presented an important new study that linked visual imagery and dates recorded on monuments to specific positions of the planets. Her analysis of these date patterns was later published in *A Forest of Kings,* coauthored with David Freidel. In what has to be one of the longest footnotes in the book, she outlined iconographic elements associated with dates corresponding to planetary positions of Venus, Jupiter, and Saturn (Schele and Freidel 1990:444–446, n. 47). Her ability to weave together discussions of iconography, political history, and astronomy was compelling and led other scholars to new avenues of investigation.

In a subsequent study, Anthony Aveni and Lorren Hotaling (1994) used statistical analysis to investigate the astronomical patterning of what they referred to as "culturally tagged" dates. Analyzing the astronomical dates published by Schele and Freidel (1990:444–447), along with related sets generated by Schele (1982:Appendix 4, chart 10), Floyd Lounsbury (1982, 1989), and John Justeson (1989), they studied the patterning in terms of real astronomical events. Aveni and Hotaling found that previously published studies often cited the greatest elongation of Venus as an event of significance, but the pattern of dates actually revealed that maximum altitude of the planet was the more notable event. Nonetheless, their analysis provided support for studies linking Maya dates to events involving Saturn and Jupiter, especially dates recording the retrograde position of these two planets. In this light, I began to study date patterns associated with God K, whose attributes suggested a possible celestial association. God K, first identified in the Postclassic codices (Schellhas 1904), is very prominent on Classic

Maya monuments. My study reveals that God K is associated with *k'atun-* endings involving Jupiter and Saturn events, especially in late Classic Maya times (C.E. 600–850). Furthermore, there seems to be a clear link between certain God K images and dates coinciding with Jupiter's position in retrograde, when the planet seems to stop and then move backward in the sky. Before looking at these dates, it is important to understand why God K is a good candidate for studies of an astronomical nature.

Imagery of God K

God K's celestial context is clear in a number of images. A Postclassic Maya mural painting from Tulum depicts a skyband with a winged God K (Figure 8.1). This type of celestial imagery extends back to Classic period times, as seen in the winged God K under a skyband on the capstone of the Temple of the Owls at Chichen Itza, probably dating between C.E. 800–900 (Figure 8.2). Cacao pods frame God K's legs. Cacao, the chocolate bean, was the principal currency for Mesoamerica; hence God K is a sky deity associated with great wealth. On page 25 of the New Year pages in the *Dresden Codex,* Thompson (1972:91) notes that God K appears with a glyph passage saying that cacao is God K's food (Figure 8.3).

Continuity is evident when tracing the visual imagery of God K back through time, but there are variations in details. The Postclassic God K has an upturned snout with branching elements (Figures 8.1, 8.3, and 8.4). Sometimes God K's snout has a mirror inset, best seen on *Dresden Codex* page 12a (Figure 8.3). In the Classic period, God K carries a mirror on his brow (Figure 8.5). Sometimes a

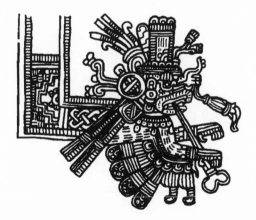

Figure 8.1. God K's celestial aspect as winged deity on sky band in Late Postclassic mural from Tulum (after Taube 1992:Figure 34c).

Figure 8.2. Winged God K in jaws of coiled serpent with sky band arching overhead on painted capstone from Terminal Classic Temple of the Owls at Chichen Itza, Structure 5C7 (after Tozzer 1957:Figure 384).

Figure 8.3. Ben New Year with God K in temple of east, *Dresden Codex*, page 25b (after Villacorta and Villacorta 1977).

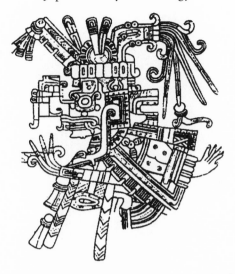

Figure 8.4. Late Postclassic God K bound like prisoner in murals of Mound 1, Santa Rita, Belize (after Taube 1992:Figure 32f).

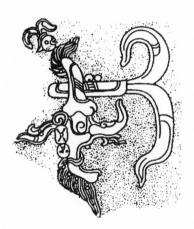

Figure 8.5. Late Classic God K with smoking celt or mirror emanating from mirror on brow, Pier C of House A at Palenque (after Robertson 1985b:Figure 38).

torch emerges from the mirror, its smoke resembling cigar smoke or the smoke from fires (Figure 8.6; Schele and Miller 1983:Figure 3n). More commonly, a smoking celt or axe emanates from God K's mirror (Figure 8.5). In Classic and Postclassic glyphic writing, God K's head with a mirrored brow is his name, but sometimes a smoking mirror by itself can name God K in the Classic period (Figures 8.7 and 8.8).

God K's nocturnal nature is evident in images from the Palenque Palace that

Figure 8.6. Classic period relief of God K at Sayil has both serpent leg and smoking mirror of Central Mexican Tezcatlipoca (after Taube 1992:Figure 34a).

Figure 8.7. Classic glyph for God K representing smoking mirror (after Schele and Miller 1983:Figure 3i).

Figure 8.8. God K's Postclassic portrait head glyph with elongated snout bearing smoking mirror (after Taube 1992:Figures 32a and b).

Figure 8.9. Mirror-browed God K wearing T510f star, West Court of Palenque Palace (after Robertson 1985b:Figure 358).

show the mirror-browed God K wearing a star glyph (Figure 8.9). Stela 31, a fifth-century monument from Tikal, depicts God K with a smoking celt emerging from a forehead mirror with markings like the glyph for night known as *ak'bal* (Figure 8.10).

Linda Schele (1976:29) originally pointed out that the ruler is the incarnation of God K at Palenque. Subsequently, she noted that "God K's mirror-in-hand" (T1030d:670) is a glyph compound denoting the presentation or display of God K at the time of an heir-designation ceremony at Palenque (Schele 1984a:304). Although she modified her position somewhat in more recent publications, as noted below, it is evident that God K is the Classic Maya god of lineage and rulership. In this light, it is interesting that a number of Maya rulers incorporate God K in their personal names or titles (Schele and Mathews 1998:319–324). God K is seen in the headdress of Stormy Sky (Sian Kan K'awil or K'awil Chaan)

Figure 8.10. Early Classic God K with smoking celt emanating from *ak'bal* mirror brow, Tikal Stela 31 (after Miller 1986:Plate 19).

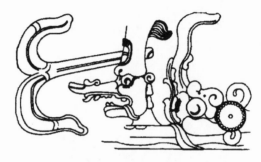

Figure 8.11. God K's head emerges from jaws of double-headed serpent flanking portrait of ruler on North Palace Substructure, Palenque (after Robertson 1985b:Figure 339b).

on Tikal Stela 31, which records his accession to the throne (Figure 8.10; Miller 1986:54, 82). The headdress shows God K's torso on a sky glyph, transforming Stormy Sky's personal name into a costume accessory (Coggins 1990:84).

On Maya lintels and stelae, God K frequently appears in the jaws of a double-headed serpent, an image like the God K scepter used by Maya rulers as a royal insignia (Cohodas 1982:113; Stuart 1984:18–19). On an architectural relief from the North Staircase of the Palace at Palenque, God K's head emerges from the jaws of a double-headed serpent flanking the portrait of a ruler (Figure 8.11). The double-headed serpent with an upturned bulbous nose seems to embody the front head of the Cosmic Monster, as seen on Palenque House E and on Lintel 3 of Tikal Temple IV (Figure 8.12; Milbrath 1999:227, 281, Figure 5.7g, Plate 15). On the other hand, God K's serpent foot often seems to represent a naturalistic snake, as on the Sayil relief (Figure 8.6). God K's serpent foot and smoking mirror have led him to be compared to the Aztec god Tezcatlipoca, considered to be a lord of the night sky (Coe 1982:47, 54; Robicsek 1979:126).

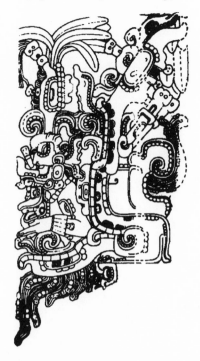

Figure 8.12. God K in jaws of Cosmic Monster arching over ruler's head, detail of Tikal Lintel 3, Temple IV (after Jones 1977:Figure 11).

God K's Name

God K can be identified as the sky god called Bolon Dzacab in Colonial period sources. The Motul dictionary glosses Bolon Dzacab as "perpetual thing" (eternal), certainly appropriate for a celestial god. The link between God K and Bolon Dzacab, first proposed by Eduard Seler at the turn of the century, is now widely accepted (Seler 1960–1961:I:76–377; 1990–1998:I:96–97; Taube 1992:73). The Dzacab element in his Colonial period name is no doubt derived from *ts'akab',* meaning lineage, ancestry, cast, or generation (Barrera Vásquez 1980:873). Bolon means nine, and Eric Thompson (1972:90) translated Bolon Dzacab as "nine generations." He proposed that this name may be linked with the nine lords of the underworld (Thompson 1970:227, 280). In the *Dresden Codex* New Year pages, the scene of the Etz'nab years on page 26 shows God K with the number nine, evoking the name Bolon Dzacab. Thompson (1970:Figure 7b–h) illustrates various Classic period examples of God K's name associated with the number nine, although he misidentified the smoke elements in his name glyph as vegetation.

Stuart's (1987:15) phonetic reading of God K's name as *k'awil (kauil)* provides support for linking God K with maize, the principal source of sustenance (Taube 1992:78). Nonetheless, recent interpretations of *k'awil* suggest that the term refers to sculptures or "idols," as well as obsidian, flint, and stone axeheads associated with lightning (Freidel et al. 1993:194–200; Schele and Mathews 1998:115, 412–413, Figures 5.3, 5.12). Schele and Mathews (1998:115, 185–187, 412–415, Figure 5.12) say that God K was a patron deity of a number of Maya cities and the spirit of deity statues and the Vision Serpent.

The *Cordemex Dictionary* defines *k'awil* as "food," noting that the term also refers to a deity who provides food (Barrera Vásquez 1980:386–387). The dictionary entry also points out that because *il* is a common suffix, the significant element in the name may be *k'aw*, the name used in Yucatan for a bird in the family of Icteridae. This bird seems to be a great-tailed grackle (*Quiscalus m. mexicanus;* Howell and Webb 1995:Plate 65). In the area of Tikal, this bird is known by its Maya name, *k'au* (Smithe and Trimm 1966:262). The association with maize is probably because grackles love to eat maize.

Although *k'awil* is now more commonly used in translating God K's name, an alternate reading for his name at Palenque is *tahil*, meaning "obsidian mirror" or "torch mirror," based on the torch in God K's mirrored brow; this reading suggests a connection with the K'iche' god Tohil (Taube 1992:75–76; Tedlock 1985:365). Tohil, the K'iche' god of lightning and storms, was the lord of a K'iche' lineage at the time of the conquest. God K is similarly connected with lineage and lightning. As Karl Taube points out, God K's headdress elements—mirrors, smoking axes, fire, torches, and cigars—all may allude to lightning. Apparently, God K is linked with meteorological phenomena, especially storms and lightning.

God K in Calendar Cycles

Landa describes Bolon Dzacab (Bolon Zacab) as a god worshipped in New Year ceremonies; he was associated with the year-bearer K'an, and he was honored every four years (Tozzer 1941:139–140). In the *Dresden Codex* (25–26), God K appears in the New Year pages in ceremonies associated with year-bearers named Ben and Etz'nab (Figure 8.3). The Sun God (God G) is also represented on the same page as God K in the Ben and Etz'nab New Year ceremonies. Clearly God K is distinguished from the sun itself, but he plays a prominent role in the New Year ceremonies celebrating the annual cycle of the 365-day vague year.

Returning to God K's celestial associations, we can conclude that this deity is somehow connected with the solar year but is clearly distinguished from the Sun God. Investigating the cycles of the planets indicates that only Saturn and Jupiter show a notable relationship with the solar year. The solar year ends only 13 days before Saturn completes its 378.1-day synodic period, bringing it back to the same position relative to the earth and sun. Jupiter is seen in the sky for about a year during its synodic period, being visible for a mean interval of 367 days before disappearing in conjunction with the sun (Aveni 1980:Table 6). Thus it is possible that God K is somehow connected with these planets in their relationship to the annual cycle.

God K also appears in the *tun*-Ajaw cycle represented in Late Postclassic murals from Mound 1 at Santa Rita, Belize (Figure 8.4; Gann 1900; Thompson 1960:198, 251). On the east portion of the north wall, God K appears with the date 1 Ajaw in a sequence of deities associated with different Ajaw dates that end the 360-day *tun*. These are read from right to left, following the *tun*-Ajaw sequence: 12, 8, 4, 13, 9, designating five *tuns* (360-day "years"), but following 9 Ajaw the sequence skips 5 Ajaw and shifts to 1 Ajaw. This unusual sequence may refer to a set of five *tuns* linked with the *k'atun* 1 Ajaw. God K's association with 1 Ajaw at Santa Rita is an interesting detail in light of a pattern linking Jupiter events to *k'atuns* ending 1 Ajaw during the Classic period noted by Thompson (1960:228). As we will see, there are other reasons for linking God K to Jupiter.

God K is prominent in the *k'atun* cycle of the *Paris Codex* on pages 2–12. Owing to the structure of the *k'atun* cycle, each of the thirteen *k'atuns* was associated with a different Ajaw date (the sequence of Ajaw dates for the *k'atun*-endings is: 1, 12, 10, 8, 6, 4, 2, 13, 11, 9, 7, 5, 3). God K's head is carried to the new *k'atun* lord in each of the *k'atuns* in the *Paris Codex*, making him a sort of embodiment of the *k'atun*, a period approximating twenty years (Milbrath 1999:230). Each *k'atun* incorporated a period of 19.71 years (20 × 360 days), and the entire cycle of the thirteen *k'atuns* in the "Short Count" ran for about 256 years. David Kelley (1985:238) notes that the interval between successive conjunctions of Jupiter and Saturn is between nineteen and twenty years, close to the length of a *k'atun*. The conjunction of Jupiter and Saturn at such intervals cannot be expected to align with a specific date in the *k'atun* cycle over long periods of time, but a pattern would certainly be notable over the course of the centuries. In conjunctions between Jupiter and Saturn, Jupiter is the dynamic actor in the scenario, essentially running laps around the slower-moving Saturn. In this light, the God K head carried to the enthroned *k'atun* lord in the *k'atun* cycle of the *Paris Codex* may symbolize Jupiter transported across the sky to a new encounter with Saturn.

God K is named in an 819-day cycle known to refer to Jupiter and Saturn in Late Classic texts. The 819-day cycle has a high incidence of Jupiter and Saturn events in the Classic period inscriptions, according to John Justeson (1989:103). The 819-day phrases often name God K in the fifth position (Kelley 1976:57–58, Figure 17; Thompson 1960:Figure 35, numbers 2–3). A companion glyph (T739) in the fourth position also is used as Glyph Y of the Supplementary Series where it is governed by a seven-day cycle that may be a "planetary week" (Yasugi and Saito 1991).

Jupiter Events and God K on Maya Monuments

The patterning of images and dates on monuments from a number of Maya sites suggests that God K encodes a relationship between Jupiter and Saturn. God K is especially connected with Jupiter's retrograde, a period when the planet seems to stop forward motion at the first stationary point and then apparently moves backward until it reaches its second stationary point, when it again resumes forward motion (Milbrath 1999:231–240). Before focusing on monuments from Palenque, Tikal, and Yaxchilan, I will highlight God K images from a variety of sites to show that this seems to be a fairly widespread phenomenon. All dates are noted in the Julian calendar using the GMT2 correlation constant, which makes the Julian day number equal to the Maya day number plus the correlation constant 584,283.

The Osario at Chichen Itza, recently restored in a project directed by Peter Schmidt (1999), displays numerous God K images on the panels covering the stepped pyramid. Profile bird figures have God K's face with a branching snout, recalling the features of Postclassic images of God K (Figure 8.1). Other bird figures seem to have Chaak's face. Recent decipherment of the dates on the southeast pillar, one of four pillars that supported the roof of the pyramid's superstructure, indicates the inscriptions date to C.E. 998, falling in the Early Postclassic period. Graña-Behrens et al. (1999) identify two dates; the first noted is 2 Ajaw 18 Mol (May 6, 998), and the second is 10 K'an 2 Sotz' (January 30, 998). Their free translation of the whole text is: "On 2 Ahaw 18 Mol, this is the image of the ruler; erected was the stone. [It happened] on the day 10 K'an 2 Zotz' in the 11th Tun of the K'atun 2 Ajaw" (Graña-Behrens et al. 1999:Table 1). It is noteworthy that the May date falls in Jupiter's period of retrograde motion (from February 21 to June 24, 998; Meeus 1997), and the date also coincides with a time when Saturn and Mercury were in conjunction with the moon in its last quarter. The January Calendar Round date 10 K'an 2 Sotz' combined with a Short Count *tun*-Ajaw denoting *tun* 11 in the *k'atun*-ending 2 Ajaw correlates with the Long Count date 10.8.10.6.4 (January 30, 998). This was the new moon. The first visibility of Venus as the Evening Star and the last visibility of Mercury as the Morning Star also took place within a week of this date. The January and May dates bracket Jupiter's retrograde period during which Jupiter made its transition from the morning to the evening sky. In late January C.E. 998 Jupiter was visible overhead at dawn, and by early May Jupiter had shifted to the eastern horizon at dusk. Throughout the year, Jupiter was positioned in Libra, identified as a bird constellation in the *Paris Codex* (Milbrath 1999:Table 7.1), an intriguing detail given that God K has an avian aspect in the Osario reliefs.

Three Seibal monuments, all bearing prominent God K images, help confirm a link between God K and the cycles of Jupiter and Saturn. Stelae 8, 9, 10, and 21 all record a single Calendar Round date, 5 Ajaw 3 K'ayab, the end of the *k'atun* 10.1.0.0.0. All show the ruler with an image of God K, but each God K is in a different position (Schele and Mathews 1998:Figures 5.10, 5.14, 5.17, 5.21). On Stela 10, the ruler's headdress bears the God K image, whereas the other three monuments show the ruler holding God K images: one is a manikin scepter (Stela 21), another is a head in the ruler's hand (Stela 8), and the third is at the ruler's feet on the tail end of a serpent bar (Stela 9). Thus we seem to have four different manifestations of God K all linked with the same date. The *k'atun*-ending (November 24, 849) is a date that coincides with the retrograde periods of both Jupiter and Saturn, only nine days before Saturn's second stationary point. Clearly this *k'atun*-ending had a propitious relationship between the cycles of Jupiter and Saturn, providing a direct connection between the *k'atun* end and the retrograde period of both planets. The two planets being simultaneously in retrograde motion at the *k'atun* end would not be seen again until C.E. 1165 *k'atun* 12 Ajaw, 10.17.0.0.0.

At Naj Tunich, a God K portrait glyph appears with the date 13 Ajaw, referring to the *k'atun*-ending 9.17.0.0.0 13 Ajaw 18 Kumk'u (January 18, 771; Stone 1995a:142, Figure 6.27). This is intriguing because God K's head is also represented in the *k'atun*-ending ceremonies of the Postclassic period. The 13 Ajaw date falls less than three weeks after the first stationary point of Jupiter (January 1, 771; Meeus 1997). Saturn was also in retrograde motion on this date. Such correlations probably led the Maya to focus on observations of these two planets at the *k'atun* end, especially in the period between C.E. 751 and 869 when every *k'atun*-ending coincided with the retrograde motion of both these planets.

A posthumous portrait of Yax Pac (Yax Pasaj) of Copan seems to relate to the midpoint of Jupiter's retrograde motion on a date (9.19.10.0.0) marking the halfway point counting up to the *k'atun*-ending 10.0.0.0.0 (C.E. 830). On Stela 11, Yax Pac wears the smoking mirror of God K, making this a rare portrait of a deceased ruler in the guise of God K (Fash 1991:177, Figure 108). The stela bears the date 8 Ajaw, inferred to be 9.19.10.0.0 8 Ajaw 8 Xul, marking the halfway point of the *k'atun (lahuntun)*. On this date (April 30, 820), Jupiter was on the eastern horizon at dusk, approximately at the midpoint of its retrograde motion (February 18 to June 20; Meeus 1997). Furthermore, Jupiter was in conjunction with the full moon on that night (Milbrath 1999:234).

Monuments from a number of other sites show a similar pattern linking God K images to dates when Jupiter was in retrograde motion. These include the majority of stelae depicting God K at Naranjo, as well as a number of other monuments, such as Bonampak Stela 1 and Dos Pilas Stela 15 (Milbrath 1999:234–235). Other God K monuments from these sites show dates that correspond to Saturn's retrograde motion, such as Lintel 4 from Bonampak and Dos Pilas Stela 14, which precisely marks Saturn's first stationary point (Milbrath 1999:234). There are, however, a number of God K monuments at Dos Pilas that do not fit the pattern, but many of these seem to mark subdivisions of the *k'atun*, indicating that the count to the next *k'atun*-ending takes precedence (Milbrath 1999:235). The strongest case for associating God K monuments with positions of Jupiter and Saturn in retrograde motion is evident in monuments from Palenque, Tikal, and Yaxchilan, certainly among the most important Late Classic Maya sites.

God K and Jupiter at Palenque

At Palenque, God K is the youngest of three astronomical brothers born in primordial times, according to Classic Maya texts at Palenque (Berlin 1963; Robertson 1991; Schele 1976:10). God K appears as GII of the Palenque Triad in mythological texts of the Cross Group; here GII's birth year is recorded as 2697 B.C.E. (1.18.5.4.0 1 Ajaw 13 Mak). The records indicate there were three astronomical brothers with GI (Venus) as the eldest, GIII (the sun) as the middle brother, and GII as the youngest (Milbrath 1999:205). This evokes connections with a modern Mopan tale about a set of three brothers in which Venus is the eldest brother and the Sun God is the middle child; the youngest is Mars or Jupiter (Milbrath 1999:232; Thompson 1930:120–123, 138).

God K is prominent in the Temple of the Inscriptions at Palenque, a pyramid that houses the tomb of Pakal II, who appears in the guise of God K at the base of a cosmic tree on the Sarcophagus Lid (Figure 8.13; Robertson 1991:18; Schele 1976:17). The scene has an astronomical context; Pakal is surrounded by a skyband, and God K and the Jester God emerge from either end of a bicephalic sky serpent (Schele and Mathews 1998:Figure 3.16). On the edge of the lid, Pakal's death or some other event related to his death is recorded on the Calendar Round corresponding to August 26, 683 (6 Etz'nab 11 Yax; 9.12.11.5.18). David Stuart has deciphered the event glyph as "he entered the road" (*och b'ih;* Freidel et al. 1993:76–77, Figure 2.12; Schele 1992:133). Heinrich Berlin (1977:137) notes that this event (T100:585) refers to the end of a reign, and it may signal death or apotheosis. This expression probably alludes to Pakal's apotheosis rather than his death (Coggins 1988:74–75). Like Yax Pac's image of apotheosis at Copan, Pakal's image on the Sarcophagus is associated with a date marking the retrograde period of Jupiter. Pakal's apotheosis date coincides with Jupiter's first stationary point (August 28, 683; Meeus 1997; Milbrath 1997, 1999:234). It seems significant

Figure 8.13. Pakal's apotheosis as God K took place when Jupiter reached its first stationary point in c.e. 683, detail of Sarcophagus Lid of Temple of Inscriptions at Palenque (after Robertson 1985a:Figure 73).

that Pakal's son, Kan B'alam II, was not inaugurated as the new ruler until Jupiter had begun to move forward again four months later (Milbrath 1999:234).

All three temples of the Cross Group at Palenque show different aspects of God K, indicating there may be at least three manifestations of God K at Palenque. The Temple of the Sun shows Kan B'alam at the time of his accession in January of 684 holding a manikin of God K with a smoking brow (Figure 8.14). The Temple of the Cross (Figure 8.15) depicts a similar scene, but here God K is associated with a small figure, originally identified as the deceased Pakal by Linda Schele (1976:13) but now recognized as Kan B'alam at his heir-designation event when he was six years old (Bassie-Sweet 1991:158, 203–204; Robertson 1991:20–21; Stuart 2000:16). The young Kan B'alam stands on a skeletal head with an elongated snout and the number nine *(b'olon)*, which probably alludes to the Bolon Dzacab aspect of God K, based on comparison with images so identified by Thompson (1970:Figure 7p). The Temple of the Foliated Cross depicts God K emerging from a spiral shell with a maize plant in hand (Figure 8.16; Dütting 1984:23; Robicsek 1979:115; Stuart 1978:167). Again, young Kan B'alam appears at his heir-designation event, but here he stands on God K's shell, indicating a direct link between the future ruler and a maize aspect of God K. The young ruler is like a sprouting maize plant, a future source of sustenance for his people.

By studying a pattern of dates in the life of Kan B'alam, Lounsbury (1989) correlated Palenque monuments with Jupiter's retrograde motion, although he did not identify specific imagery that refers to Jupiter. Both Kan B'alam's heir designation in June of 641 (9 Ak'bal 6 Xul; 9.10.8.9.3) and his accession in Janu-

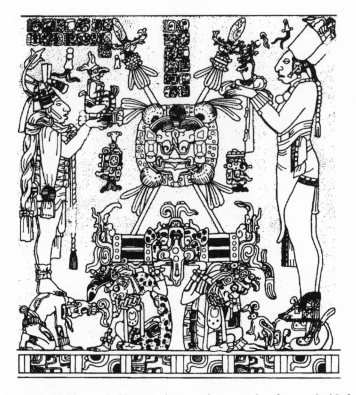

Figure 8.14. Kan B'ahlam II holding God K manikin on right of a war shield, from Late Classic Temple of the Sun, Palenque (after drawing by Linda Schele).

ary of 684 (8 Ok 3 K'ayab; 9.12.11.12.10) were timed by Jupiter's departure from the second stationary point, which means that the planet was resuming forward motion (Lounsbury 1989:Table 19.1). The heir-designation date also correlates with Saturn's approach to the first stationary point (June 26, 641; Meeus 1997; Milbrath 1999:233).

Temple XIV at Palenque shows that after his death Kan B'alam continued his relationship with God K and the planet Jupiter (Figure 8.17). The display of God K is mentioned followed by a reference to 9 Ajaw 3 K'ank'in (9.13.13.15.0; October 31, 705), a date that falls about three years and nine months after the death date (3 × 365 days + 260 days). Lounsbury (1989:250, Figure 19.5) links this post-humous date with Jupiter's departure from its second stationary point (second stationary point on October 21, 705; Meeus 1997). On this date, the moon passed by Jupiter in retrograde motion, and Saturn was also in retrograde motion (Milbrath 1999:233–234).

Figure 8.15. Young Kan B'alam II standing on Bolon Dzacab aspect of God K at time of heir designation in C.E. 641 faces mature Kan B'alam II at forty years of age when he was crowned king in C.E. 684, Temple of the Cross at Palenque (after Schele and Miller 1986:Figure II.6).

God K and Jupiter at Tikal

Turning to the site of Tikal, we find another set of monuments to test for a possible pattern linking God K images to Jupiter's retrograde period. The most important image in this respect may be Tikal Stela 20, a monument with only one date (Figure 8.18). Here Ruler B (also known as Yaxkin Chaan K'awil or Yik'in Chan K'awil) wears a headdress crowned by God K. The ruler's mouth mask is decorated with a star glyph, suggesting an astronomical context. This stela is from one of the many Twin-pyramid complexes apparently devoted to *k'atun* ceremonies. The inscribed date records the first *k'atun*-ending of the ruler's reign on 2 Ajaw 13 Sek (9.16.0.0.0; May 3, 751; Jones 1977:45, Table 1). The *k'atun*-ending 9.16.0.0.0 provides a very good correlation with Jupiter's first stationary point on May 2, 751 (Meeus 1997). Saturn was also in retrograde motion, and Mars rose at dawn, while Venus was visible near its maximum altitude, an

Figure 8.16. At time of his heir designation, youthful Kan B'alam II stands on shell housing God K, who holds sprouting maize that embodies young ruler; on the opposite side Kan B'alam II appears fully mature at time of accession, Temple of the Foliated Cross at Palenque (after drawing by Linda Schele).

auspicious interlocking of astronomical events with the calendric cycles marking the end of a *k'atun* (Milbrath 1999:237). This *k'atun*-ending was surely the focus of major ceremonies involving Jupiter, for the planet stood still to honor Ruler B on the first *k'atun* completed in his reign.

Other Tikal monuments bear dates that mark the halfway point or *lahuntun* leading up to the exceptional *k'atun* 9.16.0.0.0, when Jupiter reached its first stationary point at the end of the *k'atun*. The *lahuntun* date 3 Ajaw 3 Mol (9.15.10.0.0) opens the inscription on Lintel 3 of Temple IV. This date (June 24, 741) approximates Jupiter's first stationary point (July 10, 741; Meeus 1997). Here God K appears in the jaws of a Cosmic Monster arching over the ruler's head (Figure 8.12; Jones 1977:Figure 11). The lintel depicts God K holding a mirror glyph in his hand, positioned like the flat-hand mirror compound used to mark different Venus positions in the Venus table of the *Dresden Codex* (Milbrath 1999:Figure 5.7a). The opening inscription on Lintel 2 from Temple IV bears the same date, but here Ruler B holds his God K manikin scepter as a giant jaguar stands alongside the ruler (Jones 1977:Figure 12). Other God K monuments at

Figure 8.17. Apotheosis of Kan B'alam II on October 31, 705 (Julian), correlates with time when Jupiter departed from second stationary point; Lady Ahpo Hel holds manikin of God K, just as moon held Jupiter in conjunction, from Temple XIV at Palenque (after Schele and Miller 1986:Figure VII.2).

Tikal also bear dates linked with the retrograde periods of Jupiter and Saturn, including the lintel from Structure 5D-52, Lintel 3 from Temple I, and Stelae 1 and 5 (Milbrath 1999:237–239).

Helen Alexander's (1992:Table 1) study of dates on Tikal Stela 31 suggests that the *k'atuns* ending 8.17.0.0.0 (October 18, 376) and 8.18.0.0.0 (July 5, 396) correlate with Jupiter's first stationary point (October 11, 376, and May 30, 396; Meeus 1997) and that the *k'atun*-ending 9.0.0.0.0 (December 5, 435) coincides with the midpoint of Jupiter's retrograde motion (October 1 to January 29; Meeus 1997). It seems that the *k'atun*-endings began to be linked with Jupiter's retrograde periods at least as far back as the fourth century C.E. Alexander also notes a number of other dates on Stela 31 that seem to coincide with periods of Jupiter's retrograde motion, including *lahuntun*-endings (8.18.10.0.0 and 8.19.10.0.0). Alexander uses the Tuckerman tables and the Voyager computer program to calculate the timing of Jupiter's retrograde motion. The tables compiled by Meeus (1997) provide more precise dates. These tables confirm that the above-mentioned dates fall within the retrograde period, but only the 8.17.0.0.0 date approximates Jupiter's first stationary point, and 8.19.10.0.0 is not the midpoint but actually falls about a week after the first stationary point. It is also

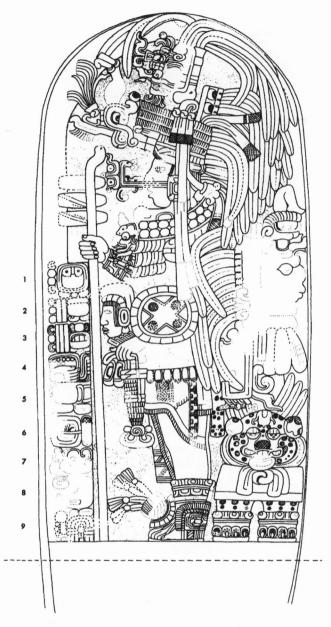

Figure 8.18. Yaxkin Chaan K'awil (Ruler B) wearing star mask and headdress crowned by God K at time of Jupiter's first stationary point, Tikal Stela 20 (after Jones 1977:Figure 15).

noteworthy that the Initial Series date on Stela 31 (9.0.10.0.0; October 16, 445) falls in Jupiter's retrograde period and also coincides with the heliacal set of Mars (Milbrath 1999:239).

One of the earliest known images of God K appears on the Leyden Plaque, probably also from Tikal. Here the ruler Moon Zero Bird holds a double-headed sky serpent that bears God K and the Sun God in its two jaws (Schele and Miller 1986:121, Plate 33b). The recorded date, 8.14.3.1.12 1 Eb 0 Yaxk'in (September 14, 320), corresponds approximately to Jupiter's heliacal rise just prior to the fall equinox. Jupiter's dawn rise so close to the fall equinox coordinated the cycles of the sun and Jupiter, perhaps leading to an early association between the cycles of Jupiter and the solar year.

God K and Jupiter at Yaxchilan

A random sampling of Maya monuments with God K images suggests a strong correlation with Jupiter events, especially retrograde motion, but a more thorough test of the hypothesis can be made by studying all the God K monuments from one site. Yaxchilan provides the best test for this study because the site provides a good sample of dated monuments bearing God K images. The dates for the Yaxchilan monuments are summarized in Table 8.1, and their correlation with Jupiter events is noted when the date falls in the retrograde period or in a seven-day window on either side of retrograde. This is a very rigorous test because the planets move very slowly around the retrograde period and the precise stationary point is hard to determine using only naked eye observations. Indeed, Aveni and Hotaling (1994:S40) allow a more generous thirty-day window in their analysis. Table 8.1 shows that at Yaxchilan, eight of the fifteen monuments that have God K images bear dates that coincide with Jupiter's retrograde. This is 53 percent of all monuments with God K images, a figure that seems significant in terms of statistical analysis. Jupiter's mean period of retrograde (120 days) added to the seven-day window on either side of retrograde indicates that Jupiter's retrograde period can be considered to be 33 percent of its synodic period (120 + 7 + 7 or 134 days in its total synodic period of 399 days [Milbrath 1999:235]). In a random sample of dates using a seven-day window, you would expect only around 33 percent of the dates to coincide with retrograde, but the God K monuments at Yaxchilan show more than 50 percent of such dates. The first date in Table 8.1 accurately pegs the midpoint of Jupiter's retrograde, and the next three fall within seven days of the first or second stationary points of Jupiter. The correlation is strengthened by the fact that the sample is not subject to the problems inherent in selecting the date that works best. All the Yaxchilan monuments in Table 8.1 bear only a single date, except Stela 1, which has two dates, both coinciding with Jupiter's retrograde motion.

Table 8.1

Yaxchilan Depictions of God K Associated with Jupiter's Retrograde[a]

Stela 11	9.15.19.1.1 (5/29/750[b])	1st st. pt. 3/28/750
		2nd st. pt. 7/28/750
Lintel 42: God K event	9.16.1.2.0 (6/6/752[b, c])	1st st. pt. 6/8/752
Lintels 6 and 43	9.16.1.8.6 (10/10/752[b, c])	2nd st. pt. 10/5/752
Lintel 7: God K event	9.16.1.8.8 (10/12/752[c])	2nd st. pt. 10/5/752
Lintel 40	9.16.7.0.0(3/27/758)	2nd st. pt. 4/29/758
Stela 1: 819-day event	9.16.8.16.10 (2/14/760)	1st st. pt. 1/27/760
		2nd st. pt. 5/30/760
Stela 1	IS 9.16.10.0.0 (3/11/761)	1st st. pt. 2/27/761
		2nd st. pt. 6/30/761
Lintel 38	9.16.12.5.14 (6/23/763)	1st st. pt. 5/7/763
		2nd st. pt. 9/5/763

---

[a]Stationary points from Meeus 1997; monument dates from Tate 1992.
[b]Date also coincides with Saturn's retrograde period.
[c]Date within 7 days of a stationary point.
   Note that when date is very close to one stationary point, only one is given. When date falls closer to midpoint in retrograde, both dates are given to show where it falls relative to the retrograde period.

On this stela, God K may have a dual nature, taking a celestial position at either end of the skyband over the ruler's head (Figure 8.19).

   Three other Yaxchilan lintels that depict God K bear dates approximating Jupiter's first stationary point, falling within twenty-one days of the stationary point. This includes Lintel 39, recording a bloodletting event on June 25, 741 (4 Imix 4 Mol; 9.15.10.0.0; Tate 1992:Appendices 2, 3). This date is about two weeks before Jupiter's first stationary point (July 10, 741; Meeus 1997). Lintels 32 and 53 bear a Calendar Round of 6 Ben 16 Mak (October 23, 709; 9.13.17.15.13), a date that Tate (1992:Appendix 2) correlates with the position of Saturn and Jupiter aligned together (within two degrees) at stationary points. This date is less than three weeks before Jupiter's first stationary point (November 10, 709; Meeus 1997). Because the superior planets slow down as they approach retrograde, it seems that an approximation of the Jupiter event is acceptable. Thus we can add three more monuments to the eight recorded in our table, increasing to 73 percent the number of God K monuments linked with dates corresponding to the retrograde period of Jupiter.

   When Jupiter was not at the appropriate position for a royal ritual involving

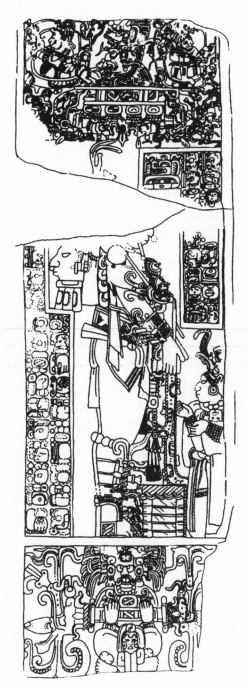

Figure 8.19. Sun God holding skeletal serpent at base; overhead double-headed sky serpent with God K in its jaws, from Late Classic Yaxchilan Stela 1 (modified after Tate 1992:Figure 124).

God K, Saturn's stationary point may have been considered a suitable substitute. Bird Jaguar IV with the God K manikin appears on Lintel 1 at the time of his accession on 11 Ahaw 8 Sek (9.16.1.0.0 or April 27, 752). This date is twenty-five days after Saturn's first stationary point (April 2, 752; Meeus 1997), and it may be significant that Mars was also in retrograde on this date (second stationary point on May 5, 752; Meeus 1997).

God K events are noted in glyphic texts on four Yaxchilan monuments, all of which depict a ruler holding a God K manikin (Lintels 3, 7, 42, 52; Tate 1992:Appendix 2). God K events on Lintels 7 and 42 correlate with a stationary point of Jupiter, and the God K event on Lintel 42 relates to a time when Saturn was also at its first stationary point (Table 8.1). The God K event on Lintel 52 coincides with Saturn's second stationary point (February 3, 766; Meeus 1997). Lintel 3 records a *hotun*-ending (9.16.5.0.0; April 6, 756), and the same one appears on Lintel 54, also depicting the ruler holding a God K manikin. Neither Jupiter nor Saturn was in retrograde on the *hotun* date recorded on these two monuments, but the date is a subdivision of the *k'atun* that could be used to track the position of Jupiter in relation to Saturn.

Allowing a twenty-one-day window on either side of retrograde indicates that thirteen of fifteen monuments with God K imagery from Yaxchilan have dates relating to the retrograde periods of Jupiter or Saturn. Six of these correspond to the retrograde periods of both planets (Lintels 6, 32, 42, 43, 53, Stela 11). Five bear dates linked only with the retrograde of Jupiter (Lintels 7, 38, 39, 40, Stela 1). Of the four remaining, two bear dates that relate only to Saturn's retrograde period (Lintels 1, 52). This leaves only two God K monuments (Lintels 3, 54) that cannot be connected to retrograde events involving Jupiter or Saturn; even these may be linked given the fact that the *hotun*-ending on these two monuments (9.16.5.0.0) marks the first quarter of the *k'atun* following the spectacular *k'atun*-ending 9.16.0.0.0, when Jupiter and Saturn were both in retrograde motion at the *k'atun* end. Certainly the positions of Jupiter and Saturn would have been observed on this *hotun*-ending.

Not all Yaxchilan monuments that bear dates coinciding with Jupiter's retrograde depict images of God K (Milbrath 1999:237). These reliefs show activities related to the ballgame, warfare, and blood offerings, events that also may be related to observations of Jupiter (Lintels 23, 24 [underside], 25, Stela 18, Step VII, Structure 33; Step I, Structure 44; Milbrath 1999:237; Schele and Freidel 1990:444–446; Tate 1992:Appendices 2, 3, Figures 98, 99, 111, 145, 154).

Looking at the entire sample of dates Tate (1992) published for Yaxchilan, there are a total of 109 different dates of which 26.6 percent (29 of 109 dates) fall in Jupiter's retrograde period or within seven days on either side of retrograde. This figure falls below the expected random frequency of 33 percent, using a seven-day window, but when we narrow our focus to those monuments depicting God K, the percentage bearing dates relating to Jupiter's retrograde is relatively high at 53 percent. Allowing a twenty-one-day window brings the percentage up to 73 percent, providing strong evidence that God K is associated with Jupiter's retrograde motion.

God K and Jupiter in Cultural Context

The data presented here indicate that God K embodies the planet Jupiter and the *k'atun* cycle involving observations of Jupiter and Saturn. The most commonly recorded events on Classic period monuments were *k'atun*-endings (Justeson 1989:104). Study of *k'atun*-endings in the Classic period reveals why Saturn and Jupiter played a prominent role. Between 8.11.0.0.0 and 8.15.0.0.0 (C.E. 258–337), Saturn was in retrograde at each *k'atun*-ending. From 8.16.0.0.0 to 8.19.0.0.0 (C.E. 357–416), both Saturn and Jupiter were in retrograde motion at the *k'atun* end. From 9.0.0.0.0 to 9.3.0.0.0 (C.E. 435–495), Jupiter was in retrograde motion at the *k'atun* end. Neither planet was in retrograde in the *k'atun*-endings 9.4.0.0.0 to 9.12.0.0.0 (C.E. 514–672), a period that overlaps with the hiatus, a temporary halt in the erection of Maya monuments (Sharer 1994:210). At Tikal, where the hiatus lasted the longest, monuments were not erected until 9.13.0.0.0 (C.E. 692), when Saturn reached its first stationary point at the *k'atun* end. Saturn's retrograde also marked the subsequent *k'atun* 9.14.0.0.0 and 9.15.0.0.0.

Analyzing texts in Temple XIX at Palenque, David Stuart (2000) notes that God K is mentioned in relation to 9.14.2.9.0 9 Ajaw 18 Sek (May 17, 714), a date one-half *hotun* after *k'atun*-ending 9.14.0.0.0. The May date marks the midpoint of Jupiter's retrograde motion (March 14 to July 14), clearly indicating an interest in Jupiter positions in relation to subdivisions of the *k'atun*. By 9.16.0.0.0 in C.E. 751, Jupiter joined Saturn in retrograde motion at the *k'atun* end, a pattern that extended through August 11, 869 (10.2.0.0.0). For almost 120 years, Saturn and Jupiter continued their dance of retrograde motion at the *k'atun* end. This epoch coincides with a heightened interest in *k'atun* ceremonies at sites such as Tikal, which recorded its last inscription on the *k'atun*-ending 10.2.0.0.0 (Harrison 1999:166–167, 192).

For the next thirteen *k'atuns,* from C.E. 889 to 1125, neither Saturn nor Jupiter was in retrograde, but both planets were always close together at *k'atun* end, their distance apart averaging about seven degrees. By August 2, C.E. 1145 (10.16.0.0.0), Jupiter once again approached its first stationary point (August 7, 1145) at the *k'atun* end, and it was in retrograde motion at the next *k'atun*-ending. Both planets were in retrograde motion at the *k'atun*-endings from C.E. 1165 to C.E. 1263 (11.1.0.0.0), dates that overlap with the Venus tables (Milbrath 1999:172–173). From C.E. 1283 to 1323, only Saturn was in retrograde motion at the *k'atun* end.

For the rest of the Postclassic, the two planets were not in retrograde motion at the *k'atun* end.

God K is often depicted on monuments commemorating the *k'atun* end, but he is also seen on a number of monuments bearing other types of dates, many of which can be linked with the retrograde periods of Jupiter and Saturn, especially at Yaxchilan, Palenque, and Tikal. God K might have more than one planetary aspect because when a Jupiter event is not apparent, Saturn seems to act as a substitute. God K is also part of the 819-day count that seems to relate to Jupiter and Saturn events, pointing to a likely association with these two planets. Classic period representations of God K connect him with astronomy, lineage, rulership, and lightning. His imagery often has celestial associations, including sky bands, sky glyphs, and stars. As a god of thunder and lightning, God K shares the role of Jupiter in ancient Rome (Zeus in ancient Greece). Perhaps this notion has an explanation in folklore linking Jupiter to storms. God K is the deity most often seen with Maya rulers, making him a god of the royal lineage. Indeed, rulers often bore God K's name as an honorific title. Jupiter was known as the king of the planets in classical antiquity, and apparently the Maya visualized Jupiter as the king's planet. It seems noteworthy that Sahagún links the classical Jupiter with Tezcatlipoca, the Aztec god of kings who is God K's counterpart (Coe 1982:47; Milbrath 1999:230; Nicholson 1971:412). God K's role as the god of Maya kings also presents an overlap with ancient European traditions identifying Jupiter as the planet of kings. There is a natural basis for the association with kings. Jupiter is rarely absent from the sky (mean disappearance interval thirty-two days), unlike Venus, which often visits the underworld and is never seen overhead. Among the planets, Jupiter is second only to Venus in brilliance. Steady, strong, and ever present, Jupiter makes a perfect celestial ruler, the counterpart to the good ruler on earth.

9

Ritual Circuits as Key Elements in Maya Civic Center Designs

Kathryn Reese-Taylor

In his study *Chamulas in the World of the Sun,* Gossen (1974) recognized the inherent relationship between public performances and spatial arrangement of civic centers. Specifically, he identified the importance of ritual cycles within the landscape of the Chamula township by noting that large sections of town were associated with particular times during the course of a day, various ages during the human life span, and specific times during the year (Figure 9.1). Furthermore, he observed that the attendant ceremonies conducted in these spaces constituted a ritual circuit within the precincts of Chamula.

Although Gossen's study is noteworthy because it explicitly links modern practices with the built environment, it is not an isolated undertaking. Many other scholars have also recognized and described ritual circuits among the contemporary, ethnohistoric, and Prehispanic Maya.[1] Indeed, given the frequency with which Mayanists comment on the pilgrimage routes and ritual paths of both the elite and non-elite, it seems clear that ceremonial processions have been crucial religious practices for the Maya since at least the Late Preclassic period (300 B.C.E.–C.E. 250). Nevertheless, although many studies have discussed the presence of ritual paths in the Prehispanic landscape of the Maya in a general fashion (Coe 1965a; Freidel and Sabloff 1984; Freidel et al. 1993; Levanthal 1999; Walker 1990), few have actually tied individual ceremonial paths in the geography of specific settlements to explicit ritual events (Ashmore 1991; Looper 2001; Maca 1999; Newsome 1999; Reese 1996; Reese-Taylor 1999). Moreover, none have attempted to illustrate multiple circuits in a particular geography, even though ethnohistoric and ethnographic documents confirm that the Maya conducted more than one type of ritual within their ceremonial precincts.

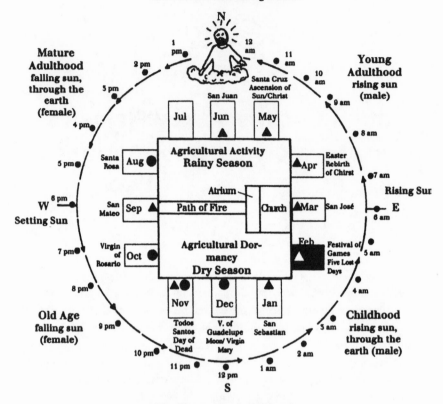

Figure 9.1. Chamulan model of the cosmos (Freidel, Schele, and Parker 1993; drawing by Linda Schele, © David Schele).

This chapter focuses on multiple ritual circuits within individual landscapes. In essence, I propose that there are distinct types of ritual circuits and that the incorporation of one or more of these ritual circuits is requisite to the design of a proper Maya civic center. The analysis centers on two primary questions: (1) what is the nature of specific ritual circuits? and (2) how did the Maya incorporate these ritual circuits into the design of their civic/ceremonial spaces? In order to answer these questions, I have used a direct historical approach. First, by examining the ethnohistoric and ethnographic literature, I identified the physical features of a particular ritual's processional path. Then, by comparing those characteristics to specific features within Maya settlements, I demarcated particular routes of procession and linked them to express ceremonies. Because Cerros and Tikal have comparable architectural forms and plans and both were the subjects of long-term research programs, I have centered my discussion of multiple paths on these two important cities.

What Constitutes a Ritual Circuit?

Ritual circuits feature movement from one location to another during the course of a political or religious ceremony. The movement is punctuated by stops to perform ritual acts at stations, specific locales along the circuit. The ritual acts at the stations may take place over a period of minutes, hours, days, weeks, months, or years, and the subsequent movement between stations may be of short or long duration. Movement from one locale to another is usually by means of a formal procession of actors.

Ritual circuits and their attendant processions have been an integral component of Maya liturgical performance since at least 300 B.C.E. The ritual circuits themselves, however, are rarely fully described in the ethnographic, ethnohistoric, or Prehispanic literature. Instead, the accounts focus on the actions performed at the specific stations within the overall circuit. Nevertheless, the detailed and varied descriptions available suggest that each procession was part of a specialized rite performed to a specific end. As a consequence, the processional routes within a ritual circuit were unique, designed to fulfill the needs of specific ceremonies. On the basis of the ethnohistoric and ethnographic descriptions of processions, I have defined three general categories of ritual circuit: ritual circumambulation; periphery/center circuits; and base-to-summit-of-mountain circuits.

Ritual Circumambulation

Descriptions of ritual circumambulation are provided by Classic period hieroglyphic texts as well as by modern ethnographic accounts from Chiapas and the Guatemalan highlands. Characterizing all accounts is a counter-clockwise movement from one location on the landscape to another at specific points in the ceremonial cycle.

Evon Vogt (1969) proposed that the primary function of contemporary circumambulation rituals within Zinacanteco society was to maintain boundaries. He suggested that when members of a community circumambulate a territory or a feature they are "saying symbolically 'these are our lands'" (Vogt 1969:391). This functional interpretation coincides well with Classic period texts, which state that space is defined by ritual circumambulation (Freidel et al. 1993).

In Gossen's study of the Tzotzil Maya, the ritual circuit of Chamula follows the path of the sun on its daily passage across the sky and into the underworld. The performances construct a landscape that mirrors the cosmos because the ritual acts of the Chamulans mirror the actions of the supernaturals (Gossen 1974:57). The cultural landscape of the Chamula municipio is divided into four quadrants that correspond to various cycles of time: a twenty-four-hour day; a solar year; a single lifetime; the cycles of birth, death, and rebirth; and, finally, four cycles of creations.

According to Vogt (1968, 1969, 1988), circumambulatory processions are also performed in Zinacantan on the days of the patron saints San Lorenzo (August 10) and San Sebastian (January 20). These processions involve all the civic and religious officials of the community (Vogt 1988). Ritual circumambulation is performed during *K'in Krus,* May 3, as well.[2] All the shamans living in a lineage or water hole group (groups of lineages that share a water supply, usually a spring in a limestone sink) pay homage to the ancestors who first found the land and the water holes used by the group and to the Earth Lord, who lives inside the earth and owns all the land and water holes. Vogt (1994:178) states, "During the ceremonial circuit, ritual is performed at the water hole, at the houses of the mayordomos, and at the Kalvaryo where the ancestors are waiting for their gifts." The ceremony itself consists of processions to various cross-shrines located in caves, in households, and on hilltops where participants offer prayers, candles, and copal incense to their ancestors and the Earth Lord. Indeed, the construction of cross-shrines at various stations of the ritual circuit seems to weave the locale and its inhabitants (human or spirit) into the cultural fabric of Zinacantan (Vogt 1994:182).

In the highlands of Guatemala, circumambulation to local shrines is an integral part of initiation ceremonies for daykeepers (Tedlock 1982). On the day after his or her initial presentation to the ancestors, the teacher takes the novice to the Nima Sab'al, the "nine-place" shrine where the initiate is presented to the altar. During the following 260-day cycle, the newly initiated daykeeper is further presented to the "six-place" shrine *(wakib'al).* This shrine is located at Paclom, a hill in the center of town that is considered the "heart" *(c'ux)* or center of the Momostenango world. Paclom is also spiritually connected to four inner hills placed in the four cardinal directions and surrounding the village within a radius of three kilometers. The daykeeper is presented at each of these hills in addition to Paclom (Tedlock 1982:71). Ritual obligation to make offerings at each shrine location is a continuing responsibility for all initiated daykeepers.

In addition, initiated priest-shamans among the highland Maya have duties that include making offerings at lineage shrines during each 260-day cycle (Tedlock 1982:76–77). These shrines are located on the hilltops surrounding various villages, expanding the ritual obligations of the priest-shaman to include both directional and kinship markers on the landscape. The ritual offerings made at each of the shrines along the ritual circuit symbolically establish the sacred landscape of the community as a whole and define the ceremonial territory of the individual kin groups.

These ethnographic examples of ritual circumambulation mirror textual accounts from the inscriptions of Palenque of similar rituals. In the hieroglyphic texts from the Tablet of the Cross, the laying out of directions is explicitly recorded. In this passage, First Father, as the Maize God, dedicated or laid out the Six Sky, Eight House Partitions place by "circumambulating" space. Then, according to the Tablet of the Cross, after space was organized, he turned or spun the Raised-Up Heart place, a metaphorical reference to initiating the passing of time (Freidel et al. 1993).[3] I have argued elsewhere (Reese 1996), as have Matthew Looper (1995c) and, most recently, David Freidel and Barbara MacLeod (2000), that this textual account records a mythic circumambulation ritual.

During the Late Formative period two architectural complexes embody the mythic version of the Eight House Partitions place where, according to the texts from the Temple of the Cross, the directions of the world were laid out. They are Structure 6 at Cerros and Structure H-X from Uaxactun (Figures 9.2 and 9.3).

Although Structure H-X from Uaxactun is oriented east-west, and Structure 6 from Cerros is oriented north-south, each complex consists of eight structures, with the four largest structures placed in the cardinal directions and the remaining four smaller structures placed in the intercardinal directions. These unique and highly formalized complexes mirror precisely the Eight House Partitions place as described in the Palenque texts. According to the texts, the Raised-Up Sky Place, Eight House Partitions is the location where the three realms of the world were separated and the directions laid out.

The masks that adorn the facades of Structure H-X, Sub-3 express the creation theme at the time of separation. On the upper tier, the serpent emerges from the mouth of a mountain or *witz* mask, and the *tzuk* head, which signifies partition, is held in its mouth (Freidel et al. 1993; Grube and Schele 1991). The snake emerging from the *witz* mask marks this structure as a Kan Witz or "Snake Mountain," one of two primordial mountains in Maya cosmology (Schele and Mathews 1998:43), and the *tzuk* glyph refers to the primordial acts of creation in which the three levels of the cosmos were divided and the cardinal and intercardinal directions were laid out (Freidel et al. 1993:140).

The basal tier of Structure H-X, Sub-3 consists of another *witz* mask with a cleft forehead and foliation growing from either side of its head. Schele and Kappelman (2001) have identified this image as Sustenance Mountain, the counterpart of Snake Mountain. In the *Popol Vuh,* Sustenance Mountain was the location where the gods obtained the maize used for fashioning the first humans.

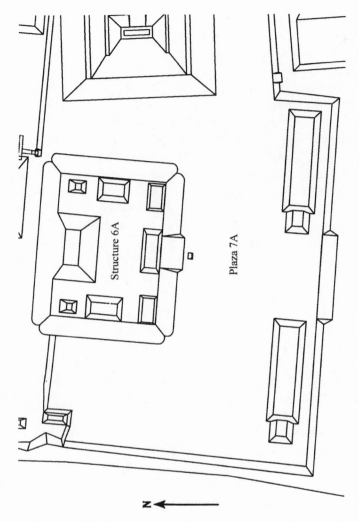

Figure 9.2. Plan view of the Structure 6 complex at Cerros, Belize (drawing by the author).

Therefore, the imagery depicted on the Structure H-X, Sub 3 facades defines two primordial locations, directly associating this architectural complex with events of creation (Schele and Kappelman 2001).[4]

The mask remnants on Structure 6B from Cerros also picture a snake adjacent to the basal mask on the lower tier (Figure 9.4). Like its counterpart, Structure H-X, Sub-3 at Uaxactun, the snakes on this structure identify it as Snake Mountain, a primordial location. In addition, the twisted cords of the upper panel also associate the structure with creation. In recent articles, Kappelman

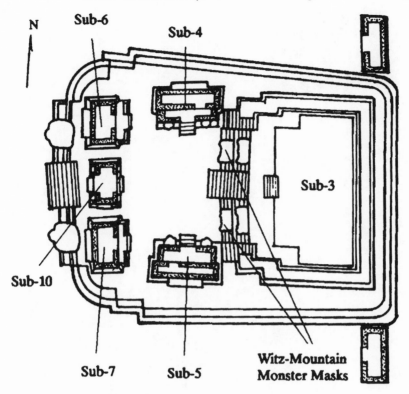

Figure 9.3. Plan view of Group H-X from Uaxactun, Guatemala (Schele and Freidel 1990; drawing by Linda Schele, © David Schele).

and Looper (Kappelman 1997; Looper 1995c; Looper and Kappelman 2000) suggest that twisted cords are symbolic of the *sak nik* (white flower) cords, which appear at the instant that First Father separates the three levels of the cosmos and lays out the directions, providing a means of communicating between the newly formed realms of the cosmos.[5] Therefore, both the snake head and twisted cord present on the Structure 6B panel establish this architectural complex as a setting for acts related to creation. Similar to the people of Chamula, the Prehispanic Maya re-created a cosmic geography wherein rulers could reenact the actions of the gods.

The arrangement of the platforms around the periphery of Structure H-X, as well as Structure 6A, lent itself well to processions of circumambulation. In a proposed re-creation, the ruler would have entered the perishable superstructure atop the platform at the apex of the arrangement. There he symbolically entered other realms, via bloodletting, and communicated with the gods and ancestors, gaining powers for the actions to follow. His exit from the building and appear-

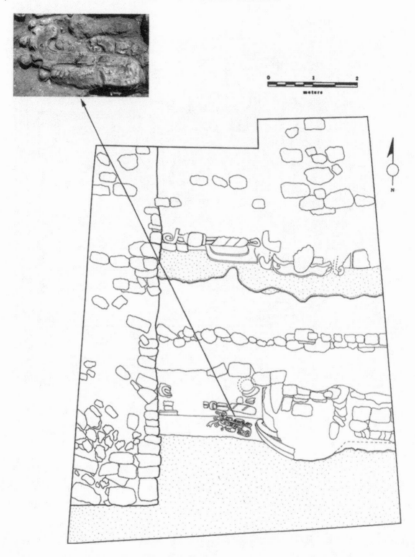

Figure 9.4. Plan view of Structure 6B facades (adapted from Freidel 1986b).

ance before the gathered audience signaled his rebirth as First Father, thereby displaying his supernatural ability to perform acts of creation.

Following his communication with the supernaturals, the ruler, as the embodiment of First Father, raised the sky from the sea and laid out the directions of the cosmos. This feat was accomplished by a specific action, ritual circumambulation of the platforms located at the cardinal and intercardinal directions.

The North Acropolis at Tikal, a Late Classic version of an Eight House place,

N

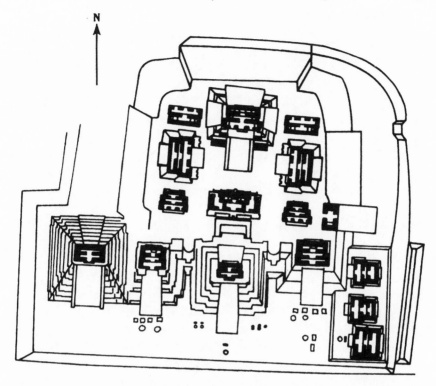

Figure 9.5. Plan view of North Acropolis, Tikal, Guatemala (Schele and Freidel 1990; drawing by Linda Schele, © David Schele).

is identical in design and orientation to the Structure 6 complex at Cerros (Figure 9.5). The Eight House layout of the North Acropolis is dated by C14 to the early part of the seventh century and is hypothesized to be part of a large renovation of the North Acropolis that coincided with the death of Animal Skull, Tikal's twenty-second ruler. Along with the construction of a number of new buildings, activity in the North Acropolis also included the destruction, defacement, and relocation of many stelae during this time period.

Jones (1991) notes that the destruction and rebuilding activity is best interpreted as two sequential events: one of destruction in which Tikal appears to have been defeated by Caracol and the second that entailed the restoration of the Tikal lineage to power. If this is so, then the ruler who embarked upon the great renovation of the North Acropolis harkened back to an earlier period for his template, one wherein he aligned his act of re-creating the heart of Tikal with First Father's act of creating the world. This is an exceptional reference to Late Formative architectural symbolism that occurs at a historically significant transition point for Tikal.

In these circumambulations around the periphery of a structure, the ruler, as First Father, was marking his domain, in this case the land lying within the cardinal and intercardinal directions. In a symbolic act parallel to that of the contemporary Zinacantecos, the ruler proclaimed to his audience that "these are our lands."[6]

Banner Processions from Periphery to Center

The second type of ritual circuit involves processions from the periphery to the center, often featuring actors who carry staffs, banners, or other ceremonial objects. This tradition of parading from surrounding areas to a central location is still practiced in the Maya lowlands (Coe 1965a; Vogt 1969, 1988, 1994). In his study of ancient community structure among the Maya, Michael Coe (1965a) suggested that ritual procession from periphery to center functioned as a mechanism to strengthen integration and social solidarity within towns or villages comprised of dispersed settlements.

According to Evon Vogt (1969, 1988, 1994), important Zinacanteco leaders, carrying ritual staffs, regularly move in processions from outlying areas to the civic center. Elaborate processions occur on the days of the patron and involve all the civic and religious officials of the community. Each individual wears the full costume of his rank and carries the appropriate scepter. The participants are arranged in rank order during the procession and when seated at the bench in front of the town hall (Vogt 1969, 1988, 1994).

Vogt (1988) also recorded Year Renewal ceremonies, which are conducted three times a year. During these ceremonies, all the male shamans from the surrounding hamlets assemble in the ceremonial center. The participants in the Year Renewal ceremonies are also dressed in costumes symbolic of their rank and carry bamboo scepters. Again, individuals are arranged in rank order for the processions according to how many years they have been shamans (Vogt 1988).

Ethnohistoric accounts also record New Year or Year Renewal ceremonies. According to the Maya calendar, the New Year falls on a different day each year during a four-year cycle. In 1539, the year-bearer days in Yucatan were K'an, Muluk, Ix, and Kawak, and it was the ceremonies surrounding this set of Year Bearer days that Landa recorded (Bricker 1981). Each of these ceremonies involved processions from the center to the periphery of a community, and individuals in the processions carried ritual objects, including standards.

For example, in the days preceding a K'an year, a hollow image of Kan u Uayeyab was made of clay and placed on a pile of stones at the south entrance of a town. After cleansing the image of Kan u Uayeyab, all the lords, priests, and other men placed the image on a standard and carried it to the house of the sponsor. At the end of the Wayeb or five "nameless days" period, the participants carried the image of Kan u Uayeyab to the eastern entrance, where it stood for a year (Tozzer 1941:139–143). Similar ceremonies were performed on the days preceding the Muluk, Ix, and Kawak New Years. Images were carried from one of the four cardinal directions located in the periphery of the kingdom to the center and then back out to guard a new point. In this way, all of the cardinal directions were traversed in a counter-clockwise fashion, and the connection between the four corners of the kingdom and the center was renewed.

Coe (1965a) uses the ethnohistoric account of Year Renewal ceremonies by Landa and accounts from the *Book of Chilam Balam of Chumayel* (Roys 1933) as a model for the community organization of ancient Maya settlements. He suggests that various sectors in a community are defined based on kinship and that the concomitant procession from each sector to the center, the locus of centralized authority, symbolizes rotating political authority among the various lineages, akin to the cargo system found among contemporary Maya.[7] Chase (1985:118–124) also draws on Landa's accounts of Wayeb ceremonies to explain the distribution of censers and caches within the ceremonial landscape of Santa Rita Corozal.

Ritual processions with banners are depicted in several formats during the Classic period. Banners are long, slender staffs topped with a feather-rimmed disk or ball carried during large ritual processions, such as those depicted in Structure 1 at Bonampak.[8] The murals cover the interior walls of the three rooms within this structure, and in each room the artists have illustrated an important episode in an heir-designation ceremony (Miller 1986; Schele and Miller 1986). In the scene located on the upper register of Room 1, a small child is presented to the court on 9.18.0.3.4 (December 14, 790). Lord Chan Muwan and several of his wives oversee the ceremony, which was designed to ensure the peaceful transition of power from one ruler to the next. The second scene in Room 1 takes place 336 days later and portrays Chan Muwan and the principal officials of Bonampak dressing for a public performance. This performance is pictured on the lowest register and took place on 9.18.1.2.0 (November 15, 791), an auspicious day when Venus first rose as Evening Star. Three central figures, Chan Muwan and two other lords, are clad in full regalia, complete with feathered backracks. They dance at the center of a great procession. Musicians and other performers in unusual costume flank the dancers on the right. A procession of lesser nobles, two carrying large feathered banners, form on the left of Chan Muwan and his fellow performers (Figures 9.6a and 9.6b; Miller 1986; Schele and Miller 1986).

A Late Classic Maya vessel also depicts warriors processing with banners and implements of war (Figure 9.7). Several of the individuals hold decorated spears, identified by the diagnostic laurel leaf-shaped spear point, and others hold banners affixed with feathers and circular disks.

Processions are also an important component of the sculptural program at the

a

b

Figure 9.6. *(a)* Procession scene from lower register of Room 1, west side, Bonampak, Guatemala; *(b)* Procession scene from lower register of Room 1, east side, Bonampak, Guatemala (Freidel, Schele, and Parker 1993; drawings by Linda Schele, © David Schele).

Late/Terminal Classic site of Chichen Itza. In the Temple of the Warriors, a long colonnaded portico surrounds the primary building on both the north and east sides. Carved on the separate columns are individual figures dressed in the regalia of warriors, priests, and court officials. The figures are arranged according to rank, and Wren and Foster (1995) have suggested that they symbolize the processions that took place on the great plaza located in front of the temple. In addition, on the registers of the Lower and Upper Temple of the Jaguars, associated with the Great Ballcourt, low relief carvings also depict individuals of various rank participating in processions.

At Cerros, the evidence for a banner ritual procession that links center to periphery is circumstantial. During excavations at the base of Structure 6, archaeologists uncovered a large, squarish monolith with rounded corners that measures approximately 1.4 × 1.4 meters. It sits on a low-lying stone platform constructed of loaf-shaped stones and situated approximately two meters south of the Structure 6A staircase basal tread (Figure 9.8).

A circular hole that appears to have been cut is inset 40 centimeters from the

Figure 9.7. Late Classic vessel depicting warriors processing with banners (K5763, photograph © Justin Kerr).

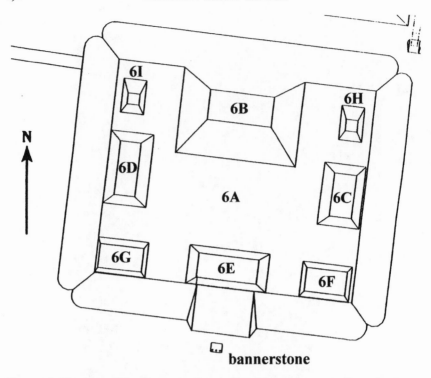

Figure 9.8. Plan view of the Structure 6A complex with bannerstone at base of stair-case, Cerros, Belize (drawing by the author).

west edge and 60 centimeters from the south edge of the monolith. The hole is approximately 15 centimeters in diameter and between 10 and 15 centimeters deep. Twenty centimeters to the east of the hole and inset 60 centimeters from the south edge is another carved hole of the same approximate dimensions. The spacing of the two holes implies that a third hole should have been present, establishing a linear, triadic pattern. No third hole was detected on the surface, but the area where the third hole should have been is heavily damaged.[9]

Previously, I proposed (Reese 1996) that the holes in the Cerros monolith functioned as banner holders. Although bannerstones are unusual, remarkably similar examples have been recovered from the sites of Nakbe (Hansen 1993), Blue Creek (Guderjan 1998:107; Weiss 1995, 1996), Copan (Fash et al. 1992), and Dos Pilas (Demarest et al. 1995). The presence of a bannerstone at the base of Structure 6A implies that this locale may have been the terminus for a procession, such as one of those described in the previous examples (Figure 9.8).

Although the evidence from Cerros is circumstantial, the evidence for periphery/center processions with banners at the site of Tikal is more compelling. Although bannerstones are lacking at the base of the North Acropolis, an unusual

0   **50 M**

Figure 9.9. Stela 9, Tikal, Guatemala (adapted by the author from Jones and Satterthwaite 1982:Figure 13).

group of stelae were erected in the Great Plaza from 9.2.0.0.0 to 9.4.0.0.0 or C.E. 465 to 514 (Figure 9.9; Jones and Satterthwaite 1982:23). These stelae all depict the ruler in profile with a vertically held staff very similar to the banners described above. The placement of these "staff stelae" at the base of the acropolis suggests that staffs in some way were part of the ceremonies that occurred there (Christie 1999).

   Even more convincing, however, is the actual layout of epicentral Tikal (Figure 9.10). Puleston (1983) identified an area within Tikal that extends out from the center approximately 0.5 kilometer to the east, south, and west and 1 kilometer to the north. This area consists of a dense concentration of public buildings,

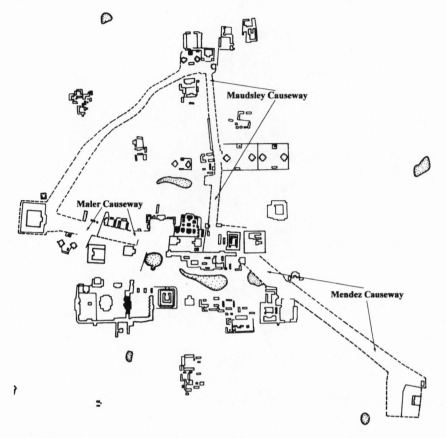

Figure 9.10. Map of epicentral and central Tikal (redrawn by the author from Schele and Freidel 1990).

sparsely interspersed with residences. It is united by a series of *sakbeob* (white paths) that extend out from the North Acropolis and the Great Plaza to the north, west, and southeast. With the exception of the Mendez *sakbe,* all other *sakbeob* terminate within the epicenter. The Mendez Causeway terminates outside of the epicenter at an arrangement of public buildings atop a platform.

Although it is clear that *sakbeob* provided dry pedestrian paths over lowlying areas and were integrated into water management systems (Reese 1996; Scarborough 1980, 1983a, 1983b, 1985a), their primary function appears to have been ceremonial.[10] Ethnohistoric evidence suggests that they were important venues of ceremonial action and were invariably associated with religious structures (Freidel and Sabloff 1984:82–83). Specifically, Landa (in Tozzer 1941:174) described ceremonial processions between various settlements along *sakbeob,* Molina Solis described pilgrims visiting temples and shrines along a route (in

Villa Rojas 1934:207–208), and Lizana also noted four great causeways oriented to the cardinal directions used primarily for pilgrimages to the oracle at Izamal (in Villa Rojas 1934:198). Finally, on Cozumel Island, the *sakbeob* run from the centers of settlement out to peripheral shrines and shrine groups (Freidel and Sabloff 1984:84).

At Tikal, the arrangement of the causeways, radiating out from the center, provides unambiguous evidence for periphery/center processions. The causeways inherently connect the heart of Tikal to the outer limits of the ceremonial precinct, and, just as on Cozumel Island, all of the *sakbeob* at Tikal lead to religious structures: the Mendez Causeway links the North Acropolis and the Great Plaza with the Temple of the Inscriptions group in the southeastern sector of the site; the Maudsley Causeway links the Great Plaza with Group H, the ceremonial structures located at the northern edge of the ceremonial precinct; and the Maler Causeway links the Great Plaza with Temple IV, the western edge of the civic/ceremonial center (Figure 9.10). Although causeways may have served a more prosaic function, such as components in water management systems or as major footpaths, they performed an equally important ritual function as routes for processions, likely in an episodic cycle renewing center/periphery relationships, much like the New Year ceremonies recorded by Landa.

Processions from Base to Summit of Mountain

The third type of ritual circuit proceeds from the base to the summit of a mountain and is seen in various contemporary ceremonies throughout Mesoamerica. This type of procession unites the three realms of the cosmos. As actors ascend from one level to another, they symbolically progress from the underworld through the human world and into the heavens.

During the Festival of Carnival in Chamula, the final destination of the ceremony is the summit of the hill, Kalvaryo. As Victoria Bricker (1981:130) noted in her book *Indian Christ, Indian King,* the main activity is the pilgrimage that the Pasiones (religious sponsors of Carnival) and their assistants, Los Flores, make to cross-shrines in the town centers. The culminating act of the ceremony, however, is the parade up the hill to Kalvaryo by the Pasiones and Los Flores, all of whom carry large banners decorated with effigies of the Sun-Christ and flags.

Other instances of procession from base to mountain summit have been recorded among contemporary societies in Oaxaca. Heather Orr (1997, 2001) has built a convincing argument for base-to-summit processions as a fundamental act performed at the site of Dainzu. On the basis of a comparison with modern religious practices in Oaxaca involving processions, she links such base-to-summit-of-mountain processions with supplications for rain.

The Maya too incorporate base-to-mountain-summit circuits in their site

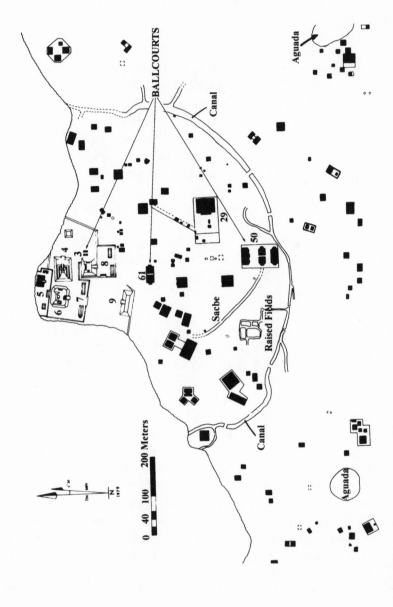

Figure 9.11. Map of Cerros civic center (adapted from Scarborough 1991).

plans. A recent study by Richard Levanthal (1999) points to processions on the staircases of structures, a proposal that is supportive of base-to-summit ritual circuits. Specifically, Levanthal proposes that the processions of Maya rulers up the staircases of large temple structures at Xunantunich symbolized the transformation of the king from a human ruler into a god. The transformation was done before an audience and was based on the precept that the ruler was both simultaneously human and divine.

Often ritual circuits correlate with other aspects of site planning, such as directionality, and this is the case for the base-to-summit-of-mountain circuit at Cerros. Several scholars (Ashmore 1989, 1991; Houk 1996; Koontz 1994; Masson and Orr 1998; Reilly 1994a; Sugiyama 1993) have suggested that Mesoamerican sites have a predominant north-south alignment for organization of sacred landscape. Likewise, Cerros is noted for its north-south axis delineated by ballcourts (Reese 1996; Scarborough 1991:34), and the settlement also displays a descending topographic slope from north to south (Figure 9.11). A group of raised plazas in the north of the civic center directs the water runoff to the south of the site where it is captured in a reservoir system formed by several *sakbeob* (Scarborough 1980, 1983a, 1983b, 1985a, 1985b, 1991). This sophisticated water catchment system not only provided water during the dry season for the raised fields located in the southern periphery of the settlement but also caused a large swampy area to form in the southern portion of the main civic center, especially during the rainy season. This dichotomy between the north, an elevated area with a concentration of human-constructed mountains, and the south, a depressed area, is the expression in the physical landscape of two important mythic locations: Xibalba in the south, which lies under the waters of the underworld, and the heavens in the north, where spirits of the deceased ascend to live in perpetuity.

The three ballcourts oriented along this north-south axis provide a path through which this landscape may be traversed (Figure 9.11). Elsewhere I have argued (Reese 1996) that ballcourts at Cerros served as transitional paths between the three different realms of the cosmos.[11] In addition, I propose that the ballcourts provided paths for ritual processions, linking a watery mountain base with a summit located on the raised plazas.

The base-to-summit-of-mountain ritual circuit is also seen at Tikal. The complex of buildings at the heart of Tikal includes the North Acropolis and the Great Plaza. The structures are built on a natural rise. To the south of the Great Plaza is the Palace Complex, and just south of this elite residential compound is the Palace Reservoir, constructed in a low-lying area (Figure 9.12). Here again, we see the topographic slope from elevated area of dense temple structures in the north to low-lying water catchment zone in the south.

Because many of Tikal's rulers were entombed in this northern complex, it seems clear that the symbolic mountains of the North Acropolis were designed

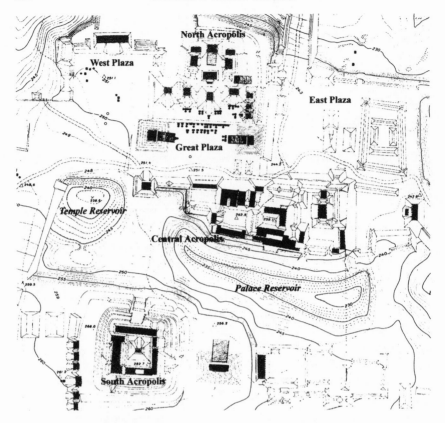

Figure 9.12. Map of North Acropolis, Great Plaza, Palace Reservoir, and South Acropolis, Tikal, Guatemala (adapted from Coe 1967).

to be the earthly embodiment of the "heavens of the north" (Ashmore 1991). Equally transparent is the identification of the Temple and Palace Reservoirs as the watery underworld of Xilbalba. Furthermore, the processions would have been facilitated by the wide path constructed between the two reservoirs, running from the South Acropolis to the Great Plaza (Figure 9.12). This path is much wider than is necessary for pedestrian traffic flow or water control, as attested to by the width of the path lying on the eastern margin of the Palace Reservoir. The eastern path (or check dam) is much more narrow, yet allows for comfortable movement of two people abreast, whereas the western path is much wider with space for as many as eight people to traverse the circuit side by side.

Tikal's ritual circuit from low-lying water locale in the south to mountain summit in the north is the quintessential expression of the Mesoamerican north-south template. As we enrich this template by adding human actors moving along a ritual path that connects one area of the site with another, however, our perception of the Maya civic center shifts from rigid cosmogram to dynamic performance venue (cf. Kappelman 2001; Looper 2001; Orr 1997, 2001; Reese 1996).

Concluding Remarks

In conclusion, ritual circuits appear to have been significant factors in the design of Maya civic centers. This is expected because most Mayanists now agree that large civic/ceremonial centers provided the venues for public performances. Ritual processions along various circuits served the diverse needs of a complex society, and in the Maya area, three functions have been defined. Processions along ritual circuits serve to mark boundaries, promote social cohesion, and unite the different realms of the cosmos. Moreover, because the functions of ritual circuits vary, their paths also differ within individual landscapes, resulting in master plans for Maya centers that include multiple ceremonial pathways punctuated by various architectural stations.

Ritual circuits were only one of many design considerations used by Prehispanic architects and city planners, however. As scholars of early urban centers, we must identify the multiple functions of cities and their concomitant design considerations. Furthermore, although economic and administrative factors have long been taken into account, we are still only beginning to identify other factors that affect the final design of these great cities. For example, the demands of water management systems needed to be integrated with the needs of large and small performance spaces. In addition, all of these solutions had to conform to the dictates of the surrounding topography in an aesthetically pleasing manner. Only in identifying these multiple factors and their interrelationships, however, will we be able to understand the developmental forces that produced these great Prehispanic metropolitan spaces.

Acknowledgments

I would like to extend my thanks to David Freidel, Julia Kappelman, and two anonymous reviewers for providing insightful comments on earlier drafts of this chapter. I also am grateful to Andrea Stone for her editorial assistance and her patience in dealing with my hectic schedule and to Judith Knight for her help during the final production stages of this publication. My sincere appreciation is also extended to FAMSI, particularly Sandra Noble and Sylvia Thibado, for assistance in obtaining permission to publish several of Linda Schele's drawings and to Justin Kerr for his permission to use one of his photographs. My thanks are given as well to David Freidel who also granted permission for me to use illustrations. In addition, I would like to thank David Schele for his generosity in sharing the work of Linda Schele with scholars throughout the world. Finally, I would like to express my deepest gratitude at having known and worked with Linda Schele. She had a profound influence on my work as both a Mesoamerican scholar and an educator, and I am fortunate to be able to acknowledge her not only as a mentor but also as a friend.

Notes

1. Ritual circuits among the contemporary Maya have been studied by Bricker (1981), Freidel et al. (1993), Tedlock (1982), and Vogt (1968, 1969, 1988, 1994); ethnohistoric accounts of Maya ritual circuits have been described by Freidel et al. (1993), Landa (in Tozzer 1941:146, 174), Lizana (in Villa Rojas 1934:189), and Molina Solis (in Villa Rojas 1934:207–208); and Prehispanic ritual circuits have been investigated by Chase (1985:118–124), Coe (1965a), Cogolludo (in Tozzer 1941:109), Freidel (1976, 1981; Freidel and Sabloff 1984; Freidel and Schele 1988a, 1988b, 1989), Levanthal (1999), Looper (1995a, 2001), Maca (1999), Miller (1986), Newsome (1999), Reese-Taylor (Reese 1996; Reese-Taylor 1999), Schele and Miller (1986), Walker (1990, 1996), and Wren and Foster (1995).

2. This ceremony is conducted not only at the beginning of the rainy season but also at the end (Vogt 1988:13–14).

3. A more literal translation of the text follows. After 542 days, First Father, Hun Nal Ye, entered the sky at Lying-Down Sky, First Three Stone Place. Subsequently, on 13 Ik' and the last day of Mol, "it was made proper or circumambulated (as an alternative translation), the Raised-Up Sky Place, the Eight House Partitions, is its holy name, the house of the north."

4. Snake Mountains are also prevalent in the cosmology of culture groups from highland Mesoamerica. In the creation myth of the Mexica, Coatepec or "Snake Mountain" is a mountain surrounded by water from which a snake emerges bearing the implements for paradigmatic warfare (Koontz 1994; Reese 1996; Schele and Kappelman 2001; Schele and Mathews 1998:43).

5. Looper and Kappelman (2000) also discuss the relationship between snakes and twisted cords in their recent article.

6. In a recent paper presented at the 6th Annual Maya Weekend sponsored by the University of California at Los Angeles, Elizabeth Newsome (1999) also used ethnographic and ethnohistoric data to suggest that radial pyramids were the locus of ritual circumambulations, especially during k'atun-ending ceremonies. The ritual circumambulation of these structures would serve the same function as the circumambulation of Eight House structures.

7. Jeffrey Stomper (2001) has recently proposed that the various sectors within the Copan polity were organized according to lineage.

8. In earlier literature, banners also have been referred to as ballcourt markers (Laporte 1988).

9. See Koontz (1994) and chapter 7, this volume, for a complete discussion of bannerstones.

10. In addition to serving as ceremonial paths, Kurjack and Garza (1981:308) have noted that the *sakbeob* at Dzibilchaltun function to link discrete building complexes to each other as well as to the site core. The clustering of vaulted architecture along the causeways supports this interpretation. Also, Stomper (2001) has suggested that on an even larger scale, the causeway systems of other sites (such as the Coba-Yaxuna, Uci-Cansahcab, and the Izamal-Ake) served to connect distant satellite communities and distinct sites together. He has observed that although clearly these causeways were used for transport, their underlying purpose was to unite symbolically two or more communities.

11. Others have also noted the placement of Maya ballcourts at points of transition between different areas within settlements. The implication of this arrangement is that, like their cosmological counterparts, earthly ballcourts serve as portals linking locations with distinct cosmological significance (Ashmore 1989, 1991; Fox 2001; Gillespie 1991; Houk 1996; McDougal 1997; Tedlock 1985).

10

The Toponyms of El Cayo, Piedras Negras, and La Mar

Marc Zender

Some forty years ago, three major epigraphic revolutions drastically altered the prevailing understanding of the ancient Maya landscape. Proskouriakoff's (1960) demonstration that the content of the Maya script was largely historical (rather than solely religious or chronological) in nature, Knorosov's (1953, 1958, 1965) "phonetic" approach, and Berlin's (1958) discovery of "emblem glyphs" would eventually allow the reconstruction of ancient political organization (Houston 1987, 1992, 1993a; Mathews 1988), the association of city-states with ancient dynasties (Mathews 1991; Schele and Grube 1994b, 1995), and the interaction of these dynasties with respect to larger, more powerful city-states exercising hegemonic influence (Martin and Grube 1995). It is Berlin's (1958) discovery—emblem glyphs incorporating toponyms used in lordly titles of origin and political affiliation—that led to Stuart and Houston's (1994) seminal decipherment of "place names," a category of glyphic collocations that first made available for scrutiny ancient Maya concepts of place, identity, and ethnicity. They recognized that toponyms were regularly employed in titles of the form *aj*-TOPONYM "he of such-a-place" and TOPONYM-*ajaw* "lord of such-a-place" to signal origin, rank, or both (Stuart and Houston 1994). They also pointed out that many texts employ these place names to record explicitly the location of ancient actions, whether fields of battle, places of burial, or the locales of kingly ceremony (Stuart and Houston 1994). With this breakthrough, epigraphers could finally read *where* (rather than merely *when* and at the behest of *whom*) events referred to in the texts had taken place and begin to build approximations of the spatial arena of ancient sociopolitical interaction.[1]

Previously Identified Upper Usumacinta Toponyms

With the recognition of toponyms in the inscriptions, a number of recent studies have located and discussed locales of importance to the region here under consideration. Stuart and Houston (1994:31–33) have shown that the main component of Piedras Negras's emblem glyph, *Yokib'*, also appears, albeit very rarely, as a toponym, as on Altar 1 of that site (Stuart and Houston 1994:Figure 36a, b). Their work has also made possible the identification of a *Siyan Chan* toponym for Yaxchilan—again, an element well known from this site's emblem glyph but rarely employed as a toponym proper. There is also some suggestive evidence from both inscriptions (Anaya et al. 2002; David Stuart, personal communication 2001) and geographical modeling that another site, *Hix Witz*, or "Jaguar Hill"—known to us from inscriptions at Piedras Negras and Yaxchilan and on unprovenanced Peten ceramics—is perhaps to be equated with El Pajaral and/or Zapote Bobal, in the Peten (Figure 10.1). A little further afield, Stanley Guenter (1998) and Alexandre Safronov (personal communication 2000) have recently proposed that *Maan*—a site mentioned prominently in the inscriptions of Yaxchilan, Piedras Negras, Motul de San Jose, and Tikal—is to be identified with La Florida (Figure 10.1).[2] These recent identifications are very exciting and open up entirely new avenues for the exploration of dynastic politics, warfare, and alliances. As further toponymical expressions are tied to specific archaeological sites, the task of discovering the identities of those remaining is greatly simplified.

This said, it was until recently quite troubling that our toponym record in the Upper Usumacinta did not address in any significant manner its largest site, Piedras Negras, nor any of the smaller sites known to have been most directly under its hegemonic influence. Mathews's (personal communication 1997) recent work at El Cayo has greatly assisted in filling in this gap, with clear references to an El Cayo toponym. With the first of Piedras Negras's dependencies identified, the rest of them, and that of Piedras Negras itself, are more easily identified.

Yaxniil, the El Cayo Toponym

At least as early as 1989, Stuart and Houston (1994:43) had noted peculiar "general and specific place references" in the context of a burial event on El Cayo Panel 1. In the absence of any further, unequivocal El Cayo inscriptions, however, they were unable to confirm the identity of this toponym with El Cayo. Moreover, available photographs and drawings of the monuments were not clear enough for them to propose a reading for the collocation (cf. Stuart and Houston 1994:Figure 46). With the discovery in 1994 of El Cayo Altar 4, however, we are

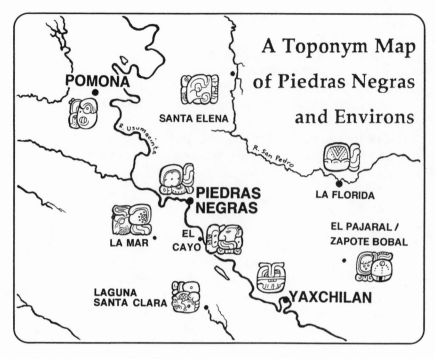

Figure 10.1. A toponym map of Piedras Negras and environs (drawing by the author).

now in a much better position to assess these texts and to assign convincingly a toponym to El Cayo itself.[3]

The top of Altar 4 (Figure 10.2a) portrays the *sajal,* or "subordinate lord," Aj Chak Wayib' K'utiim, the ruler of El Cayo, holding an incense bag and casting copal incense before an incensario laden with bundled offerings, amate paper, and pitch pine. The incensario sits atop a three-legged stone altar that may represent El Cayo Altar 4 itself. For our purposes, however, the text directly in front of the figure's face is most important. After calendrical and verbal information that tie this event to the 9.15.0.0.0 *k'atun*-ending (C.E. 731), we are given the names and titles of the ruler (Figure 10.3e). The final glyph block (B4) reads **AJ-YAX-ni-la** > *aj yaxniil,* "he of *Yaxniil.*"[4] The texts on supports 1 and 2 of the altar also mention *Yaxniil* as the place of origin of the protagonist's father—one Ochnal K'utiim Ch'ok *Aj Yaxniil* (Figure 10.3c)—and, perhaps more important, as the city of *Yaxniil* of which the central seat of power, the *yax ahkal-ha'* (Figure 10.3d) or "green many-turtles-water," is but one part.

With these identifications in hand, we are much better equipped to understand some later passages on El Cayo Panel 1. The burial event (Figure 10.3a)—which can be associated with the date 9.16.12.2.6 (C.E. 763)—reads *'i-cham-ø*

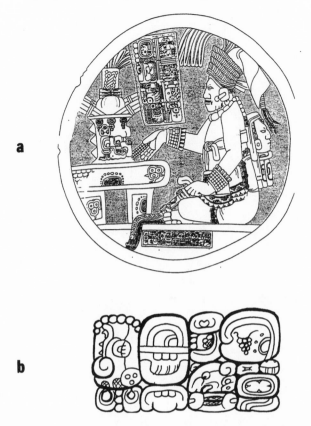

Figure 10.2. El Cayo Altar 4 and colophon. *(a)* El Cayo Altar 4, top (drawing by Peter Mathews); *(b)* El Cayo Altar 4, top, sculptor's signature: Dɪ-Eɪ (drawing by the author).

muhk-aj-ø t-u-ch'e̓n yax-niil, "it was then that he died (and) was buried in his grave at *Yaxniil.*" The name of the dead ruler, perhaps the same individual portrayed on El Cayo Altar 4, is immediately followed by the accession of his son under the auspices of Piedras Negras Ruler 4, an event that makes a great deal more sense when we understand that *Yaxniil* must surely refer to El Cayo, one of Piedras Negras's closest neighbors. The final passage of El Cayo Panel 1 (Figure 10.3b) is the long title string of one Chan Panak Wayib' Aj Chak Suutz' K'utiim, the *sajal,* he of *Yaxniil,* who acceded on 9.17.1.5.9 (C.E. 772) and was almost certainly the grandson of Aj Chak Wayib' of Altar 4 fame. This means that we can now convincingly associate the *Yaxniil* toponym with some three generations of El Cayo rulers; it is strong evidence, indeed, that *Yaxniil* can be securely placed on a toponym map of the Upper Usumacinta (Figure 10.1).

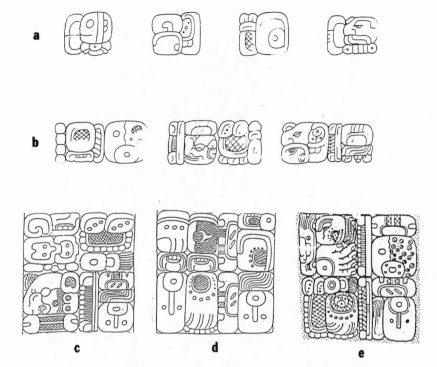

Figure 10.3. *Yaxniil* toponyms at El Cayo. *(a)* El Cayo Panel 1, D12-C14 (drawing by the author); *(b)* El Cayo Panel 1, M11-N13 (drawing by the author); *(c)* El Cayo Altar 4, Support 1, E'2-F'3 (drawing by Peter Mathews); *(d)* El Cayo Altar 4, Support 3, I'3-J'4 (drawing by Peter Mathews); *(e)* El Cayo Altar 4, Top, A3-B4 (drawing by Peter Mathews).

K'in-'a as the Piedras Negras Toponym

Epigraphers have long known that Piedras Negras lords regularly took a title read *k'in-ajaw,* or "Sun Lord" (Figure 10.4) (Coe 1992:266–267; Mathews 1993: 97–98, 110, 124; Stuart 1985:183). The title has a long and distinguished pedigree, and there are strong indications that the title dates back to at least Middle Classic times at the site. On Piedras Negras Lintel 2, for instance, Ruler C carries the *k'in-ajaw* title associated with a date in the early sixth century (Figure 10.4a). Similarly, Piedras Negras Ruler 1 is twice named as a *k'in-ajaw* (Figures 10.4b and 10.4c), as is Ruler 2 (Figures 10.4d and 10.4e), and Ruler 3[5] and Ruler 4 (Figure 10.4f) carry this title at least once each. Clearly, we can trace this title through some two hundred years of Piedras Negras's history. Unfortunately, the title's longevity has not simplified its interpretation, which has frequently been taken as either priestly in nature (Mathews 1993:97–98; Schele and Miller 1986:149; on

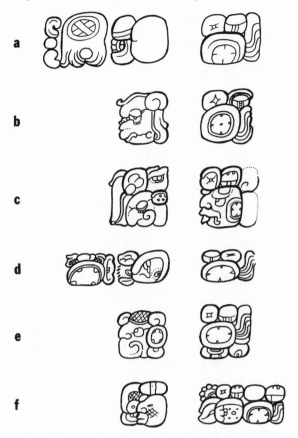

Figure 10.4. Rulers of Piedras Negras with *k'in-ajaw* titles. *(a)* "Turtle Tooth," Piedras Negras Lintel 2: R1-R2; *(b)* Yo'onal Ahk (Ruler 1), Piedras Negras Stela 25, front: C1-B2; *(c)* Yo'onal Ahk (Ruler 1), "Denver" Panel: A1-A2; *(d)* Ruler 2, from a Paqal Incised ware vessel; *(e)* Ruler 2, "Hellmuth" Panel: B3-A4; *(f)* Ruler 4, El Cayo Lintel 1: D6-F1 (drawings by the author).

analogy with the modern *ah-k'in,* cf. Barrera-Vásquez 1980:401) or as a reference to the Maya Sun God (himself named either *k'in-* or *k'inich-ajaw*).

I would suggest, however, that on analogy with other toponym titles in the Maya lowlands—such as *yokib'-ajaw* for "lord of *yokib'* (the place)"—the term *k'in-ajaw* might best be translated as "lord of *K'in* (the place)." Evidence for this comes in a number of forms, though perhaps most clearly on El Cayo Altar 4. As already discussed, this altar is largely concerned with the El Cayo ruler Aj Chak Wayib' K'utiim, his parentage, and his whereabouts and actions on the occasion of a prestigious *k'atun*-ending (Figure 10.2a). A substantial colophon appears below the main scene (Figure 10.2b), however, which reads in part *y-ux-*

ul-ø siya(j)-chan-ahk ch'ok-k'in-ajaw, or "it is the carving of Sky-Born-Turtle, the young lord of *K'in* (the place)." The toponym pattern, noted above, immediately suggests that Siyaj Chan Ahk should be a young (i.e., nonruling) lord of a place called *K'in.* Because El Cayo's toponym is *Yaxniil,* however, this raises the question of whence the young sculptor hailed.

There can be little doubt that El Cayo Altar 4 betrays very strong Piedras Negras affiliations in terms of epigraphic, iconographic, and even rhetorical styles. The very rare collocation [2]**tzu-ja** > *tzuhtz-aj-ø,* "was closed" (in reference to the fifteenth *k'atun*) at A2 (Figure 10.2a) for instance, is identical to that on Piedras Negras Panel 3 (cf. Judd 1948:122), carved some fifty years later. Similarly, the naturalistic pose of the ruler—coupled with iconographic details that would not be out of place on any of the later Piedras Negras monuments—strongly suggest that more than artistic influence is at work here; rather, this sculpture was most likely executed by someone trained at Piedras Negras itself. As Montgomery (1994:*pace*) has demonstrated, this was hardly uncommon. His study of preserved scribal signatures shows that many El Cayo monuments were actually carved by master sculptors from the regional capital, Piedras Negras. These considerations suggest that Siyaj Chan Ahk was a *ch'ok-ajaw,* or "young lord" of Piedras Negras and offer compelling evidence that the *k'in-ajaw* collocation is a toponymical title referencing Piedras Negras itself. Where is the evidence that the *k'in* portion of this title can be separated from the *ajaw* portion, however? That is, where are the clear-cut "origin" and "location" variants that typify other toponymical constructions in the script?

One variant of this title—more explicitly framed in terms common to toponyms—turns up on the lintels of Laxtunich, a site located somewhere between Yaxchilan and Piedras Negras (and likely closer to Piedras Negras, if we can rely to any degree on the travel narrative of Dana Lamb and Ginger Lamb [1951]). At least two of Laxtunich's three known lintels contain the signature of a sculptor known as Mayuy Ti' Yopaat *Aj K'in-'a,* or "Mayuy Ti' Yopaat of *K'in-'a* (the place)" (Figure 10.5b). The stylistic and sculptural canons employed in these lintels—especially the better-known Kimbell Panel now located in Fort Worth, Texas (Figure 10.5a)—are very strongly evocative of Piedras Negras sculpture and forcibly remind one of Piedras Negras Panel 3 and Stela 12 in particular. The curtained palaces, naturalistic poses, tiered stairway, and throne compositions (as well as general quality of carving) all strongly suggest that this sculptor was of the Piedras Negras school (see Montgomery 1994 for an excellent analysis of this school). Laxtunich Lintel 1 (Mayer 1991:Plate 53) is just as strongly influenced and bears God N collocations that otherwise occur only at Piedras Negras and Pomona, its other subordinate site. These considerations all strongly reinforce the possibility that Mayuy Ti' Yopaat's place of origin was none other than Piedras Negras and therefore that *Kin-'a* was its toponym.

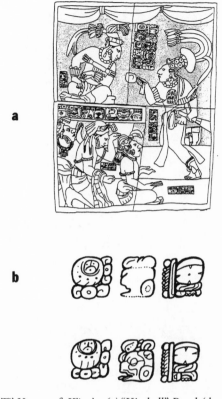

Figure 10.5. Mayuy Ti' Yopaat of *K'in-'a*. *(a)* "Kimbell" Panel (drawing by Linda Schele, © David Schele, in Schele and Miller 1986:Figure III.5); *(b)* the scribal signatures of Mayuy Ti' Yopaat (drawing by the author).

That the *k'in-ajaw* title is toponymical rather than priestly in nature is perhaps best demonstrated by its usage at Piedras Negras itself. The daughter of Piedras Negras Ruler 3 (Yo'onal Ahk II) and Lady Winik Haab' Ajaw, presumably born at Piedras Negras proper, is named on her birth as an *ixik-k'in-ajaw*, or a "noble lady of *K'in* (the place)" (Figure 10.6). That she is given this title at her birth— rather than at an official "accession" ceremony of some sort—strongly suggests that this is an ascribed status rather than an achieved one. This renders its identification with either a priestly office or a deity name more than a little problematic. More likely, she was given the title because she was born at Piedras Negras and was therefore "from" there. This finds support in the observation that whereas Ruler 3, his daughter, and his son (the eventual Ruler 4) all carry the *k'in-ajaw* title, his wife, known to be of foreign extraction, never does. Indeed, whereas references to the Lady Winik Haab' Ajaw never fail to mention her city of origin (La Florida, glyphic *Maan*) in the second component of her name

Figure 10.6. Nominal glyphs of Lady Huuntahn Ahk K'in Ahaw, Piedras Negras Stela 3: C7-D7 (drawing by the author).

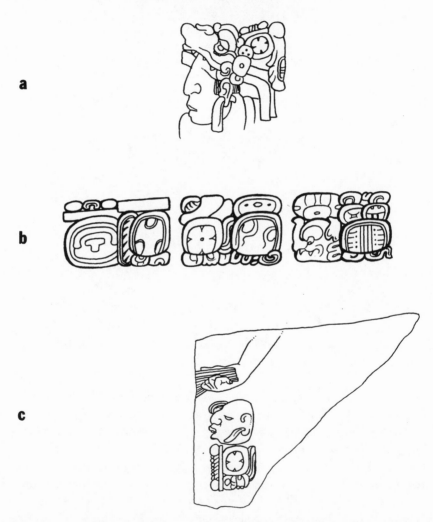

Figure 10.7. War references to Piedras Negras at Palenque. *(a)* Aj K'in Nal as a captive at Palenque, House C lower panels; *(b)* The "axing" of Piedras Negras by Chak Suutz', Tablet of the Slaves: E3-J1; *(c)* Aj K'in'a as a captive at Palenque, East Alfarda of Temple XXI: A2 (drawings by the author after Linda Schele in Schele and Mathews 1993:179).

phrase, this component is replaced in the name phrase of her daughter by the *k'in-ajaw* title, which may be among the strongest pieces of evidence that the title is toponym related. Taken together, the *k'in-'a* ~ *k'in-ajaw* patterns of occurrence seem a strong indication that *k'in-'a* was the actual Piedras Negras toponym and that the *'a*, "water" component was either hidden, elided, or bumped by the *ajaw* component when combined into *k'in-'(a)-ajaw* titles.

The importance of this newly identified toponym to an understanding of local or regional political history cannot be overestimated. One of the captives portrayed on the lower panels of House C at Palenque wears the hieroglyphic badge *aj-k'in-nal,* or "he of the *K'in* place," in his headdress (Figure 10.7a).[6] The hieroglyphic caption naming this individual includes the collocation **a-ku,** *ahk* or "turtle," an element very common in nominal phrases at Piedras Negras and much rarer elsewhere. Most important, we know that these captives were taken in the context of a war against Pomona, a site that had close associations with Piedras Negras at this time (Schele 1995b). Numerous captives from a **wa-**"bird" site mentioned only in the inscriptions of La Corona Palenque, and Piedras Negras suggest that the site will yet be found on the border between these respective kingdoms.[7] Moreover, an earlier defeat of Palenque on 9.9.11.12.3 (November 10, C.E. 624) at the hands of Piedras Negras Ruler 1 (as recorded on Piedras Negras Stela 26) helps establish a traditional enmity between these two centers (Schele and Mathews 1993:80–81). As such, this campaign can be seen as a war against the larger Piedras Negras polity, which lends additional strength to the identification of this toponym.

The most important ramification for the identification of the *K'in-'a* toponym as Piedras Negras is far too complex a topic to consider here, and a more detailed analysis must be saved for a larger work (Guenter and Zender 1999). Nevertheless, it is clear from Palenque's Tablet of the Slaves that Chak Suutz' of Palenque attacked *K'in-'a* (Piedras Negras) on 7 Ik' 5 Sek, or 9.14.13.11.2 (May 7, C.E. 725) (Figure 10.7b). The recurrence of the 5 Sek date—as well as the identification of Chak Suutz' as the captor of nobles from the court of Piedras Negras Ruler 3 (Yo'onal Ahk II), named as the captives' liege (on the Tablet of the Orator)— makes it certain that the Orator and Scribe panels of the Palace and the Temple XXI alfardas record the outcome of this battle (Guenter and Zender 1999). Most important for our purposes here, however, is the fragmentary East Alfarda (Figure 10.7c), which depicts a captive scribe still holding a handful of paintbrushes. He is identified with the hieroglyphic caption *aj k'in-'a*, "he of *K'in-'a* (i.e., Piedras Negras)."

The evidence, then, is remarkably unequivocal that Piedras Negras's toponym was *K'in-'a*. Lesser nobles hailing from this city referred to themselves as *aj k'in-'a* or "he of K'in-'a," and kings took the title *k'in-('a)-ajaw* or "*k'in-'a* lord." The translation of the toponym is less clear, though one might suggest either "Sun-

Water" or perhaps even "Hot Water."[8] Indeed, there is some suggestive evidence that this latter translation might prove the correct one and that it refers to the unique and extensive series of steam baths at the site of Piedras Negras (see Proskouriakoff 1946:xii, 27–29 for evocative reconstructions of the P-7 baths and Child in Houston et al. 1998 for the results of new excavations of these structures). If so, the **K'IN-'a** compound will need to be transliterated with an infixed -h- as *k'ihn-'a* (not *k'in-'a*). Infixed -h-was not often recorded by Maya scribes (or even by later Spanish friars), so this does not present us with any particularly vexing orthographic difficulties. It is, however, far from proven that the intention of the scribes in writing **K'IN** was indeed "hot" rather than "sun," and so we must leave the question in abeyance for the moment. Whether the "hot" interpretation proves to be correct or not, the *k'in-'a* toponym surely identifies Piedras Negras and can confidently be added to a map of Upper Usumacinta place names (Figure 10.1).

T'ul Tuun, "Rabbit Stone," as the Toponym of La Mar

First discovered by Teobert Maler in 1897, La Mar has been subsequently lost again and is in desperate need of a new archaeological reconnaissance. The site had three known stelae, all of which are now in public and private collections and all of which share a great many compositional features and hieroglyphic references with art commissioned in the reign of Piedras Negras Ruler 7 (Montgomery 1994). Indeed, on current evidence, La Mar's written history spans only the period between the accession of Mo' Ahk Chaahk[9] on 9.17.12.4.9 (ca. C.E. 783, as per Stela 1) and his celebration of a *hotun*-ending with Piedras Negras Ruler 7 on 9.18.5.0.0 (ca. C.E. 796, as per La Mar Stela 3 and Piedras Negras Stela 12). That said, we have an extraordinary number of depictions of this La Mar ruler (at least four) at both his home site and at Piedras Negras, and it is through him and his titles that we can most clearly identify the La Mar toponym.

Work on the toponym in question (Figure 10.8)—which couples a "rabbit head" with **TUUN-ni** in most spellings—began with Stuart and Houston (1994:37, Figure 42), who observed that:

> at the site of Piedras Negras, are references to a place we call "Rabbit Stone" (perhaps *T'ultun*), so read because of the two components of their glyphs. An important retainer of the last-known lord at the site was the *ahaw* of this place [fig. 8a], and another individual mentioned on Piedras Negras Stela 40 merely came from "Rabbit Stone," at least to judge from the "*Ah*-Rabbit Stone" expression on the side of the monument [fig. 8b]. The location of this place cannot be pinpointed, although it must surely

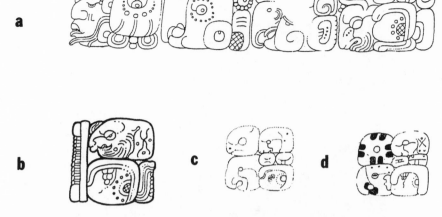

Figure 10.8. T'ul Tuun Ajaw collocations at Piedras Negras and *Sak Tz'i'*. *(a)* Piedras Negras Throne 1: B1-E1 (drawing by John Montgomery); *(b)* Piedras Negras Stela 40: C11 (drawing by the author after Stephen Houston in Stuart and Houston 1994:40); *(c)* "Brussels" Panel: A1 (drawing by John Montgomery); *(d)* "Denver" Panel: A6 (drawing by John Montgomery).

have been in the neighbourhood of Piedras Negras [square brackets added and figure numbers amended].

Building on these identifications, John Montgomery (1994:326) noted the regular association of the "Rabbit Stone" toponym with Mo' Ahk Chaahk and commented that "La Mar may be the location referred to as the 'Rabbit-Stone' place." A review of these data is necessary in order to observe whether the case for La Mar as "Rabbit Stone" could not be made more forcefully.

To begin with, Piedras Negras Panel 3 of Structure O-13—which depicts an evening gathering and the drinking of hot cocoa *(tik-al kakaw)* at the court of Ruler 4 (Itzam K'an Ahk II)—also contains, to the right of the main scene (Figure 10.9a), an assemblage of what are "perhaps one or two of his [Ruler 4's] sons and possibly the future ruler of La Mar as a young boy" (Montgomery 1994:64). The small boy second from the right is named in the hieroglyphs beneath his feet (Figure 10.9b) as none other than Mo' Ahk Chaahk, here labeled a *ch'ok,* or "youth." Of most interest, this places the future La Mar ruler at Piedras Negras on 9.15.18.3.15 (July 27, c.e. 749). Given his height and dress I would venture that he could not be much older than ten or twelve years of age in this scene, which would place his birth date about c.e. 737–739. Mo' Ahk Chaahk stands with two other youths—one of them quite possibly the young Ruler 5, the other most likely the sculptor who carved this exquisite panel. At least one full step be-

a   b

Figure 10.9. Mo' Ahk Chaahk at the Court of Ruler 4. *(a)* Close-up from a reconstruction of Piedras Negras "Lintel 3" (drawing by M. Louise Baker in Judd 1948:122–123);
(b) Mo' Ahk Chaahk, Piedras Negras Panel 3: W'-B" (drawing by the author).

hind them, arms crossed over his chest, stands Jasaw Chan K'awiil, an *ak'uhuun*
or "almner," who keeps a watchful eye over his charges.

   This juxtaposition of skilled nobles suggests that Mo' Ahk Chaahk was raised
and trained in the capital city, which in turn has profound implications for our
appreciation of Late Classic political affiliations and the spread of sculptural/
glyphic styles. That Mo' Ahk Chaahk was so trained is strongly confirmed at his
9.17.12.4.9 (ca. C.E. 783) accession date on La Mar Stela 1 (Figure 10.10c). Not
only is the seated ruler quite clearly named as Mo' Ahk Chaahk (Figure 10.10a)
but also he has gained the title *ak'uhuun* (Figure 10.10b), probably after years of
study with his master in Piedras Negras. As he was likely born within a few years
of C.E. 738, this would make him about forty-five years of age at the time of his
accession. Some ten years later, on 9.18.1.8.18 and 9.18.3.6.19 (ca. C.E. 793), La
Mar and Piedras Negras coordinated an attack on Pomona (Schele and Grube
1994b). Mo' Ahk Chaahk is depicted on La Mar Stela 3 (Figure 10.11) during the

Figure 10.10. Mo' Ahk Chaahk on his accession. *(a)* Mo' Ahk Chaahk, La Mar Stela 1: A4; *(b) ak'uhuun* collocation on La Mar Stela 1: B4; *(c)* Mo' Ahk Chaahk himself, La Mar Stela 1 (drawings by the author).

latter attack, spear in hand, clutching his bearded captive Aj K'eech Aat Took' by the hair (Figure 10.11a). Again, his hieroglyphic moniker leaves no doubt about his identity (Figure 10.11c). Some fifty-five years of age at this point, he is still depicted as a hale and hearty warrior.

The final depiction of Mo' Ahk Chaahk occurs on Piedras Negras Stela 12 (Figure 10.12) some days after the second battle waged at Pomona. There, standing proudly in the same battle raiment that he wore on La Mar Stela 3, he is clearly labeled hieroglyphically (Figure 10.12a) as Mo' Ahk Chaahk *aj-lajuun-*

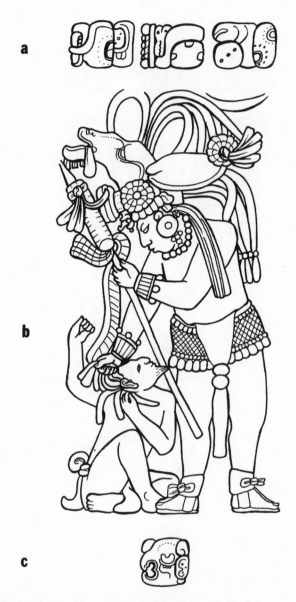

Figure 10.11. Mo' Ahk Chaahk capturing Aj K'eech Aat Took' of Pomona. *(a)* La Mar Stela 3: C1-C3; *(b)* La Mar Stela 3, front; *(c)* Mo' Ahk Chaahk collocation, La Mar Stela 3: A3 (drawings by the author).

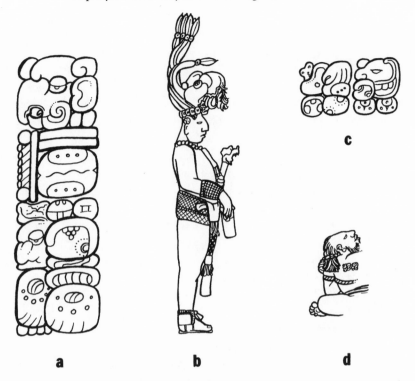

Figure 10.12. Mo' Ahk Chaahk at Piedras Negras. (a) Piedras Negras Stela 12: 5–8; *(b)* Mo' Ahk Chaahk, Piedras Negras Stela 12, front; *(c)* Aj K'eech Aat Took', Piedras Negras Stela 12: 51–52; *(d)* Aj K'eech Aat Took' as a captive, Piedras Negras Stela 12 (drawings by the author).

b'aak "Rabbit Stone"-*ajaw b'akab',* or "Mo' Ahk Chaahk, he of ten captives, the lord of 'Rabbit'-Stone, the *b'akab'.*" Lest any doubts should remain as to the identification of this figure with that on La Mar Stela 3, huddled at the feet of Mo' Ahk Chaahk (Figure 10.12d) is his bearded prisoner from that stela, hieroglyphically labeled on his back (Figure 10.12c) as Aj K'eech Aat Took', the *sajal* (presumably of the contemporary Pomona king K'ooch K'in B'ahlam). That Mo' Ahk Chaahk never takes the "Rabbit Stone" emblem on his own monuments is immaterial to this identification because there his point of origin would have been common knowledge. Rather, it is at Piedras Negras (on Stela 12 [Figure 10.12a] and Throne 1 [Figure 10.8a]) that this designation was needed to single him out as someone from a "foreign" city. Taken all together, these patterns make a very forceful case for the association of the "Rabbit Stone" emblem and toponym with La Mar, and it too can be added to a map of Upper Usumacinta place names (Figure 10.1).

How are we, then, to read this toponym? Although Boot (1997) has recently suggested a syllabic value *lo* for the T759 "Rabbit" sign, Stuart (Stuart et al. 1999:56; David Stuart, personal communication 2000) points out that this reading is based on an erroneous series of substitutions, which leaves us for the moment without a reliable syllabic reading for T759. This is, however, no detriment to our understanding of T759 in the "Rabbit Stone" context, where its behavior forcefully suggests a logographic value. That is, because all meaningful Maya nominal and verbal roots are CVC in form (Zender 1999:22, 34–35) and because T759 alone must spell out some quality, state, or condition of the **TUUN** sign always following it in this context, a logographic value is indicated. This is reinforced most especially by spellings of this collocation on Piedras Negras Throne 1, E1 (Figure 10.8a) and Piedras Negras Stela 12 (Figure 10.12a), where the "rabbit" occupies its own distinct space within the collocation, clearly pointing to a reading of "Rabbit"-**TUUN-ni-AJAW-wa** for "'rabbit'-*tuun-ajaw*," or "Lord of Rabbit-Stone."[10] Kaufman and Norman (1984:133) reconstruct **t'uhl* "rabbit" for Proto-Ch'olan, with cognates from all Ch'olan and Tzeltalan languages. The infixed -h- of this reconstruction is still unclear, however, because Yucatec has *t'u'ul* (Bastarrachea et al. 1992:123) and otherwise provides evidence of original infixed -h- in long vowels with high tone (e.g., Yuc. *k'áak'* < pM **q'ahq'*) (Bastarrachea et al. 1992:99; Kaufman and Norman 1984:123). At the moment, then, we are quite justified in following Stuart and Houston's (1994:37) more conservative reading of **T'UL** "rabbit" for the sign in question—and **T'UL-TUUN** for the La Mar toponym—with the caveats that the internal vowel was surely complex (i.e., probably cueing either *t'u'ul* or *t'uhl*, if not **t'u'hl*) and that definitive phonetic complementational and substitutional evidence is still required to strengthen this proposal (and cf. Schele and Miller 1983:42–46 for a different view). Whether this toponym has some prominent local significance (landforms, architecture, or mythemes) may also influence this proposal, though it will have to await the refinding of this site and further archaeological and epigraphic investigations.

The identification of La Mar as *T'ul Tuun* has far-reaching historical and political implications and privileges historiographers with a much firmer grasp of regional politics in the Upper Usumacinta. By way of example, one set of wars recorded on unprovenanced panels now in Brussels and Denver—between Piedras Negras and her allies on the one hand and unidentified *Sak Tz'i'* on the other—becomes even more interesting now that we have one variable fewer in our analyses. That is, knowing the point of origin of the *T'ul Tuun* combatants (Figures 10.8c and 10.8d) facilitates a more convincing association of other toponyms with their geographic locales. My colleagues and I have detailed these war events and have used them to "home in," as it were, on the location of *Sak Tz'i'* itself, which we believe to be located in the vicinity of Laguna Santa Clara (Figure 10.1) (Anaya et al. 2002; Zender 1998). Moreover, with the concerted set of toponym identifications here proposed or defended, we are also in a much better position to understand the changes in Piedras Negras foreign policy and the processes by which relationships with vassals were maintained. We are now in the position to move beyond the *what, when* and *where* of Maya history as recorded in its hieroglyphs and consider the whys and hows of these historical particularities. As further toponyms are identified, seemingly unrelated historical episodes yield their connections and reveal political alliances and the means by which such alliances were perpetuated. As the decipherments and identifications proliferate, so too, inevitably, does our understanding of the ancient Maya deepen.

Acknowledgments

I owe a large debt (both academic and personal) to the late Linda Schele, who in 1994, after a talk on Maya cosmology given at the University of British Columbia, Vancouver, Canada, encouraged me to learn something of the history of Mayan languages if I was really interested in becoming an epigrapher. In all of the years following that first meeting, Linda never flagged in her words of advice and encouragement, and I am truly grateful to have had the privilege of her acquaintance. I also thank Peter Mathews, Armando Anaya, Stan Guenter, and David Kelley for three years of very stimulating exchange on Maya script, archaeology, and history. I am also very grateful to Stephen Houston, Simon Martin, David Stuart, and Søren Wichmann, whose valuable comments on an earlier version of this chapter have improved it immeasurably. To these fine scholars must go a great deal of the credit for whatever is meritorious in this chapter and to myself alone the fault for whatever errors of interpretation remain.

Notes

1. *How* and *why,* the next great frontiers, will require the close association of epigraphers, ethnographers, and archaeologists in all stages of project planning into this millennium.

2. See, for instance, La Florida Stela 7, C4 (Graham 1970:449, Figure 6b) and the clear affiliations of *Maan* (La Florida) and *Ik'* (Motul de San Jose) lords on a vase in the Dumbarton Oaks collection (cf. Reents-Budet 1994:94, 152, 176–177, 261).

3. Peter Mathews (personal communication 1997) first identified the *Yaxniil* toponym as belonging to El Cayo. The defense for such an identification and the connections proposed in this section, however, are mine.

4. This may relate to *ni',* which is common to most Mayan languages as a word

meaning "nose," "tip," "top," "peak," or "mountain" (Kaufman and Norman 1984: 127; Laughlin 1975:252). The *-il* is a common derivational suffix. Hence, "Green Prominence" is a possible translation for the *Yaxniil* toponym.

5. Although not illustrated here, Ruler 3 clearly takes this title on a stingray spine from Burial 5 at Piedras Negras (cf. Coe 1959:Figure 56b).

6. The *-nal* "inhabitant, resident" and *-'a* "water" compounds regularly substitute for one another in the context of toponyms and toponym titles in the inscriptions (e.g., *ux-witz-'a* and *ux-witz-nal* for Caracol, Belize.

7. It is possible, though by no means certain, that this site will turn out to be Santa Elena, Tabasco (David Stuart, personal communication, 2000).

8. Itzaj *k'inal*, "warm" (Hofling and Tesucún 1997:392), Ch'orti' *k'ihn*, "heat, warmth," and Ch'orti' *k'ihna'*, "warm or hot water" (Wisdom 1950:85); cf. Proto-Ch'olan *k'ix-in*, "warm" (Kaufman and Norman 1984:124).

9. The most complete spelling of this ruler's name occurs on Piedras Negras Throne 1, D1-E1 (Figure 10.8a), where the reading order and constituent elements are clearly **MO'-'o-AHK-CHAAHK,** or Mo' Ahk Chaahk, for what is elsewhere most often written in only one glyph block.

10. Recently, Simon Martin (personal communication 2000) has identified a series of important substitutions of the "Rabbit-Stone" toponym that cast some doubt on the logographic status of T759 entertained herein. On Tonina Monuments 72 and 84, and again on Piedras Negras Panel 4, we encounter the variant spellings T759-**e-TUUN-ni.** Utilizing these and other contexts, Dmitri Beliaev and Albert Davetshin (personal communications 2000 and 2001) have suggested a syllabic value of **pe** for T759, a reading that would have the advantage of explaining the observed orthographic variation in the "Rabbit Stone" toponym in terms of an occasionally unspelled final glottal-stop (i.e., **pe-TUUN-ni ~ pe-'e-TUUN-ni**). If they are correct, the toponym would actually read *pe'-tuun*, with the meaning of "carried-stone" or something similar (cf. Yucatec *pe', "llevar o traer en las manos"* (Barrera Vásquez 1980:642; Bastarrachea et al. 1992:112).

II

Quirigua Zoomorph P

A Water Throne and Mountain of Creation

Matthew G. Looper

About ten years ago, when I took my first undergraduate course in Precolumbian art, I recall seeing for the first time Alfred P. Maudslay's photographs of Quirigua sculpture that were reprinted in Michael Coe's (1987) textbook *The Maya.* Like many before me, I was impressed by the grandeur of the monuments as well as by their rich iconography and wondered whether there might be some way to decode this imagery in order to understand better these great works of art. A few years later, while attending Linda Schele's 1989 workshop on Copan, the answer came to me. As Linda explained the texts of Waxaklajun Ub'ah K'awil's (18-Rabbit's) great stelae, I realized that hieroglyphic texts could be used as a basis for interpreting iconography. Later work with Linda as a graduate student reinforced this methodology and prepared me for my work at Quirigua.

This chapter presents interpretations of the iconography of one of the most impressive works of Maya art known: Zoomorph P at Quirigua. In her 1983 dissertation and subsequent article, Andrea Stone (1983, 1985) interpreted Zoomorph P and related monuments at Quirigua as cosmic diagrams, conceptualized as realms and images of creation. In the present chapter, I attempt to explore this idea through analyses of the monument's texts and iconography in light of recent reconstructions of Classic Maya mythology of cosmogenesis in which Linda Schele served as the fulcrum. This study points to the richness of the zoomorphs of Quirigua as epigraphic and iconographic sources and suggests that, like medieval sculpture programs, their imagery may be repeatedly analyzed, each time revealing new insights.

As one of the largest, best-preserved, and most elaborately carved monuments at Quirigua, Zoomorph P inspires awe today, as it has since its discovery by

Frederick Catherwood in 1840 (Figure 11.1). A sandstone boulder measuring 3 meters long, 3.5 meters wide, and 2.2 meters high, the sculpture was set in place on a low terrace on the southern side of the Ballcourt Plaza, adjacent to the acropolis. Its foundation consists of three huge stone slabs. The front face of the sculpture faces northward, toward the ballcourt. In front of Zoomorph P lies a large (3.6 meters long) and flat (0.5 meters thick) sandstone monument known as Altar P', discovered in 1934 (Morley 1935:107–108). Both of the monuments were dedicated by the king known as Sky Xul, the fifteenth ruler of Quirigua, to celebrate the 9.18.10.0.0 period-ending (September 15, C.E. 795) (Stone 1983:38).

Stylistically, the zoomorph and its altar are typical of late Quirigua sculpture, which feature little undercutting and minimal definition of form by mass. Instead, extremely elaborate, often interlocking calligraphic shapes play across the stones' surfaces. The superficial emphasis of the sculpture is especially prominent in Altar P', in which forms wrap abruptly from the upper surface to the sides of the monument. Although teams of sculptors doubtlessly worked on both of these monuments, the uniform treatment of each sculpture suggests that its carving was closely overseen by a master. The somewhat rougher execution of Altar P' relative to Zoomorph P, however, suggests that either each monument was executed by a different workshop or that more highly skilled artists were concentrated on the zoomorph. Unfortunately, no sculptors' signatures are preserved on the monument, so the artists remain anonymous.

The dedication text for Zoomorph P is inscribed on the sculpture's south face in several panels (Figure 11.2). It begins with the date 9.18.5.0.0 4 Ajaw 13 Kej, followed by a complex dedication sequence. The clearest portion of this passage begins at C4a, naming the monument as a "4 Ajaw stone," followed by a dedication verb. The next few signs (C5b–D9a) seem to refer to the monument as a "13 Kawak building" (Grube et al. 1991:109) and as the *kuch,* or "seat." The reading of the T178 compound as *kuch,* "seat, container," is based on a decipherment by Barbara MacLeod (personal communication 1993). In its appearance on Zoomorph P, as elsewhere, T178 is superfixed to a sign that I interpret as a conflated **ku** and the "breasts" sign that is probably a **chu** syllable (C6a, C8b). This combination of signs may function as a phonetic spelling for the T178 logograph.[1] As in other examples, the collocation is possessed using T126 **ya,** which would seem to indicate that the possessed form of this word was *yakuch.* I would offer two possible analyses of this word: (1) *y-ak-kuch*—"his fixed/seated/covered container" (Yuc. '*ak* or '*ah* "settled, or seated firmly," as in '*ahkuuns* "seat firmly" [Bricker et al. 1998:2]; *ak* "cover" [Barrera Vásquez 1980:4–5]); (2) *y-aj-kuch*—in which *aj* is an agentive (Barrera Vásquez 1980:3).

The text further indicates that the monument is possessed by K'ak' Tiliw Chan Yoat (C6b–C7) and Waxaklajun Ub'ah K'awil (C9). Elsewhere known as

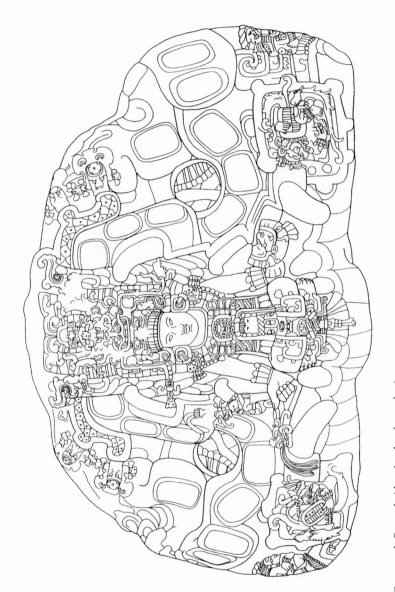

Figure 11.1. Zoomorph P, north (drawing by the author).

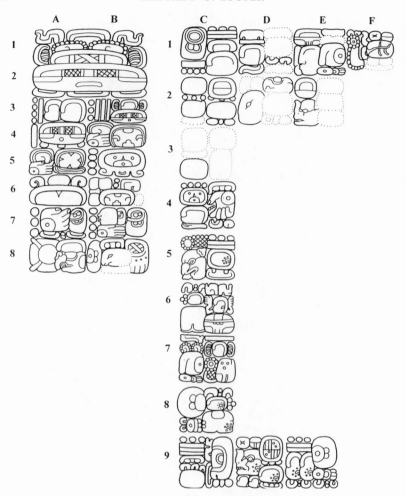

Figure 11.2. Zoomorph P, south dedication text (drawing by the author).

'Kawak Sky', K'ak' Tiliw was the fourteenth ruler of Quirigua, who defeated the king of Copan, Waxaklajun Ub'ah K'awil, and who preceded Sky Xul to the throne (Jones and Sharer 1980; Kelley 1962). This reference suggests that the zoomorph is a ceremonial throne that commemorated the historic interaction of K'ak' Tiliw and his adversary.[2] Further on in the text, at D9b, appears confirmation of this interpretation. Here, a combination of T593 (**TZ'AM?** or **tz'a?**) with a subfixed **ma** syllable suggests a reference to the zoomorph as *tz'am*, or "throne" (Schele and Looper 1996:155).

Analysis of earlier sculpture programs at Quirigua reveals additional cosmic significance of this zoomorph. The east text of Stela C consists of an elaborate description of the creation of the cosmos on 13.0.0.0.0 4 Ajaw 8 Kumk'u (August 13, 3114 B.C.E.), preserving details of the narrative unknown from other texts. In this account, a key event in the creation is the setting of three stone thrones by an assembly of deities. Each throne has a specific identity, the first being a jaguar throne, the second a snake throne, and the third a water throne. As I have shown elsewhere (Looper 1995b), this text introduces a program of three monuments, Stelae C and A and Zoomorph B, the final monumental commissions of K'ak' Tiliw. Each cosmic throne is represented on one monument in the program, the first two appearing on Stelae C and A. The third throne, a water throne, corresponds to Zoomorph B. In that Zoomorph B, like Zoomorph P, is rendered in the form of the "Cosmic Monster," a polymorphic crocodilian (Schele and Miller 1986:45; Stone 1983), it is likely both sculptures represent the third stone throne of creation. In order to test this interpretation, it is essential to consider the imagery of Zoomorph P in detail.

The crocodilian portrayed on Zoomorph P is cleverly compressed to fit a nearly spherical boulder. In addition, the aquatic imagery typical of the Cosmic Monster is pronounced, emphasizing the monument's identity with the third creation stone, the "water" throne. On the north face (front) of the monument, the monster's mouth is open wide, its huge blunt teeth framing a portrait of the king (Figure 11.1). Scrolls at the edges of the mouth frame miniature portraits of Chaak, the Maya deity of lightning and rain. The Chaaks hold T593 glyphs, out of which they decant water (Thompson 1962:220). If this glyph is read **tz'a,** the glyphs may function in this context to indicate the action of the Chaaks because *tz'aa* means "moisten" in Yucatec.

The monster's eyes are represented as bulging hemispheres, with heavy lids and crossed-band eyeballs. Fourteen oval glyphic cartouches define the curve of the mandibles and eyebrows. Four additional cartouches mark the upper part of the forelegs, which extend back on both sides. Above the mouth, lobed water lily pads emerge from behind the king's tall headdress. These pads are adorned with personified flowers, marked with *k'an*-crosses, recalling the imagery of the watery underworld (see Hellmuth 1987).

On the sides of Zoomorph P, the monster's legs are almost totally obscured by detail, save the four clawed feet that point northward toward the front of the monster (Figure 11.3). Each leg bears a cuff, framed by a rope and fringe. Glyphic cartouches and columnar texts mark the rear legs of the beast. These texts begin the lengthy dedication inscription, which continues to the right, covering most of the south face (Figure 11.4). Usually, the Cosmic Monster bears an emblem called the "Quadripartite Badge" on or in place of its tail. This emblem is characterized by a bowl or plate marked with a sun glyph, a shell, a stingray spine, and a crossed-banded element (Schele and Miller 1986:45). In the case of Zoomorph P, however, the Quadripartite Badge is replaced on the south face by a

Figure 11.3. Zoomorph P, west (drawing by the author).

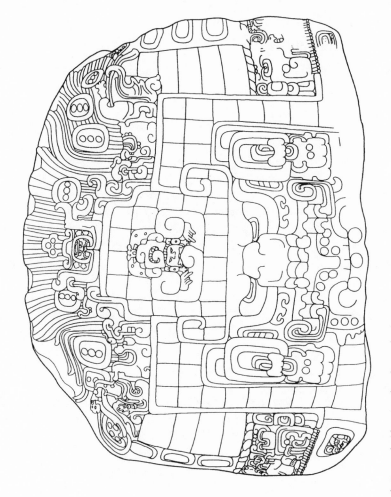

Figure 11.4. Zoomorph P, south (drawing by the author).

head of the Principal Bird Deity, a being that is also associated with the Cosmic Monster (Stone 1983:123). On Zoomorph P, the Principal Bird Deity grasps a large shell in its beak, and its crest arches toward the upper surface, framed by the tail of the monster, which is marked with triple-dotted ovals. The stepped glyphic panel that serves as the bird's crown is accented by a personified water curl in the center.

The upper surface of the monster is carved in the form of a personified mountain or hill (Figure 11.5b; see Stuart 1987:17–23). The main face is represented frontally, elaborate dotted *kawak* signs emphasizing its stony quality. On both sides, the cheeks of the upper mountain are merged with the cheeks of profile mountain personifications, with the noses pointed downward. On both sides of Zoomorph P, the profile mountain monsters' noses frame winged beings with skeletal heads, eyeball collars, and long curling fingers (Figure 11.3). These may be compared to representations of insects on Classic period ceramics (see Paredes et al. 1996:53–54). In the context of the zoomorph, the location of these insects in the nostrils of the mountain monsters probably evokes the insects found in caves and places of burial, which the Maya conceived as mountainous.

If the monumental group of Zoomorph P and Altar P' are observed from the adjacent stairway of the acropolis, additional significance of this mountain image is revealed. Viewed at this angle, the mountain face of the Zoomorph P upper surface merges with the half-quatrefoil of Altar P' (Figure 11.5). Thus, the two monuments are analogous to images of the Maya creation mountain, which features the Maize God resurrecting from a cleft in the earth as on the Palenque Temple of the Foliated Cross main panel and Bonampak Stela 1 (Freidel et al. 1993:Figure 3:8). In place of the Maize God, the designers of the Quirigua program have cleverly substituted the image of Sky Xul on the north side of Zoomorph P, under the mountain monster's forehead. Like the example of the mountain from Palenque, the mountain at Quirigua is shown "floating" on the primordial sea represented as the crocodilian below. Cavorting on the face of the mountain are five miniature beasts, their contorted figures squeezed into the monster's cheeks (Figure 11.3). On the east side is the figure of an iguana, characterized by crest, tail, long fingers, and reptile marking on its back. A long-lipped monkey is adjacent, and below is a hybrid being that has the head of a snake or bat and a feline paw. On the west appear two full-figure beasts: a rat on the left and what seems to be an anthropomorphic snake on the right. Several of these animals hold T593 glyphs from which they decant water, like the Chaaks on the monument's north face. These animals seem to take the place of the Hero Twins, who are shown on Classic Maya pottery assisting the resurrection of the Maize God by pouring liquid on his mountain of emergence (see Freidel et al. 1993:66, Figure 2:4). It is possible that these creatures are analogues of the animal

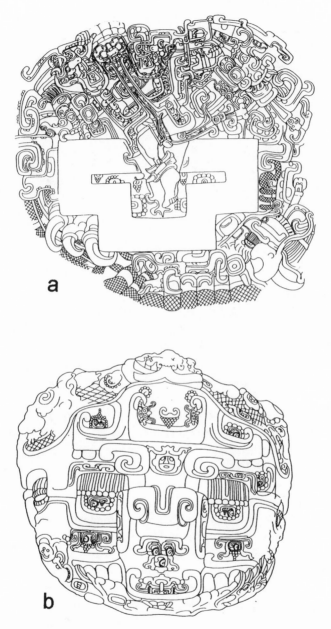

Figure 11.5. *(a)* Altar P' (drawing by the author); *(b)* Zoomorph P, viewed from above (drawing by the author).

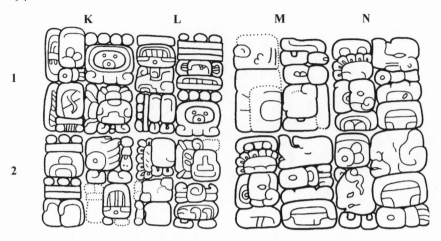

Figure 11.6. Altar P', detail of text (drawing by the author).

helpers that lead humans to the mountain of abundance, as described in the creation myths of the *Popol Vuh* (see Tedlock 1985:163).

Reinforcing the creation theme of Zoomorph P is the iconography of Altar P', which displays a large image of the god Chaak (see Coe 1978:76; Stone 1983:156). The appearance of this deity seems to refer to his mythological guise as the god of lightning, who splits open the mountain of creation or its analogue, a turtle, allowing the Maize God to be reborn (see Karl Taube, cited in Freidel et al. 1993:423; Taube 1986). Out of the deity's mouth emerge two streamers that branch and terminate in large personification heads. Glyphic elements on these "breath" cords mark them as *sak nik ik'(?)*, "white flower breath/spirit(?)."[3] As pointed out by Stone (1983:155), the same termination heads that mark the Chaak's breath cords on Altar P' dangle from the ends of the cords that descend from the sky as shown on Quirigua Stela A. Recent work by Linda Schele, myself, and others has shown that these cords are a fundamental element of Maya creation mythology, representing "cords of heaven" that descended on 13.0.0.0.0 4 Ajaw 8 Kumk'u. These cords are both cosmic "umbilici" that accompany the birth of gods into the world as well as a metaphor for the king's connections to the supernatural world (see Freidel et al. 1993:128; Kappelman 1997; Looper 1995a:131–134, 167; Looper and Kappelman 2000; Taube 1994:659–660). Glyphic elements on these "breath" cords mark them metaphorically as "white flowers," thereby stressing their associations with birth.

The elaboration of the cords of heaven on Altar P' seems to have been motivated by a passage in the monument's text (Figure 11.6). At L1b2-N2, the text gives an account of the events of 13.0.0.0.0 4 Ajaw 8 Kumk'u as a paradigm for the period-ending. Although some of the text is eroded, key glyphs at N1-M2 are legible. These are presented as a couplet, beginning with the word *uhub'il* (N1a). If we interpret *hub'il* as a variant of Yucatec *hub'nal,* "cord, string, twisted thread" (Barrera Vásquez 1980:239), it is possible that this passage may refer to the twisted cords of heaven. This interpretation is strengthened by the next glyphs (N1b1), which include a snake head and a glyph for "white." As mentioned above, the cords of heaven were called "white flower" and were commonly represented with snake heads (Freidel et al. 1993:Figure 4:2). The Altar P' text continues at N1b2 with glyphs reading *yax chan,* or "first sky," an apparent reference to the nascent sky, which is being put in order during cosmogenesis. The fact that this phrase is coupleted (N1-M2) seems likely to be a reference to the cords of heaven because the cords of heaven are always represented as doubled. On Quirigua Stelae F, C, and A, celestial cords are shown falling to the east and west, thereby evoking the orientation of the ecliptic. On Altar P', the doubled form of the "white flower" cords of heaven are reflexed in the twin breath cords of the Chaak that also fall toward the east and west (Figure 11.5a). In sum, the prominent imagery of the cords of heaven on Altar P' reinforces the imagery of the Chaak splitting open the mountain of creation. In this way, the monument's text and image work together to present the contemporary period-ending as a replay of cosmic ordering. This symmetry is further stressed by the fact that both creation and monument dedication fell on the day 4 Ajaw.

As repeatedly demonstrated by Linda Schele and her colleagues, the imagery of creation appears in art from many Maya sites (Freidel et al. 1993; Schele and Mathews 1998; Schele and Villela 1996). At each site, its significance as a paradigmatic act of cosmic ordering is contextualized in order to sacralize historical or dynastic events. One of the most concise of these depictions appears on the Palace Tablet of Palenque, which shows the king K'an Joy Chitam (K'an Xul) taking the emblems of rulership from his parents seated on the three creation thrones (Looper 1995b; MacLeod 1991; Schele and Villela 1996:29, Figure 11a). In this example, the acceding king's throne is adorned with *xok* fish heads, which identify it with the third throne of creation, the "water" throne. This image calls to mind another great set of accession thrones, those depicted on the "niche" stelae of Piedras Negras (e.g., Stelae 6, Proskouriakoff 1960:455, Figure 3). In each of these stelae, the imagery of the Cosmic Monster is prominent, and on some, as on Stela 6, water lilies emphasize the identity of the scaffold structures with the aquatic third throne of creation. In sum, even though their representational mode is altogether different, the Piedras Negras niche stelae and Zoomorph P represent the same underlying concept—the ruler acceding in the context of the third throne of creation. The representation of this act on Zoomorph P, however, is extremely conservative. Its display of the king seated inside the mouth of the crocodilian recalls some of the most ancient representations of royal power in Mesoamerica, such as the Olmec Relief 1 at Chalcatzingo.

Another correspondence of the Piedras Negras accession stelae and Quirigua Zoomorph P is the prominence of the image of the Principal Bird Deity. On the Piedras Negras stelae, the bird grasps the cords of heaven in its beak. This iconography may be interpreted both as a reference to the ritual rebirth of the king upon accession and as a metaphor for the ties between the king and the supernatural sources of his power (see Taube 1994). On Zoomorph P south, the huge bird holds a bivalve shell in its beak. This shell is a common element of the "water group" glyph (T38) that reads **k'u** or **K'UHUL/CH'UHUL** "divine" (see Houston and Stuart 1996). It seems plausible that this image evokes the celestial powers that manifest in the ruler's ceremonial rebirth through accession.

Evidence from Zoomorph P's hieroglyphic texts suggests that the monument is more than a generic accession throne in that it specifically commemorates the accession of Sky Xul. On the cartouches that appear on the monster's rear legs, six glyphs do not form a sentence and seem to be names of the monument. Following a standard reading order from east to west and left to right, the upper cartouche on the southeast side (V1, Figure 11.7) is read first. Although slightly eroded, the mirror-image signs may be **IK'** "black"(?), a shell-in-hand sign, and a snake with upturned nose. A similar combination of signs appears on Zoomorph G, at M'5, apparently naming the locus of Sky Xul's accession on October 15, 785 (Figure 11.8). On Zoomorph G, the compound is possessed, beginning with what is probably the "white flower" collocation that refers to breath and to the cords of heaven. In the Zoomorph P cartouche, the scribe may have used a shorthand version of this glyph, rendering it merely as the square-nosed snake head that represents the cords of heaven in iconography. In the next block of Zoomorph G is the shell-in-hand sign and the "black"(?) glyph that appears on Zoomorph P. Finally, a T4 **NAH** on Zoomorph G indicates that the place of accession is a building. In sum, the close correspondence of the location of accession of Sky Xul given in Zoomorph G and Zoomorph P cartouche V1 suggests that Zoomorph P represents specifically the throne of accession of Sky Xul.

The other five cartouches on the legs refer to the iconography of the monument. The second cartouche (V2) is partly broken, but a **CHAAK** or GI head is legible. The third (V3) is composed of the glyph for stone, *tun,* followed by a crocodile head with a **NAL** toponymic marker. The first cartouche on the southwest leg (W1) is a bird head with a nasal emanation that substitutes for the "impinged bone" glyph, read by Barbara MacLeod (in Schele 1992:232–235) as **KUN,** "seat, container" and by Stuart et al. (1999:15) as **CH'EEN,** "cave, cliff." Thus, cartouches V3 and W1 seem to name the monument as a "stone crocodile place seat/cave." The second cartouche on the west side (W2) reads *ujun nal,* "his Maize God," followed by a combination of a mirror and water lily–skull combination (W3). These last two glyphs seem to refer to the monument in terms of the resurrecting Maize God, who springs from a turtle, mountain, or water lily

Figure 11.7. Zoomorph P, cartouches on legs, SE and SW (drawing by the author).

monster. The reference seems to be to the complex of Zoomorph P and Altar P', which represent the cleft in the mountain of creation. In fact, the Chaak shown on Altar P' may be the referent of the **CHAAK** glyph appearing at V2. Thus, the leg cartouches seem to summarize some of the key protagonists and location of the cosmic events represented in the monumental program.

Finally, it should be noted that several of the details of the monument's iconography seem to indicate the particular day on which the zoomorph was dedicated, the 9.18.5.0.0 period-ending. In particular, some of the sculpted details may be astronomical references to the appearance of the night sky on this date, September 15, C.E. 795. In *Maya Cosmos* (Freidel et al. 1993), Linda Schele interpreted the Cosmic Monster as a representation of the Milky Way when positioned in its east-west conformation, and on the night of dedication of Zoo-

M'   **N'**

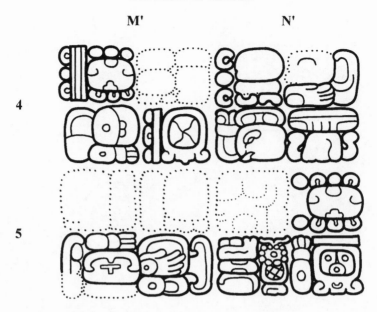

Figure 11.8. Zoomorph G, detail of text (drawing by the author).

morph P, the Milky Way was indeed visible in this form at midnight. Four oval cartouches on the north face of the monument, placed on the monster's forelegs, represent animals that may refer to constellations visible at the time (Figure 11.9). Two of the animals, a God N–turtle and a snake, are likely to have been identified with the ecliptic constellations of Gemini and Sagittarius, respectively, which appear at the east and west horizons when the Milky Way stretches across the sky (see Freidel et al. 1993). The other two cartouches show a *bak'tun* bird and a crocodile, two beings that do not correspond to ecliptic constellations that readily appear in Classic iconography or in the *Paris Codex,* pages 23 and 24 (see Freidel et al. 1993:Figure 2:32).

Interestingly, the beings on the monster's four cuffs are represented in association with stylized snakes and twisted cords—imagery that refers to the Maya cords of heaven that we know as the ecliptic. This suggests that these four beings represent planets, the moon, or the sun; and indeed, the figure appearing on the northwest cuff holds a moon sign. Her appearance on this cuff may refer to the fact that on the night of dedication of Zoomorph P, the moon appeared in Gemini, the constellation that is registered by the adjacent turtle cartouche. Although exact correspondences are still elusive, the other three cuff figures probably personify the other three bright planets that were visible on the night of dedication: Mars and Venus, which appeared in the vicinity of Libra just after sundown, and Saturn, which rose with the moon after midnight. The four

NE

NW

Figure 11.9. Zoomorph P, cartouches on forelegs (drawing by the author).

smaller cartouches that appear on the feet of the monster may also refer to the locations where these celestial bodies appeared, but this is not certain.

In summary, Zoomorph P and Altar P' were commissioned by Sky Xul as the primary commemorative monuments for his third period-ending festival on 9.18.5.0.0. As a celebration of cosmic renewal, the period-ending was considered to be a replay of the events of cosmogenesis, which occurred on 13.0.0.0.0 4 Ajaw 8 Kumk'u. Fortuitously, the 9.18.5.0.0 period-ending fell on 4 Ajaw, the same position in the *tzolk'in* calendar as creation. The designer or designers of the Quirigua program capitalized on this symmetry by focusing the imagery of both monuments on creation themes. The major monument, Zoomorph P, reflects this through its imagery of the mountain of creation and supernatural throne. Altar

P', in addition to containing a textual narrative of creation, expands the imagery of the zoomorph, depicting the moment in which the lightning deity Chaak assisted the birth of the Maize God from the creation mountain.

The theme of renewal embodied by the myths of creation and the period-ending provided Sky Xul with a means of legitimizing his reign and his dynasty. In particular, the text inscribed in cartouches on the north face of Zoomorph P describes the founding of the dynasty of Quirigua in C.E. 426. These events gain deeper meaning in light of the paradigm of cosmogenesis. Likewise, the diagram formed by Zoomorph P and Altar P' places the king in the same structural position as the resurrecting Maize God. In this way, the program emphasizes the nature of the king's accession as a ritual rebirth. In fact, the king's headdress on Zoomorph P north is laden with botanical imagery, such as floral medallions in its flanges, a large **TE'**, "tree, plant" personification in the headdress, and a personified **SAK NIK,** or "white flower" sign at the top. As such, the ruler is given a ritual guise as *ukit nik,* or the "patron of flowers," as the Maize God was sometimes entitled (Freidel et al. 1993:84, Figure 2:19a). Surely, his sacrifices and erection of stones would cause the gods to be reborn and bring sustenance to his people.

Acknowledgments

I wish to acknowledge the generous support of the Instituto de Antropología e Historia of Guatemala for the research conducted at Quirigua, the results of which are reported in this chapter. Research funding was provided by the National Science Foundation (No. DBS 9307752), the William J. Fulbright Foreign Scholarship Board, and the Foundation for the Advancement of Mesoamerican Studies, Inc.

Notes

1. On Copan Altar Q, E2, the T178 logograph is subfixed by a clear "breasts" sign without *kawak* markings.

2. It should be noted that Zoomorph G is also glyphically identified as a throne. At O2, the monument is referred to with the T150 "throne" logograph.

3. The T503 sign was read by MacLeod (in Schele 1992:21–22) as **NAL** ("maize") when outside of the day-sign context. More recently, however, Stuart et al. (1999) suggested that the glyph is read the same as the day-sign, **IK'**. In Yucatec, this word means "spirit," "life," "breath," and "wind" (see Barrera Vásquez 1980:266). The death expression, then, may record the expiration of the "white flower spirit" of a person.

12

New Dance, Old Xius

The "Xiu Family Tree" and Maya Cultural Continuity after European Contact

Constance Cortez

The page known as the "Xiu Family Tree" (Figure 12.1) is the only extant illustrated genealogical tree from colonial Yucatan. Created between 1558 and 1560,[1] the "Xiu Family Tree" is part of the *Xiu Family Chronicle,*[2] a series of documents called *probanzas de hidalguía,*[3] or "proofs of nobility." These petitions were written on behalf of the Xiu family, one of the most powerful Maya families controlling the northern Yucatan Peninsula prior to the coming of the Spaniards. The texts were primarily directed toward the Spanish Crown and proved Xiu nobility by means of recording services to the Crown.

Although the "Xiu Family Tree" and the *probanzas* that it accompanies were initially directed toward the Spaniards, they were also meant to satisfy the informational and aesthetic needs of the Xiu family in whose keeping they would remain until the late nineteenth century. Because of these requirements, the page's artist and scribe had to be someone capable of bridging the enormous cultural gap created by the conquest—someone who could produce a document that could be visually and mentally accessed by both cultures.

The page's author, Gaspar Antonio Chi,[4] was, in part, a product of the conquest. As a child, Chi had received an extensive education from the newly arrived mendicant friars. By 1549, Franciscans had established a convent and school in the Xiu capital, Mani (Tozzer 1941:73). As part of the process of conversion, they encouraged the chiefs (particularly those of high status) to allow their sons to attend. Although Chi's father was a member of the Chi lineage and a priest of the old religion, Gaspar Antonio's mother was a Xiu. After the death of Gaspar Antonio's father, his mother's family had taken on the primary responsibility for raising the young boy. Because of his association with such a preeminent family,

Figure 12.1. The Xiu Family Tree (Tozzer Library of Harvard College Library, Harvard University).

Chi was encouraged to attend school at the Mani convent. It was at Mani that Gaspar Antonio honed his linguistic capabilities. As was common among the indigenous elite of Yucatan, Chi was conversant not only in Yucatec Maya but also in Nahuatl (Tozzer 1941:45). At Mani, he readily acquired knowledge of Spanish and Latin (Karttunen 1994:84–113). His aptitude for languages placed him in a privileged position at an early point in his life.

It is also likely that it was at Mani that Chi first came into contact with European models of the Tree of Jesse on which the "Xiu Family Tree" would be based. Images such as these were brought to the Americas by mendicants in the form of loose prints and immediately incorporated into fresco programs in the newly built churches. They quickly became part of the repertoire of visual tools used to instruct and convert indigenous people and were essential in conveying notions of both genealogical and spiritual ascendancy (Cortez 1995:86–94).

Visual representations of the Tree of Jesse appeared in Europe during the eleventh or mid-twelfth century (Ladner 1979:250; Watson 1934:1). By the sixteenth century, the theme was both widespread and popular. Based on a biblical passage from Isaiah (11:1–5),[5] the image relates to the prophecy foretelling the founding of the house of David. In most illustrations, Jesse is portrayed asleep at the base of a tree with a hand supporting his head (Figure 12.2). The tree springing from the area of his loins represents subsequent generations. The root of the tree corresponds visually and conceptually with the sleeping progenitor, Jesse. The Virgin Mary is equated with the trunk of the tree, and the fruit or the blossoms of the tree are associated with Christ.[6]

In Chi's version, the Christian patriarch has been replaced by the male progenitor of the Xiu lineage, Tutul Xiu, who mimics the typical pose of Jesse. Here, Xiu reclines at the base of a tree that springs from his backside and supports his head with one hand. Like Jesse's kin, Xiu's descendants are part of the tree and are named in the blossoms of the branches.

Although the use of a biblical model and European style implies a high degree of assimilation of Old World ideology and iconography, Chi's page contains both textual and iconographic elements that are inconsistent with European images of the Tree of Jesse. Rather, these elements are derived from two Mesoamerican traditions in place prior to European arrival: those of the Maya region and of Central Mexico.

Some explanation is necessary here to explain the family's connection to Central Mexico. Although Tutul Xiu was recognized as a Maya lord, his family's roots were either in Central Mexico or in an area that was in contact with Central Mexican traditions. Citing Daniel Brinton's earlier work, Sylvanus G. Morley (Morley and Roys 1941:16, n. 1) points out that the family name itself may be of Nahuatl derivation, coming from *xiuitl,* meaning "plant," "herb," "turquoise," or "blue-green." Alternatively, Karl Taube (personal communication 1995) believes the name "Xiu" to be "derived from *xiuhtototl,* the 'lovely cotinga,' a turquoise colored blue bird seen on the headdresses of Xiutecuhtli and 'Toltecs' at the (Central Mexican) site of Tula and by the Maya at Chichen Itza."[7]

The best-known visual evidence supporting the connection between the Xiu and Central Mexico involves the crown worn by the Maya progenitor. Morley (Morley and Roys 1941:19) initially noted the similarity between the Aztec

Figure 12.2. *Dresden Codex,* page 28 (after Lee 1985:51).

xiuhuitzolli and Tutul Xiu's crown. He also links the crown worn by Xiu with the Xiu patronym, viewing the latter as a kind of linguistic pun. Jeff Kowalski (1987:56) also notes the importance of the crown and cites Diego de Landa's sixteenth-century treatise, which recounts that when "the Xiu arrived their only weapons were the atlatl and darts, typical Mexican highland weapons."

While referencing the Central Mexican origin of his family, Gaspar Antonio Chi also made sure that the family's Maya identity was clear. This was accomplished by the insertion of a caption located in the area of Tutul Xiu's head. Morley (Morley and Roys 1941:30) reconstructed the caption as:

(Hu)n (U)itzil
chac ome
(hala)ch Tutul Xiu

He has translated this as:

Hun Uitzil Chac,[8]
his own blood,[sic]
the true Tutul Xiu.

The first phrase of the name, *Hun Uitzil Chac,* can be read as "one mountain Chaak." Beyond being part of Tutul Xiu's titles, the word "Chaak" is also the name of rain-associated supernaturals that the Maya believed inhabited mountains. It is in keeping with Maya tradition for rulers to carry deity-associated appellatives in the list of titles attached to their name. For instance, the title *B'akab',* the generic name for deities that hold up the four corners of the world, seems to have been favored in the Classic period by Maya elites. At the Postclassic site of Chichen Itza in Yucatan, deity-associated appellatives seem to be all but nonexistent with the one possible exception of the title *Yahaw Watab* ("the lord of wherever/everywhere").[9] This may be comparable to the Nahuatl, *Tloque Nahuaque* ("lord of the near, lord of the nigh").[10]

Likewise, the name of the woman on the Xiu Family Tree underlines the family's connection to the Maya. The association here is clearly through marriage. Her identification as the wife of Tutul Xiu is based on Morley's (Morley and Roys 1941:30–31) reading of the caption located to the right of her head. The incomplete script reads:

Yx. . . .
ticul mu . . .
hun . . *tzi* . . .

Morley has reconstructed this as:

Yx . . . [proper name, of]
Ticul, [wife of]
Hun [Ui]tzil [Chac]

Because the page has been damaged, the personal name of the woman pictured on the Xiu page is unknown. It is believed, however, that she came from Ticul because the name of the town is clearly indicated below the *Yx* prefix. The town lies well within the Mani territory that eventually came to be controlled by the Xiu. Even though there exists a slim possibility that the woman came from Central Mexico,[11] it seems more likely that the foreign-born Tutul Xiu married into a local Maya family in order to validate his lineage. Although Landa does not explicitly mention such exogamous marriages, Tozzer (1941:31) believes that the following passage indicates its presence in the case of the Xiu family: "And there [around Mayapan], they [the Xiu] began to settle and to construct very good buildings in many places; and the people of Mayapan became very good friends with them and were glad to see that they cultivated the land as the natives do; and in this way those of Tutul Xiu subjected themselves to the laws of Mayapan and thus they intermarried, and as the lord Xiu of the Tutul Xius was such he came to be very much esteemed by everybody."

This type of exogamous marriage seems to have been common in expansionist cultures throughout Mesoamerica. Owing to the political, economic, and symbolic significance of such alliances, women in these instances are prominent subjects in both historical and visual representations dating from earlier periods and from precontact Central Mexico (Marcus 1992:223–259). The placement of women within such contexts reveals not only the nature of rulership and political alliances but also indigenous attitudes about high-status women and their ideal functions in Mesoamerica (Cortez 1995).

Perhaps the most significant elements linking the Xiu page to Mesoamerican traditions are the offering, the cave, and the hill located in the bottom region of the page. All three are essential components that appear in the visual definition of Mesoamerican lineage. In the case of the Xiu image, the elements convey notions of reciprocity between the great ancestor and his descendants and connect the ancestor to concepts of cyclical renewal.

At the bottom of the page, burning crossed deer legs placed in a basket have been situated before the darkened opening of a cave. At the time of the conquest, the Yucatec Maya practiced a type of ancestor worship that required periodic auto-sacrifice, animal sacrifice, and burnt offerings (McAnany 1995; Pohl 1981, 1988; Tozzer 1941:63). This practice seems to reflect the Maya belief that caves located in mountains not only were the source of the sustaining rains that water their crops but also housed protective ancestors or supernaturals (Carlson 1981b:201; Pohl 1981:522).

This grouping of mountains, moisture, and ancestors has early correlates in Mesoamerica. For instance, some of the same elements—hills, caves, and the concept of origins—can be found at the Classic period site of Teotihuacan in the Pyramid of the Sun. The huge structure was built to mark an ancient natural cave, once the site of an underground spring (Heyden 1975:141). Doris Heyden (1975, 1976, 1981) has convincingly argued that pyramid, cave, and spring are early manifestations of a pan-Mesoamerican preoccupation with natural elements and ancestors. Heyden not only traces the roots of this phenomenon back to earlier Olmec practices but also shows the same ideological concepts present in later Aztec visual culture and writing especially as it is connected to Chicomoztoc, the seven-lobed cave of Aztec ancestral emergence.

It should also be mentioned that the Aztecs incorporated the natural components of water and hill into their definition of the city. The Nahuatl term for "town," *altepetl,* literally means "water-hill"—a word that combines the most essential natural elements in the founding of an Aztec city (Karttunen 1992:9). This concept would not have been lost on the Xiu, given their links to Central

Mexico. As will be recalled, the Xiu page served as a frontispiece for *probanzas,* documents reinforcing the family's right to their traditional lands. It would therefore be in keeping with the intent of the documents to show Tutul Xiu on a hill thus referencing not only his status as a great progenitor but also the geopolitical entity under Xiu control—the city or perhaps even the region itself.

The deer legs found at the bottom of the Xiu page are more in keeping with Maya conventions associated with sacrifice. An example of this is found in the Postclassic deer offering placed before the world tree illustrated in the *Dresden Codex,* page 28 (Figure 12.2). There are obvious problems in terms of the disparate contexts of the three offerings: the Xiu context is one of death and homage to ancestors, and the Dresden image is associated with New Year ritual activities. These differences can be reconciled if we view the imagery of both in a broader context of sacrifice as an act marking rites of passage. In the Dresden example, the rebirth and renewal are associated with the new year, hence, time; on the Xiu family page, the rite of passage is death. Because death did not represent ultimate finality to the Maya, it can also be viewed as a "rebirth," albeit rebirth into a supernatural realm. Landa remarks on the afterlife in his discussion of colonial Maya beliefs regarding the posthumous fates assigned to good-versus-evil Maya (Tozzer 1941:131–132):

> This people has always believed in the immortality of the soul, more than many other nations, although they have not reached such a high state of civilization; for they believed that there was another and better life, which the soul enjoyed when it separated from the body. They said that this future life was divided into a good and bad life—into a painful one and one full of rest. The bad and the painful one was for the vicious people, while the good and the delightful one was for those who had lived well according to their manner of living. The delights which they said there were to obtain, if they were good, were to go to a delightful place, where nothing would give them pain and where they would have an abundance of foods and drinks of great sweetness, and a tree which they call the *yaxche,* very cool and giving great shade, which is the ceiba, under the branches and the shadow of which they would rest and forever cease from labor. The penalties of a bad life, which they said that the bad would suffer, were to go to a place lower than the other, which they called *Metnal,* which means "hell," and be tormented in it by the devils and by great extremities of hunger, cold, fatigue and grief. They maintained that there was in this place a devil, the prince of all the devils, whom all obeyed, and they call him in their language Hunhau. And they said that these lives, bad and good, had no end for the soul.

Figure 12.3. Tota, Our Father (after Durán 1971:Plate 14).

The three elements of mountain, cave, and offering found on the Xiu page can be understood as a unified iconographic complex found throughout Mesoamerica and can be traced back to the Olmec (Freidel et al. 1993:138–139). In the Maya area, for example, this complex is known to have been associated with the creation of people and was made manifest in site construction. Huge pyramidal bases alluded to sacred mountains of creation, and temples atop these bases represented caves in which rulers could access ancestors. The plaza below represented the primordial sea, a "portal to the Otheworld" (Freidel et al. 1993:139).

The foundation of peoples and their lineages also reflects concepts of time and ancestral power while exemplifying the sacrificial obligation of child to father. This is especially true if the world tree is taken into consideration. In the case of the Aztecs, the tree known as Tota ("Our Father") (Figure 12.3) was the focus of ritual slated for the end of the ritual year (Durán 1971:160–163). During the Feast of Etzalcualiztli, an artificial forest was set up in the plaza of the Aztec sacred precinct of Tenochtitlan. Tota was placed at the center of this "forest" and was surrounded by four smaller trees. The smaller trees were connected to the larger one by straw ropes. All of these trees had been harvested earlier from a common site, a place called the "Hill of the Stars" at Culhuacan. In the context of lineages, it seems significant that the term "Culhuacan" has general associations with places of origin for ancestors and royal dynasties (Gillespie 1989; Heyden 1976;

Leibsohn 1993). In essence, the trees and the New Year can all be understood as emerging from a hill associated with earlier generations.

More direct genealogical associations can also be made. The cords that bind the smaller trees to the large central tree are associated with both auto-sacrifice and umbilical cords (Durán 1971:160–163). The implication is one of filial relationship—the binding of the father (Tota) to the sons—in this case, the four trees. In the Xiu example, the relationship between patriarch and future generations is indicated not only by the cartouches in the tree connected to Xiu but also by the presence of four smaller trees situated at the base of the image. Clearly, these function in much the same way as the smaller trees that surround Tota in the Aztec example. All of these elements, then, reinforce the relationship between Tutul Xiu and the descendants who benefited from the work of their great ancestor.

An image reproduced in 1656 by Cogolludo (Figure 12.4) also provides a key to the relationship between past and present generations while associating great ancestors with actual calendrical time. This image is a reproduction of a painting of a "coat of arms" possibly produced as early as 1541. According to Cogolludo (cited in Morley 1920:472–473), the thirteen heads represent members of the Xiu elite who were killed by the Cocom family at the notorious 1536 Massacre of Otzmal. According to the many accounts of this event,[12] in 1535 there was a severe drought on the peninsula that resulted in large-scale starvation. With the hope of ending the drought, the lord of the district of Tutul Xiu, Nappol Chuuah, decided to make the pilgrimage through Cocom territory to Chichen Itza to make offerings at the cenote there. In the previous century, the Xiu had attacked the Cocom and killed many of their kinsmen. Nonetheless, in 1535, believing that the Cocom would leave these old enmities behind in such a time of need, the Xiu leader led forty nobles, including Gaspar Antonio Chi's father, through Cocom territory after securing a promise of safe conduct from the Cocom leader. After three days of entertaining the Xiu at the town of Otzmal, the Cocom massacred all of those present. It was here that Gaspar Antonio's father had an arrow shot through his eye. This event is significant because it exemplifies the historic feud between the Cocom and Xiu lineages as well as for the fact that it left the fatherless Chi dependent on his mother's kinsmen.

In the Cogolludo image, two of the members of the Xiu entourage are represented. The head of the family, Nappol Chuuah ("Ah Napot Xiu"), is situated at the top left of the shield, and Gaspar Antonio's father, Ah Kin Chi, is located just opposite and facing the Xiu leader. The original from which Cogolludo took his rendering was still in existence as late as 1841 and was commented on by Stephens (quoted in Morley 1920:473), who noted that the tree in the center of the image was "growing out of a box, representing the sapote tree at Zotuta under which the murder was committed."

Figure 12.4. Coat of arms (after Morley 1920:Figure 73).

In their analysis of Cogolludo's "coat of arms," both Sylvanus Morley (1920: 472–487) and William Gates (1931) chose to discount to a great extent the historic readings of Stephens and Cogolludo, electing instead to privilege the image's role as a "*k'atun* wheel"—a visual device used in marking the progression of calendrical time in twenty-year increments. Such *k'atun* wheels are found in many of the *Books of Chilam Balam,* volumes recording and prophesying the nature of the *k'atun.*[13] In the Cogolludo image, "Ah Napot Xiu" corresponds to the initial *k'atun* from which time is being reckoned. As time progresses, one proceeds in a counterclockwise fashion until the head of Ah Kin Chi is reached and a cycle of 260 years is completed.

In more orthodox versions of *k'atun* wheels, such as those from the *Chilam Balams of Chumayel* and *Kaua* (Figure 12.5), the thirteen *k'atuns* are presented in a circular format. Each *k'atun* is indicated by a head that is emblematic of the day glyph Ahaw, meaning "lord" or "ruler." Rather than mentioning the names of specific personages, the day name Ahaw and a numerical coefficient are placed

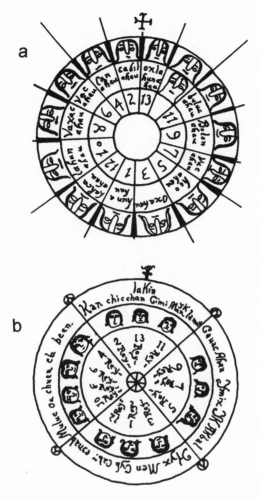

Figure 12.5. *(a)* *K'atun* wheel from the *Chilam Balam of Chumayel* (after Gates 1931:6); (b) *k'atun* wheel from the *Chilam Balam of Kaua* (after Gates 1931:6).

under the head. In the Kaua version, the Spanish word for "king," *rey,* is used in lieu of *ahaw.* In both instances, the starting point of the *k'atun* count is marked with a cross that appears in relation to *k'atun* 13 Ahaw. The Kaua wheel is further elaborated by clearly demarcated quadrants and a tiny bird stationed atop the cross. Surely these two aspects refer to cardinal directions and Precolumbian world trees that often have a single bird perched in the uppermost branches.

Morley also believed that names inscribed under each of the heads in the Cogolludo manuscript were added later (Figure 12.4). This he attributes to memory lapses on the part of the Maya vis-à-vis the proper Ahaw dates and their corresponding coefficients.[14] Apparently, bad memory was catching, for he noted two other Maya sources where the passage of time was reckoned in terms of some of these same lords.[15] The tree at the center of Cogolludo's coat of arms received no comment from Morley at all.

Although it is probable that Morley and Gates were correct in their association of *k'atuns* with this page, it seems also as likely that the historical reading relayed by Cogolludo and Stephens, via different Maya sources, was just as correct. Reconciliation of these disparate points of view is possible if the presence of the tree is taken into consideration. In Cogolludo's "wheel," the tree is situated inside an offering bowl that in turn rests on a square support. There are flames (crossed deer hooves?) surrounding the base of the tree. The tree, its container, and the square support are all situated before a darkened cave entrance. It is clear that Cogolludo's rendition of the original is a bit confused and that, in the original, the tree grew directly out of a square element that represents dressed masonry. It is probable that this square support corresponds to the *tun* element in Dresden representations of the foliated *akantun* ("set-up stone")[16] and that the container, not mentioned by Stephens, rested in front of the tree and not below it.

Like the Xiu image, the tree of Otzmal, under which the pilgrims were murdered, can be viewed as a site of sacrifice. In their attempt to set right the drought besieging the peninsula, the victims became martyrs. As such, they became prescriptive of the correct behavior associated with ancestors who try to intercede on behalf of their community. That these thirteen Xiu ambassadors should be associated with *k'atuns* is not surprising, then. The events—the historic pilgrimage and the pilgrims' sacrifice at Otzmal—were immediately recontextualized by later generations of Maya who placed them in their proper context of cyclical time—cyclical time that required sacrifice and devotion for its maintenance.[17]

In regards to time and the Xiu founder, Tozzer (1941:28, n. 154) cites earlier sources that credit Tutul Xiu with the introduction and perpetuation of the calendar system in use by the Maya at the time of the conquest. Whether true or not, the attribution of this knowledge to the Xiu lord underscores the importance of temporal control as a definitive marker of function for ancestral elites. The offering at the base of the tree can be understood, then, as a reciprocal response on the part of the Xiu descendants who, by their actions, insure successful continuity of both time and the lineage.

Notes

1. Two alternative dates have been suggested for the page's initial production. William Gates (Landa 1937:123) believes that the first installment of the page was completed by 1548 and associates this date with the baptism of the hereditary leader

of the Xiu lineage, Kukum Xiu, at Mani in 1548. Alternatively, Morley (Morley and Roys 1941:170–181) assigns this page a later date of between 1558 and 1560—a date that may associate the document with the creation of the Mani Land Treaty of 1557 (*Crónica de Maní*), which effectively established the boundaries of Mani, the Xiu capital (see Landa 1937:133 for drawing of map). As I will show, the later date is more likely. A second installment was made to the page in 1690 by Juan Xiu.

2. Produced between c.e. 1557 and 1817, the *Xiu Family Chronicle* has been summarized by William Gates (Landa 1937:120–139). An English translation of all of the documents is to be found in volume 2 of an unpublished manuscript by Sylvanus G. Morley and Ralph L. Roys (1941) that is available at the Tozzer Library, Harvard.

3. According to Morley (Morley and Roys 1941:2), "During the Spanish Colonial Period, [a *probanza*] was a recital of services to the Crown by a claimant for *encomienda* (title to land given by the king), pension, or land grant, supported by sworn statements of witnesses as to the truth of the claimant's contentions."

4. Tozzer (1941:45, n. 219) was one of the first scholars to suggest that Gaspar Antonio Chi drew up the Mani land treaty. Morley (Morley and Roys 1941:170–171) concurs and attributes the page to Chi based on a long line of evidence. (See also Morley and Roys [1941:175–176, n. 1] for a recitation of Robert S. Chamberlain's criteria for the dating of the page and his commentary on the page's calligraphic qualities.)

5. According to Isaiah, Chapter 11:

Then a shoot will spring from the stem of Jesse,
And a branch from his roots will bear fruit.
And the Spirit of the Lord will rest on Him,
The spirit of wisdom and understanding,
The spirit of counsel and strength,
The spirit of knowledge and the fear of the Lord.
And He will delight in the fear of the Lord,
And He will not judge by what His eyes see,
Nor make a decision by what His ears hear;
But with righteousness He will judge the poor,
And decide with fairness for the afflicted of the earth;
And He will strike the earth with the rod of His mouth,
And with the breath of His lips He will slay the wicked.
Also righteousness will be the belt about His loins,
And faithfulness the belt about His waist.

And the wolf will dwell with the lamb,
And the leopard will lie down with the kid,

And the calf and the young lion and the fatling together;
And a little boy will lead them.
Also the cow and the bear will graze;
Their young will lie down together;
And the lion will eat straw like the ox.
And the nursing child will play by the hole of the cobra,
And the weaned child will put his hand on the viper's den.
They will not hurt or destroy in all My holy mountain,
For the earth will be full of the knowledge of the Lord
As the waters cover the sea.

Excerpted from *Master Study Bible* (1981).

6. For the association of specific tree parts with biblical characters, see Gertrude Schiller (1972:2:15). In the Judeo-Christian tradition, the Tree of Jesse is related to a broader group of images including the "Tree of Knowledge," the "Tree of Life," and, by extension, the cross upon which Christ was crucified. All three of these trees can be associated with the Garden of Eden (Underwood 1950:101). Conceptual differences between the tree of knowledge (evil; death) and the cross (good; resurrection) are reconciled in the *Holy Cross Legend* by the fact that the tree of life "later furnished the wood for the Cross of the Savior" (Ladner 1979:236). See also Rab Hatfield (1990:135) for a synopsis of this legend as it is found in James of Varagine's *Golden Legend*.

7. Alfred Tozzer made another linguistic connection between the family and Central Mexico in his commentary on the "Xiu Family Tree." Tozzer (1941:30, n. 159) accepted the notion of the family's Nahuatl (or Nahuatl-influenced) cultural identity and cited as evidence the presence of the name Ah Cuat Xiu (son of Ah Uitz) in the branches of the tree as proof of the family's Central Mexican connections. According to Tozzer, *cuat* is the Maya variant of the Nahuatl term *coatl,* or "snake."

8. Stuart (1987:23) has noted the use of the title as early as the Classic period at Yaxchilan (Lintel 45). The title also appears in a variety of colonial sources. According to Tozzer (1941:n. 159): "We learn from the *Relación* of Teav (Teabo) (RGY [1983:]1:287) that the name of the first Tutul Xiu of Uxmal was Hunuikilchac (Hun Uitzil Chac), 'lord of Uxmal, a most ancient city and well renowned for its buildings, a native of Mexico.' In addition to the above, Morley and Roys have noted this founder's name twice each in the Chilam Balams of Mani and of Tizimin. The four references have to do with three priests, Kauil (Chel), Napuc Tun, Xupan Nauat and Hun Uitzil Chac of Uxmal." The reference to the priests in relation to Tutul Xiu may be significant. According to Landa (Tozzer 1941:141), priests were the recipients of deer leg offerings during the New Year ceremony. Such an offering is depicted in front of the reclining Maya patriarch.

9. Translation by Ruth Krochock (personal communication 1995).

10. Although the latter phrase seems to be used by the Aztecs exclusively to describe the deity located in the highest Aztec heaven, the use of a comparable phrase in Postclassic Maya inscriptions to describe the deified ruler may represent a conceptual melding of the Aztec term and the Maya practice and would establish yet another link between the Itza and the culture of Central Mexico.

11. The garment worn by the Xiu woman is a *huipil*—a later Central Mexican import into the Maya region (Anawalt 1981:213–214).

12. This event is recounted in Landa's *Relación* (Tozzer 1941:54), and Morley (Morley and Roys 1941:81–82) lists fourteen other postconquest sources where accounts of the tragedy are mentioned.

13. Gates (1931) compares the Cogolludo wheel to corresponding *k'atun* wheels in the *Chilam Balam of Kaua* and the *Chilam Balam of Chumayel*. Morley (1920) also includes the *Chilam Balam of Mani* in his analysis.

14. The *k'atun* always began on the day Ahaw ("Lord") that was symbolized by a disembodied head.

15. These two sources are the *Chilam Balam of Kaua* and the *Chilam Balam of Mani* (Morley 1920:482).

16. There is some debate over the correct reading of the "tree" present in *Dresden Codex* 28. In his commentary on Landa's *Relación,* Tozzer (1941:141, n. 663) notes that it is the statue on the "standard" (Sp. *palo* = pole, stick) that is referred to as *k'ante* ("yellow wood"). Following Thompson's (1972:92) reading, MacLeod and Puleston (1979:74) refer to this element as *akante',* thereby privileging the "wood" *(te')* symbol located in the trunk of the tree. Schele and Grube (1997) have identified the "tree" as the *akantun,* the "set up stone." (See Tozzer 1941:n. 669 for a variety of translations for *akantun.*)

17. Morley (1920:484) is baffled by the association of Ah Napot Xiu's name with *k'atun* 3 Ahaw in both the *Chilam Balam of Kaua* and the *Chilam Balam of Mani* inasmuch as *K'atun* 3 Ahaw ended a century after the death of Napot Xiu at Otzmal. If we assume, however, that such historic events are reconciled not only with the past and the present but also with the future, associating Napot Xiu's name with a future *k'atun* would only validate the importance of his death and the cyclical nature of recurring events.

13

The Workshops on Maya History and Writing in Guatemala and Mexico

Nikolai Grube and Federico Fahsen

It is not widely known the extent to which Linda Schele became engaged in the Maya Revitalization Movement in Guatemala. Her passion for the Maya was more than an academic interest in a field of research. Linda felt deep love and respect for the Maya, not only for the ancient people who populated famous cities, such as Palenque, but more and more the actual, living Maya of Guatemala, Mexico, Honduras, and Belize. We have never seen Linda in such a cheerful interchange as with Maya villagers from highland Guatemala or the Yucatan Peninsula. She was not a cultural or social anthropologist and had neither training nor experience doing fieldwork, yet she got along very well with the "others." Her capacity to laugh at herself and her enthusiastic creativity opened doors that remained closed to many other people from "our" society. Federico and Nikolai were greatly privileged by joining Linda in these intellectual and emotional adventures into the world of the living Maya.

The Beginnings of the Workshop

Our narrative begins with a "Taller de Lingüística Maya," a meeting of linguists in Antigua Guatemala held by the Centro de Investigaciones Regionales de Mesoamérica (CIRMA) in June 1987. For many years, these academic meetings have been run by Maya linguists and cultural activists in cooperation with a few foreign linguists. The 1987 *taller* ended with an excursion of the entire group to the site of Copan, where Linda happened to be—she spent a sabbatical at Copan meticulously recording the entire corpus of hieroglyphic inscriptions at the site. The Maya group, led by Martín Chacach, a Kaqchikel who then was the director of the Proyecto Lingüístico Francisco Marroquín (PLFM), asked Linda to be their guide through the history of Copan. Linda took the entire day to lead the Maya through the site or, more correct, to give an energetic, inspired, and passionate "performance" of the sculptural program created by the rulers of Copan. Although Linda's Spanish was not (and never became) the most perfect, she was able to communicate her ideas and to get the entire group involved in the enterprise of decipherment. Linda understood how to link the messages recorded in the inscriptions to ideas and concepts of the Maya. She showed that a lot of hieroglyphic vocabulary has indeed survived in modern Mayan languages, and she invited the Maya to contribute their ideas and alternative interpretations. Her deep passion for Copan and the ancient Maya must have created a lasting impression on the group. They realized that Linda's involvement was more than purely academic and that she enjoyed teaching and sharing her insights.

Martín Chacach, who later became one of Linda's dearest friends, asked her during lunch on one of these days whether she would be interested in giving a three-day course on epigraphy for the Maya that same summer. Linda's reply was positive, and she later told us that she felt greatly honored by this invitation extended by Maya intellectuals. Until then, academic interchange between Maya and foreign scientists was limited to cooperation with linguists and social anthropologists. In Guatemala, Maya research was an asymmetrical relationship where Maya were confined to the role of informants; the agenda of research projects and the motives and concerns for investigations and publications were not written and defined by the Maya themselves. Only a few foreign scholars have attempted to challenge these relations. One was Terry Kaufman, an American linguist who had started to offer professional linguistic training to Maya in the Instituto Lingüístico Francisco Marroquín as early as 1970. He was soon joined by other linguists such as Nora England and William Norman, who provided skills to the Maya that were not available to them in Guatemala (Warren 1998:x). Still, this kind of interaction in which scholars returned knowledge to the Maya was confined to those sciences that simply by the pure nature of the "object" studied addressed the needs, thoughts, and demands of present-day Maya. Other sciences, such as history, archaeology, and epigraphy, never, or only indirectly, saw themselves confronted with issues related to contemporary Maya.

The Lack of Access to the Past

Maya archaeology was, and still is, dominated by foreign scholars; most of the leading Guatemalan archaeologists have received their education abroad and belong to the "Ladino" sector of Guatemalan society. Although the national institutions in charge of the cultural heritage demand reports written in Spanish from each archaeological project, the actual publications about the excavations, such as at Tikal, Piedras Negras, and El Mirador, are issued in English, a language inaccessible to the Maya. New insights into prehispanic Maya civilization hardly make their way to the Guatemalan public, and they reach even less the Maya themselves. Although in the past decade more Guatemalans have become high-ranking and internationally recognized archaeologists, there is yet not a single Maya in a responsible position involved in an archaeological excavation. This is in part because Maya university students prefer to study careers that are closer to their immediate needs. The history, or more precisely, the historiography of the Maya, whether prehispanic or modern, is shaped by foreigners. This is not to say that the Maya do not produce history, but their history, written, for example, in the sixteenth-century *Anales de los Kaqchikeles* and in the *Popol Vuh* and recounted and modified every day in what we call oral traditions, has not the power of that version of history that is produced by scientists, the shamans of our society. The different narratives about history hardly overlap. Cultural anthropologists study Maya oral history because of their research interests in discourse analysis or the reconstruction of local histories. The agenda of their research is based on the requirements of the academic community in their countries of origin.

In order to be heard, Maya historians have to adopt a "Western" academic discourse and express their history in the paradigms of science. The institutions where this kind of history is written and debated, universities and national research institutions, however, are hardly accessible to the Maya. The Maya are underrepresented in the academic system of Guatemala as well as in Mexico. Only about 1 percent of the young Maya population of the country receives a university education (Allebrand 1997:113). According to Demetrio Cojtí (1995), one of the leading Maya intellectuals of Guatemala, the universities are not made for the Maya and exclude topics that are relevant to the Maya people. The universities do not offer classes designed to promote and study Maya history. Furthermore, there are no classes dedicated to the study of Maya documents or where Maya could learn their ancient writing system. Cojtí states that Maya, in order to learn about the history of their people, have to leave their country and study abroad. Although this situation has changed recently, especially because of the academic program of the Universidad Rafael Landívar, which has given full scholarships and five-year grants to roughly one thousand Maya students (10 percent of the total enrollment), there are still hardly any contacts between archaeologists and Maya intellectuals. Prehispanic history is still in the hands of people outside the Maya world.

The meeting between the members of the Proyecto Lingüístico Francisco Marroquín and Linda was a happy circumstance. In Linda they met a scholar who originally came from outside the academic establishment and who had always felt a deep obligation to share her knowledge and passion for what she was doing. Linda had extensive experience teaching workshops to enthusiastic lay people from a variety of backgrounds. At the same time Linda met a group of Maya eager to learn about their past, Maya who all had had previous experience in cooperating with foreign scientists. Thus Linda went to Antigua to start the first workshop. Assisted by linguists Kathryn Josserand and Nicholas Hopkins, she gave a three-day introduction on Maya hieroglyphic writing to a group of approximately twenty-five Maya from the Proyecto, by then the leading independent linguistic institution in Guatemala. The workshop, and until 1996 all following workshops, was housed in a room of the former monastery of La Compañía de Jesús in Antigua. The room was otherwise used as the ceramic laboratory for CIRMA and was stuffed with broken incense burners, utilitarian ceramics, and large storage vessels from Cakhay and many other archaeological sites in the highlands of Guatemala. Ironically, before it was acquired by the Jesuits for their monastery, this site was the house of Bernal Díaz del Castillo, who wrote *La Verdadera Historia de la Conquista de la Nueva España (The True History of the Conquest of New Spain)*.

The first *taller* ended successfully, and Linda was invited to come back. In 1989, after her usual visit to Copan, Linda once again traveled to Antigua and gave a workshop on the Tablet of the 96 Glyphs from Palenque. The thirty participants, all members of the Proyecto Lingüístico Francisco Marroquín, were especially interested in the syntax of the text, the use of semantic couplets and metaphors that parallels linguistic features of their own forms of verbal art. The five-day course ended with the translation of the hieroglyphic inscription of the tablet from its original Classic Ch'ol into the languages of the participants involved: Kaqchikel, K'iche', Mam, Ixil, Q'anjob'al, Q'eqchi', and Poqomam. Martín Chacach proudly presented Linda with a hieroglyphic thank-you letter; it was written in the Kaqchikel language but used Maya hieroglyphic signs (Figure 13.1). It was probably the first time that hieroglyphs were used to write a modern Mayan language.

The Institutionalization of the Antigua Workshops

The next year, Linda and Nikolai Grube met again at Copan for research on the newly discovered hieroglyphic inscriptions. Linda asked Nikolai to join her in teaching the next workshop about the making of history in the inscriptions and political program of Shield Jaguar II and Bird Jaguar IV of Yaxchilan. The workshop was organized so that there would be two days of introduction to Maya hieroglyphic writing, followed by three days during which the history of Yaxchilan would be summarized and two days of work in small groups. Because the group was very large, Linda and Nikolai divided the teaching so that Linda would teach the inscriptions of Shield Jaguar II and Nikolai those of his succes-

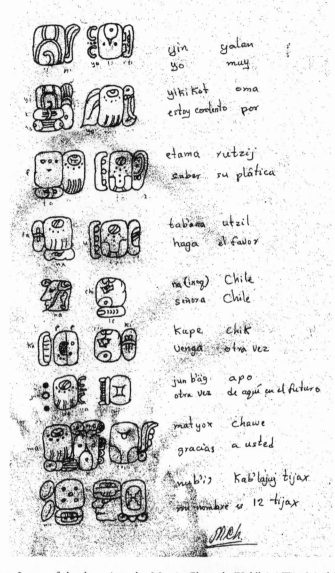

yin	yalan
yo	muy
yikikot	oma
estoy contento	por
etama	rutzij
saber	su plática
tabana	utzil
haga	el favor
na (ixoq)	Chile
señora	Chile
kape	chik
venga	otra vez
jun b'äg	apo
otra vez	de aquí en el futuro
matyox	chawe
gracias	a usted
nub'i	Kab'lajuj tijax
mi nombre es	12 tijax

MCh.

Figure 13.1. Letter of thanks written by Martín Chacach (Kab'lajuj Tijax) in hieroglyphs. This was the first Maya letter written in Kaqchikel using Maya hieroglyphs.

sor, Bird Jaguar IV. For Nikolai this was the first time that he discussed Maya hieroglyphic inscriptions with Maya intellectuals. Although he had spent years of fieldwork in a Yucatec Maya village in central Quintana Roo in Mexico, it seemed to him that there was no reason for them to talk about hieroglyphs or the prehispanic past. For him, there was no way that prehispanic history and the agenda of modern Maya could ever be joined. There was this dead culture on the one side and contemporary Maya on the other side who presented themselves as the inheritors of a colonial past. The Yaxchilan workshop for the first time confronted him with Maya intellectuals who had become the architects of a national movement for ethnic vindication, searching for strategies to establish new connections to their precolonial past. For them, the past was more than just a matter of academic interest; prehispanic history as uncovered by the recent advances in Maya epigraphy was a central element in the definition of a Maya identity. Nikolai and Linda suddenly saw themselves in an influential position that required a maximum of responsibility. There was a group of powerful intellectuals, among them Demetrio Cojtí, Martín Chacach, Narciso Cojtí, José Mucía Batz, David Yilos, E. Espinoza, Raxche' Demetrio Rodríguez, and José Chaclan, who were national and even international disseminators of ideas and knowledge and who treated Linda and Nikolai with the greatest possible confidence.

On the last afternoon of this workshop the participants presented the results of their small work groups. It seems that the presence of women on the Yaxchilan lintels had made an especially deep impression. Seeing women portrayed on important monuments sparked discussion of gender roles in Maya society and showed that women were held in high respect and even held high offices in ancient Maya society. Nikolai's reply that women held power and became true rulers only four times in Maya history, always in situations of dynastic crisis, was countered by the statement that the function women have in Maya society is exactly what makes them so powerful—they are vehicles of continuity and stability; female power was only more secretive and not as outward and public as male claims. Nikolai soon recognized that debating Maya history was more than just presenting it: this was a workshop in the best sense of the word, where our point of view was challenged. Often we found ourselves confronted with issues we had never considered, at least never discussed in a public context. More than once we had to confess ignorance and irritation.

In 1991 it was difficult to accommodate a hieroglyphic workshop in the time schedules of the PLFM. Instead of teaching a weeklong course on hieroglyphic writing, Linda and Nikolai invited a new group of young Maya linguists who had constituted themselves in Antigua in 1990 using the name *Oxlajuuj Keej Maya Aj'tz'iib'* ("Thirteen Deer" Maya Authors, OKMA). The name derives from the day in the 260-day cycle *(Cholq'iij)* when they came together for the first time

Figure 13.2. Discovering Mixco Viejo in 1992. The students around Linda are members of Oxlajuuj Keej Maya' Aj'tz'iib' (photograph by Nikolai Grube).

during a visit to Mixco Viejo, the old capital, probably of the Poqom, north of Guatemala City (Figure 13.2). This visit was an opportunity to debate the continuities between Classic period Maya architecture and Postclassic architecture and civilization of the highlands.

The Involvement of Maya Daykeepers

By 1992 the hieroglyphic workshops in Antigua already had become a kind of institution. They were announced and broadcast nationwide in the new Maya media that were created everywhere in connection with and in response to the celebrations of the Quinto Centenario. The topic of the 1992 *taller* was highly significant: that year Linda and David Freidel, in conjunction with many of their colleagues, had made significant progress in the understanding of Maya creation mythology as represented in the inscriptions of Palenque and Quirigua. For the first time it became possible to establish links among the creation of the universe in 3114 B.C.E.; Maya imagery and iconography on sculpture and painted ceramics; the narrative of the creation of the world as recounted in the *Popol Vuh;* modern beliefs about Maya cosmology; the creation of maize; and other related issues (Freidel et al. 1993). Although young linguists and cultural activists constituted the core of the participants, for the first time there were also Maya daykeepers in this group, specialists in prognostication using the 260-day calendar, such as Rodolfo García Matzar, Manuel Pacheco, Florentino Ajpacaja Tum, and Luis Morales Choy. They were an important addition to the group of participants, most of whom came from a more urban context and were university-educated intellectuals. The daykeepers brought in knowledge that the other participants could not contribute—not only the knowledge of the ancient calendar but also deep insights into Maya cosmology and religious ceremonies as celebrated in the rural areas.

This workshop became highly interactive. We were no longer the authoritative experts, but equals. We debated the same issues, simply from two different perspectives. Discussions of a single scene on a painted vase could occupy the entire day, for instance the well-known scene of the dressing of the Maize God. The daykeepers observed that the idea that the young maize plant is dressed before it comes out as a tender sprout is widely known and even present in metaphorical phrases describing its birth. This creation workshop had a deep impact on the participants because it provided strong arguments that contemporary Maya religion, so-called *costumbre,* had its roots in religious beliefs of the Classic period. The Guatemalan sociologist Mario Roberto Morales, one of the strongest critics of the Maya movement, calls contemporary Maya spiritualism a new invention without authentic historical roots: *"esos rituales que los mayas se están inventando expresan hibridación"* (Blanck and Colindres 1996:23). Together with the daykeepers, we debated and defined the Preclassic roots of Maya shamanism and the continuity of some of the basic concepts of Maya spirituality.

After a week of intense workshops, the group traveled together with Linda and Nikolai to Copan, where they intended to study the manifestation of Maya creation mythology in the sculpture and inscriptions of the site. They were accompanied by German journalists, who published a long article on the Maya movement and especially on the rediscovery of the past by contemporary Maya in the popular magazine *Geo.* The issue of the revitalization of Maya culture was regarded by the editors as having such interest that the article became the main contribution in an issue of the journal entirely dedicated to the Maya.

In 1993, the leading Guatemalan epigrapher, Federico Fahsen, who had visited the workshops in 1991 and 1992 but had not actively taught, joined Linda and

Nikolai. Federico came from an entirely different background; trained as an architect, he became a politician and ambassador of Guatemala to the United States during one of the country's most difficult times. It was in the United States where Federico began to do research on Maya hieroglyphic writing and where he came into contact with Linda and other colleagues. In the 1990s, Federico became closely involved in the Maya movement as a friend, advisor, and intermediary between the movement and governmental institutions. As a member of the Commission on Sacred Sites, he took one of the leading roles in the peace process, although the task of the commission to produce a comprehensive survey of the country's Maya religious centers finally failed. Late in 1999, however, new efforts were being undertaken with his participation.

Federico's involvement in the *talleres* has been of greatest significance: being a member of the country's European-identified elite, his participation has become a visible mark of the structural changes that Guatemala has undergone in recent years. Federico since then has participated in all additional workshops and continues to interact with Maya intellectuals and leaders of the Maya movement. The theme of the 1993 workshop was the *Dresden Codex*. This codex is of great importance for the Maya movement, Maya spirituality, and Maya priests today. Maya daykeepers have learned to read the day signs and numerals in the codices, but they had no access to the decipherment of the noncalendrical passages. Maya shamans in rituals use copies of the *Codex;* they are placed on altars and mountain shrines. The Maya movement instrumentalizes the codices as a sign of an authentic prehispanic literary culture that rivaled that of Europe. The burning of the codices by Diego de Landa has been interpreted as a sign of European intolerance of and disrespect for their sacred knowledge. Images of the codices are used widely in Maya publications and pamphlets published by Maya activists. Participants in this workshop learned not only to read the Venus and eclipse pages of the *Dresden Codex* but also to write their own calendars and prediction tables.

A New Workshop in Yucatan

That same year the three of us received an invitation to give a hieroglyphic workshop for a Maya cultural group in Valladolid, Yucatan. Grace Bascope, a student at Southern Methodist University, established contact with this group. After the end of the Guatemalan workshop, Linda and Nikolai traveled to Yucatan—Federico was unable to attend because of other commitments. In Saki/Valladolid, Linda and Nikolai met a mixed group of cultural activists, mostly bilingual teachers, who had founded Mayaon ("we are Maya"), an organization defending and promoting Maya culture and language in the Yucatan Peninsula. This was an entirely different group with a completely different history.

Whereas the participants in the Guatemalan workshops represented a variety of highland languages, such as K'iche', Kaqchikel, Mam, Poqomam, Poqomchi', Q'eqchi', Q'anjob'al, Popti', Tz'utujiil, and occasionally other languages, such as Ixil and Mopan, the Yucatecan group had the same linguistic background. The lingua franca of the Guatemalan group was Spanish, the only language common to all of them (although Kaqchikel and K'iche' are becoming kinds of indigenous linguae francae). The first language of the Yucatec group was Yucatec Maya. Spanish was used only in those situations where the lack of technical vocabulary would make the use of Yucatec difficult or impossible. Most of the instruction would therefore take place in Spanish because the vocabulary for talking about Maya epigraphy would still have to be created. Nikolai, who had spent a lot of time in a monolingual Maya village in Quintana Roo, occasionally attempted to switch to Yucatec; however, the use of Yucatec excluded Linda from the discourse and therefore was limited to informal conversations. Another difference of the Yucatec workshop was its rural setting. Although the first workshop took place in the offices of the local INI (National Institute for Indigenous Affairs) on the outskirts of Valladolid, all other workshops thereafter were housed in a large Maya-style thatched roof house constructed as the seat of Mayaon's cultural activities in the entrance to the village of Chichimila. Finally, the Yucatec Maya movement is much more limited in its ambitions and not a large, nationwide phenomenon as in Guatemala. The deep schism that runs through Guatemalan society and makes it possible to identify "Maya" and "Ladinos" as opposing groups does not exist in Yucatan, where a process of *mestizaje* can be observed that did not transform Maya into "Ladinos" but allowed both groups to live together. Yucatec Maya is not only used in the rural countryside but is also the language of some of the urban middle class. In public discourse, the intention to preserve Maya culture and language is always present. Nevertheless, the Maya themselves view this public meddling with great skepticism. Although Yucatec Maya have become archaeologists and anthropologists, access to precolonial history is still extremely limited. One of the factors certainly is the reluctance of Mexican archaeologists and historians to accept the recent breakthroughs in the reading of Maya hieroglyphs (Coe 1992:208–209). Another factor that has prevented Maya history from becoming widely disseminated is the focus on Central Mexico as the core of Mexican identity. Official Mexican history includes the biographies of the Aztec kings and their heroic fight against Spanish colonialism and so do most Mexican schoolbooks. The Yucatan Peninsula has witnessed a different history and in regard to its culture and historic ties was more closely connected to its southern neighbors of Belize and Guatemala than to the distant capital.

The first weeklong workshop in Yucatan was dedicated to a general introduction to Mayan writing. The similarity of the Yucatec Mayan language to the

Figure 13.3. Front page of *Iximuleew,* a Maya newspaper published monthly in Guatemala under the auspices of the Academia de las Lenguas Mayas (ALMG). The name of the newspaper is also written with syllabic signs.

Ch'olan language of the hieroglyphs greatly facilitated the teaching; participants basically had to learn only the hieroglyphic signs; once they recognized the signs they often were able to read a text based on their knowledge of the language. Because all participants had Maya names, it was a great surprise and joy for them to discover their last names—Balam, Kauil, Chan, Itza, and Cocom—written in the inscriptions.

The Revival of Maya Hieroglyphs

In July 1994, Linda, Federico, and Nikolai gave another workshop in Antigua, hosted by OKMA. The topic of this workshop was hieroglyphic inscriptions on Maya ceramics. Maya hieroglyphic writing had already found wide dissemination and was employed by Mayan cultural activists in a variety of public contexts. Whereas in earlier years hieroglyphs had been used merely as a decorative device, Maya writing now had become meaningful, and hieroglyphic messages, written in syllabic signs, adorn Maya newspapers, documents, posters, and invitations to family fiestas (Figure 13.3). For their identifying logos, Maya activist forums use hieroglyphs that spell their name. Our intention was to provide Maya activists with ancient models for such texts. Hieroglyphic inscriptions on ceramics present a hieroglyphic formula, which has been deciphered as a complex dedication phrase presenting many variants (Coe 1992). The study of these phrases would allow Maya to create their own dedication inscriptions for houses, public buildings, sacred places, and works of art. During that workshop students painted their own pots and ceramics with texts to their liking as exercises for future texts of all kinds.

After the first Yucatec workshop for Mayaon turned out successfully, we were asked to return. In August 1994 we gave a workshop on the creation of the universe that focused strictly on the episode of the birth, death, and rebirth of the Maize God. This was an issue of greatest interest to the bilingual teachers who were all working in remote villages where agriculture and related ceremonies dominate most of the activities. We were thrilled to see that the past year's workshop was highly successful insofar as some of the participants had become fully literate in hieroglyphic writing (Figure 13.4). As bilingual teachers they had soon integrated ancient Maya writing into their curriculum. Crisanto Kumul, a teacher from Sisbikchen, Yucatan, and one of the leading intellectuals of the Mayaon group, had written poems and short stories in Yucatec and used hieroglyphs to write these down. He had soon turned into a real expert not only on Maya writing but also on Maya culture in general and continues to publish commentaries on issues related to Maya cultural history in regional Yucatec newspapers, such as *Por Eso* and *Novedades de Yucatan.*

In 1995 other Maya groups contacted us asking for workshops on topics related to Maya history and religion. A group of Maya shamans organized in COCADI (Coordinadora Cakchiquel de Desarrollo Integral), a Kaqchikel organization located in Boko/Chimaltenango that, among other activities, attempts to organize and coordinate activities of Maya shamans, invited us to conduct another workshop on Maya cosmology and the creation of the universe. Here we were exposed to a large group of shamans from all over the highlands who had rejected Christianity, seeing both Catholicism and the various Protestant churches as forms of colonialism. Some of the participants are nationally known representatives of Maya spirituality, such as Simon Taquira, Domingo Tac Txay, Emilio Saluj, Pedro Tum Coy, and Ruberto Poz. This "shamanic wing" of the Maya movement was much more rooted and experienced in Maya spirituality than the university-trained Maya who represented the majority of our previous workshops. Often illiterate in our alphabetic writing system, these shamans quickly learned to read Maya hieroglyphs. Although most of them had received only minimal formal education in the Guatemalan school system, they were self-conscious opponents who criticized and challenged our interpretations even more than those members of the Maya movement who were used to classroom settings. We repeated the workshop with the same topic with the linguists and cul-

Itzamna Kawil Uuk.

Figure 13.4. A hieroglyphic text written by Itzamna Tiburcio Kawil Uc, a ten-year-old Maya from Tepich, Quintana Roo. The text reads *Itzamna K'awiil Uk ku k'at oltzi tech yabach utzil* "Itzamna Kawil Uc wishes you all the best."

tural activists from the OKMA group, the "academic wing" of the Maya movement (Warren 1998:189–190).

Participants in the COCADI workshop also asked us to give a creation workshop in the Kaqchikel village of San Andres Semetabaj. This workshop, conducted by Linda and Federico, was the first held in a Maya village with the participation of an extremely heterogeneous group that included village elders, Catholic Action activists, Maya leaders, members of women's organizations, local high school students, and, of course, shamans. At their request, two more two-day workshops were conducted in San Andres, this time by Federico only, and in 1997 and 1998 another pair of two-day meetings were held in Xelaju/ Quetzaltenango with many of the Maya shamans of the COCADI group.

Finally, Linda and Nikolai met in Valladolid again for a third workshop under the auspices of Mayaon (Figure 13.5). This was dedicated to the *Dresden Codex*

Figure 13.5. Studying the hieroglyphic lintels in the upper level of the Monjas, Chichen Itza. Linda is joined by bilingual Yucatec schoolteachers from Mayaon, Valladolid (photograph by Nikolai Grube).

and was highly stimulating for all parties involved. Linguistically, the language of the *Dresden Codex* is very close to actual Yucatec Maya (although it preserves many Ch'olan archaisms). Furthermore, the *Dresden Codex* was probably written somewhere on the Yucatan Peninsula and therefore is culturally significant for modern Yucatec Maya. Although the majority of attendants were teachers, some of them came from very traditional family backgrounds and had parents who trained them in shamanic knowledge. Their knowledge about sacred plants, manifestations of the rain god Chaak, and food offerings contributed greatly to a more sophisticated understanding of the *Dresden Codex*. Many new discoveries and even new decipherments were made that still await their proper publication.

Discussing Historical Discourse

In 1996 OKMA in Antigua volunteered again to house the annual glyph workshop. We decided to confront the Maya with a theme that was rarely discussed in the Maya movement: warfare and alliances in the Classic period. Although Maya activists acknowledge the existence of conflict and warfare between their groups, this is still a kind of taboo issue. In the light of ongoing unresolved land disputes between Maya communities and speakers of different Mayan languages, tales of conflict clearly challenge the image of unity of the Maya movement. Furthermore, it cannot be denied that there is a strong competition between representatives of different linguistic groups about resources and political presence, which has also lead to occasional conflicts within the Maya movement. Maya leaders fear that "scientific" (and therefore authoritative) statements about warfare among Maya in the past could be used by their critics and political opponents to split the Maya movement. Opponents of the Maya movement also used the internal conflict between the Maya as an argument justifying the Spanish invasion. It turned out, however, that the group assembled in Antigua did not want to cover up this enmity. Rather, they sought to parallel warfare and conflict with those of many other nations before their formal unification took place. They added that it would be useless to hide the truth; instead, understanding the agendas of previous conflicts now could help to prevent them in the present and future.

Though the selection of the topics of the workshops initially was done by us, this has changed in recent times. It cannot be denied, however, that the Maya at first relied on our authority as scientists and translators of their past. We have been aware of this hierarchy and the colonial dilemma implied by our position and have often discussed these issues both among us and together with the Maya. There is no simple solution to avoid these unequal relationships. To resign being a teacher would have made no contribution to rectify the injustices of the colonial situation at all. We believe together with Linda that we do not have a right to keep back information from the Maya. Our intention was to open a door for an intellectual interchange, a long conversation about history that would sensitize both parties involved. We hoped to decolonialize the making of history by placing the means of its production in the hands of the Maya. We are aware that this will involve more than just the workshops. This plan requires a strategy for changing the academic discourse and its political and economic context in general. Linda has approached this goal very pragmatically by providing scholarships for Maya students, invitations to Maya to attend workshops at the University of Texas at Austin, and financial support for independent Maya research projects (such as the monolingual K'iche' dictionary written by Florentino Ajpacaja Tum).

In 1996 we also returned to Yucatan to conduct a workshop on the topic of dedication texts, which we had given before in Antigua. This theme was selected not only because some members of Mayaon were interested in this genre of texts as a model for their own use of Maya writing but also because it enabled us to focus on hieroglyphic inscriptions from Yucatan, where this genre of texts is especially common. The 1996 workshop in Yucatan was the last in which Linda participated. On the last evening, a very spirited discussion articulated Maya rights and dreams of a Maya nation, dreams that went even beyond those of the Guatemalan Maya movement and that were fueled by recent developments in Chiapas.

Linda's Legacy

Linda and Nikolai planned to meet in Antigua for the July 1997 workshop to be hosted by OKMA. Shortly before final arrangements were made, Linda discovered that she had cancer and cancelled all plans for the summer. In the same message informing us about her state, she added a final sentence: "Don't forget we were going to do Quirigua and Copan!" We, the two authors, took this as a quest to continue the workshops without Linda and conducted a workshop for sixty members of the grown OKMA research group, which culminated in a three-day trip to Copan and Quirigua. In Valladolid, Nikolai was in charge of a workshop on Yucatec history, which focused on the interpretation of indigenous chronicles as well as the reading of hieroglyphic inscriptions from Yucatan. While the workshop was held, festivities took place to celebrate the 150th anniversary of the beginning of the Caste War. Being the leading cultural group in Yucatan, Mayaon was involved in many of the activities accompanying the celebrations. Not surprisingly, the anniversary made the group extend the debate on Maya history to include the changes that took place in the colonial period. A most intense discussion centered around the question of whether there is a "project" in Yucatec Maya and in Maya history in general. How much do the different Maya groups have in common? Can prehispanic history actually help the Maya movement to become international and to cross the borders between the present states of Mexico, Guatemala, and Belize, which have significant Maya populations?

Linda's untimely death was widely bemoaned by all groups of Maya shamans, leaders, and intellectuals. At the time of her death she had become a symbol for cooperation between Western scholars and the Maya. The priority that contemporary Maya had received toward the end of her life was widely recognized and appreciated. Her publications, although still awaiting Spanish translation, have become most influential among Maya scholars and historians. The burial of her ashes above Lake Atitlan in a Maya ceremony, conducted by Maya shamans from all over the Guatemalan highlands, has even increased the respect of leading Maya intellectuals for her. Linda has certainly turned into an icon, associated with the uncovering of Maya history and thought. Her willingness to share her insights was almost unlimited. She enthusiastically supported the Maya in public presentations but also through sometimes very private acts of solidarity and help. Continuing without the "Linda icon" was difficult, but fortunately, the organizational structures of the *talleres* were so well established that we were able to conduct a workshop on the history of Tikal in 1998 that climaxed in a four-day trip to Tikal, Uaxactun, Yaxha, and Topoxte. In 1999, we gave a weeklong workshop on Palenque in Antigua, once again under the auspices of OKMA. This was fueled by the new discoveries from Temple XIX at Palenque and new insights about Maya theology, sacred images, and the religious obligations of vassal lords that in some ways paralleled the structure of present-day *cofradías*. Nikolai went once again to Valladolid. He had been asked to provide a general introduction on Maya writing in cooperation with Mayaon, but this time the invited participants included mainly people from rural hamlets who had never before had access to recent information on the prehispanic past. Many participants came from the village of Xocen and included local authorities. Their interest in the past was enormous. A visible sign of their desire to reconnect with their precolonial roots is the construction of a local Temple of the Talking Cross in the form of a Maya temple in Puuc style.

We have made plans to continue the workshops for the Maya in the future, incorporating other volunteers from our academic world and other Maya groups. The future of these meetings and the directions they will go is in the hands of the Maya. We feel our obligation to return knowledge of the past to its inheritors. Even more important than the sheer facts is the command of the resources from which history is made. Access to the primary sources of their history—whether inscriptions, chronicles written in the sixteenth and seventeenth centuries, or even archaeological data—is the key for the creation of a new Maya history, a history free of European prejudices and academic biases. There are various reasons why epigraphy plays a special role. It is not only that epigraphers were the first to make their sources available. It is the transparency of epigraphy that makes it a dynamic field where an infinite number of minds can contribute ideas, reassess problems, and unmask falsehoods. Epigraphers leave their data as found. They neither destroy nor frame it in such a way that alternative interpretations are impossible. The reading of hieroglyphs gives us some of the most tangible and useful insights we have into the Maya past. The past uncovered by epigraphy is not the same as the past described in the *Anales de los Kaqchikeles* or other documents written in the colonial period. It is a precolonial past that in many conventional histories is covered quickly because, as was believed by European historians, it left few traces and had no historical future. Whereas most historical narratives about the Maya and the history of European and Maya encounters were written by Europeans selecting only documents written by the Spaniards, Maya historians now turn to their side of the history, focusing on indigenous accounts. Hieroglyphic writing is seen as particularly authentic, ancient, and undisturbed by foreign views. It is no great surprise that documents written in hieroglyphic writing became a prime focus of interest for Maya historians striving to reconstruct their own view.

Since Linda started to give workshops, not only the passive knowledge of the script has disseminated widely but also its active use has been reinforced. Although Maya hieroglyphic writing probably has never been used by the genetic forefathers of present-day highland Maya groups (this is a point of major discussion and discrepancy between us and some Maya activists who claim that the K'iche' and other groups had hieroglyphic codices), it is regarded by them as "their script" in the same way as Tikal is "their past" (and in the same way that we Europeans and North Americans link "our" past to Greece). Hieroglyphic writing was (probably) restricted to the Ch'olan-speaking elite of the great lowland cities. Its appropriation can be seen as a sign that the Maya movement indeed is a "pan-Maya" movement, which strives to incorporate all Maya groups. Maya history is not understood as the history of different groups but as a common trajectory with different local manifestations. We have often been accused of falsifying history by establishing forced links between contemporary highland Maya and the great lowland Maya civilization. If Maya study their history, we were told, they should devote themselves to the history of their particular group; they should research the history of the K'iche', the Poqomam, and so on. It is indeed important not to ignore local histories and the less known and less spectacular histories of the highland Maya. In fact, Maya historians do read and study documents that deal with the history of their linguistic group (Warren 1998:198). The issue is more complex, however. We try not to impose our often very different view on the Maya; rather, the desire to connect to Tikal and Copan derives from the Maya themselves. The Maya say that there is a strong interest by critics of the Maya movement to disconnect them from glorious and highly symbolic "ruins" of a long-buried past. Official history very often admires the breathtaking architecture and intellectual achievements of the ancient Maya and insists that the collapse of the great cities and then the Spanish Conquest along with the process of *mestizaje* terminated the independent trajectory of Maya history where Maya existed as the subjects, not as the objects, of history. In the process of revitalization and development of a new Maya consciousness, the reinterpretation of history becomes as important for the Maya as it has been for other nations in the past two hundred years (Hobsbawm 1983).

Many Maya have developed an alternative literacy in hieroglyphs. They use hieroglyphic messages in a variety of public spaces (Sturm 1996). Because of its intrinsic symbolic value, Maya hieroglyphic writing is employed as an icon of self-consciousness in publications, address cards, letterheads, newspapers, and inscriptions on community centers. This literacy is not confined to the urban Maya elite. Through publications, small workshops, and finally also its teaching in

Maya schools, hieroglyphic literacy is astonishingly popular. We have seen small children who were able to write their names in Maya script. In order to adapt the script to the phonology of highland Mayan languages, the Maya have developed a system of diacritics that, added to certain syllabic signs, converts them into their highland equivalent (Schele and Grube 1996:133).

We became involved in the Maya movement accidentally. When Linda was asked by Martín Chacach to give a workshop at Copan, she did not foresee that this was the beginning of a long process of cooperation. In 1987 the Maya movement had hardly taken shape, and nobody imagined the dimensions the movement would take. As the recuperation and rewriting of history is one of the central issues of revitalization movements in general (Wallace 1956), so the appropriation of ancient history became one of the major concerns of the Maya movement. Kay Warren (1998) observes that the efforts of the Maya movement focus on cultural issues. She interprets this emphasis as a Maya strategy of survival based on fatal experience with European-style revolutionary or armed movements. Until now, the movement has been more successful than any other earlier attempt to regain public space. The knowledge that writing and history played a vital part in the survival of Maya culture today was a source of great happiness for Linda. She regarded this work and the contact with contemporary Maya as the most important task in her life.

Appendix

In September 1999, Nikolai interviewed Lolmay, a young Maya intellectual from San Andres Semetabaj, Department of Solola, Guatemala. Lolmay, who uses his Maya name both in private and in public contexts rather than his Christian name, Pedro García Matzar, has been part of the OKMA research group since its founding. He has assisted in all workshops that we held in Antigua and has become fully literate in Maya hieroglyphic writing. Lolmay is one of the leading Maya linguists and cultural activists as well as author of books and articles on the Kaqchikel language, Mayan linguistics in general, and language politics in Guatemala. We include a text of the interview here. The English translation is by the editor; the original Spanish text follows.

Q: Considering all of the economic, social, and political problems of the Maya people of Guatemala, don't you think that epigraphy workshops represent a luxury, something attractive but of little urgency for the Maya people?

Lolmay: I think that depends on the point of view of analysis. First, because of the social situation of the community, its interests are going to be food, housing, access to potable water, and other material things; people don't perceive the importance and necessity of an education, much less the knowledge of history. The situation of the workshops is similar. For the majority of the population, they are exotic, part of a historical past that would be good to know. Nevertheless, for the professional and intellectual Maya, it is important to know our own history, which soon will be written according to our vision.

Q: Given that there exist so many Mayan linguistic groups in Guatemala, what importance does history and cosmology of the Classic period assume for the highland Maya? There are many critics who say that the highland Maya should study the history of *their* people, written in the *Annals of the Kaqchikels*, the *Popol Vuh*, etc.

Lolmay: I believe that too is a question of individual perspective. First, some academics want to break the bond uniting us with our ancestors, that is, that the Maya of the Classic period disappeared and the various contemporary groups are different, as seen in their history preserved in the more recent documents, such as the *Popol Vuh*, the *Annals of the Kaqchikels,* and others. I believe that this perspective lacks vision because it does not consider the similarity of life of the Classic period with the life recounted in the aforementioned documents, nor even with the life of today. Nevertheless, there are differences. In fact, they represent distinct eras, and different things existed, but one can see the chain of connection.

Q: What aspects of the Classic culture are of greatest importance for the Maya movement?

Lolmay: I believe that the most relevant aspects of the Classic period which assume much importance for the Maya movement are diverse, and I would like to mention a few. Social organization: in spite of the failure [i.e., the Classic Maya collapse] for specific reasons which are already known, the social organization is interesting to observe in that we might have a similar organization without the mistakes which they had. Today, one speaks of the meaning of concepts of state and nation. What will our approach be if we do not know what their organization was in the Classic period? Education: presently, one speaks of a Maya university, also of a Maya education. But how can one begin if one does not know the history of the education of the Maya? There are ideas about what was Maya education, but they are still vague. Knowledge of different branches of science, among which can be mentioned astronomy, botany, architecture, medicine, and linguistics. For us, it is highly interesting to learn that the writing of the Classic period is based on a very profound knowledge of their language. Perhaps in the future, we can develop a new "Maya ethnolinguistics" based on Maya linguistic concepts and also a linguistic terminology derived from Maya words, for example.

Q: How is the work of Linda Schele seen by the present-day Maya?

Lolmay: I believe that the intellectuals think that she came to open the door that was closed between the foreign scholars and Maya people. She revealed part of the history that was unknown to us; she came to teach us that the pictures meant something, that they were more than just decoration, that they tell us our vision of our history. She taught us to write in the same manner as our ancestors, and, as a consequence, a great number of Maya organizations have their names written in hieroglyphs.

P: En frente de todos los problemas económicos, sociales y políticos del pueblo maya en Guatemala, ¿no piensas que los talleres de epigrafía representan un lujo, algo bonito pero de poca urgencia para el pueblo maya?

Lolmay: Yo pienso que depende del punto de vista de donde se analiza, primero porque si se ve la situación social de una comunidad, su interés va a ser su alimentación, su vivienda, acceso a agua potable y otras cosas materiales; no se ve la importancia y la necesidad de una educación, y mucho menos de la historia. Es algo similar la situación de los talleres, entonces quizá para la mayoría de la población sea algo muy interesante, exótico. Y ya quedó en el pasado histórico y sería bueno saberlo. Sin embargo, para los profesionales y la intelectualidad maya es importante para conocer nuestra propia historia, que dentro de poco se escribirá de acuerdo a nuestra visión.

P: Dado que existen tantos grupos lingüísticos mayas en Guatemala, ¿qué importancia asume la historia y la cosmología del tiempo clásico para los mayas del altiplano? Hay muchos críticos que dicen que los mayas del altiplano deberían estudiar la historia de sus pueblos, escrita en los *Anales de los Kaqchikeles,* el *Poopol Wuuj,* etc.

Lolmay: Creo que también es una cuestión de enfoque. Primero porque algunas personas estudiosas quieren romper ese lazo de unión con nuestros ancestros, es decir que los mayas de la época clásica desaparecieron y los diferentes grupos actuales son diferentes, por lo que su historia deben de verla en los documentos más recientes, tales como el *Poopol Wuuj,* los *Anales de los Kaqchikeles* y otros. Pienso que esta situación es falta de visión, debido a que no se ponen a pensar en la similitud de vida de la época clásica con la vida que relatan dichos documentos y aún relacionados con la vida de hoy. Sin embargo hay diferencias; de hecho son épocas distintas. Se viven cosas diferentes pero se puede ver la cadena de unión.

P: ¿Qué aspectos de la cultura clásica son de alta importancia para el movimiento maya?

Lolmay: Creo que los aspectos más relevantes de la época clásica que toman mucha importancia para el movimiento maya son diversos y quiero mencionar algunos. La organización social: A pesar de que fracasó por distintas razones que ya se conocen, es interesante ver y conocerlos para poder tener una organización similar sin los errores que se tuvieron. Hoy día se habla de la definición de conceptos de estado y nación. Entonces, ¿como será nuestro planteamiento si no conocemos cómo fue la organización en la época clásica? La educación: Actualmente se habla de una universidad maya, también de una educación maya. Pero, ¿como se puede echar a andar si no se conoce la historia de la educación de los mayas? Existen ideas sobre lo que fue la educación Maya pero todavía son muy vagas. El conocimiento de diferentes ramas de las ciencias y las ciencias mismas, dentro de las que se pueden mencionar la astronomía, la botánica, la arquitectura, la medicina, y la lingüística. Para nosotros es sumamente interesante descubrir que la escritura de la época clásica está basada en conocimientos muy profundos de su lengua. Tal vez en el futuro podríamos desarrollar una nueva 'etnolingüística maya' que se basa en conceptos lingüísticos mayas y también una terminología lingüística derivada de palabras mayas, por ejemplo.

P: ¿Como está visto el trabajo de Linda por los mayas actuales?

Lolmay: Yo creo que los intelectuales piensan que ella vino a abrir la puerta que estaba cerrada entre los estudiosos extranjeros y la gente maya. Ella dió a conocer parte de la historia que estaba desconocida por nosotros; ella vino a enseñar que los dibujos significaban algo, que eran más que solamente adorno, que nos relatan nuestra visión de nuestra historia. Ella nos enseñó a escribir de la misma forma que escribían nuestros antepasados y como consecuencia gran número de organizaciones mayas utilizan su nombre escrita con jeroglíficos.

14

The Schele Icon and Maya Mania

The Growth of Public Interest
in Maya Epigraphy

Elin C. Danien

The field of Maya studies has gone through many stages on the road from un-
fettered exploration and adventure (Brunhouse 1973, 1975; Stephens 1841, 1843;
Waldeck 1838) through early professionalization (Mason 1937; Morley 1943; Spinden 1913) to the current academic and scientific stance of the discipline (Coe
1990; Fry 1980; Peregrine and Feinman 1996). Concomitantly, public fascination
with the Maya, awakened in the nineteenth century by Stephens, grew in the
twentieth. The somewhat romanticized popular books written for public con-
sumption by Morley (1946) and Thompson (1954) offered comfortable ways to
think about a mysterious people who had lived and died a thousand years ago.
They were books by people on the inside, written to be read by people on the
outside, permitting the reader a glimpse into the otherwise closed and rather
esoteric realm of the professional archaeologist. The reader could settle back
comfortably in an easy chair and enjoy the vicarious thrills that gave rise to the
descriptive phrase "armchair archaeologist."

As the discipline matured, however, its reports became more specialized and
less accessible to the interested but uninitiated public. With the rise of the "New
Archaeology" in the 1960s, the proliferation of "self conscious scientism" (Wilk
1985) carried its interpretations ever further away from general understanding.
This lack of attention to the larger public followed on and may have stemmed
from the sometimes rancorous and ultimately successful removal of archaeology
from its earlier museum-centered role to a home in academic departments of
anthropology and archaeology (Conn 1998; Darnell 1969).

Comparable developments were taking place in the decipherment of Maya
hieroglyphic inscriptions as control of the field shifted from the dedicated ama-

teurs of the nineteenth and early twentieth centuries to become the property of the academy. Most Mayanists adhered to Thompson's theory that the Maya writing system was incapable of recording the complexities and nuance of spoken language. Heinrich Berlin's (1958) recognition of the emblem glyph did little to alter this belief. The well-regarded Tatiana Proskouriakoff (1960) had to overcome initial skepticism with her breakthrough discovery that the inscriptions of Piedras Negras were of a historical nature. Even when Thompson (1960:v) admitted the validity of her argument, the discussion remained within the academic world. The attack on Knorosov's phonetic approach (for details, see Coe 1992) is indicative of the level of rejection and outright antagonism that met any attempt by an "outsider" to unlock the secrets of ancient Maya writing.

All Mayanists are familiar with the now almost mythic tale of Linda Schele's 1970 visit to Palenque and how that experience changed her from a studio artist and art teacher to a student of Maya epigraphy; how less than three years later, in 1973, at the first Mesa Redonda she and Peter Mathews identified the Palenque king list; and how her discoveries helped bring the ancient Maya from a prehistoric people to a people with a history, a history recorded in texts she was instrumental in deciphering (Coe 1992).

The scholarly work she inspired is evidenced by many of the chapters in this volume. Here I consider a different area of her contributions, one that may not be as well recognized or appreciated within the academy: the annual glyph workshops she initiated and their influence on an ever-growing constituency. The workshop concept is hardly original, but the way in which the Maya glyph workshops operate offers a salutary example of the necessary ingredients for splendid achievement. The reasons for that success are not limited to the workshop format and perhaps might be applied more frequently to traditional teaching environments with equal success.

The Development of Glyph Workshops

Schele's glyph workshops grew out of a series of small meetings organized in 1974 by Elizabeth Benson, director of Pre-Columbian Studies and curator of the Pre-Columbian Collection at Dumbarton Oaks in Washington, D.C., where Floyd Lounsbury, Peter Mathews, David Kelley, and Linda Schele continued the pioneering work begun in 1973 at Palenque. They thrashed out the form of structural analysis that would prove so constructive in the ensuing years.

While still teaching art at the University of South Alabama, Linda Schele was invited to give a series of lectures at the University of Texas at Austin. That initial offering in November 1977 was organized by Professor Nancy Troike under the auspices of the Institute of Latin American Studies and the Departments of Anthropology, Linguistics, and Art. The flyer promised a "non-technical" explanation. Those who have heard Linda speak know that a technical explanation would have been hard put to survive her sometimes salty, down-home southern speech. One of her talents was the ability to phrase the most esoteric problem or solution in language the layperson could understand and work with. Word quickly spread about the exciting approach that built on the research of many others, refined it, and brought it to a new, more productive level.

In the spring of 1978, Schele was a visiting lecturer at Austin and used the opportunity to present the first Maya Hieroglyph Writing Workshop in the form it would maintain for the next five years. Over a two-day weekend she explained concepts and deciphered inscriptions. I was fortunate enough to attend that March 1978 meeting and was amazed to find a large and diverse audience of about 150, comprising archaeologists, linguists, art historians, students, and the interested public. To describe the format, I can do no better than to quote Michael Coe (1992:217): "These are basically one-woman performances by the charismatic Linda, a born show-woman if there ever was one, taking her rapt audience effortlessly through the most difficult material, from Knorosovian phoneticism to parentage statements." Her enthusiasm, exhortation, and inspiration swept everyone along with the joy of discovery.

In 1983 the Texas Maya Meetings expanded to include an advanced seminar, a five-day workshop that followed the weekend lectures. Instead of merely sitting in an auditorium and listening to Schele speak, participants now had the opportunity to work in groups, putting theory into practice. In these small groups, beginners worked along with the more experienced, the amateur person along with the professional, and they all knew that anyone might have the thrill of actually deciphering inscriptions and, perhaps, coming up with a previously unknown reading.

That same year, 1983, the University of Pennsylvania Museum offered its own version of a Maya weekend. As the recently appointed public programs coordinator and inspired by my attendance at that 1978 Texas Maya Meeting, I had structured the Penn weekend from the beginning as a public event designed to introduce glyph decipherment to museum members and the interested public. The presenter was Dr. Christopher Jones, a Penn archaeologist and epigrapher, whose seminal paper identifying parentage glyphs (Jones 1977) was a landmark in glyph decipherment. Jones prepared a workbook for the event (Jones 1983), although he doubted that more than twenty-five people would come. I had anticipated about seventy-five. That first year brought 125 people, all nonprofessionals. The workshop had been designed as a single event, but it was clear that the concept evoked a strong response in a broad audience. There was an immediate decision, reached even before the end of the weekend, to continue it on an annual basis.

We experimented with several formats until we settled on one that seemed to meet the needs and expectations of our audience. During two days of lectures, a dozen or so scholars presented the latest findings on many aspects of ancient Maya culture; concomitant glyph workshops were geared to glyphers of all levels of expertise. Unlike the Texas workshops, where Schele alone led the weekend workshop, at Penn each group had a different leader. This combination of workshops and lectures worked well for Penn, and in 1985 the Texas Meetings added a two-day symposium to precede the weekend workshop. The two workshops complemented each other, with Penn providing shorter, more varied workshops led by different scholars using their own worksheets and with Texas working with a single group of inscriptions.

Hundreds of people attended each of the workshops. Indeed, many people came to both Austin and Philadelphia. They came from every state and from Mexico, Honduras, Belize, Guatemala, Canada, France, and England. These meetings quickly evolved from their early approach of presentations by professionals to an audience composed of amateurs. It became an interactive meeting ground for amateurs and professionals. All the participants were engaged in seeking out the structure of the inscriptions, locating the clauses, and recognizing certain formulaic phrases. They argued, they discussed, and they taught each other. Ideas could be floated and new readings suggested by everyone. Academic credentials were of less importance than intellectual creativity.

The Workshops Increase

The workshop concept took on a life of its own. Linda's students and colleagues started their own annual glyph workshops in different regions of the country. In 1988 Tom and Carolyn Jones gave the first of their annual workshops at Humboldt State University in Arcata, California. Dorie Reents-Budet and Sharon Mujica began a series of annual workshops through Duke and the University of North Carolina starting in 1992. The following year Cleveland State University initiated an annual weeklong celebration of all things Maya, called *Kinal Winik,* and glyph workshops were a centerpiece. In 1996 Peter Mathews, who had led workshops at Texas and at Cleveland, started his own workshops at Calgary. In 1998, Kent Reilly initiated an introductory workshop at Southwest Texas State, scheduled to precede immediately the Austin meetings, to prepare rank beginners for the intensive work ahead of them.

Such annual workshops served only to whet the appetite of nonprofessionals for access to this intellectual adventure. In Philadelphia, an amateur glyph group was started by the Pre-Columbian Society at the University of Pennsylvania Museum as an outgrowth of the first Penn Maya Weekend. It meets monthly and has been doing so since 1984. An offshoot of the Philadelphia organization, the Pre-Columbian Society of Washington, D.C., has a similar glyph group. In addition, there are informal glyph groups in Minneapolis, Chicago, Albany, and Denver.

In 1988, anthropologists and linguists Kathryn Josserand and Nicholas Hopkins began what they call "taking the glyphs on the road." Since then, this couple alone has logged fifty-five workshops in towns in Mexico, Guatemala, Texas, Louisiana, Minnesota, Pennsylvania, Florida, Illinois, North Carolina, Tennessee, California, and Washington, D.C.! Other itinerant workshops were led by people such as Barbara MacLeod and Karen Bassie-Sweet. At Maya meetings that ostensibly have nothing to do with glyphs, such as the California Maya meetings at UCLA and at Brevard Community College in Florida, glyphers gather surreptitiously to compare readings and exchange new information (John Harris, personal communication 1998).

Maya meetings around the country continue to attract hundreds of people each year. The appeal seems universal. In 1989 a lengthy *New York Times* article reported on a California symposium that had considered the current state of Maya epigraphy (Blakeslee 1989). At the end of this two-page article, the reporter included a few lines about the forthcoming Penn weekend. She listed a phone number along with the information that amateurs could participate. Those amateurs promptly jammed the phone lines. That year, attendance went from two hundred to four hundred and has now leveled off at somewhat more than five hundred people each year. Although some of the attendees are academics, most are not. They are lawyers, bankers, business people, artists, homemakers, senior citizens, and adolescents, many of whom return each year. They have one common and passionate abiding interest: the study of Maya glyphs.

Additions and Supplements

Some who came to the workshops as beginners have become, through talent and tenacity, expert epigraphers in their own right. Their newfound mastery has resulted in the publication of books of scholarly as well as popular import, all developing out of the workshops themselves. The reports given by participants in the Texas advanced seminar are available in a series of publications edited by Tom Jones and Carolyn Young (Jones) (1988, 1989, 1990, 1992, 1994, 1996). John Harris, a retired research chemist, and Steve Stearns, a computer specialist, participants in both the Texas and the Penn Maya workshops, have written an introductory text on deciphering Maya hieroglyphs (Harris and Stearns 1992). Although specifically designed as a self-teaching tool, the book has been applauded by professionals (see Houston 1993b) and has been used in university courses around the country (Michael Coe, John Harris, personal communications 1996). Justin Kerr, a preeminent fine arts and museum photographer and enthusiastic participant in the Texas and Penn meetings, focused his interest on the glyphs and iconography of Maya ceramics. This led to a continuing series of books illustrating the hundreds of Maya vessels photographed by Kerr and in his database. The books, self-published by Justin Kerr and Barbara Kerr (Kerr 1989, 1990, 1992, 1994, 1997, 2000), include articles by noted scholars on ceramics-related epigraphic and iconographic discoveries.

The Maya Mystique

What does it all mean? Why does the fire burn so fiercely in the glyphers' bellies? Archaeology has always had its devotees. Fascination with the ancient Maya finds parallels in the mystique surrounding Egyptology, biblical archaeology, and the like. Part of the answer may lie in the changing demographics of the United States. The combination of longer life spans, broad educational background, earlier retirement, greater disposable income, and a healthy economy have led to an increase in the demand for more fulfilling activities in the later years of longer lives. This gave rise to the development of greater depth and breadth in nontraditional, continuing education, a model that has come to be known as "lifelong learning" (Lerner and King 1992; Oliver 1999). As mature students have filled such course rosters in community colleges and universities, their needs and demands have prompted major changes in didactic approaches (Cohen 1995; Cross 1981; Edelson and Malone 1999; Usher and Bryant 1989).

Another part of the explanation is supplied by the ease of modern travel, which simplifies access to erstwhile mysterious and unapproachable sites. The ruined cities of the enigmatic Maya are now only a plane trip away. In addition to visits by individual travelers, once off-the-beaten-path sites have become the daily destination of "study tours" led by art historians, historians, cultural anthropologists, and archaeologists. Organizations such as the EarthWatch Institute of Boston sponsor excavations that solicit (for a fee) volunteer, short-term labor and provide those volunteers with an adventurous, educational vacation. Such opportunities encourage the travelers, once returned to their home cities, to seek more intensive exploration of the ideas and cultures encountered. "Lifelong learning" has created an environment that makes continuing education a natural part of the adult life cycle. Still, the question remains: In this expanding universe of educated, interested, and intellectually curious avocational Mayanists who have the advantage of ease of travel, volunteer opportunities, and access to more traditional learning settings, why do hundreds of people continue to make an annual journey to Austin, Philadelphia, and other Maya meetings?

The Workshop as Commune

A comparison of the workshop structure with other educational approaches reveals some important distinctions. Most of the nontraditional learning environments, whether in the classroom or the field or on study tours, have a hierarchy consisting of the provider of information—classroom teacher, tour leader, or field archaeologist—and the recipients, who may be students, tourists, or volunteer laborers. A workshop, however, is a totally interactive activity. The leader works with the participants as they decipher, analyze, and interpret. The workshop leader serves as a guide, not a pedant. Participants in one workshop frequently find themselves functioning as leaders in future sessions.

Unlike almost every other academic endeavor in the new world of lifelong learning, in the hieroglyphic workshops professionals and amateurs freely interact, as do scholars of various disciplines, including archaeology, iconography, epigraphy, and art history. No college degree, advanced or otherwise, grants precedence in this difficult, exacting, and exciting intellectual voyage. Only hard work, tenacity, and intellectual discipline are required. The reward is occasionally discovery, and frequently the camaraderie of the quest.

Participants as Zealous Mavericks

There are multiple reasons for an interest in deciphering Maya hieroglyphs, and my assessment of those who come to the glyph workshops, based on almost two decades of personal experience and interaction, is not meant as a scholarly analysis. Rather, it stems from personal conversations and observation of hundreds of people over the years. Those for whom decipherment develops into more than a passing interest tend to be intrigued by the fact that glyphs have seemed an insoluble puzzle. Despite the easy access to sites and the knowledge based on excavation, Maya writing still holds secrets. Even as the structure of the writing system is revealed, the glyphs themselves still guard their ultimate meaning from professional and amateur alike. There are yet readings to be disputed, phonetics to be decided, interpretations to be argued. For people who scorn the ordinary venture, the chance to be part of an unusual band of intellectual explorers is magnetic. The glyph workshops provide a unique opportunity to join others for whom this quest is paramount, to be immersed for days in a vast sea of inscriptional lore without the distraction of life's ordinary demands.

Schele, the Evangelist, and Danien, the Jewish Mother

The individual styles of the Texas and Pennsylvania meetings reflect the differences in their conception. Linda Schele had been transformed by her experience at Palenque. It shaped her life, and she exhorted those who came to Texas to join with her in this great experience. Her charismatic personality, no less than her message, charmed and convinced those who came to Texas. By following her lead, anyone could be taught to understand the principles of Maya writing. Anyone—professional or nonprofessional—willing to work at it could make valid contributions to the burgeoning corpus of glyph interpretation. Maya enthusiasts were galvanized by the thought that they, too, might be part of this special gathering and help reveal the written words of the Maya.

At Penn, the approach was somewhat different. Because the first Maya meeting was planned as a public event, it was understood that participants would probably be less knowledgeable about hieroglyphs and perhaps a bit more hesitant than at Texas. Everyone was gathered in and welcomed at a huge buffet, where they were offered tempting morsels of knowledge in a warm, nonjudgmental atmosphere. Introductory workshops predominated. Participants were presented with new ideas, applauded when they did well, and encouraged if at first they failed to understand. This initial stance continued in future meetings, with a focus on bringing in the novice and developing that elementary interest. Those who showed a more intensive desire went on to the more advanced workshops and were encouraged to join the monthly glyph meetings. Many have gone on to include the Texas Meetings in their annual glyph immersion.

Conclusion

When they first began, the Maya glyph workshops were suspect in many academic circles. Schele's personality and her leaps of epigraphic interpretation gave pause to many epigraphers and archaeologists. They thought she lacked sufficient data for her readings, that she ignored conflicting archaeological discoveries, and that she projected a romantic and magical aura that is the antithesis of modern archaeological method (e.g., Pyburn 1998, 1999). The Penn meetings, because of their public nature, often were considered to be nonscholarly and not worthy of professional attention or participation. For the participants, none of these considerations mattered. At neither meeting was a lack of academic credentials a barrier to participation. All who came were welcomed and invited to share in the work and in the discovery. Texas worked them harder (Linda Schele, personal communication 1988); Penn encouraged them to try.

Through these meetings and others, thousands of nonprofessionals have gained an understanding of and love for the rather esoteric study of Maya hieroglyphs. As the astonishing number of participants continued to grow, and the high level of intellectual inquiry was maintained, the academic world changed its views, and its reluctance to participate has evaporated. Professionals who once were averse to having their names connected with such a public venture now are eager to be part of the Penn meetings. They have learned to communicate with people outside the ivy-covered walls. Hundreds of nonprofessionals have been welcomed to an esoteric, previously mysterious environment; they have been encouraged to contribute to the pool of epigraphic knowledge. They have felt the excitement of discovery that underlies seemingly dry scholarship. Perhaps more important, they have been introduced to and understand the methods and frustrations that lurk on the cutting edge of discovery. They can communicate this understanding to a broader general public that will, ultimately, have a voice in deciding the level of support for archaeological research and the protection of archaeological sites. This may be the most significant result of all.

Acknowledgments

I wish to express my appreciation to Andrea Stone for her patience, firm hand, and unfailing good humor. I am grateful to Kathryn Josserand, Nick Hopkins, Dorie Reents-Budet, Karen Bassie-Sweet, Sharon Mujica, Peter Keeler, and Justin Kerr, who shared with me their experiences and their memories. Naturally, in the timeworn manner of all academic presentations, I take full responsibility for any misuse of their data. I apologize to anyone whose name may have been omitted from this very brief look at the past twenty years of popular glyph decipherment. It was through oversight, not intent.

Appendix 1

Bibliography of Linda Schele's Publications

Andrea Stone

Books

Freidel, David, Linda Schele, and Joy Parker
  1993 *Maya Cosmos: Three Thousand Years on the Shaman's Path*. William Morrow, New York.
Schele, Linda
  1982 *Maya Glyphs: The Verbs*. University of Texas Press, Austin.
  1997 *Hidden Faces of the Maya*. Alti, San Diego.
  1997 *Rostros ocultos de los mayas*. Impetetus Communications, Mexico City. [Spanish translation of *Hidden Faces of the Maya*]
Schele, Linda, and David Freidel
  1990 *A Forest of Kings: The Untold Story of the Ancient Maya*. William Morrow, New York.
  1991 *Die unbekannte Welt der Maya: Das Geheimnis ihrer Kultur entschlüsselt*. Translated by Johann George Scheffner. Albrecht Knaus Verlag GmbH, Munich, Germany. [Translation of *A Forest of Kings*]
Schele, Linda, and Peter Mathews
  1998 *The Code of Kings: The Language of Seven Sacred Maya Temples and Tombs*. Scribner, New York.
Schele, Linda, and Mary Ellen Miller
  1986 *The Blood of Kings: Dynasty and Ritual in Maya Art*. George Braziller, New York.

Monographs

Schele, Linda, and Peter Mathews
  1979 *The Bodega of Palenque, Chiapas, Mexico*. Dumbarton Oaks, Washington, D.C.
Schele, Linda, and Jeffrey H. Miller
  1983 *The Mirror, the Rabbit, and the Bundle: Accession Expressions from the Classic*

Maya Inscriptions. Studies in Pre-Columbian Art and Archaeology 25. Dumbarton Oaks, Washington, D.C.

Single-Authored Articles

Schele, Linda

1974   Observations on the Cross Motif at Palenque. In *Primera Mesa Redonda de Palenque, Part I,* edited by Merle Greene Robertson, pp. 41–62. Robert Louis Stevenson School, Pebble Beach, California.

1976   Accession Iconography of Chan-Bahlum in the Group of the Cross at Palenque. In *The Art, Iconography, and Dynastic History of Palenque, Part III,* edited by Merle Greene Robertson, pp. 9–34. Proceedings of the Segunda Mesa Redonda de Palenque. Robert Louis Stevenson School, Pebble Beach, California.

1977   Palenque: The House of the Dying Sun. In *Native American Astronomy,* edited by Anthony Aveni, pp. 42–56. University of Texas Press, Austin.

1979   The Palenque Triad: A Visual and Glyphic Approach. *Acts du XLIIe Congrès International des Americanistes, 1976,* vol. 7, pp. 407–423. Musée de l'Homme, Paris.

1979   Highland Rabbits and Lowlands Lords. *Actes du XLIIe Congrès International des Americanistes, 1976,* vol. 8, pp. 281–295. Musée de l'Homme, Paris.

1979   Genealogical Documentation on the Tri-figure Panels at Palenque. In *Tercera Mesa Redonda de Palenque,* vol. 4, edited by Merle Greene Robertson and Donnan Call Jeffers, pp. 41–70. Pre-Columbian Art Research and Herald Printers, Palenque and Monterey, California.

1981   Sacred Site and World-View at Palenque. In *Mesoamerican Sites and World-Views,* edited by Elizabeth Benson, pp. 87–114. Dumbarton Oaks, Washington, D.C.

1984   Human Sacrifice among the Classic Maya. In *Ritual Human Sacrifice in Mesoamerica,* edited by Elizabeth Benson, pp. 7–48. Dumbarton Oaks, Washington, D.C.

1984   Some Suggested Readings of the Event and Office of Heir-Designate at Palenque. In *Phoneticism in Mayan Hieroglyphic Writing,* edited by John Justeson and Lyle Campbell, pp. 287–305. Institute for Mesoamerican Studies Publication 9. State University of New York at Albany.

1985   Balan-Ahau: A Possible Reading of the Tikal Emblem Glyph and a Title at Palenque. In *Fourth Palenque Round Table, 1980,* vol. 6, volume editor Elizabeth Benson, general editor Merle Greene Robertson, pp. 59–65. Pre-Columbian Art Research Institute, San Francisco.

1985   The Hauberg Stela: Bloodletting and the Mythos of Classic Maya Rulership. In *Fifth Palenque Round Table, 1983,* vol. 7, volume editor Virginia Fields, general editor Merle Greene Robertson, pp. 135–151. Pre-Columbian Art Research Institute, San Francisco.

1985   Color on Classic Maya Architecture and Monumental Sculpture of the Southern Maya Lowlands. In *Painted Architecture and Polychrome Monumental Sculpture in Mesoamerica,* edited by Elizabeth Boone, pp. 31–49. Dumbarton Oaks, Washington, D.C.

1988   The Xibalba Shuffle: A Dance after Death. In *Maya Iconography,* edited by Elizabeth Benson and Gillett Griffin, pp. 294–317. Princeton University Press, Princeton.

1989   A Brief Note on the Name of a Vision Serpent. In *The Maya Vase Book,* vol. 1, edited by Justin Kerr, pp. 146–148. Kerr Associates, New York.

1990   House Names and Dedications at Palenque. In *Visions and Revisions in Maya Studies,* edited by Flora Clancy and Peter Harrison, pp. 143–157. University of New Mexico Press, Albuquerque.

1991   The Demotion of Chac-Zutz': Lineage Compounds and Subsidiary Lords at Palenque. In *Sixth Palenque Round Table, 1986,* vol. 8, volume editor Virginia Fields, general editor Merle Greene Robertson, pp. 6–11. University of Oklahoma Press, Norman.

1991   An Epigraphic History of the Western Maya Region. In *Classic Maya Political History: Archaeological and Hieroglyphic Evidence,* edited by T. Patrick Culbert, pp. 72–101. Cambridge University Press, Cambridge.

1991   The Owl, the Shield, and Flint Blade: In A.D. 378, the Maya Learned the Art of Conquest. *Natural History* 11:6–11.

1992   The Founders of Lineages at Copán and Other Sites. *Ancient Mesoamerica* 3(1):130–139.

1992   A New Look at the Dynastic History of Palenque. *Supplement to the Handbook of Middle American Indians: Epigraphy,* vol. 5, edited by Victoria R. Bricker, pp. 82–109. University of Texas Press, Austin.

1992   Religion und Weltsicht. In *Die Welt der Maya: Archäologishe Schätze aus Drei Jahrtausenden,* edited by Eva Eggebrecht, Arne Eggebrecht, and Nikolai Grube, pp. 197–214. Verlag Philipp Von Zabern, Mainz, Germany.

1994   Some Thoughts on the Inscriptions of House C. In *Seventh Palenque Round Table, 1989,* volume editor Virginia Fields, general editor Merle Greene Robertson, pp. 1–11. Pre-Columbian Art Research Institute, San Francisco.

1995   The Olmec Mountain and Tree of Creation in Mesoamerican Cosmology. In *The Olmec World: Ritual and Rulership,* edited by Jill Guthrie, pp. 105–117. The Art Museum, Princeton University, Princeton.

1995   Sprouts and the Early Symbolism of Rulers in Mesoamerica. In *The Emergence of Lowland Maya Civilization: The Transition from the Preclassic to the*

Early Classic, edited by Nikolai Grube, pp. 117–135. Acta Mesoamericana 8, A. Saurwein, Möckmuhl, Germany.

1996   History, Writing, and Image in Maya Art. *Art Bulletin* 78(3):412–416.

1996   Im Zeitalter der vierten Schöpfung: Religion und Kosmologie in der Welt der Maya. *Mannheimer Forum* 95/96:157–222. R. Piper GmbH, Munich, Germany.

1998   The Iconography of Maya Architectural Façades during the Late Classic Period. In *Function and Meaning in Classic Maya Architecture,* edited by Stephen Houston, pp. 479–517. Dumbarton Oaks, Washington, D.C.

Coauthored Articles

Fash, Barbara, William Fash, Sheree Lane, Rudy Larrios, Linda Schele, Jeffrey Stomper, and David Stuart

1992   Investigations of a Classic Maya Council House at Copán. *Journal of Field Archaeology* 19:419–422.

Freidel, David, and Linda Schele

1988   Kingship in the Late Preclassic Maya Lowlands: The Instruments and Places of Ritual Power. *American Anthropologist* 90(3):547–567.

1988   Symbol and Power: A History of the Lowland Maya Cosmogram. In *Maya Iconography,* edited by Elizabeth Benson and Gillett Griffin, pp. 44–93. Princeton University Press, Princeton.

1989   Dead Kings and Living Temples: Dedication and Termination Rituals among the Ancient Maya. In *Word and Image in Maya Culture: Explorations in Language, Writing, and Representation,* edited by William Hanks and Don Rice, pp. 233–243. University of Utah Press, Salt Lake City.

1993   Maya Royal Women: A Lesson in Precolumbian History. In *Gender in Cross-Cultural Perspective,* edited by Caroline B. Brettel and Carolyn F. Sargent, pp. 74–78. Prentice Hall, Englewood Cliffs, New Jersey.

Grube, Nikolai, and Linda Schele

1994   Kuy, the Owl of Omen and War. *Mexicon* 16(1):10–17.

Grube, Nikolai, Linda Schele, and Federico Fahsen

1991   Odds and Ends from the Inscriptions of Quirigua. *Mexicon* 13(6):106–112.

Josserand, Kathryn, Linda Schele, and Nicholas Hopkins

1985   Linguistic Data on Maya Inscriptions: The *ti* Constructions. In *Fourth Palenque Round Table, 1980,* edited by Elizabeth Benson, pp. 87–102. Pre-Columbian Art Research Institute, San Francisco.

Mathews, Peter, and Linda Schele

1974   Lords of Palenque: The Glyphic Evidence. In *Primera Mesa Redonda de Palenque, Part 1,* volume editor Merle Greene Robertson, general editor Merle Greene Robertson, pp. 63–76. Robert Louis Stevenson School, Pebble Beach, California.

Schele, Linda, and Maricela Ayala

1993   De poesía e historia: el Tablero de los Glifos de Palenque. *Vuelta* 17(203): 25–27.

Schele Linda, and David Freidel

1990   The Maya Message: Time, Text, and Image. In *Art as a Means of Communication in Pre-Literate Societies,* edited by Dan Eban, pp. 303–340. Israel Museum, Jerusalem.

1991   The Courts of Creation: Ballcourts, Ballgames, and Portals to the Maya Otherworld. In *The Mesoamerican Ballgame,* edited by Vernon Scarborough and David Wilcox, pp. 289–315. University of Arizona Press, Tucson.

Schele, Linda, and Nikolai Grube

1996   The Workshop for Maya on Hieroglyphic Writing. In *Maya Cultural Activism in Guatemala,* edited by Edward Fischer and R. McKenna Brown, pp. 131–140. University of Texas Press, Austin.

Schele, Linda, Nikolai Grube, and Erik Boot

1998   Some Suggestions on the K'atun Prophecies in the Books of Chilam Balam in Light of Classic-Period History. In *Memorias del Tercer Congreso Internacional de Mayistas (9 al 15 de julio, 1995),* pp. 399–446. Instituto de Investigaciones Filológicas, Centro de Estudios Mayas, Universidad Nacional Autónoma de México, Mexico City.

Schele, Linda, and Julia Guernsey Kappelman

2001   What the Heck's Coatepec? In *Landscape and Power in Ancient Mesoamerica,* edited by Rex Koontz, Kathryn Reese-Taylor, and Annabeth Headrick, pp. 29–53. Westview Press, Boulder, Colorado.

Schele, Linda, and Matthew Looper

2002   Seats of Power at Copán. In *Copán: The Rise and Fall of a Classic Maya Kingdom,* edited by William Fash and E. Wyllis Andrews V. School of American Research Press, Santa Fe, New Mexico, in press.

Schele, Linda, and Peter Mathews

1991   Royal Visits and Other Intersite Relationships among the Classic Maya. In *Classic Maya Political History: Archaeological and Hieroglyphic Evidence,* edited by T. Patrick Culbert, pp. 226–252. Cambridge University Press, Cambridge.

Schele, Linda, and Khristaan Villela

1996   Creation, Cosmos, and the Imagery of Palenque and Copan. In *Eighth Palenque Round Table, 1993,* vol. 10, volume editors Martha Macri and Jan McHargue, general editor Merle Greene Robertson, pp. 15–30. Pre-Columbian Art Research Institute, San Francisco.

Villela, Khristaan, and Linda Schele

1996   Astronomy and the Iconography of Creation among the Classic and Colonial Period Maya. In *Eighth Palenque Round Table, 1993,* vol. 10, volume editors Martha Macri and Jan McHargue, general editor Merle Green Robertson, pp. 31–44. Pre-Columbian Art Research Institute, San Francisco.

Notebooks for the Texas Meetings

Schele, Linda

1978   *Notebook for the Maya Hieroglyphic Writing Workshop at Texas.* Institute of Latin American Studies, University of Texas at Austin, Austin.

1979   *Notebook for the Maya Hieroglyphic Writing Workshop at Texas.* Institute of Latin American Studies, University of Texas at Austin, Austin.

1980   *Notebook for the Maya Hieroglyphic Writing Workshop at Texas.* Institute of Latin American Studies, University of Texas at Austin, Austin.

1981   *Notebook for the Maya Hieroglyphic Writing Workshop at Texas.* Institute of Latin American Studies, University of Texas at Austin, Austin.

1982   *Notebook for the Maya Hieroglyphic Writing Workshop at Texas.* Institute of Latin American Studies, University of Texas at Austin, Austin.

1983   *Notebook for the Maya Hieroglyphic Writing Workshop at Texas.* Institute of Latin American Studies, University of Texas at Austin, Austin.

1984   *Notebook for the Maya Hieroglyphic Writing Workshop at Texas.* Institute of Latin American Studies, University of Texas at Austin, Austin.

1985   *Notebook for the Maya Hieroglyphic Writing Workshop at Texas.* Institute of Latin American Studies, University of Texas at Austin, Austin.

1986   *Notebook for the Maya Hieroglyphic Writing Workshop at Texas.* Institute of Latin American Studies, University of Texas at Austin, Austin.

1987   *Notebook for the Maya Hieroglyphic Writing Workshop at Texas.* Institute of Latin American Studies, University of Texas at Austin, Austin.

1988   *Notebook for the Maya Hieroglyphic Workshop at Texas.* Institute of Latin American Studies, University of Texas at Austin, Austin.

1989   *Notebook for the 13th Maya Hieroglyphic Workshop at Texas. The Dynastic History of Copan.* Department of Art and Art History, College of Fine Arts, and the Institute of Latin American Studies, University of Texas at Austin, Austin.

1990   *Notebook for the 14th Maya Hieroglyphic Workshop at Texas. Tikal: The Early Dynastic History.* Department of Art and Art History, College of Fine Arts, and the Institute of Latin American Studies, University of Texas at Austin, Austin.

1991   *Notebook for the 15th Maya Hieroglyphic Workshop at Texas. Yaxchilan: The Life and Times of Bird-Jaguar.* Department of Art and Art History, College of Fine Arts, and the Institute of Latin American Studies, University of Texas at Austin, Austin.

1992   *Notebook for the 16th Maya Hieroglyphic Workshop at Texas. The Group of the Cross at Palenque: A Commentary on Creation.* Department of Art and Art History, College of Fine Arts, and the Institute of Latin American Studies, University of Texas at Austin, Austin.

Schele, Linda, and Nikolai Grube

1994   *Notebook for the 18th Maya Hieroglyphic Workshop at Texas. Tlaloc-Venus Warfare: The Peten Wars 8.17.0.0.0–9.15.13.0.0.* Edited by Timothy Albright. Department of Art and Art History, College of Fine Arts, and the Institute of Latin American Studies, University of Texas at Austin, Austin.

1995   *Notebook for the 19th Maya Hieroglyphic Workshop at Texas. The Last Two Hundred Years of Classic Maya History: Transmission, Termination, Transformation Post-9.15.0.0.0.* Department of Art and Art History, College of Fine Arts, and the Institute of Latin American Studies, University of Texas at Austin, Austin.

1997   *Notebook for the 21st Maya Hieroglyphic Workshop. The Dresden Codex.* Department of Art and Art History, College of Fine Arts, and the Institute of Latin American Studies, University of Texas at Austin, Austin.

Schele, Linda, and Matthew Looper

1996   *Notebook for the 20th Maya Hieroglyphic Forum at Texas. The Inscriptions of Quirigua and Copan.* Department of Art and Art History, College of Fine Arts, and the Institute of Latin American Studies, University of Texas at Austin, Austin.

Schele, Linda, and Peter Mathews

1993   *Notebook for the 17th Maya Hieroglyphic Workshop at Texas. The Dynastic History of Palenque.* Department of Art and Art History, College of Fine Arts, and the Institute of Latin American Studies, University of Texas at Austin, Austin.

Copán Notes

Note: The Copán Notes Series is published by the Copán Mosaics Project and the Instituto Hondureño de Antropología e Historia, Honduras.

Fahsen, Federico, Linda Schele, and Nikolai Grube

1995   The Tikal-Copán Connection: Shared Features (Version 2). *Copán Note 123.*

Grube, Nikolai, and Linda Schele

1987   U Cit Tok, the Last King of Copán. *Copán Note 21.*

1987   The Date on the Bench from Structure 9N-82, Sepulturas, Copán, Honduras. *Copán Note 23.*

1988   Cu-Ix, the Fourth Ruler of Copán and His Monuments. *Copán Note 40.*

1988   A Venus Title on Copán Stela F. *Copán Note 41.*

1988   A Quadrant Tree at Copán. *Copán Note 43.*

1990   Two Early Classic Monuments from Copán. *Copán Note 82.*

1990   A New Interpretation of the Temple 18 Jambs. *Copán Note 85.*

1990   Royal Gifts to Subordinate Lords. *Copán Note 87.*

1990   Two Examples of the Glyph for "Step" from the Hieroglyphic Stairs. *Copán Note 91.*

1992   Yet Another Look at Stela 11. *Copán Note 106.*

Grube, Nikolai, Linda Schele, and Federico Fahsen

1995   The Tikal-Copán Connection: Evidence from External Relations (Version 2). *Copán Note 121.*

Grube, Nikolai, Linda Schele, and David Stuart

1989   The Date of Dedication of Ballcourt III at Copán. *Copán Note 59.*

Grube, Nikolai, David Stuart, and Linda Schele

1989   A Possible Death Reference for Yax-K'uk'-Mo'. *Copán Note 60.*

Looper, Matthew, and Linda Schele

1994   The Founder of Quiriguá, Tutum-Yol-K'inich. *Copán Note 119.*

Morales, Alfonso, Julie Miller, and Linda Schele

1990   The Dedication Stair of "Ante" Temple. *Copán Note 76.*

Schele, Linda

1986   Paraphrase of the Text of Altar U. *Copán Note 5.*

1986   The Founders of Lineages at Copán and Other Maya Sites. *Copán Note 8.*

1986   The Figures on the Central Ballcourt Marker of Ballcourt IIa at Copán. *Copán Note 13.*

1986   Moon-Jaguar, the 10th Successor of the Lineage of Yax-K'uk'-Mo' of Copán. *Copán Note 15.*

1986   Interim Report on the Iconography of the Architectural Sculpture of Temple 22. *Copán Note 19.*

1987   The Figures on the Legs of the Scribe's Bench. *Copán Note 24.*

1987   Some Ideas of the Protagonist and Dating of Stela E. *Copán Note 25.*

1987   A Possible Death Date for Smoke-Imix-God K. *Copán Note 26.*

1987   A Brief Commentary on a Hieroglyphic Cylinder from Copán. *Copán Note 27.*

1987   Wan, the "Standing up" of Stela A. *Copán Note 28.*

1987   New Data on the Paddlers from Butz'-Chaan of Copán. *Copán Note 29.*

1987   Stela I and the Founding of the City of Copán. *Copán Note 30.*

1987   The Inscription on Stela I and Its Altar. *Copán Note 31.*

1987   The Reviewing Stand of Temple 11. *Copán Note 32.*

1987   The Surviving Fragments of Stela 9. *Copán Note 33.*

1987   A Cached Jade from Temple 26 and the World Tree at Copán. *Copán Note 34.*

1987   The Dedication of Structure 2 and a New Form of the God N Event. *Copán Note 35.*

1987   Two Altar Names at Copán. *Copán Note 36.*

1987   Notes on the Río Amarillo Altars. *Copán Note 37.*

1987   New Fits on the North Panel of the West Doorway of Temple 11. *Copán Note 38.*

1988   Revisions to the Dynastic Chronology of Copán. *Copán Note 45.*

1988   Altar F' and Structure 32. *Copán Note 46.*

1989   A House Dedication on the Harvard Bench at Copán. *Copán Note 51.*

1989   A New Glyph for "Five" on Stela E. *Copán Note 53.*

1989   The Numbered Katun Titles of Yax-Pac. *Copán Note 65.*

1989   A Brief Commentary on the Top of Altar Q. *Copán Note 66.*

1989   Some Further Thoughts on the Quirigua-Copán Connection. *Copán Note 67.*

1990   "End of" Expression at Copán and Palenque. *Copán Note 69.*

1990   The Early Classic Dynastic History of Copán: Interim Report 1989. *Copán Note 70.*

1990   The Glyph for "Hole" and the Skeletal Maw of the Underworld. *Copán Note 71.*

1990   Preliminary Commentary on a New Altar from Structure 30. *Copán Note 72.*

1990   Further Comments on Stela 6. *Copán Note 73.*

1990   A New Fragment from Altar J'. *Copán Note 74.*

1990   Early Quiriguá and the Kings of Copán. *Copán Note 75.*

1990   Speculations from an Epigrapher on Things Archaeological in the Acropolis at Copán. *Copán Note 80.*

1990   Lounsbury's Contrived Numbers and Two 8 Eb Dates at Copán. *Copán Note 81.*

1990   Commentary on Altar G'. *Copán Note 89.*

1990   A Possible Death Statement for 18-Rabbit. *Copán Note 90.*

1991   Venus in the Monuments of Smoke-Imix-God K and the Great Plaza. *Copán Note 101.*

1991   Another Look at Stela 11. *Copán Note 103.*

1992   The Initial Dates on Stelae 2 and 12. *Copán Note 104.*

1993   A Reexamination of U-Yak-Chak. *Copán Note 111.*

1995   The Texts of Group 10L-2: A New Interpretation. *Copán Note 118.*

1995   The Text in Temple 21a. *Copán Note 120.*

Schele, Linda, Federico Fahsen, and Nikolai Grube

1994   The Floor Marker from Motmot. *Copán Note 117.*

Schele, Linda, and Barbara Fash

1991   A New Assessment of Smoke-Monkey, the 14th Successor in the Line of Yax-K'uk'-Mo'. *Copán Note 97.*

1991   Venus and the Reign of Smoke-Monkey. *Copán Note 100.*

Schele, Linda, and Nikolai Grube

1987   The Brother of Yax-Pac. *Copán Note 20.*

1987   The Birth Monument of Butz'-Chaan. *Copán Note 22.*

1988   The Father of Smoke-Shell. *Copán Note 39.*

1988   A Future Marker on a Hand Scattering Verb at Copán. *Copán Note 42.*

1988   Stela 13 and the East Quadrant of Copán. *Copán Note 44.*

1990   Six-Staired Ballcourts. *Copán Note 83.*

1990   A Tentative Identification of the Second Successor of the Copán Dynasty. *Copán Note 84.*

1990   The Glyph for Plaza or Court. *Copán Note 86.*

1990   Building, Court, and Mountain Names in the Text of the Hieroglyphic Stairs. *Copán Note 92.*

1990   A Preliminary Inventory of Place Names in the Copán Inscriptions. *Copán Note 93.*

1991   Speculations on Who Built the House under Temple 11. *Copán Note 102.*

1992   New Information on the Earlier Date on the Ante Stair. *Copán Note 105.*

1992   The Founding Events at Copán. *Copán Note 107.*

1992   Venus, the Great Plaza, and Recalling the Dead. *Copán Note 108.*

1994   Who was Popol-K'inich? A Re-evaluation of the Second Successor in the Line of Yax-K'uk'-Mo' in Light of New Archeological Evidence. *Copán Note 116.*

Schele, Linda, Nikolai Grube, and Federico Fahsen

1990   A Suggested Reading Order for the West Side of Stela A. *Copán Note 88.*

1993   The Tikal-Copán Connection: The Copán Evidence (Version 2). *Copán Note 122.*

1994   The Xukpi Stone: A Newly Discovered Early Classic Inscription from the Copán Acropolis, Part II: Commentary on the Text (Version 2). *Copán Note 114.*

Schele, Linda, and Rudi Larios

1991   Some Venus Dates on the Hieroglyphic Stair at Copán. *Copán Note 99.*

Schele, Linda, and Matthew Looper

1994   The 9.17.0.0.0 Eclipse at Quiriguá and Copán. *Copán Note 115.*

Schele, Linda, and Alfsonso Morales

1990   A New Fragment from Structure 22–6th at Copán, Honduras. *Copán Note 78.*

1990   Some Thoughts on Two Jade Pendants from the Termination Cache of "Ante" Structure at Copán. *Copán Note 79.*

Schele, Linda, and Elizabeth Newsome

1991   Taking the Headband at Copán. *Copán Note 96.*

Schele, Linda, and David Stuart

1986   Te-Tun as the Glyph for "Stela." *Copán Note 1.*

1986   The Chronology of Altar U. *Copán Note 3.*

1986   Butz'-Chaan, the 11th Successor of the Yax-K'uk'-Mo' Lineage. *Copán Note 14.*

1986   Waterlily-Jaguar, the Seventh Successor of the Lineage of Yax-K'uk'-Mo'. *Copán Note 16.*

Schele, Linda, David Stuart, and Nikolai Grube

1989   A Commentary on the Restoration and Reading of the Glyphic Panels from Temple 11. *Copán Note 64.*

1991   A Commentary on the Inscriptions of Structure 10L-22A at Copán. *Copán Note 98.*

Schele, Linda, David Stuart, Nikolai Grube, and Floyd Lounsbury

1989   A New Inscription from Temple 22a at Copán. *Copán Note 57.*

Stuart, David, Nikolai Grube, and Linda Schele

1989   A Substitution Set for the "Ma Cuch/Batab" Title. *Copán Note 58.*

1989   A New Alternative for the Date of the Sepulturas Bench. *Copán Note 61.*

Stuart, David, Nikolai Grube, Linda Schele, and Floyd Lounsbury

1989   Stela 63, a New Monument from Copán. *Copán Note 56.*

1986   Yax-K'uk'-Mo', the Founder of the Lineage of Copán. *Copán Note 6.*

1986   Interim Report on the Hieroglyphic Stair of Structure 26. *Copán Note 17.*

Stuart, David, Linda Schele, and Nikolai Grube

1989   A Mention of 18 Rabbit and the Temple 11 Reviewing Stand. *Copán Note 62.*

Texas Notes

Note: The Texas Notes on Precolumbian Art, Writing, and Culture are published by the Center for the History of Art of Ancient American Cultures (CHAAC), Art Department, University of Texas at Austin, Austin.

Fahsen, Federico, and Linda Schele

1991   A Proposed Reading for the Penis-Perforation Glyph. *Texas Notes on Precolumbian Art, Writing, and Culture No. 8.*

1991   Curl-Snout under Scrutiny, Again. *Texas Notes on Precolumbian Art, Writing, and Culture No. 13.*

Grube, Nikolai, and Linda Schele

1991   Tzuk in the Classic Maya Inscriptions. *Texas Notes on Precolumbian Art, Writing, and Culture No. 14.*

1993   Naranjo Altar 1 and Rituals of Death and Burials. *Texas Notes on Precolumbian Art, Writing, and Culture No. 54.*

1993   Un verbo nakwa para "batallar o conquistar." *Texas Notes on Precolumbian Art, Writing, and Culture No. 55.*

1993   Pi as bundle. *Texas Notes on Precolumbian Art, Writing, and Culture No. 56.*

1994   Tikal Altar 5. *Texas Notes on Precolumbian Art, Writing, and Culture No. 66.*

1994   New Observations on the Loltun Relief. *Texas Notes on Precolumbian Art, Writing, and Culture No. 74.*

Looper, Matthew, and Linda Schele

1991   A War at Palenque during the Reign of Ah-K'an. *Texas Notes on Precolumbian Art, Writing, and Culture No. 25.*

Schele, Linda

1990   The Palenque War Panel: Commentary on the Inscription. *Texas Notes on Precolumbian Art, Writing, and Culture No. 2.*

1990   Ba as "First" in Classic Period Titles. *Texas Notes on Precolumbian Art, Writing, and Culture No. 5.*

1991   Further Adventures with T128 Ch'a. *Texas Notes on Precolumbian Art, Writing, and Culture No. 9.*

1991   Some Observations on the War Expressions at Tikal. *Texas Notes on Precolumbian Art, Writing, and Culture No. 16.*

1991   A Proposed Name for Río Azul and a Glyph for "Water." *Texas Notes on Precolumbian Art, Writing, and Culture No. 19.*

1993   Creation and the Ritual of the Bakabs. *Texas Notes on Precolumbian Art, Writing, and Culture No. 57.*

1994   New Observations on the Oval Palace Tablet at Palenque. *Texas Notes on Precolumbian Art, Writing, and Culture No. 71.*

1995   An Alternative Reading for the Sky-Penis Title. *Texas Notes on Precolumbian Art, Writing, and Culture No. 69.*

Schele, Linda, and Federico Fahsen

1991   A Substitution Pattern in Curl-Snout's Name. *Texas Notes on Precolumbian Art, Writing, and Culture No. 12.*

Schele, Linda, Federico Fahsen, and Nikolai Grube

1992   El Zapote and the Dynasty of Tikal. *Texas Notes on Precolumbian Art, Writing, and Culture No. 34.*

Schele, Linda, and Nikolai Grube

1994   Some Revisions to Tikal's Dynasty of Kings. *Texas Notes on Precolumbian Art, Writing, and Culture No. 67.*

1994   Notes on the Chronology of Piedras Negras Stela 12. *Texas Notes on Precolumbian Art, Writing, and Culture No. 70.*

Schele, Linda, Nikolai Grube, and Federico Fahsen

1992   The Lunar Series in Classic Maya Inscriptions: New Observations and Interpretations. *Texas Notes on Precolumbian Art, Writing, and Culture No. 29.*

Schele, Linda, and Paul Mathews

1994   The Last Lords of Seibal. *Texas Notes on Precolumbian Art, Writing, and Culture No. 68.*

Schele, Linda, and Peter Mathews

1990   A Proposed Decipherment for a Portion of Resbalon Stair 1. *Texas Notes on Precolumbian Art, Writing, and Culture No. 3.*

Schele, Linda, Peter Mathews, Nikolai Grube, Floyd Lounsbury, and David Kelley

1991   New Readings of Glyphs for the Month Kumk'u and Their Implications. *Texas Notes on Precolumbian Art, Writing, and Culture No. 15.*

Schele, Linda, Peter Mathews, and Floyd Lounsbury

1990   Redating the Hauberg Stela. *Texas Notes on Precolumbian Art, Writing, and Culture No. 1.*

1990   Untying the Headband. *Texas Notes on Precolumbian Art, Writing, and Culture No. 4.*

1990   The Nal Suffix at Palenque and Elsewhere. *Texas Notes on Precolumbian Art, Writing, and Culture No. 6.*

Schele, Linda, and Khristaan D. Villela

1991   Some New Ideas about the T713/757 "Accession" Phrases. *Texas Notes on Precolumbian Art, Writing, and Culture No. 27.*

1994   The Helmet of the Chakte. *Texas Notes on Precolumbian Art, Writing, and Culture No. 63.*

Selected Unpublished Papers

Schele, Linda

1979   The Puleston Hypothesis: The Water-Lily Complex in Classic Maya Art and Writing.

1986   The Tlaloc Heresy: Cultural Interaction and Social History. Paper presented at Maya Art and Civilization: The New Dynamics, a symposium sponsored by the Kimbell Art Museum, Fort Worth, Texas.

1989   Brotherhood in Ancient Maya Kingship. Paper presented at the New Interpretation of Maya Writing and Iconography Symposium, Albany, New York.

1995   The Wars of Hanab-Pakal. Paper presented at the 1995 Mesa Redonda de Palenque, Palenque, Mexico.

Schele, Linda, Peter Mathews, and Floyd Lounsbury

1983   Parentage and Spouse Expressions from Classic Maya Inscriptions.

Appendix 2

Schele-ana: Memories of Linda Schele

The Living Maya, The Mukta Antz Chingón, and Me:
A Tale of Life and Death

Duncan Earle

One of the numerous traditions I have trouble believing are no longer with us is the parties Linda used to have during the Austin Maya meetings. While I was living in that fair city I frequented the gatherings and was always stimulated by the conversations I was able to have among the crowds. One year, as the numbers grew beyond the available space of her East Side home, I fled the teeming masses by hopping onto a sofa. When I turned to see who else it had rescued, there was Linda, just gazing out at all the people with a face between pride and wonder. I saw a chance in that moment to raise an issue of huge importance to me and Maya studies—as well as to the survival of the current Maya peoples—that had been one to dog me already for over fifteen years: the meaningful connections between the ancient Maya and the cultural beliefs and practices of the present ones.

Being an ethnographer of the Maya who had previously studied archaeology, I knew there were strong connections. But I also knew that since before the time of Kubler's "radical disjunction" concept, the idea that too much had changed with the colonial impact to find the past in the present, Mayanists were not receptive to analogies across time that went beyond the basic notions of maize farming and a few scattered "survivals" such as the 260-day calendar. The evidence for cultural meaning in Preclassic and Classic times was largely in elite artifacts; glyphs demarcating elite activities; elite funerary pots; a few codices, no doubt of specialized manufacture; and so on. In fact, as it became increasingly evident that the writing and sculpture were products and depictions of royalty rather than deities, the connections with the present seemed to many more untenable than ever.

I knew this was in error. Every Maya studies conference I went to, each paper I read, each new discovery pointed only further toward ideas I had been exposed to while living with the K'iche' and Tzotzil Mayas. I became certain that the domestic locus of maize production in ancient times led to a conjoining of elite and commoner ideology and a glorification not of the walled-off city but of the rural farmer-hunter by those in power. I had read the Postclassic documents that said the K'iche' king would ceremonially plant a milpa each year. I had seen the farm houses elaborated on pyramids in Yucatan. The Hero Twins episodes in the *Popol Vuh* taking place in a rural farmhouse rather than in a palace also confirmed for me the importance of this connection between commoner and elite culture. Even the elaborate evidence of elite propaganda on their public monuments led me to see the Maya rulers as seeking approval and support from their followers, the hinterland farmers, not an alienation from them. For me, elites created an elaborated, ramified version of the cultural grammar of everyday farmer life, in part to justify themselves before their supporters in an idiom of mutual intelligibility. For this reason, I thought that when the elites were killed or acculturated or impoverished by the colonial Spanish, their belief system did not disappear. I also knew that for the sake of the survival of the current indigenous people, this connection should be appreciated by a world of influential people who so love the ancient Maya. The terrible slaughter of nearly two hundred thousand Mayas in Guatemala in the early 1980s would be more difficult to repeat if these connections of continuity to the great ancient civilization were made.

But such a position in those days, nearly a decade ago, was still controversial. The leap from Classic pottery to the 1550s *Popol Vuh* (by Michael Coe) was hard enough for many to embrace, but ethnographic analogy for many remained beyond the pale. With this in mind I took up a discussion with Linda and at first found her to be as resistant as the next Mayanist. But as I noted specific analogies I saw at work, and as I began to describe Chamula Tzotzil ceremonial events associated with the Festival of Games (K'in Tahimoltik), she became intrigued. Then she did what I would not have expected anyone to do in this situation, what I would later call doing "a Linda." She said to me, "Let's go, then, you and I. I will pay for the trip, and you show me what you are telling me, and if I can see it, I will concede the point." An idle promise just to shut me up, get me off the couch? I came away from the party bemused that she might be serious. I hoped. I burned incense.

Months passed, and I heard nothing. Then in the fall of 1991, Linda called me up and asked if I were still ready to give her a tour of Chamula in "Crazy February" if she footed the bill. "Don't say it unless you mean it," I stammered. She did. We went. She explained that when the University of Texas at Austin gave her the endowed chair, it came with some money attached to it, money most people just sucked up. But she kept hers in a fund to use only for educational and research purposes, for just such a situation as the one she was presenting to me. Her endowed chair would provide the money for us to explore my hypothesis and my challenge, in San Juan Chamula, in the Mexican state of Chiapas, in the lost days of Carnival—Mayan style.

That trip, as well as another to Chichicastenango and the caves of Utatlan the following summer, are chronicled in the book *Maya Cosmos* (1993), which she wrote with David Freidel and Joy Parker. I remember with such awe how she was able to "see" the details of ceremonial practices that I and other ethnographers had missed. She also became an instant hit with the Chamulas because in place of the prohibited camera she produced a sketch pad and pen. A crowd would form around her as she rendered scenes of ritual activity in all their smoke and pomp and drama. She kept quizzing me about whether this was alright to do from a Chamula standpoint, if the prohibition toward photos extended to drawings, which I knew it did not. I finally translated for an official who explained to her an essential point separating art from photographic recording. "You shall never capture who we are, what we do, with your pen, for all its verisimilitude. You will always make errors that show God your imperfection and make your image fallible and unable to capture the soul of our faces. It will only be enough to remember."

It was decided in the respectful crowd around her sketching that her images were *"chingón"*—a word borrowed from Spanish to mean "great" or "excellent," despite its sexual and derogatory origin of *chingón,* a big "f*cker." *"Ep chingón li mukta antz"* was said again and again, and finally Linda asked me, "What is with this phrase, *"chingón mukta antz"* they keep saying to each other?" "They say you are great at drawing," I said with a poorly concealed smirk. Then she pinned me down for etymologies. "Well," I said, *"mukta* means big, they say you are big, a big woman, *mukta antz.*" And *chingón?* She had heard this word in other contexts, and it dawned on her they were calling her the Chingón Big Woman. I cringed, expecting her to be upset. On the contrary, she let out a huge laugh and proceeded to call herself by that name for the rest of the trip! To those who knew the meaning, I could not explain why she liked it, and those who did not understand the words were mystified why she thought it was so funny. She loved it.

On the last day of the trip she wanted to see Zinacantan, and I wanted to show her Romeria, the grave site for the eastern Chamulas. All the time in Zinacantan I tried to move us along so there would be time for the other visit. Linda began to get ticked at me, not seeing what was so important about Romeria and me unable to articulate why I thought it was a must see. Finally I found myself winding around the curves of the road to Tenejapa, saying, "Just another few turns" while she groused that we were going to miss a dinner date she had arranged—that is, until she saw the *camposanto* (graveyard) appear before us; then she became quiet as I drove the car off the road and onto a bit of green lawn before the towering crosses that overlooked the graves, each grave topped with a "door" of planks. The graves stretched off west and south to the horizon, and the evening light gave a special feel to the hallowed ground. The crosses were decorated with evergreens and mountain flowers and moss, standing a good forty feet above us. She got out with that special quickness and barely containable excitement and focus that spoke of inner revelation and discovery. It was the culmination of a series of realizations about the continued importance of the cross symbol, from early times to now, as a kind of cosmic world tree (and portal) connecting earth and cosmos, creation and history, the past and the present, and life with death and renewal. It was in fact an appropriate symbol to stand for the whole issue of connection between the ancients and the Mayas of today, even as it was one of the elements of ritual practice that most convinced Linda that the past and the present are continuous. The poignancy of her revelations there before the dead Maya ancestors, standing beneath crosses that connected Maya tombs to the heavens, were to fall again upon me much later, when I last saw her alive.

We talked about a shared theory about Maya concepts of death, immortality, and afterworlds, outside the little Austin conference held to commemorate her just a year ago, in which I had just done the prayers announcing and presenting her before the ancestors and had burned the requisite copal incense. As we spoke I saw Romeria again, reflected upon all the work she had afterward done for the current Maya, teaching courses on the glyphs just for them, making a place in her research life for their voices and concerns, bringing them to the Austin conference to share knowledge, and so much more. She had liberated for them their history and writing, revealing its genius after five centuries of silencing and death. She had come to cultivate in Maya studies, in the time between Romeria and this sad moment, a love and respect for the living Maya that would never allow again the serious scholar of the past to ignore the present. Between that amazing Chamula graveyard and her own descent toward the jaws of the Earth Monster at the root of the world tree, the Mukta Chingón Antz had resuscitated interest in the living Maya within a field dedicated to understanding their dead. And so she lives forever, in Heart of Sky, Heart of Earth. *Tanato,* see you later, Linda.

This Will Blow Your Mind

Gillett Griffin

In a burst of excitement generated by the extraordinary revelations of the First Mesa Redonda de Palenque, Elizabeth Benson invited Linda Schele in the autumn of 1974 to give a talk at Dumbarton Oaks. Suddenly, Linda was coming up to the northeast, and there was the opportunity to have her talk at Princeton several days before her talk at Dumbarton Oaks. The problem, I discovered, was that there was too little time to schedule a lecture hall. All of the rooms in the

Department of Art and Archaeology were taken. So I decided to use my own home for the talk.

I was able to print an invitation and a poster, and I collared and phoned everybody potentially interested in hearing and meeting Linda. My home is small and not one bit suited for a lecture. Every chair was pressed into service. People sat on the floor, radiators, stairs, or chair arms or stood at the edges and in corners of the space that serves as dining room and living room. As I recall more than forty people showed up. No one could have been comfortable.

I expected Linda to give a nice Palenque travelogue. And this she began to do. The slides were good, and she was dynamically excited as she always was. There were pictures of the site in general, the rain forest, the Palace, the Cross Group, and, finally, the Temple of the Inscriptions. She told of the discovery of the tomb and showed pictures of the descent into the tomb chamber. She flashed on the screen Merle Greene Robertson's remarkable photograph, later made into a poster, of the Sarcophagus Lid. Then, for the next hour or more she explained the complex iconography.

Her audience, stiff from sitting in cramped quarters or standing in awkward places, was finally able to move to get drinks or food. A very few—as I remember, only those with baby-sitters—fled, thanking Linda. Most stayed on to ask questions or talk with her. It had been a magical Linda evening.

Several days later I went to Washington, to Dumbarton Oaks, to hear Linda speak. It may have been the first time outside of her talks at Palenque or those to her classes in Mobile that I had heard her speak in public. Dumbarton Oaks is a most elegant atmosphere. In those early days Linda loved to surprise her audience in various ways. First of all everyone expected to see a bright young professor—neat, tailored—possibly with a briefcase or a sheaf of neatly typed notes. She would shamble onto whatever platform or stage from the wings, looking like a bewildered janitor. She wore thick glasses. Her hair looked as if a bowl had been placed upside down on her head and all the hair below trimmed. She usually wore a shirt tucked into her Levis, over which, for formality's sake, she wore a plaid wool shirt unbuttoned, which hung over her pants. When she began to talk it was with a slow deliberate southern drawl. She would speak without notes and often would inject colorful and quaint vocabulary. It took a while for her audiences to adjust, but as she progressed they would begin to grasp that this was someone special.

Dumbarton Oaks had never encountered such an original. In the hush occasioned by her appearance, she began in her slow southern drawl, "Last Monday I was in Gillett Griffin's house to give a talk on Palenque. When I got to Merle Greene Robertson's picture of the Sarcophagus Lid and began explaining it—it all came to me!" I realized with a jolt that all of that iconography revealed itself to her as she had spoken.

She came to Princeton to talk many times. She always stayed with me. In those days she smoked and drank a lot. We would sit up listening to music and talking about all sorts of things. And suddenly we would notice that birds were chirping—it was dawn. Often she had not put her slides together before we went to bed to get some rest. She would never tell me what she was going to lecture on to my class; she would simply announce, "I'm going to blow your mind." And she always did.

The Rabbit Woman

Elizabeth P. Benson

In 1973 Professor Floyd Lounsbury of Yale University was a visiting scholar at Dumbarton Oaks, where I was in charge of Pre-Columbian Studies, and in December he and I went to Palenque to a Mesa Redonda organized by Merle Greene Robertson, who was living with her husband, Bob, in a house they had built there, at La Cañada. Floyd had been working on the codices, but, shortly before going to Palenque, he had begun to look at the monumental Maya inscriptions and some related glyphs on vases.

The first Palenque Mesa Redonda was small and intimate; I think that there were no more than thirty-five of us. One was Linda Schele; I had heard of her from Gillett Griffin of Princeton, who had met her earlier at Palenque and been impressed. Another was Peter Mathews, an undergraduate at Calgary, a student of David Kelley's. Both Linda and Peter had begun to work on the Palenque glyphs.

We spent the afternoons in the site, which looked very different then, especially the Palace and the Cross Group. Often there were informal sessions in the ruins. At Merle's house, we sat on the floor and talked, and we had sessions in a small *champa* near an enclosure with two spider monkeys who were quieter than the howler who attended a later Mesa Redonda. That howler was a former pet who returned to hang around in a tree near a big *champa* that had been built across from Merle's house. Occasionally, the monkey would come down and roar. One afternoon, Francis Robicsek flew in to give a paper. Shortly after he had started to read it, the howler came down low in the tree behind him and joined in. Francis tried valiantly to talk against the howling. Finally, he asked, "What *is* that?" Linda called out, "That's your cousin!"

At the first Mesa Redonda, a magic intellectual chemistry occurred when Linda, Peter, Floyd, and Jeffrey Miller, a Yale graduate student, began to talk together. By the end of the meeting, they had produced a king list for Palenque. Everyone was excited, and there was a wonderful sense of new possibilities. The king list was not a final one; Linda and Peter worked over the years to refine it. But the initial list was an extraordinary accomplishment.

At the end of that fiscal year, I had money in the budget at Dumbarton Oaks, and I decided to bring together for a day and one-half as many as possible of the people who had worked on the Palenque inscriptions. I invited Heinrich Berlin, who had written a breakthrough article on the emblem glyphs associated with Maya sites, but he wrote me that he would not come; he was no longer concerned with "those things with which I used to toy of yore." Floyd, Linda, Peter, and Merle came, as well as Michael Coe, David Kelley, George Kubler, and Tatiana Proskouriakoff, who had written a breakthrough article on history in Maya inscriptions. Linda and Tania sat across the long table from each other; physically and socially, they were two very different personalities. Tania was thin and sharp, reserved and self-contained and clearly not quite approving of the large, earnest Young Turk sitting across from her. I had not structured the meeting, and it did not go well. No one had much to say. The Sunday morning session was a little better, and then Tania, Mike, and George went to the airport, and the others hung around quietly for a while, browsing in books alone or talking quietly two by two. Then something changed: they began to come together, and there was a wonderful moment when they were all on the floor around a copy of Maudslay, and they got a new glyph. Each of them knew or saw something that the others didn't. I said to myself, "That's my group—Linda, Floyd, Dave, Peter, and Merle." I got them together several times after that, and later they continued to get together on their own. Every now and then, I received a postcard with a batch of indecipherable English inscriptions on it.

In 1974 Linda and Peter produced an inventory of the storeroom at Palenque, which included many sculptural remains with inscriptions. Dumbarton Oaks published it in 1979. In 1975–76, Linda was a fellow at Dumbarton Oaks, and, for part of her stay, Floyd was there as a visiting scholar. Later, she worked at Dumbarton Oaks with Robert Rands, a specialist in Palenque ceramics. Linda also contributed to several Dumbarton Oaks conferences and their publications and to a Maya conference and publication at Princeton. One of her triumphs was the glorious 1986 *Blood of Kings* exhibition and catalogue at the Kimbell Art Museum and the Cleveland Museum of Art, a collaboration between Linda and Mary Ellen Miller of Yale.

I have many personal memories: visits at Linda's houses and at my houses, the times when she was a fellow at Dumbarton Oaks, the semester when I replaced her and Terry Grieder at the University of Texas at Austin (and she was in town part of the time for good company). Earlier, when Linda was teaching at the University of South Alabama, in Mobile, she invited me to lecture. She met me at the airport and took me to a party at the home of a herpetologist and a potter (Linda gave me some of her pottery). Linda had told them that I played with Mike Coe's pet pine snake, so, as she egged them on, they handed me a nine-foot, thirty-pound boa named Bertha. Soon, David Schele came in and started toward me. But, seeing Bertha's head going back and forth beside my head, her vibrating tongue moving in and out, and the rest of her wrapped around me,

David said, "I'll talk to you later." Linda was laughing. I felt like the queen facing a serpent on a Yaxchilan lintel. Linda did not hold Bertha that day, but she dealt with large snakes in another way when she later interpreted the Vision Serpent in Maya iconography.

Among other memories is the afternoon we spent at Palenque exploring the Maya aqueducts, wading through the accumulation of water and mud, getting too dirty to ride back to town in anyone's car. At the International Congress of Americanists in Paris, where Linda gave papers on "The Palenque Triad" and "Highland Rabbits and Lowland Lords," we were roommates in a hotel on the Ile St. Louis. I had the sheer joy of taking her into the Sainte Chapelle, which is, of course, formed almost entirely of gorgeous stained glass, almost literally a jewel. She loved it.

Linda was a presence: generous, quick-witted, open-minded, good-humored (mostly), and intellectually stimulating. A rugged individualist, her individualism influenced many people. She was both earthy and spiritual. She had a good eye; she taught people to see. She made fine drawings of Maya sculpture and glyphs, painted big luminous paintings, played the recorder, read science fiction, and liked the art of Gustav Klimt. She had the gift of enjoying. She enjoyed talking, joking, explaining, enthusing.

Recently, I found a cache of letters from some twenty years ago. Most are signed with a wonderful rabbit drawing. In fact, a good deal of the subject matter of those letters concerned rabbits. The Maya associated the rabbit with the moon. In that part of the world, people do not see a man in the moon; they see a rabbit. Maya depictions of the Moon Goddess show her holding a rabbit. Linda thought of her *nahual,* or animal alter ego, as a rabbit, and some of her early work dealt with rabbits. Rabbit and deer are interchangeable in much Maya folklore; sometimes they are brothers. Linda recognized that rabbit and deer skulls are interchangeable in the emblem glyph that identifies the site or lineage of Palenque.

Linda died in the spring of 1998. In June the Art Museum of Princeton University gave a large and splendid party in honor of Gillett Griffin's seventieth birthday. Many of Linda's friends were there. Standing under a huge tent placed on the grass between university buildings, I looked over and saw, near a building at the end, a rabbit hopping along the lawn. It stopped, looked toward the tent, and then went on.

Working with Linda

David Kelley

It was always difficult trying to keep up with Linda, whether climbing a pyramid, publishing new ideas and material, or making great leaps of interpretation. This was obvious the first time I met her at Dumbarton Oaks during that Palenque conference in 1974 arranged by Betty Benson. I had developed some new ideas about the Palenque dynasty during my sabbatical in England and was expecting to be well ahead of the pack, but she and Peter were tremendously ahead of me. After the main conference, Linda, Peter, Merle, and I stayed on and worked together on the earlier part of the sequence. Linda explained to us that the plants depicted on Pakal's coffin referred somehow to lineages. I said that in that case, there should be linguistic evidence to support the view. Floyd and I knew that Landa's letter -l- (ele) corresponds to *le*, "leaf," and that seemed a promising starting point. Betty got us various dictionaries. Checking in K'iche', we found that *le* meant both "leaf" and "lineage," to my considerable astonishment. No matter what ways of checking we used, Linda kept coming up with good answers. Even more striking, she never retreated to her own expertise for justification. Instead, she wanted to understand both the basis of objections and of support from an unexpected area. She decided fairly rapidly that she had to get some understanding of linguistics as well as a much fuller knowledge of Mayas outside Palenque. Peter graduated from Calgary and went on to be Floyd's student at Yale. Linda had received a Dumbarton Oaks fellowship and commuted between Washington and Yale to attend Floyd's classes, so the three of them saw each other fairly often, but I saw them less frequently.

On one occasion I was staying at my home in Jaffrey, New Hampshire, and they came up to visit me. We began talking about the *Dresden Codex*. Soon a copy was spread on the floor across most of the parlor. We were particularly interested, that day, in the transitions from one section to another and in parallels between sections. From Linda, there were occasional excited cries on the order of "Oh, look, this must mean . . . "; Floyd might point out that "the mathematical structure demands . . . ," or "there is a textual parallel between this passage and . . . "; Peter was often the one who pointed out Mayan inscriptions with relevant texts and more frequently the one to say "no, that can't be because . . . " I was the one who cited parallel material in the Borgia or Vienna codices or Polynesia or China. Gradually, it became clear that the eclipse table was related in some fashion to the Serpent Number table and that specifiable dates in that table led into the following elaborate ninety-one-day tables. Any of us was apt to say, "Yes, and if so, then . . . ?" It was a wonderful combination of good fun, intellectual stimulation, disagreements—often vehement and occasionally lasting—but frequently followed by arrival at conclusions we all accepted yet none of us could have reached alone.

On the road to Merida, singing the song of the Chaaks and getting drenched; in Guatemala, looking at helmeted figures from Piedras Negras; at Palenque, listening to howler monkeys and talking about the glyph for the howler monkey; or in Calgary, giving evidence to justify a particular reading (on my demand), pulling texts out of her head and jointly looking at others, with a new reading falling out on the way—wherever I saw Linda, she was enthusiastic and perceptive. It was difficult keeping up with Linda, but whenever I could, it was well worth it.

Writing on Through with Linda

David Freidel

Staring at that little screen, I watched the magic little square bounce along, writing as I talked, backing up and fixing and moving on. It was well after midnight, and Linda and I were at the end of another marathon conversation, trying to put down in some coherent way a big picture of what had happened to take the Maya from the Preclassic into the Classic and how it could be seen in the art. As she typed at that Heathkit Zenith and I watched in fascination, the words just tumbled out of my mouth. Some sentences into it Linda paused and looked at me. "David, have you said this before?" "No" I said, "it just came to me now." We went on, and as she typed she changed and added to the text. I responded to her elaborations and new directions as I saw them appear on the screen. When done, we printed it out on the daisy wheel printer, stared at it for a while, and called it a night.

That was how we moved from talking to writing together, which we continued to do intensively for more than a decade, publishing five articles and two books. What hooked us, I think, was the surprise we would experience periodically, the surprise that came with this peculiarly disciplined kind of improvisation. We came at problems with different memories, different training, and a shared optimism that defied all the false leads and dead ends that must litter free-flowing thought experimentation. We also shared a sense of the organization of Maya thought and art that lent itself to the methods of structuralism. Analysis of diadic relations, triadic relations, and concentric dualism (quincuncial order) were some of the elements of our methodology. Structural analysis is well represented in the study of Maya religion and ritual, as in my teacher Evon Vogt's *Tortillas for the Gods* elucidating the practices of the Zinacanteco Maya in Chiapas. Linda had already shown a predilection for structural analysis in her study of the tri-figure compositions at Palenque, and she embraced structuralism enthusiastically. When in Jerusalem for a conference once, she had the opportunity to meet Claude Levi-Strauss and declared to him that she was a structuralist. In the wake of poststructuralism and postmodernism, Levi-Straussian structuralism may be no longer fashionable, but I think that this way of looking at iconographic and conceptual patterns is reflected in Linda's recent work, such as her article on world trees and creation mountains. When we thought about this methodology, and we always discussed why we were working with particular methods, we concluded that it was appropriate because, as Linda put it, the Maya themselves appeared to be thinking in such structural patterns. Her favorite aphorism was "let the data drive the models." And while that ideal must remain exactly that, an ideal, it reflected her goal of seeing the field progress, even if that meant discarding some favorite idea.

When Linda invited me to write *A Forest of Kings* with her, she made it an absolute condition that I get a decent computer and that I learn the word processor that she was using, Nota Bene. She had in mind a new way of collaborating, one that went beyond the mutual writing on the same text at the same time. She wanted to send disk versions of drafts and have us just write through them and send them back. The drafts of chapters became another medium for the kind of mutual exploration of the material we had always undertaken when aiming for a written result. Linda taught me how to think Maya history through that book. She also showed me how to move open-eyed into serious controversies over such history. The chapter on the Tikal conquest of Uaxactun was an example of how to make a hypothesized event the centerpiece of a productive pattern in evidence spanning all the relevant categories of data—art, architecture, and artifactual contexts, as well as epigraphy. Despite the sustained skepticism of such formidable scholars as David Stuart that there ever was such a war, the Tikal conquest of Uaxactun continues to be a productive hypothesis in the hands of epigraphers and archaeologists such as Federico Fahsen and Juan Antonio Valdés. The final resolution of this matter remains to be seen, and it will be settled by means of evidence that, through interpretation, holds an enduring consensus. But there is no doubt that Linda set an agenda for the discussion of war and conquest in Maya civilization that will be forever consequential.

Linda observed that *A Forest of Kings* was my chance to get inside the envelope of Maya history, but *Maya Cosmos* was her chance to really know that the contemporary Maya peoples were linked to their ancestors in profound and compelling ways. After embarking on that effort, Linda never left the Precolumbian Maya arena of discovery, but she truly dedicated herself to sharing what she could of that insight with living Maya. *Maya Cosmos* set our moral compass on the Maya of today as surely as the star patterns set the creation story of the ancient Maya. Her discovery that the Maya story of creation was painted in the Milky Way and the stars centered our book so decisively that Linda had to tell it as a story. It was as if we had been groping toward something with our draft chapters and finally laid hands on it. It's not like other, more expert Mayanists hadn't been working with celestial patterns. Barb MacLeod literally laid a foundation with her discovery of the Three Stone Place; the Tedlocks had seen such patterns among the K'iche'. It's just that what we had in our heads and in our drafts when Linda saw the living Milky Way linked up history, religion, mathematics, and astronomy in ways that we had never anticipated.

The idea of Classic Maya history is here to stay, thanks in large measure to Linda. The idea of Classic Maya religion as a coherent great vision informing an enduring civilization's political, social, military, and commercial institutions is taking hold in the vital new efforts of many outstanding Mesoamericanists.

Spider Eyes

Merle Greene Robertson

Linda and I were the first to discover that God K played such a special role at Palenque; at least that's what we thought back in 1971. I had been working at Palenque with Bob Rands since 1964 doing drawings and was now taking photographs for the *Sculpture of Palenque* volumes. Linda was working and living with my husband, Bob, and me at our home, Na Chan Bahlum, in La Cañada. Whenever we weren't photographing we were exploring the ruins over and over again.

How did Linda happen to be with me? That goes back a year to when Linda, David, and two of her students made a stop at Palenque on her tour of Mexico gathering photographs for the university archives. They spent several days at Palenque, every minute of which was spent at the ruins. We hit it off right from the start. The morning they were to leave for sites further up the peninsula, Linda was up at dawn for one last look at the ruins. Two days later, who should Bob and I see at our door but Linda and party? She simply could not go on without returning to Palenque. She had been "bitten" by the "Palenque Bug" as had I in 1962 when I stopped off after completing a season's work with the University of Pennsylvania at Tikal.

It was great having Linda at the house and also stimulating, as every archaeologist working in the area stopped off for a day or two at Palenque. Na Chan Bahlum became headquarters for roving Mayanists on the way to or from their sites, as well as for those who came solely to Palenque. Many were the evenings when stimulating conversations took place between an illustrious variety of scholars; even a partial list of our guests can be mind-boggling. Two particularly unusual visitors whom Moises Morales brought over after rescuing them from their overturned jeep were the Lacandon, young Chan Boar, and his Canadian wife, Grace. They had been to Mexico City, supposedly to have his wife's visa corrected so that she could stay in Mexico. Actually, what was happening was that the rest of the Lacandon Indians wanted to get rid of her, and Chan Boar wanted to take another wife, which was their custom, but she would not let him. Linda, Bob Robertson, my husband, Bob Rands, and I spent a great deal of our time politely listening, but it was Linda and Bob Rands who very graciously spent the whole day listening to this story over and over.

Linda, Bob, and I gloried in all that we were absorbing and having such fun with our stream of never-ending guests. One evening Gillett Griffin, David

Joraleman, Paul Gendrop, Bob, and I were sitting on our patio discussing things Maya, as usual, when we came up with the idea that it would be great if we could get a few people we knew to come to Palenque for a week and just talk about Palenque. We sent out letters to people we thought might be interested, and when Bob and I returned to Pebble Beach three weeks later, the telephone was ringing as we entered our house. It was Mike Coe. He said, "Let's do it this Christmas." It was then September. Well, it happened. Thirty-five people came over Christmas in 1973. Everyone made their own arrangements, paid their own bills, and what was intended to be a get-together of Mayanists turned out to be a turning point in the study of Maya history and epigraphy.

Our first meetings were held in the living area of Na Chan Bahlum. The windows were covered with black cloth, and the white wall served as a screen for projecting pictures and note writing. Delegates sat on anything there was to sit on, including beds, chairs, and boxes. Coffee was constantly brewing, and anyone who wanted a drink just helped themselves. You can't imagine a more enthusiastic crowd.

Jeffrey Miller (who died in Merida just a few days after the second Mesa Redonda) played a very important role at this conference. He had brought dozens of Maya dictionaries, which he spread out on the dining table. Jeffrey, Linda, and Peter Mathews (then a sprouting young student of Dave Kelley's at Calgary) spent every spare moment going over these dictionaries. The highlight of the entire conference happened the last day. Linda, Peter, and Jeffrey spent most of the day at the ruins going over hieroglyphs, then returned to the house and spent the rest of the time conferring with Floyd Lounsbury, the great linguistic scholar we were so fortunate to have with us. That evening history was made when they came up with the Palenque king list. White paper was taped on the wall, and Linda drew the glyphs, noting who were the kings. Next came the chore of naming them. We were all thinking in terms of English nicknames. Moises Morales spoke up and said, "But this is a Spanish-speaking country; they should be Spanish names." Then Fray Facunda Ramírez from Tumbala announced, "But they did not speak Spanish; they spoke Ch'ol."

We all knew that the Ch'ol names we were giving them were not the names the ancient Palencanos would have used, but Floyd assured us that the name Pakal was undoubtedly correct. The new Palenque dynasty list made news all over Chiapas. The little town near the railroad station immediately changed its name to Pakal Na, the name it retains today. The Ch'ol now had a living history. They knew the names of their ancient illustrious ancestors. Governor Manuel Velasco Saurez had a bronze plaque made for the front of the municipal building that praised the work of Pakal, the ancestor of today's Palencanos, and hoped that the present-day citizens would keep up the good work started so long ago.

Linda shared all of her thoughts on decipherment with everyone. There were no "secrets" that were just Linda's alone, sitting around waiting to be published. She used to send hastily written notes to "the crazies," as she called us (Floyd, Peter, David Kelley, Mike Coe, Betty Benson, and me). A typical letter started like this: "Merle: The enclosed letters to the Crazies are self explanatory. I can't write about the 2nd miracle that happened at D.O. when Floyd and I got together. It was beautiful and my stay was very successful. Please call me the very instant after you kiss Elizabeth [our English bull dog] when you get home."

One of the great things about working at Palenque was that we always had fun, and it was so easy to dash to the ruins to confirm something we were talking about. Then in the evening, we would all sit on our back patio of Na Chan Bahlum and relate experiences we had had. Inevitably, stories get around to "snake stories." One evening we were all telling our stories. Linda told, in wildly gesticulating terms, her story of the pet boa owned by a colleague of hers at the University of South Alabama, how the boa once got caught in the door while she was playing with it, and she couldn't get its eight-inch-round body out of the half-inch space between the door and the jamb. Finally, they had to take the door off, with Linda proudly carrying the boa around the room coiled around her neck. Of course, I had to tell my "snake" story about the time when I was staying at the ruins by myself. The electricity came on for only an hour in the evening, so most of the evening I worked by lantern light. On this particular night in the low light the wires that hung overhead took on the semblance of a serpent. I knew they were the wires, so I crawled onto my cot in the middle of the floor and blissfully went to sleep. In the morning when I got up, I saw that what I thought were wires the night before really was a snake, and a three-foot deadly *nauyaca* at that. I knew that if I climbed on a ladder and tried to kill it that it would slither down and be lost in the piles of sacks of pot shards and tools all along the wall. I stood in the front doorway and shouted for Augustine, who lived in a small Maya house by the Queen's waterfall. I shouted and shouted, but no one came until Augustine finally showed up after an hour had passed. I told him about the *nauyaca,* and he shrugged his shoulders, probably not really believing me. He took one look and, without saying a word, dashed out the door, cut a long pole with a forked end, and returned. With one thrust he had the snake's head in the fork and with his machete made fast work of the critter. All the time I was telling this story, Linda did not say a word. The next evening the same group was sitting on the patio again, when Linda dashed out yelling, "It's true, it's true." "What's true?" we all said. "Merle's snake story last night. I went out and asked Augustine."

Linda, Bob, and I had a dog. Now that is something, as we all know that Linda was a "cat" person. She and I had gone to Chinkultic, and afterwards we had bought a fifteen-inch ear of Comitan Valley corn from a street vendor and were sitting in the jeep eating it when along came a Maya man carrying a tiny puppy. He stopped at the car and asked if we wanted a dog. We both asked, *"Cuantos?"* Five pesos. Without even thinking, I pulled five pesos out of my pocket, and we had a dog. He trained himself and was the best dog we ever had. We named him Chinkultic. One night we stopped overnight at Trudy Blom's with our puppy, and at dinner Trudy saw that Linda had not finished her soup and that she had eaten only one bite of her bread. Trudy, who was a very good friend of both of us, said in a very loud voice, glaring at Linda, "I was always taught to eat *everything* on my plate." Linda had been sick the entire trip, so I said to Trudy, "But this is the first thing Linda has eaten all week as she has been so sick." Well, now everything was different. She couldn't do enough for Linda and our puppy too. She went to the kitchen and sliced off a big slice of roast beef and brought it to the table for little Chinkultik. When we returned to Palenque and took Linda to the doctor, he said that she had hepatitis. Linda never forgot the piles of candy I fed to her under doctor's orders.

All of us staying at the house one summer (Bob and I, Linda, and Donnan Jeffers) were avid readers—not just about the Maya, but anything good. Linda would read a science fiction book a night, so the place became filled with science fiction. There was one book all three of us wanted to read—*The Exodus*. Every time one of us would lay it down, one of the others would grab it instead of politely letting the first person finish it. Another pastime that went on whenever any of our friends showed up was the card game "Oh shit." This game was still played at Linda's in Texas up until the very end. Linda also loved to joke with people, so tearing down from the ruins in the dark in our Safari late at night was hilarious. John Bowles, then a high school senior, later a Harvard graduate, and now an India art specialist, was the unfortunate recipient of our frequent "spider eyes" jokes. Linda and I would yell out periodically on the wild ride down the hill to "look out for the spider eyes: there's one right there." Poor John, try as he did, he was not able to see our "spider eyes," and it wasn't until much later that he finally caught on as to what Linda and I were doing. To this day he remembers the "spider eyes" of Palenque.

When I was photographing the sculpture on Palenque piers for the Princeton books, Linda was a great help. We would have to set up the camera on the platform at the end of a fifteen-foot plank leading out from the temple in daylight and then wait until dark to start shooting. We would sit on the end of the plank out from the Temple of the Inscriptions and every night debate whether or not the Maya lived in the Palace at one time or other. At that time I was for having them live there at times, and Linda was not. One night I would win the argument, and the next night Linda would win. We did this over and over all the time we were working there.

For nearly thirty years Linda and I had a beautiful, very special friendship, sharing much of what was developing in Maya history and epigraphy all over

Mesoamerica. This was not just a professional relationship but a very special friendship that covered having fun in discovering things and both of us being artists, sharing in the beauty of what we saw both in the architecture and sculpture and in the Maya people themselves. When Linda chose me to be her mentor at the Society of Life Models Honoring New Explorers and Mentors in Chicago in February 1997, I was deeply honored but felt that it almost should have been the other way around, as I had learned so much from her.

The Age of Schele

Michael D. Coe

In the long history of Maya studies, there was once an "Age of Thompson," followed by an "Age of Proskouriakoff." There is no doubt in my mind that for over twenty-five years we have been living in an "Age of Schele." It began in 1972, when this astonishing woman burst upon the Maya scene at the First Palenque Mesa Redonda and only ended with her premature death in April 1998. I doubt whether we will ever see the likes of such a person again, for she was unique in every way.

In one respect, Linda was the Sylvanus Morley of our own times. Morley was a brilliant popularizer and enthusiast of all things Maya and a charismatic personality whom the public came to identify with the world of the ancient Maya, yet in appearance Linda was his exact opposite. Whereas Morley (whom I never knew) was said to have been small, neat, dapper, and a finicky dresser, Linda was large, careless of dress (one saw her in jeans far more than in a skirt), and incredibly ribald in speech. Her audiences, whether NASA scientists or "little old ladies from Dubuque," ate up every word and came back for more, year after year. Be that as it may, behind her Nashville twang and devil-may-care aspect was not only the visual acuity of a talented artist but also an all-encompassing mind approaching genius. In truth, she created our modern vision of what Maya civilization was all about.

In September 1998 I spent two weeks as a guest of Linda's old department in Austin, staying with David in the Schele home and having the use of her old office at the university. These weeks were an eye-opener, for they showed me aspects of Linda's life and thought that I had only surmised or knew at second hand. A case in point was the library in my bedroom, with shelves filled with what seemed to be every sci-fi paperback ever printed, hundreds upon hundreds of them, all neatly alphabetized by author. Her reading branded her as a visionary.

I was aware that, like her beloved friend and colleague Floyd Lounsbury, Linda was a highly skillful computernik, so the first thing I did when I sat behind her office desk was to switch on her computer. When the screensaver came up, it turned out to be a simulation of an endless trip through the starry universe. In addition to the usual calendrical software, Linda had installed one astronomical program after another, and I called them all up. She was a true space traveler of the mind, like her intellectual predecessors, the Maya astronomer-scribes. When Linda spoke of the Maya creation taking place among the starry heavens on a certain day five millennia ago, she knew exactly what she was talking about.

I personally consider *Maya Cosmos* (written in collaboration with David Freidel and Joy Parker) her greatest single achievement; there is no question in my mind that this great creation story was as basic to Classic Maya culture as the Book of Genesis is to Western civilization. It was Linda's all-encompassing vision that brought this to light in the first place.

How did she do this? It was not just an amassing of data—Linda had total control of an incredible quantity of facts—but, I believe, her ability to bring together all sorts of approaches to the data, with the goal of describing a mental universe that the Maya themselves would have recognized as valid and important. This ability became apparent to all of us lucky enough to hear her at that amazing 1973 meeting in Palenque. Right from the start, this young artist enlisted others in her intellectual enterprises: she was a born scholarly collaborator. In those days, it was Floyd, Peter Mathews, and Dave Kelley who teamed up with Linda to work out the dynastic history of Palenque. And it was probably Floyd who convinced her of the importance of getting into the linguistic side of decipherment, leading to her interest in Maya grammar and her eventual doctoral dissertation on the verbs.

But Linda was always a painter at heart, and a highly competent one, with incredible visual acuity. She and Miguel Covarrubias were probably the most naturally talented artists ever to draw Mesoamerican art and architecture (Tania Proskouriakoff was good at this, but I don't think she ever had the facility that these two did, and some of her reconstructions, although architecturally accurate, look labored and must have cost her great effort). The *Blood of Kings,* the great exhibition and catalogue of Classic Maya art which she put together in close collaboration with Mary Miller, was the most important contribution to this subject since Spinden's 1913 *A Study of Maya Art* and far more influential because it created a new paradigm for the Maya based not only on art history and connoisseurship but also on the very latest developments in decipherment in which Linda had played a major role. She and Mary had made it possible for those long-dead Maya kings to tell their story in their own words, and a gripping story it was. The old Thompsonian picture of a peaceful, "Apollonian" Maya was gone forever.

Linda had the common touch, there can be no doubt about that, and the public responded accordingly. I remember one night many years back when she was slated to speak at the American Museum of Natural History in New York.

I had come down from Yale with a group of my students. We were lucky to have reserved seats in the huge auditorium, for the line of people waiting to get in went right out the museum's doors and around a very large city block. Finally, Linda strode on the stage, and in five short minutes she had that audience in the palm of her hand. Speaking without notes, funny and erudite at the same time, taking occasional swigs of Coca-Cola from a bottle held in one hand, she had both amateurs and hardened professionals mesmerized. I think that the ghost of Morley would have been pleased with her.

I'm not even going to mention the nineteen successive Maya hieroglyphic workshops that she conducted every year from 1978 to 1997, for there are others who were far more involved with these than I. However, I attended three and learned much that I managed to sneak into new editions of my general book on the Maya. The one that I enjoyed the most was when I came with Gillett Griffin. When her audience seemed stumped over some difficult glyphic detail, she used her old friend as a foil, all with the greatest sense of fun: "You people don't get what I'm saying? Listen, if Gillett can get this, *anybody* can!"

Collegiality and generosity were built into Linda's ebullient, outgoing personality. I've had considerable experience in trying to get Mayanist colleagues to let me use published (and unpublished) data, photos, and drawings in my books, and it often hasn't been a very good one. Dr. Freud divided the world between anal-retentive personalities and oral ones. I'm sorry to say that all too many archaeologists, and the money-grubbing museums that they work for, fall into the first category (I won't mention names, but that isn't necessary). Linda was definitely an oral type. Her attitude was, "Mike, I'm here to help scholars, not hinder them. Go ahead and use any of my drawings, free of charge—just give me credit."

This openness and generosity of spirit clearly made her one of the great teachers of our time, and I've been privileged to know many of the outstanding students whom she trained over the years. There was always a special understanding between us Yalies and the Texans, and we were happy to send some of our very best graduating seniors down to Austin for advanced degrees. In fact, it was not long before there were complaints from enemies about an Austin–New Haven axis, but I always took this as a sign of success.

Yes, Linda had enemies, but I'm proud to say that they were my enemies, too. And yes, Linda had many friends, and I'm even prouder to say that they were my friends, too. The Maya field is an intensely competitive one, with too many scholars trying to occupy a very small academic space. I am often reminded of anthropologist George Foster's Principle of Limited Good. This is a mind-set that says that there is only so much good in the world, and therefore the more good that comes to you, the less comes to me, and vice versa. Linda's brilliant success in creating a new view of the Maya based largely on epigraphy and art history seriously annoyed an influential group of field archaeologists, who never forgave her. Instead of joining in the enterprise begun by Linda, many have chosen to ignore it or carp at it from the sidelines.

I've said that Linda was unique, and one testimony to her uniqueness was her reaching out not only to the Western-educated public but, perhaps more important, to the living Maya themselves. So many major and minor digs in the Maya area end with the archaeologists packing it all up and leaving for home, perhaps with the bones of the greatest Maya kings stuffed into shoe boxes or paper bags, and that is that. The Maya themselves—who are in some cases their own workmen—hear no more of it. In her final years, Linda, along with Nikolai Grube and Federico Fahsen, held seminars in Guatemala and in Yucatan to re-introduce Maya intellectuals to the wonderful writing system that their own ancestors had created almost twenty-four centuries ago. As the native peoples of Mesoamerica begin to reclaim their ancient heritage after five centuries of heinous oppression, Linda will be seen as a true pioneer—a pioneer in redressing this very large sin of omission on the part of professional archaeologists who ought to have had more of a social conscience.

What will Linda's legacy be? It is an established fact that the reputations of great individuals often suffer an eclipse after their death, and it wouldn't surprise me if this happened to Linda (a nasty anonymous obituary in the *Times* of London was probably a harbinger of things to come). Real appreciation sometimes comes only after several decades have passed and a new generation can view things more dispassionately. Certainly, as far as the Maya decipherment is concerned, it is now time to test rigorously all past glyphic interpretations and readings, including Linda's, in the context of the grammar and syntax of the ancient written language. Many of the readings from the "Age of Schele" have been, and will continue to be, changed. But does this alter my view of Linda? Not a bit!

I look at Linda as a mighty creator figure, who almost single-handedly made the study of the Maya truly interdisciplinary. Neither Morley nor his Carnegie successor, A. V. Kidder, had been able to do that. I think that her great goal was to re-create the material, mental, and artistic universe of the preconquest Maya in a way that they themselves would recognize as true. She may have gotten some of the details wrong, but I feel certain that her overall vision will surely hold up.

We are told that "God is in the details," but surely He is also in visions.

Remembrances of Linda Schele at the University of Texas at Austin

Dorie Reents-Budet

As often happens in life, momentous occasions are not recognized until years later. So it is with the arrival of Linda Schele in 1977 at the University of Texas at Austin and the gathering together of an assortment of dedicated and excited students. Little did we realize that our individual and collective pursuits, under the inspiration of Linda, would set the stage for and help determine the pattern of one of the most remarkable programs in Mesoamerican culture history.

When Linda first came to the University of Texas at Austin, she encountered a small group of students spread throughout the university, from the Departments of Anthropology, Art History, and Latin American Studies, to the Department of Physics. Because we were being trained in different fields, and because each of us had a very different background, we were able to contribute unique skills and viewpoints to our collective efforts. We merged into a productive whole inspired by Linda's enthusiasm for Maya art and hieroglyphic writing and her vision for an interdisciplinary approach to Precolumbian studies.

As an "outsider" to the academy, Linda was not restrained by what she viewed as artificial constraints on models of thoughtful inquiry and sources of pertinent data. She constantly encouraged us to explore any relevant source of information, to pursue any methodology that seemed to lead down productive paths, and to interact with fellow students and professionals both inside and outside the discipline of art history. This openness is one of the strengths of Linda's intellectual approach, and its practice has well served her first group of graduate students during the early 1980s.

An important social component of the successful academic environment created by Linda was her approach to her students. She did not view us as students to be instructed but instead as participants in the process of revealing ancient Mesoamerican history. She led us to understand that, in her mind, each person had an equal chance to discover an unknown fact, the reading of a hieroglyph, or the meaning of an iconographic sign. Such individual empowerment only strengthened our dedication to the collective pursuit of Maya and Mesoamerican culture history.

The productivity of this intellectual environment is best exemplified by the 1980 graduate seminar in Maya hieroglyphic writing taught by Linda. We formed small groups to tackle the monumental inscriptions of the major lowland sites of the Classic period. This was one of the most memorable times in my career as a Mayanist, when, together with Andrea Stone and Robert Coffman, we deciphered the dynastic history of Caracol, Belize. Granted, during these early years of Maya glyphic studies, the phonetic and linguistic values of only a few glyphs had been established, and glyphic "decipherment" was an exercise in structural analysis, pattern recognition, and semantic glosses. Nevertheless, we were able to reconstruct the basic chronological framework of Caracol's dynasty and to identify the names of its rulers. We knew it was possible to do so by employing the structural method pioneered by Tatiana Proskouriakoff and further developed by Floyd Lounsbury, David Kelley, Peter Mathews, Jeffrey Miller, and Linda. We were quite aware that we were the first people in eleven hundred years to discern the names and know the basic histories of the rulers of this important Maya polity . . . a thrilling moment in any student's career!

Often Linda's seminars were held at her home, where we had free access to her extensive collection of photographs, photocopies, and original drawings of Maya and other Mesoamerican carved stone monuments and portable artifacts. These drawings were the crucial resource for our epigraphic and iconographic research. The seminars' venue in Linda's home also allowed us to first watch *Star Trek* episodes on television. Although this may seem merely like an excuse for a bunch of students and their professor to have fun, it actually set the stage for a more sobering realization: although we were engaged in the pursuit of history through established academic methods, all histories are only interpretations of reality and the boundary between history and mythology oftentimes is permeable. The Classic Maya, too, were carving in stone their own historical mythologies and social ideologies, just as *Star Trek* served to create modern mythologies that reflect contemporary ideologies. This understanding fostered caution in our approach to and interpretations of Classic Maya hieroglyphic texts and imagery.

Linda's belief that we all are partners in deciphering culture history has profoundly affected my own teaching philosophy. Following her model, I do not seek to instruct but rather to lead students along the path of intellectual discovery. I prefer to help them recognize their own strengths and learn how to apply these to the task at hand. I strive to instill in my students the realization that each person embodies potential, that although it may take great effort to achieve one's potential, ultimately we are constrained only by self-imposed limitations.

Because the world of Maya studies is highly competitive, Linda strongly believed that the only effective survival strategy was for each of us to carve out our own niche. If necessary, she would make an introduction or send a word of confidence on our behalf to a professional colleague. But it was entirely up to each of us to discover our research interests, formulate a research design, and then to make it from there, mostly on our own. This strategy nurtured a group of highly independent and successful professionals. In many ways, it was the correct approach during these early years when art historical investigations had not yet been accepted as a viable approach to New World culture history. During these years, Precolumbian studies was dominated almost entirely by social scientists following the path of the "New Archaeology" (archaeology in the service of testing models of social theory). Linda's writings, teaching, and lectures opened up the field such that today, art historical investigations (especially iconographic and epigraphic studies) are integral components of the exploration of Precolumbian culture history. In light of Linda's contributions that helped to make art history integral to Precolumbian studies, her students and colleagues hope Linda's forward momentum will live on (even though her department chose an anthropologist as her replacement).

The past decade has witnessed an ever-increasing competitiveness for professional positions in a shrinking job market. One of the results of this trend may be the undermining of Linda's original approach of granting independence to her graduate students. Today, the support and promotion by one's professor are requisite for a student's advancement—even his or her survival. Although the current approach may be a more efficient method of advancing a student's career, one contemplates the potential loss of intellectual and professional individualism and independence on the part of the students.

The true reward of the academic life is the privilege to pursue a subject that engages the mind, that allows one to seek new intellectual ground and to draw upon all of life's experiences in the quest to contribute to our collective knowledge and understanding of the world. A crucial part of the academic process is the concept of intellectual play—of freedom of thought and of interaction with one's colleagues without fear of ridicule. This was a fundamental component of the intellectual atmosphere created by Linda Schele during her early years at the University of Texas at Austin. One can only hope that this intellectual environment will prevail and that her spirit will live on, perpetuating a type of creative, scholarly environment where nothing is not worth considering and everything is possible.

Remembering the *Blood of Kings*

Mary Ellen Miller

Readers know that Linda and I organized the *Blood of Kings* exhibit together, but neither of us ever described our working relationship for that project at the time. So I thought I'd try to tell the story here or at least a few pieces of the story. I had known Linda since my undergraduate days, when the work of the first Palenque Mesa Redonda was rocking Maya studies and when Gillett Griffin had invited her to speak at Princeton, where I was a student. When I had looked for a graduate program in Precolumbian art history, Linda was not yet teaching at the University of Texas, and I had gone off to Yale to be George Kubler's student and also to work with Mike Coe and Floyd Lounsbury. During my first year of graduate school, Linda visited Yale one spring week—she, David Joralemon, Dicey Taylor, and I sat up half the night in Dicey's apartment looking at slides of works and talking about the future of Precolumbian studies. The following day, after Floyd's seminar, I gave Linda a ride to Princeton in my rusted-out 1973 Maverick. Linda kept the passenger window rolled down in order to keep up a steady stream of cigarettes—I don't think I ever let anyone but Linda smoke in my car. But we had a great three-hour ride, free-associating on Maya art. By the time we hit the Vince Lombardi Rest Area for a pit stop, I had also sketched out the dissertation I planned to write on Bonampak. When I dropped Linda off at

Gillett's, we were having a grand time, rewriting Maya studies and mapping out a series of books that we would write "someday."

From that moment on, Linda and I were colleagues who talked to one another about their work. Two years later, Linda was an assistant professor at Texas, and I was writing my dissertation at Dumbarton Oaks in Washington, D.C. Linda came to visit the Stuarts (George, Gene, and David) for a week over spring break, and she spent quite a bit of time at Dumbarton Oaks, where she had happily been a fellow herself a few years before. Linda and Dave Stuart helped me tackle the Bonampak glyphs; they particularly looked at the captions that royal attendants bore in the paintings and struggled with the problematic verbal statement at the end of the Initial Series. I was grateful for their assistance: with help from many corners the Bonampak dissertation was submitted in 1981.

In the early 1980s Linda and I had both finished our dissertations, and we were both assistant professors, she at Texas and I at Yale. Linda was already a well-known figure in the field, of course. From the days of the first Mesa Redonda, her leadership was clear, but without what she called the "union card," the Ph.D., she had remained a professor of art in Alabama. Once she received her Ph.D. she began to command an important role not only in Maya studies but also in art history. She turned her dissertation into a book, and she began to think about other projects. Quite interestingly, we had both begun to think about how an exhibition might serve to promulgate the changes that were taking place in the scholarly understanding of the Maya to a much broader public.

Then, remarkably, in 1983, in separate conversations with Dee Smith, an entrepreneurial young man in Fort Worth, we imagined essentially identical exhibitions of Maya art organized around the principal themes that we had come to recognize as the dominant ones in both Maya writing and art. Dee was the spark that ignited the exhibition: he came to the Mesa Redonda at Palenque that year, and he had conversations with every Mayanist he could find over a beer or a cup of coffee. At the end of the meeting, he was ready to return to Fort Worth and to begin trying to bring together the Kimbell Art Museum and a team of Schele and Miller in order to pull off a great Maya show.

And so, facilitated by Dee, during the fall of 1983, Linda and I met with Emily Sano, a curator at the Kimbell, and Ted Pillsbury, the director. We had already decided that core exhibition themes would follow the principal stages in the life of a Maya king: installation in office, success as a warrior, bloodletting, the ballgame, and death. We photocopied lots of pictures and drawings, and Ted was particularly drawn in by the Yaxchilan lintels. "Give me a title," he said, "and make it say something about blood." "The Blood of Kings" rolled right off Linda's tongue, and the name of the show was set.

Over the next eighteen months, we traveled to museums both separately and together, coming up with a list of 150 objects for the exhibition—a list that would eventually be winnowed to just 116. Linda was nearly speechless when she returned home from the British Museum, where Elizabeth Carmichael had essentially promised her every Maya object in storage. The promise of the British Museum pieces anchored the principal themes of the exhibition. My jaw dropped when a curator at the Baltimore Art Museum took me into storage and showed me a weird Jaina figurine that was not on display, so odd it had seemed. It was of course the most tortured Jaina figurine known (Plate 94, *Blood of Kings*). We traveled together to Belize in hope of negotiating loans, but after days of working in the storerooms in Belmopan, we left suspecting that no arrangement would work out—and we were correct. Linda had assembled most of a mosaic mask, though, and left the Polaroid snapshots for the director of archaeology; we'd also come upon a beautiful carved shell whose workmanship seemed almost identical to an object in the Houston Museum of Fine Arts (Plate 18, *Blood of Kings*) and whose attribution was "Blue Creek"—or what we assumed was Rio Azul's Belize extension. Linda went on a long and ultimately fruitless mission to Mexico City; I traveled with greater success to Honduras, which generously loaned key works to the show.

By the end of 1984 we had added two themes in order to accommodate the many works that were less explicitly encapsulated by a limited verbal structure in the texts: the Royal Person, to look at the special attire of a king, and Courtly Life, for the assemblage of works that both enriched palace life and in turn described it. We divided up the chapters: Linda would write about the Royal Person, Kingship and Accession, Bloodletting and the Vision Quest, and Death and the Journey to Xibalba. I would write Courtly Life, Warfare and Captive Sacrifice, and the Ballgame. Emily Sano began the complicated process of negotiating formally for the loan of works, and the Cleveland Museum of Art signed on as a second venue. We found ourselves limited to just two venues in order to accommodate the limitations imposed by the British Museum, whose contributions were so central. We were thrilled that the Kimbell took us up on our request that Justin Kerr make the photographs for the catalogue.

So in late July 1985, our minds were concentrated on these works, and we were ready to start the book. Working with the Kimbell, we knew what sort of book we were going to write, a book that would be far more than a conventional catalogue, a book that would stand as a thematic introduction to Maya art. But what of the introduction, the central narrative? This we planned to write together: Linda invited me to work in Austin, and off I went for fifteen days, moving into Linda's tiny guest room.

Both Linda and I had faced major changes in our lives in the years that had intervened since the initial conceptualization of the exhibition, both personal and professional. But for two days we did nothing but carry on about the objects, occasionally lamenting the ones we had not been able to land for the show but mostly just talking nonstop on what Linda liked to call the "gotchas," the promised loans. Only rarely did we cross to the personal. "Do you think you'll have children?" she asked. Exactly a decade her junior, I said "yes," and we talked about the difficulty of a career for women with kids. But mostly we kept our eyes on the prize: arguing the case for *Blood of Kings.*

In those early days we struggled with each other's internal clock. We had traveled together, but we had never tried to write together. I'm a morning person, up and looking for coffee and a newspaper with the sun, but Linda was a night owl. She rose at noon or later, her motor warming up slowly, with Coca-Cola and CNN. At 10 P.M. she was really cooking, lighting cigarette after cigarette with animation; at midnight she'd remember someone we should call long distance; by 1 A.M. I had collapsed. On day three we began to write pieces that would form the introduction: we started with the "Characteristics of Maya Art" (*Blood of Kings:*33), an attempt to categorize the corpus we had selected for the exhibition. After I had fallen asleep, Linda wrote on into the night, leaving a printout for me on her computer; when I awoke in the morning, I went for a short run, made coffee, and then carried on alone for a few hours, until we could start the process again. On day four we wrote the section we called "How Maya Art Works" (pp. 35–38), and at midnight we were dancing over the books in Linda's study, so pleased we were with the way we were working and even with the words we were writing. And we continued our dance every so often as we worked during the coming days, hands on each other's shoulders, celebrating the wonderful fun we were having.

In these days when we worked together, Linda usually manned the keyboard, perhaps because it was her computer, perhaps because her very up-to-the-minute Zenith ran programs unfamiliar to a Macintosh user like me. But I typed on while Linda slept, and we each deciphered the other's hand-scrawled commentary that filled the margins of what we had printed out.

In and around the writing, we were doing test tastes of the flavors of Bluebell Ice Cream, Linda's favorite brand and unknown to a northerner like me. We went to the supermarket, and I planned for what I swore would be super-healthy meals, but we would slip and find ourselves turning the ingredients for a healthy meat loaf into rich cheeseburgers instead. I met ingredients in Linda's kitchen that I hadn't crossed before (Salad Supreme sticks in my mind), and I put staples in her pantry—sun-dried tomatoes and extra-virgin olive oil—to concoct quick pasta sauces. Every once in a while we threw ourselves into novels, just for a quick escape, and Linda would convince me to watch a favorite episode of *Star Trek* from her video collection. The one time I set off in Linda's big station wagon by myself, Austin cops gave me a speeding ticket, so I learned my lesson: don't mess with Texas, a favorite line of Linda's.

Having made some progress, we needed to face the question of where to start the book. On day five we wrote the first paragraph of the book, carefully measuring our words to match the big picture we had been describing to one another, to the Kimbell, and to curators around the world as we had organized the exhibition. What was this exhibition? From that first paragraph in the book we went straight to the last paragraph on page 11, framing the question historically and then mapping the history we proposed, naming Maya kings, presenting our case. Linda and I argued through each sentence: how we would use the word *king*, for example, and which European comparisons we would draw. And then blood. We understood the role blood played in all Mesoamerican societies, but we believed that this was the unifying aspect of Maya ritual life, its mortar, as we came to say. We turned the sentence that reviewers would repeat time and again around several times before settling on just how we would put it and where in the paragraph. Sentence two: "Blood was the mortar of ancient Maya ritual life."

And then we were on a roll, completing the section that would end at the top of page 18 the next day. We called Emily Sano, our curator at the Kimbell, even before we'd completed that portion of the text: she hopped on a plane and came to Austin on a Saturday morning. In the days just before the widespread use of fax machines, she hadn't seen the text before she arrived: she sat down in Linda's reading chair, lit a cigarette, and waved us away for two hours. "You guys," she started, shaking her head slightly and holding her hands palm up when she found us later in Linda's study, "this is it. You've got it. This is great." I made up a pot of fresh coffee from one of Linda's favorites of the summer—was it hazelnut? or French roast?—and we sat down with Emily. "Now let me tell you what else I want to see: A Guide to the Gods, so that the reader can follow you once you hit the chapters." We groaned at the thought of such an additional assignment, just as we were imagining hitting our own chapters, but within forty-eight hours we had composed "Maya Gods and Icons" (*Blood of Kings*:41–55), identifying, photocopying, and pasting the illustrations that Linda would draw later.

We'd written over forty pages in ten days or so; exhausted, we hopped on a flight one morning for a day trip to Houston, where Justin and Barbara Kerr were photographing works in the Museum of Fine Arts for the exhibition. The escape from Austin was fruitful, and we began to plan a symposium to accompany the opening of the exhibition some nine months in the future. What were the questions we were *not* asking in *Blood of Kings*? What could Bill Fash tell us about early Copan or Arthur Demarest about polity organization or David Freidel about Yucatan? We were plotting the next book even as the first was launched.

Refreshed by the break and the good company of the Kerrs, I started the historiography section, "The Modern Invention of the Ancient Maya," the next morning. Linda took to this section with relish. We worked through her excellent library, pulling books off shelves and finding damning quotes from Thompson and Morley. Linda would chortle as she read Thompson and then take in a deep breath of appreciation when she read what insights Joe Spinden had had early in the century. We completed most of the introduction, chasing down footnotes and adding sites to an outline map.

Some seventy-five-odd pages later, Linda took me to the airport. Bone tired and a bit burned out, we'd done what we'd said we'd do, write the introduction—and never has a collaboration been such a joint project. Over the next three months, we'd write our separate chapters and the long entries that went with objects; Linda would add the cultural overview on pages 9–11 of the published volume. In the process of writing, Linda decided to create a final chapter, "Kingship and the Maya Cosmos," to expand beyond the concept of death. But our initial text stood—and still, quite remarkably, stands today.

On January 1, 1986, Linda called me up. "You'll never guess what I've done," she said. Well, I couldn't, and although there was no point in my trying to imagine what it would be that Linda would do, I did notice that there was no cigarette exhale on the line. "I've quit smoking," she said quietly. "The patch." "Darn," I said, ever so happy for her. "Why oh why couldn't you have quit *six months* ago!" And then a pause. "You know, Linda, the next thing I know, you'll be size 8—and maybe by the time of the *Blood of Kings* opening!" Well, of course she was not a size 8 at the opening, but she never smoked another cigarette.

Linda had collaborated with other Mayanists before—Peter Mathews and David Stuart, of course—and would do so later, with David Freidel, chiefly, and Peter Mathews once again. I went on to collaborate with other Mayanists as well, chiefly Steve Houston and Karl Taube. But only Linda and I danced. We were literally spinning around by the opening of the exhibition, for we saw our dreams come true: the *Blood of Kings* transformed the way Maya art would henceforth be seen and even the way the antiquity of the New World would be approached. Some archaeologists railed against the exhibition, and a few art historians carped, but we didn't look back: we knew we had changed the contours of the Maya field, and indeed we did.

Linda Scholastica

David Schele

Linda was raised in a Methodist family, and like many of her youthful peers, she was taken by the romance and idealism of entering the world of Methodist missionaries. Also like many of her peers, as she grew older, attended college, and observed world events, she became disenchanted with organized religion and its historical excesses. Through the thirty years I knew Linda, she never expressed any interest in joining a church and in some ways seemed even hostile to modern religion. It may have come as something of a surprise to those who knew her that, on her death bed and comatose, I made the decision to have her chrismated into the Orthodox Church. This is the short story behind that decision.

Although Linda was not interested in organized religion, she was very concerned with the spiritual aspects of life, especially as they molded the culture of different peoples. In the 1970s and 1980s, as she developed an understanding of Maya culture, she came to understand that to a very great extent the form of that culture was determined by its spiritual conception of the universe. Through the late 1980s and 1990s this concern with the spiritual intensified as she formed close working and personal relationships with a number of modern Maya, and she came to understand how deeply their present-day worldview depends on their perception of how the otherworld and its forces are structured, how they can react with it, and how its forces affect their lives. It is a measure of Linda's own acceptance of a spiritual view of the universe that she used just this approach in her presentations to a NASA committee established to determine how best to explain their programs to the public and to argue the importance of spiritual beliefs with scientists such as astronomer Carl Sagan, a determined atheist and materialist.

One of our friends for many years in Austin has been Father Robert Williams, archbishop of North America in the Old Catholic Church and a dedicated amateur Mayanist and Mixtec scholar. Several years ago the Old Catholics merged with the Orthodox Church, Western Rite, retaining Father Bob as archbishop. When Linda entered the hospital for the last time early Thursday morning, family, friends, and students quickly gathered in support, including Kent Reilly, a longtime friend and former student who had converted to the Orthodox faith. Soon Father Bob was called. He came directly from Good Friday services, an imposing figure still wearing his most elaborate vestments and carrying his bishop's scepter, and he stayed until Linda's death on the afternoon of Holy Saturday. At some point after Father Robert arrived, Kent presented me with several persuasive arguments for having Linda taken into the church.

The Orthodox Church has changed little from the early days of Christianity, and it still uses a liturgy that has remained unchanged since before the time of Pakal, a historical note that Linda would have appreciated. Also, the Orthodox Church has a methodology for offering prayers for the departed in perpetuity; Linda was so moved by the many people offering prayers for her in so many different religions around the world that I thought this continuation would have been an equally emotional experience for her. It is comforting to me to know that she is remembered at services every day of every week of every year. But more important, Orthodox priests are in the business of opening portals to the otherworld. For instance, when an ikon is painted it is just an image of a religious figure, but when it is consecrated it becomes a window into the spiritual realm through which the Orthodox, priest and layperson alike, can communicate directly with the spiritual dimension. Furthermore, during Mass the priests prepare the sacraments, then open a portal to the otherworld through which they are sent for consecration. When the sacraments return, Holy Communion can be performed. Finally, Father Bob decided to give Linda the church name Sister Scholastica, after Saint Scholastica, the twin sister of Saint Benedict. Together these two saints are credited with establishing the monastic movement in Europe, which is largely responsible for preserving learning during the Dark Ages, an endeavor that corresponded to Linda's effort to restore to the modern Maya a sense of their ancestors' history and written language.

Although Linda was becoming increasingly concerned with spiritual matters and was the eager subject of several healing and cleansing rituals performed by her Maya friends, it is not certain that she would ever have made a conscious decision to join a church on her own. However, after reflecting on the correspondences between the beliefs and practices of the Orthodox Church and the Mesoamerican world that Linda so loved, I made the plunge on her behalf. On Friday, one day before she died, Linda became Orthodox. On the next Wednesday we held Linda's funeral. Annette Morris, an artist and longtime friend, decorated the funeral home with cattail reeds and lined the aisles with marigold blossoms, Maya symbols of the place of creation and path to the otherworld. Father Robert, with Fathers Anthony and Aidan and Sister Gwen, sang the Orthodox service *Pannykhida* in one of the most noble and hauntingly beautiful funeral services I have ever witnessed.

References

Alexander, Helen

1992 Celestial Links to the Ancestors: A Pattern Analysis of Celestial Events on Twelve Dates Recorded on Tikal Stela 31. *U Mut Maya* 4:48–60.

Allebrand, Raimund

1997 Renaissance der Maya: Indianischer Aufbruch in Guatemala. In *Die Erben der Maya: Indianischer Aufbruch in Guatemala,* edited by Raimund Allebrand, pp. 69–135. Horlemann, Unkel.

Anawalt, Patricia

1981 *Indian Clothing before Cortés: Mesoamerican Costumes from the Codices.* University of Oklahoma Press, Norman.

Anaya, Armando, Stanley Paul Guenter, and Marc Zender

2002 Sak Ts'i': A Case Study of Politics and Geography in the Alto Usumacinta. *Latin American Antiquity,* in press.

Anderson, Arthur O. (editor)

1950 *Morleyana: A Collection of Writings in Memoriam Sylvanus Griswold Morley, 1883–1948.* School of American Research and the Museum of New Mexico, Santa Fe.

Ashmore, Wendy

1989 Construction and Cosmology: Politics and Ideology in Lowland Maya Settlement Patterns. In *Word and Image in Maya Culture,* edited by William F. Hanks and Don S. Rice, pp. 272–286. University of Utah Press, Salt Lake City.

1991 Site-Planning Principles and Concepts of Directionality among the Ancient Maya. *Latin American Antiquity* 2(3):199–226.

1992 Deciphering Maya Architectural Plans. In *New Theories on the Ancient Maya,* edited by Elin C. Danien and Robert J. Sharer, pp. 173–184. University Museum, University of Pennsylvania, Philadelphia.

Aveleyra de Anda, Luis

1963 An Extraordinary Composite Stela from Teotihuacan. *American Antiquity* 29:235–237.

Aveni, Anthony F.

1980   *Skywatchers of Ancient Mexico*. University of Texas Press, Austin.

1989   *Empires of Time*. Basic, New York.

1996   Maya Cosmos. *American Anthropologist* 98(1):197–198.

Aveni, Anthony F., and Lorren D. Hotaling

1994   Monumental Inscriptions and the Observational Basis of Maya Planetary Astronomy. *Archaeoastronomy* (supplement to *Journal for the History of Astronomy*) 19:S21–S54.

Baird, Ellen

1989   Star Wars at Cacaxtla. In *Mesoamerica after the Decline of Teotihuacan, A.D. 700–900,* edited by Richard Diehl and Janet Berlo, pp. 105–122. Dumbarton Oaks, Washington, D.C.

Barrera Vásquez, Alfredo (editor)

1980   *Diccionario maya Cordemex: Maya-español, español-maya*. Ediciones Cordemex, Merida, Mexico.

Bassie-Sweet, Karen

1991   *From the Mouth of the Dark Cave: Commemorative Sculpture of the Late Classic Maya*. University of Oklahoma Press, Norman.

Bastarrachea, Juan R., Ermilo Yah Pech, and Fidencio Briceño Chel

1992   *Diccionario básico español-maya, maya-español*. Maldonado Editores, Mexico City.

Berlin, Heinrich

1958   El glifo 'emblema' en las inscripciones mayas. *Journal de la Société des Américanistes* 47:111–119.

1963   The Palenque Triad. *Journal de la Société des Américanistes* 52:91–99.

1977   *Signos y significados en las inscripciones mayas*. Instituto Nacional del Patrimonio Cultural de Guatemala, Guatemala City.

Berlo, Janet C.

1983   The Warrior and the Butterfly: Central Mexican Ideologies of Sacred Warfare and Teotihuacan Iconography. In *Text and Image in Pre-Columbian Art,* edited by Janet Catherine Berlo, pp. 79–117. BAR International Series 180. British Archaeological Reports, Oxford.

1992   Icons and Ideologies at Teotihuacan: The Great Goddess Reconsidered. In *Art, Ideology, and the City of Teotihuacan,* edited by Janet Berlo, pp. 129–168. Dumbarton Oaks, Washington, D.C.

Bernal-García, Maria Elena

1988   La Venta's Pyramid: The First Successful Representation of the Mesoamerican Sacred Mountain. Paper presented in the Department of Art, September 1988. University of Texas at Austin, Austin.

Beyer, Hermann

1965   La gigantesca diosa de Teotihuacán. *El México Antiguo* 10:419–423.
[1920]

Blakeslee, Sandra

1989   Linguists Solve Riddles of Mayan Language. *New York Times* 4 April.

Blanck, Evelyn, and Félix Colindres

1996   Renacimiento maya. *Crónica* 9/436:19–24. Guatemala.

Blom, Franz

1928   Gaspar Antonio Chi, Interpreter. *American Anthropologist* 30:250–262.

Bolles, David

n.d.   Dictionary and Concordance of the Yucatecan Mayan Language. Files stored on computer diskettes, distributed by the author.

Boone, Elizabeth H.

1991   Migration Histories as Ritual Performance. In *To Change Place,* edited by Davíd Carrasco, pp. 121–151. University of Colorado Press, Boulder.

Boot, Erik

1997   T759 as Lo: Further Evidence. Unpublished manuscript in the possession of the author.

Bricker, Harvey, and Victoria Bricker

1993   Zodiacal References on the Maya Codices. In *The Sky in Mayan Literature,* edited by Anthony F. Aveni, pp. 148–183. Oxford University Press, New York.

Bricker, Victoria R.

1981   *Indian Christ, Indian King: The Historical Substrate of Maya Myth and Ritual.* University of Texas Press, Austin.

Bricker, Victoria R., Eleuterio Po'ot Yah, and Ofelia Dzul de Po'ot

1998   *A Dictionary of the Maya Language as Spoken in Hocabá, Yucatán.* University of Utah Press, Salt Lake City.

Brinton, Daniel G.

1882   *The Maya Chronicles.* Library of Aboriginal American Literature 1. Philadelphia.

Brown, Betty Ann

1988   All around the Xocotl Pole: Reexamination of an Aztec Sacrificial Ceremony. In *Smoke and Mist: Mesoamerican Studies in Memory of Thelma D. Sullivan,* edited by J. Kathryn Josserand and Karen Dakin, pp. 173–189. BAR International Series 402, pt. 1. British Archaeological Reports, Oxford.

Brüggemann, Jürgen K.

1992   *Tajín: guía oficial.* INAH, Mexico City.

Brunhouse, R. L.

1973   *In Search of the Maya: The First Archaeologists.* University of New Mexico Press, Albuquerque.

1975   *Pursuit of the Ancient Maya: Some Archaeologists of Yesterday.* University of New Mexico Press, Albuquerque.

Campbell, Lyle, and Terrence Kaufman

1976   A Linguistic Look at the Olmecs. *American Antiquity* 41 (1):80–89.

Carlson, John B.

1981a   Olmec Concave Iron-Ore Mirrors: The Aesthetics of a Lithic Technology and the Lord of the Mirror. In *The Olmec and Their Neighbors: Essays in Memory of Matthew W. Stirling,* edited by Elizabeth P. Benson, pp. 117–147. Dumbarton Oaks, Washington, D.C.

1981b   A Geomantic Model for the Interpretation of Mesoamerican Sites: An Essay in Cross-Cultural Comparison. In *Mesoamerican Sites and World-Views,* edited by Elizabeth P. Benson, pp. 143–215. Dumbarton Oaks, Washington, D.C.

Caso, Alfonso

1942   El paraíso terrenal en Teotihuacán. *Cuadernos Americanos* 6:127–136.

Chase, Diane Z.

1985   Ganned but Not Forgotten: Late Postclassic Archaeology and Ritual at Santa Rita Corozal, Belize. In *The Lowland Maya Postclassic,* edited by Arlen F. Chase and Prudence M. Rice, pp. 104–125. University of Texas Press, Austin.

Christie, Jessica Joyce

1999   Maya Period-ending Ceremonies in Architectural Space. Paper presented at the Annual Meeting of the Midwestern Mesoamericanists, February 13, University of Illinois at Chicago, Chicago.

Ciudad Real, Antonio

1952   Relación breve y verdadera de algunas cosas que sucedieron al Padre Fray Alonso Ponce en las provincias de Nueva España, siendo Comisario General de aquellas partes (1586). *Anales del Museo Nacional "David J. Guzman"* 3(9):8–102. San Salvador.

Clavigero, Abbé D. Francesco Saverio

1979   *The History of Mexico,* vol. 1. Garland Publishing, New York.
[1787]

Clewlow, Carl William, Jr.

1974   *A Stylistic and Chronological Study of Olmec Monumental Sculpture.* Papers on Mesoamerican Archaeology 5. Contributions of the University of California Archaeological Research Facility No. 19. Department of Anthropology, University of California, Berkeley.

Coe, Michael D.

1965a   A Model of Ancient Community Structure in the Maya Lowlands. *Southwestern Journal of Anthropology* 21(2):97–114.

1965b   The Olmec Style and Its Distribution. In *Handbook of Middle American Indians,* vol. 3, edited by Gordon R. Willey, pp. 739–775. University of Texas Press, Austin.

1972   Olmec Jaguars and Olmec Kings. In *The Cult of the Feline,* edited by Elizabeth P. Benson, pp. 1–12. Dumbarton Oaks, Washington, D.C.

1973   *The Maya Scribe and His World.* Grolier Club, New York.

1977   Olmec and Maya: A Study in Relationships. In *Origins of Maya Civilization,* edited by Richard E. W. Adams, pp. 183–196. University of New Mexico Press, Albuquerque.

1978   *Lords of the Underworld: Masterpieces of Classic Maya Ceramics.* The Art Museum, Princeton University, Princeton.

1982   *Old Gods and Young Heroes: The Pearlman Collection of Maya Ceramics.* Israel Museum, Maremont Pavilion of Ethnic Arts, Jerusalem.

1987   *The Maya.* 4th ed. Thames and Hudson, New York.

1992   *Breaking the Maya Code.* Thames and Hudson, London.

2000   Linda Schele. *American Anthropologist* 102(1):133–135.

Coe, Michael D., and Richard A. Diehl

1980   *In the Land of the Olmec.* 2 vols. University of Texas Press, Austin.

Coe, William R.

1959   *Piedras Negras Archaeology: Artifacts, Caches, and Burials.* Museum Monographs No. 4. University Museum, University of Pennsylvania, Philadelphia.

1967   *Tikal: A Handbook of the Ancient Maya Ruins.* The University Museum, University of Pennsylvania, Philadelphia.

1990   *Excavations in the Great Plaza, North Terrace, and North Acropolis of Tikal.* 5 vols. Tikal Reports 14. University Museum, University of Pennsylvania, Philadelphia.

Coggins, Clemency C.

1988   Classic Maya Metaphors of Death and Life. *Res: Anthropology and Aesthetics* 16:66–84.

1990   The Birth of the Baktun at Tikal and Seibal. In *Vision and Revision in Maya Studies,* edited by Flora S. Clancy and Peter D. Harrison, pp. 79–97. University of New Mexico Press, Albuquerque.

Cogolludo, Diego López de

1971   *Los tres siglos de la dominación española en Yucatán o sea historia de esta provincia,* I. Akademische Druck-ü. Verlagsanstalt, Graz, Austria.

Cohen, Norman H.

1995   *Mentoring Adult Learners: A Guide for Educators and Trainers.* Krieger, Malabar, Florida.

Cohodas, Marvin

1982   The Bicephalic Monster in Classic Maya Sculpture. *Antropológicas* 24:105–146.

Cojtí Cuxil, Demetrio

1995   *Ub'aniik ri una'ooj uchomab'aal ri maya' tinamit: Configuración del pensamiento político del pueblo maya.* Seminario Permanente de Estudios Mayas and Editorial Cholsamaj, Guatemala City.

Conn, Steven

1998   *Museums and American Intellectual Life, 1876–1926.* University of Chicago Press, Chicago.

Cortez, Constance

1995 Gaspar Antonio Chi and the Xiu Family Page. Ph.D. dissertation, Department of Art History, University of California, Los Angeles.

Cross, Kathryn P.

1981 *Adults as Learners: Increasing Participation and Facilitating Learning.* Jossey-Bass, San Francisco.

Cyphers Guillén, Ann

1984 The Possible Role of a Woman in Formative Exchange. In *Trade and Exchange in Early Mesoamerica,* edited by Kenneth Hirth, pp. 115–123. University of New Mexico Press, Albuquerque.

1992 Escenas escultóricas olmecas. *Antropológicas* 6:47–52.

1996 Reconstructing Olmec Life at San Lorenzo. In *Olmec Art of Ancient Mexico,* edited by Elizabeth P. Benson and Beatriz de la Fuente, pp. 61–71. National Gallery of Art, Washington, D.C.

1997 La gobernatura en San Lorenzo: Inferencias del arte y patrón de Asentamiento. In *Población, subsistencia y medio ambiente en San Lorenzo Tenochtitlán,* edited by Ann Cyphers, pp. 227–242. Universidad National Autónoma de México, INAH, Mexico City.

1999 From Stone to Symbols: Olmec Art in Social Context at San Lorenzo Tenochtitlán. In *Social Patterns in Pre-Classic Mesoamerica,* edited by David C. Grove and Rosemary A. Joyce, pp. 155–181. Dumbarton Oaks, Washington, D.C.

Darnell, Regna

1969 The Development of American Anthropology, 1879–1920: From the Bureau of American Ethnology to Franz Boas. Ph. D. dissertation, University of Pennsylvania, Philadelphia.

de la Fuente, Beatriz

1981 Toward a Conception of Monumental Olmec Art. In *The Olmec and Their Neighbors: Essays in Memory of Matthew Stirling,* edited by Elizabeth P. Benson, pp. 83–94. Dumbarton Oaks, Washington, D.C.

1984 *Los hombres de piedra: Escultura olmeca.* Instituto de Investigaciones Estéticas, Universidad Nacional Autónoma de México, Mexico City.

1996 Homocentrism in Olmec Monumental Art. In *Olmec Art of Ancient Mexico,* edited by Elizabeth P. Benson and Beatriz de la Fuente, pp. 41–49. National Gallery of Art, Washington, D.C.

Demarest, Arthur, Claudia Wolley, Kim Morgan, Nikolai Grube, and Hector Escobedo

1995 A Royal Palace at the Moment of the Classic Maya Collapse: Function, History, and Investigative Methodology. Paper presented at the 60th Annual Meeting of the Society for American Archaeology, May 3–7, Minneapolis.

Drucker, Philip

1952 *La Venta, Tabasco: A Study of Olmec Ceramics and Art.* Smithsonian Institution, Bureau of American Ethnology Bulletin 153. U.S. Government Printing Office, Washington, D.C.

Drucker, Philip, Robert F. Heizer, and Robert J. Squier

1959   *Excavations at La Venta, Tabasco, 1955.* Smithsonian Institution, Bureau of American Ethnology Bulletin 170. U.S. Government Printing Office, Washington, D.C.

Dunham, Peter

1980   The Maya and the Milky Way: A Descriptive Approach. Unpublished manuscript in the possession of the author.

Durán, Diego

1971   *Book of the Gods and Rites and the Ancient Calendar.* Translated and edited
[1574– by Fernando Horcasitas and Doris Heyden. University of Oklahoma Press,
1579]   Norman.

1994   *The History of the Indies of New Spain.* Translated, annotated, and with an
[1581] introduction by Doris Heyden. University of Oklahoma Press, Norman.

Dütting, Dieter

1984   Venus, the Moon, and the Gods of the Palenque Triad. *Zeitschrift für Ethnologie* 109:7–74.

Edelson, Paul J., and Patricia L. Malone (editors)

1999   *Enhancing Creativity in Adult and Continuing Education: Innovative Approaches, Methods, and Ideas.* New Directions for Adult and Continuing Education 81. Jossey-Bass, San Francisco.

Fash, Barbara, William Fash, Sheree Lane, Rudy Larios, Linda Schele, Jeffrey Stomper, and David Stuart

1992   Investigations of a Classic Maya Council House at Copán. *Journal of Field Archaeology* 19:419–442.

Fash, William F.

1991   *Scribes, Warriors and Kings.* Thames and Hudson, London.

Fialko, Vilma

1988   El marcador de Juego de Pelota de Tikal: nuevas referencias epigráficas para el Clásico Temprano. In *Primer Simposio Mundial Sobre Epigrafía Maya,* pp. 61–80. Asociación Tikal, Guatemala City.

Fields, Virginia

1989   The Origin of Divine Kingship among the Lowland Classic Maya. Ph.D. dissertation, Institute of Latin American Studies, University of Texas at Austin, Austin.

1990   The Iconographic Heritage of the Maya Jester God. In *Sixth Palenque Round Table, 1986,* vol. 8, volume editor Virginia Fields, general editor Merle Greene Robertson, pp. 167–174. The Pre-Columbian Art Research Institute, San Francisco.

Fox, John G.

2001   Testing the Boundaries: Ballcourts and Community Interaction in and beyond Mesoamerica. In *The Archaeology of Contact: Processes and Conse-quences,* edited by B. Kulle, C. Lesick, and A. Ponholz. Proceedings of the 25th Annual Chacmool Conference. Archaeological Association, University of Calgary, Calgary.

Freidel, David A.

1976   Cerro Maya: A Late Preclassic Center in Corozal District. In *Recent Archae-ology in Belize,* edited by R. Buhler. Occasional Paper 3. Belize Institute for Social Research and Action, Belize City.

1977   A Late Preclassic Monumental Mask at Cerros, Northern Belize. *Journal of Field Archaeology* 4:488–491.

1978   Maritime Adaptation and the Rise of Maya Civilization: The View from Cerros, Belize. In *Prehistoric Coastal Adaptations,* edited by B. Stark and B. Voorhies, pp. 239–265. Academic Press, New York.

1979   Culture Areas and Interaction Spheres: Contrasting Approaches to the Emergence of Civilization in the Maya Lowlands. *American Antiquity* 44: 36–54.

1981   Civilization as a State of Mind: The Cultural Evolution of the Lowland Maya. In *The Transition to Statehood in the New World,* edited by Grant D. Jones and R. Kautz, pp. 188–227. Cambridge University Press, Cambridge.

1983   Political Systems in Lowland Yucatan: Dynamics and Structure in Maya Settlement. In *Prehistoric Settlement Patterns: Essays in Honor of Gordon R. Willey,* edited by Evon Z. Vogt and Richard M. Leventhal, pp. 375–386. University of New Mexico Press, Albuquerque, and Peabody Museum of Archaeology and Ethnology, Harvard University, Cambridge.

1985   Polychrome Facades of the Lowland Maya Preclassic. In *Painted Architecture and Polychrome Monumental Sculpture in Mesoamerica,* edited by Elizabeth Boone, pp. 5–30. Dumbarton Oaks, Washington D.C.

1986a   Introduction. In *Archaeology at Cerros, Belize, Central America, Volume I: An Interim Report,* edited by Robin Robertson and David Freidel, pp. xiii–xxiii. Southern Methodist University Press, Dallas.

1986b   The Monumental Architecture. In *Archaeology at Cerros, Belize, Central America, Volume I: An Interim Report,* edited by Robin Robertson and David Freidel, pp. 1–22. Southern Methodist University Press, Dallas.

1992   The Trees of Life: Ahau as Idea and Artifact in Classic Lowland Maya Civi-lization. In *Ideology and Pre-Columbian Civilizations,* edited by A. Dema-rest and G. Conrad, pp. 115–134. School of American Research Press, Santa Fe.

1998   Linda Schele. *Anthropology Newsletter* 29–30 September. American Anthro-pological Association, Washington, D.C.

Freidel, David A., and Barbara MacLeod

2000   Creation Redux: New Thoughts on Maya Cosmology from Epigraphy, Ico-nography, and Archaeology. *PARI Journal* 1(2):1–8.

Freidel, David, and F. Kent Reilly III

1998   Olmec and Maya Royal Accession Scaffolds. Papers in Honor of Linda Schele, January 25, 1998. Department of Art, University of Texas at Austin, Austin. Unpublished manuscript in the possession of the author.

Freidel, David A., and Jeremy A. Sabloff

1984   *Cozumel Island: Late Maya Settlement Patterns.* Academic Press, Orlando.

Freidel, David, and Linda Schele

1988a   Kingship in the Late Preclassic Maya Lowlands: The Instruments and Places of Ritual Power. *American Anthropologist* 90(3):547–567.

1988b   Symbol and Power: A History of the Lowland Maya Cosmogram. In *Maya Iconography,* edited by E. Benson and G. Griffin, pp. 44–93. Princeton University Press, Princeton.

1989   Dead Kings and Living Temples: Dedication and Termination Rituals among the Ancient Maya. In *Word and Image in Maya Culture,* edited by William F. Hanks and Don S. Rice, pp. 233–243. University of Utah Press, Salt Lake City.

Freidel, David, Linda Schele, and Joy Parker

1993   *Maya Cosmos: Three Thousand Years on the Shaman's Path.* William Morrow, New York.

Freidel, David, and Charles Schuler

1999   The Path of Life: Towards a Functional Analysis of Ancient Maya Architecture. In *Mesoamerican Architecture as a Cultural Symbol,* edited by Jeff Karl Kowalski, pp. 250–273. Oxford University Press, New York.

Fry, Robert E. (editor)

1980   *Models and Methods in Regional Exchange.* SAA Papers No. 1. Society for American Archaeology, Washington, D.C.

Furst, Peter T.

1968   The Olmec Were-Jaguar Motif in the Light of Ethnographic Reality. In *Dumbarton Oaks Conference on the Olmec,* edited by Elizabeth P. Benson, pp. 149–162. Dumbarton Oaks, Washington, D.C.

1974   Morning Glory and Mother Goddess at Tepantitla, Teotihuacan: Iconography and Analogy in Pre-Columbian Art. In *Mesoamerican Archaeology: New Approaches,* edited by Norman Hammond, pp. 185–215. Duckworth, London.

Gaceta de México

1785   Descripción de la Pirámide del Tajín. *Gaceta de México* 2 de julio.

Gann, Thomas W.

1900   Mounds in Northern British Honduras. *Nineteenth Annual Report of the Bureau of American Ethnology, 1897–1898,* pt. 2, 655–692. Smithsonian Institution, Washington, D.C.

García Payón, José

1949   Notable relieve con sorprendentes revelaciones. *Uni-Ver* 1:351–359.

1951   La pyrámide del Tajín. *Cuadernos Americanos* 10(6):153–177.

1952   Totonacas y olmecas: un ensayo de correlación histórico-arqueológico *Uni-Ver* 3:27–52.

1973   El tablero de Montículo Cuatro. *Boletín del INAH,* segunda serie, 7:31–34.

Gates, William

1931   The Thirteen Ahaus in the Kaua Manuscript and Related Katun Wheels in the Paris Codex, Landa, Cogolludo and the Chumayel. *Maya Society Quarterly* 1:2–20.

Gauderman, Kimberly

1992   Father Fiction: The Construction of Gender in England, Spain, and the Andes. *UCLA Historical Journal: Indigenous Writing in the Spanish Indies,* special issue, 122–151.

Gemelli Carreri, Juan Francisco

1995   De los cúes o pirámides de San Juan Teotihuacán. In *La Pirámide del Sol,*
[1700] *Teotihuacán,* edited by Eduardo Matos, pp. 46–48. INAH, Mexico City.

Gillespie, Susan

1989   *The Aztec Kings: The Construction of Rulership in Mexica History.* University of Arizona Press, Tucson.

1991   Ballgames and Boundaries. In *The Mesoamerican Ballgame,* edited by Vernon L. Scarborough and David Wilcox, pp. 317–346. University of Arizona Press, Tucson.

1999   Olmec Thrones as Ancestral Altars: The Two Sides of Power. In *Material Symbols: Culture and Economy in Prehistory,* edited by John E. Robb, pp. 224–253. Occasional Papers No. 26. Center for Archaeological Investigations, Southern Illinois University, Carbondale.

Givens, Douglas R.

1992   Sylvanus G. Morley and the Carnegie Institution's Program of Mayan Research. In *Rediscovering Our Past: Essays on the History of American Archaeology,* edited by Jonathon E. Reyman, pp. 137–144. Avebury, Aldershot, U.K.

González Lauk, Rebecca

1988   Proyecto arqueológico La Venta. In *Arqueología,* vol. 4, edited by Alba G. Mastache, pp. 121–165. INAH, Mexico City.

1994   La antigua ciudad olmeca en La Venta, Tabasco. In *Los Olmecas en Mesoamérica,* edited by John E. Clark, pp. 93–112. Citibank, Mexico City.

1996   La Venta: An Olmec Capital. In *Olmec Art of Ancient Mexico,* edited by Elizabeth P. Benson and Beatriz de la Fuente, pp. 73–81. National Gallery of Art, Washington, D.C.

Gossen, Gary

1970   Time and Space in Chamula Oral Tradition. Ph.D. dissertation, Department of Anthropology, Harvard University, Cambridge.

1974   *Chamulas in the World of the Sun: Time and Space in a Maya Oral Tradition.* Harvard University Press, Cambridge.

Graham, Ian

1970   The Ruins of La Florida, Peten, Guatemala. In *Monographs and Papers in Maya Archaeology,* edited by W. R. Bullard Jr., pp. 425–455. Peabody Museum, Cambridge, Massachusetts.

Graña-Behrens, Daniel, Christian Prager, and Elisabeth Wagner

1999   The Hieroglyphic Inscription of the "High Priest's Grave" at Chichén Itzá, Yucatán, Mexico. *Mexicon* 21(3):61–66.

Greenleaf, Richard E.

1965   The Inquisition and the Indians of New Spain: A Study in Jurisdictional Confusion. *Americas* 22(2):138–166.

Grove, David C.

1970   *The Olmec Paintings of Oxtotitlan Cave Guerrero.* Studies in Pre-Columbian Art and Archaeology No. 6. Dumbarton Oaks, Washington, D.C.

1973   Olmec Altars and Myths. *Archaeology* 26:128–135.

1981   Olmec Monuments: Mutilation as a Clue to Meaning. In *The Olmec and Their Neighbors: Essays in Memory of Matthew Stirling,* edited by Elizabeth P. Benson, pp. 49–68. Dumbarton Oaks, Washington, D.C.

1984   *Chalcatzingo: Excavations on the Olmec Frontier.* Thames and Hudson, London.

1989   Chalcatzingo and the Olmec Connection. In *Regional Perspectives on the Olmec,* edited by Robert J. Sharer and David C. Grove, pp. 122–147. Cambridge University Press, Cambridge.

1996   Chalcatzingo's Monuments, Mounds, and Sacred Landscape. Paper presented at the 61st Annual Meeting of the Society for American Archaeology, April 11, New Orleans.

1999   Public Monuments and Sacred Mountains: Observations on Three Formative Period Sacred Landscapes. In *Social Patterns in Pre-Classic Mesoamerica,* edited by David C. Grove and Rosemary A. Joyce, pp. 255–299. Dumbarton Oaks, Washington, D.C.

Grube, Nikolai

1998   Deceased: Linda Schele, 1942–1998. *Mexicon* 30(3):50–51.

Grube, Nikolai, and Linda Schele

1991   Tzuk in Classic Maya Inscriptions. *Texas Notes on Precolumbian Art, Writing, and Culture No. 14.* Center for the History of Art of Ancient American Cultures, Art Department, University of Texas at Austin, Austin.

Grube, Nikolai, Linda Schele, and Federico Fahsen

1991   Odds and Ends from the Inscriptions of Quiriguá. *Mexicon* 13(6):106–112.

Guderjan, Thomas H.

1998   The Blue Creek Jade Cache. In *The Sowing and the Dawning: Termination,*

Dedication, and Transformation in the Archaeological and Ethnographic Record of Mesoamerica, edited by Shirley Boteler Mock, pp. 81–100. University of New Mexico Press, Albuquerque.

Guenter, Stanley Paul

1999 Where Is Man? The Case for La Florida. Unpublished manuscript in the possession of the author.

Guenter, Stanley Paul, and Marc Zender

1999 Palenque and Yaxchilan's War with Piedras Negras. Paper submitted for publication in *Ancient Mesoamerica.*

Hammond, Norman

1993 Review of *Breaking the Maya Code,* by Michael D. Coe. *Journal of Field Archaeology* 20:232–236.

Hansen, Richard D.

1993 Investigaciones arqueológicas en Nakbe, Guatemala: Resumen de la temporada de campo 1993. In *Investigaciones arqueológicas en Nakbé, Petén: El resumen de la temporada de campo de 1993,* edited by Richard D. Hansen, pp. 1–138. Regional Archaeological Investigation of the North Peten, Guatemala, University of California, Los Angeles.

Harris, John F., and Stephen K. Stearns

1992 *Understanding Maya Inscriptions: A Hieroglyph Handbook.* University Museum, University of Pennsylvania, Philadelphia.

Harrison, Peter D.

1999 *The Lords of Tikal: Rulers of an Ancient Maya City.* Thames and Hudson, London.

Hatfield, Rab

1990 The Tree of Life and the Holy Cross: Franciscan Spirituality in the Trecento and Quattrocento. In *Christianity and the Renaissance: Image and Religious Imagination in the Quattrocento,* edited by Timothy Verdon and John Henderson, pp. 132–133. Syracuse University Press, Syracuse, New York.

Headrick, Annabeth

1991 The Chicomoztoc of Chichén Itzá. Master's thesis, Department of Art and Art History, University of Texas at Austin, Austin.

1995 Teotihuacan Jihad: The Propaganda of Butterfly War. Paper presented at the 60th Annual Meeting of the Society for American Archaeology, May 3–7, Minneapolis.

Heizer, Robert F., John A. Graham, and Lewis K. Napton

1968 *The 1968 Investigations at La Venta.* Papers on Mesoamerican Archaeology No. 5. Contributions of the University of California Archaeological Research Facility. Department of Anthropology, University of California, Berkeley.

Hellmuth, Nicholas M.

1987 *Monster und Menschen in der Maya-Kunst.* Akademische Druck-ü. Verlagsanstalt, Graz, Austria.

Heyden, Doris

1975   An Interpretation of the Cave underneath the Pyramid of the Sun in Teotihuacan, Mexico. *American Antiquity* 40:2:131–147.

1976   Los ritos de paso en las cuevas. *Boletín* (INAH) October–December:17–26.

1981   Caves, Gods, and Myths: World-View and Planning in Teotihuacan. In *Mesoamerican Sites and World-Views,* edited by Elizabeth P. Benson, pp. 1–37. Dumbarton Oaks, Washington, D.C.

Hobsbawm, Eric

1983   Mass-Producing Traditions: Europe, 1870–1914. In *The Invention of Tradition,* edited by Eric Hobsbawm and Terence Ranger, pp. 263–307. Cambridge University Press, Cambridge.

Hofling, Charles, and Félix Fernando Tesucún

1997   *Itzaj Maya-Spanish-English Dictionary.* University of Utah Press, Salt Lake City.

Houk, Brett A.

1996   The Archaeology of Site Planning: An Example from the Maya Site of Dos Hombres, Belize. Ph.D. dissertation, Department of Anthropology, University of Texas at Austin, Austin.

Houston, S., H. Escobedo, P. Hardin, R. Terry, D. Webster, M. Child, C. Golden, K. Emery, and D. Stuart

1998   Between Mountains and Sea: Investigations at Piedras Negras, Guatemala, 1998. Report to the Foundation for the Advancement of Mesoamerican Studies, Inc., Crystal River, Florida. Unpublished manuscript in the possession of the author.

Houston, Stephen D.

1983   On Ruler 6 at Piedras Negras, Guatemala. *Mexicon* 5(5):84–86.

1987   The Inscriptions and Monumental Art of Dos Pilas, Guatemala: A Study of Classic Maya History and Politics. Ph.D. dissertation, Yale University, New Haven.

1992   Classic Maya Politics. In *New Theories on the Ancient Maya,* edited by Elin C. Danien and Robert J. Sharer, pp. 65–69. University Museum, University of Pennsylvania, Philadelphia.

1993a   *Hieroglyphs and History at Dos Pilas: Dynastic Politics of the Classic Maya.* University of Texas Press, Austin.

1993b   Review of *Understanding Maya Inscriptions: A Hieroglyph Handbook,* by John F. Harris and Stephen K. Stearns. *American Anthropologist* 95:484–485.

1996   Symbolic Sweatbaths of the Maya: Architectural Meaning in the Cross Group at Palenque, Mexico. *Latin American Antiquity* 7:132–151.

Houston, Stephen, and David Stuart

1996   Of Gods, Glyphs and Kings: Divinity and Rulership among the Classic Maya. *Antiquity* 70:289–312.

1998　The Ancient Maya Self: Personhood and Portraiture in the Classic Period. *Res: Anthropology and Aesthetics* 33:73–101.

Howell, Steve, and Sophi Webb

1995　*A Guide to the Birds of Mexico and Northern Central America.* Oxford University Press, Oxford.

Jones, Christopher

1977　Inauguration Dates of Three Late Classic Maya Rulers of Tikal, Guatemala. *American Antiquity* 42(1):28–60.

1983　*Deciphering Maya Hieroglyphs.* University Museum, University of Pennsylvania, Philadelphia.

1991　Cycles of Growth at Tikal. In *Classic Maya Political History: Hieroglyphic and Archaeological Evidence,* edited by T. Patrick Culbert, pp. 102–127. School of American Research Series. Cambridge University Press, Cambridge.

Jones, Christopher, and Linton Satterthwaite

1982　*The Monuments and Inscriptions of Tikal: The Carved Monuments.* Tikal Report No. 33, Pt. A. University Museum, University of Pennsylvania, Philadelphia.

Jones, Christopher, and Robert Sharer

1980　Archaeological Investigations in the Site Core of Quirigua. *Expedition* 23(3):11–19.

Jones, Tom, and Carolyn Young (editors)

1988　*U Mut Maya: An Unofficial Collection of Papers, Reports and Readings by Attendants of the 5th Advanced Seminar on Maya Hieroglyphic Writing Held at the University of Texas at Austin, March 14–19, 1987.* Tom and Carolyn Jones, Arcata, California.

1989　*U Mut Maya 2: An Unofficial Collection of Papers, Reports and Readings by Attendants of the 6th Advanced Seminar on Maya Hieroglyphic Writing Held at the University of Texas at Austin, March 14–18, 1988.* Tom and Carolyn Jones, Arcata, California.

1990　*U Mut Maya 3: A Collection of Reports from Attendants of the 7th Advanced Seminar on Maya Hieroglyphic Writing Held at the University of Texas at Austin, March 1989.* Tom and Carolyn Jones, Arcata, California.

1992　*U Mut Maya 4: A Collection of Reports from Attendants of the 8th and 9th Advanced Seminars on Maya Hieroglyphic Writing Held at the University of Texas at Austin, March 12–17, 1990, and March 11–16, 1991.* Tom and Carolyn Jones, Arcata, California.

1994　*U Mut Maya 5: A Collection of Reports from Attendants of the 10th and 11th Advanced Seminars on Maya Hieroglyphic Writing Held at the University of Texas at Austin, March 16–21, 1992, and March 15–20, 1993.* Tom and Carolyn Jones, Arcata, California.

1996   *U Mut Maya 6: Papers, Reports and Readings from the Advanced Seminars Held at the University of Texas at Austin, 1994–1996.* Tom and Carolyn Jones, Arcata, California.

Joralemon, David

1971   *A Study of Olmec Iconography.* Studies in Pre-Columbian Art and Archaeology No. 7. Dumbarton Oaks, Washington, D.C.

Joyce, Rosemary A.

1987   Gender, Role, and Status in Middle Formative Mesoamerica: Implications of Burials from La Venta, Tabasco, Mexico. Paper presented at the First Texas Symposium, "Olmec, Izapa, Maya," University of Texas at Austin, Austin.

Judd, Neil Merton

1948   "Pyramids" of the New World. *National Geographic* 93(1):105–128.

Justeson, John S.

1989   The Ancient Maya Ethnoastronomy: An Overview of Hieroglyphic Sources. In *World Archaeoastronomy: Selected Papers from the Second Oxford International Conference on Archaeoastronomy,* edited by A. F. Aveni, pp. 76–129. Cambridge University Press, Cambridge.

Justeson, John S., and Terrence Kaufman

1993   A Decipherment of Epi-Olmec Hieroglyphic Writing. *Science* 259:1703–1711.

Kampen, Michael

1972   *The Sculptures of El Tajín, Veracruz, Mexico.* University of Florida Press, Gainesville.

Kappelman, Julia Guernsey

1997   Of Macaws and Men: Late Preclassic Cosmology and Political Ideology in Izapan-Style Monuments. Ph.D dissertation, University of Texas at Austin, Austin.

2001   Sacred Geography at Izapa and the Performance of Rulership. In *Landscape and Power in Ancient Mesoamerica,* edited by Rex Koontz, Kathryn Reese-Taylor, and Annabeth Headrick, pp. 81–111. Westview Press, Boulder, Colorado.

Kappelman, Julia Guernsey, and F. Kent Reilly III

2001   Paths to Heaven, Ropes to Earth: Birds, Jaguars, and Cosmic Cords in Formative Period Mesoamerica. *Ancient Mesoamerica* 2:33–51. Center for Ancient American Studies, Barnardsville, North Carolina.

Karttunen, Frances

1992   *An Analytical Dictionary of Nahuatl.* University of Oklahoma Press, Norman.

1994   *Between Worlds: Interpreters, Guides, and Survivors.* Rutgers University Press, New Brunswick, New Jersey.

Kaufman, Terrence, and William Norman

1984   An Outline of Proto-Cholan Phonology, Morphology, and Vocabulary. In

Phoneticism in Mayan Hieroglyphic Writing, edited by J. S. Justeson and L. Campbell, pp. 77–166. Institute for Mesoamerican Studies Publication No. 9. State University of New York at Albany.

Kelley, David H.

1962   Glyphic Evidence for a Dynastic Sequence at Quiriguá, Guatemala. *American Antiquity* 27:323–335.

1976   *Deciphering the Maya Script.* University of Texas Press, Austin.

1985   The Lords of Palenque and the Lords of Heaven. In *Fifth Palenque Round Table, 1983,* vol. 7, volume editor Virginia Fields, general editor Merle Greene Robertson, pp. 235–240. Pre-Columbian Art Research Institute, San Francisco.

2000   Linda Richmond Schele. *Written Language and Literacy* 3(1):193–195.

Kerr, Justin (editor)

1989   *The Maya Vase Book,* vol. 1. Kerr Associates, New York.

1990   *The Maya Vase Book,* vol. 2. Kerr Associates, New York.

1992   *The Maya Vase Book,* vol. 3. Kerr Associates, New York.

1994   *The Maya Vase Book,* vol. 4. Kerr Associates, New York.

1997   *The Maya Vase Book,* vol. 5. Kerr Associates, New York.

2000   *The Maya Vase Book,* vol. 6. Kerr Associates, New York.

Klein, Cecelia

1988   Rethinking Cihuacoatl: Aztec Political Imagery of the Conquered Woman. In *Smoke and Mist: Mesoamerican Studies in Memory of Thelma D. Sullivan,* edited by J. Kathryn Josserand and Karen Dakin, pp. 237–277. BAR International Series 402, pt. 1. British Archaeological Reports, Oxford.

Knorosov, Yuri V.

1953   Knorosov's Deciphering of Maya Glyphs. *Current Digest of the Soviet Press* 4(50):3–10.

1958   The Problem of the Study of the Maya Hieroglyphic Writing. *American Antiquity* 23(3):284–291.

1965   Principios para descifrar los escritos mayas. *Estudios de Cultura Maya* 5:153–188.

Koontz, Rex

1994   The Iconography of El Tajin, Veracruz, Mexico. Ph.D. dissertation, Department of Art History, University of Texas at Austin, Austin.

Kowalski, Jeff K.

1987   *The House of the Governor: A Maya Palace at Uxmal, Yucatán, Mexico.* University of Oklahoma Press, Norman.

Kubler, George

1967   *The Iconography of the Art of Teotihuacan.* Studies in Pre-Columbian Art and Archaeology No. 24. Dumbarton Oaks, Washington, D.C.

1969   *Studies in Classic Maya Iconography.* Memoirs of the Connecticut Academy of Arts and Sciences No. 18. Connecticut Academy of Arts and Sciences, New Haven.

1984   Renascence and Disjunction in the Art of Mesoamerican Antiquity. In *Studies in Ancient American and European Art: The Collected Essays of George Kubler,* edited by Thomas F. Reese, pp. 351–359. Yale University Press, New Haven.

Kurjack, Edward, and Silvia Garza T.

1981   Pre-Columbian Community Form and Distribution in the Northern Maya Area. In *Lowland Maya Settlement Patterns,* edited by W. Ashmore, pp. 287–309. School of American Research Book. University of New Mexico Press, Albuquerque.

Ladner, Gerhart B.

1979   Medieval and Modern Understanding of Symbolism: A Comparison. *Speculum* 54:223–256.

Lamb, Dana, and Ginger Lamb

1951   *Quest for the Lost City.* Harper and Brothers, New York.

Landa, Diego de

1937   *Yucatan before and after the Conquest by Friar Diego de Landa with Other Related Documents, Maps, and Illustrations,* 2nd ed., edited and translated with notes by William Gates. Publication 20. Maya Society, Baltimore.

Laporte, Juan Pedro

1988   Alternativas del Clásico Temprano en la relación Tikal-Teotihuacán: Grupo 6C-XVI, Tikal, Petén, Guatemala. Ph.D. dissertation, Department of Anthropology, Universidad Nacional Autónoma de México, Mexico City.

Laughlin, Robert M.

1975   *The Great Tzotzil Dictionary of Zinacantán.* Smithsonian Contribution to Anthropology 19. Smithsonian Institution Press, Washington, D.C.

Lee, Thomas A., Jr. (editor)

1985   *Los códices mayas.* Universidad Autonóma de Chiapas, Tuxtla Gutiérrez, Mexico.

Leibsohn, Dana

1993   The Historia Tolteca-Chichimeca: Recollecting Identity in a Nahua Manuscript. Ph.D. dissertation, Department of Art History, University of California, Los Angeles.

León, Ignacio, and Juan Carlos Sánchez

1991–   Las gemelas y el jaguar del sitio El Azuzul. *Horizonte* (Año 1) 5–6:56–60.
1996

León-Portilla, Miguel

1987   *México-Tenochtitlan, su espacio y tiempo sagrados.* Plaza y Valdes, Mexico City.

Lerner, Allan W., and B. Kay King (editors)

1992   *Continuing Higher Education: The Coming Wave.* Teachers College Press, New York.

Levanthal, Richard

1999   Public Transformation and Private Kings: The Presentation of Power among the Ancient Maya. Paper presented at the 6th Annual Maya Weekend, October 16–17, University of California, Los Angeles.

Leyenaar, Ted J. J.

1988   Ulama: The Survival of the Mesoamerican Ballgame Ullamaliztli. In *Ulama : het balspel bij de Maya's en Azteken, 2000 v. Chr.–2000 n. Chr. : van mensenoffer tot sport = Ulama : the ballgame of the Mayas and Aztecs, 2000 BC–AD 2000 : from human sacrifice to sport,* edited by Ted J. J. Leyenaar and Lee A. Parsons, pp. 94–147. Spruyt, Van Mantgem and De Does bv, Leiden, Holland.

Lira López, Yamile

1998   La cerámica de "relieve" de Tajín. Paper presented at the XXV Mesa Redonda de la Sociedad Mexicana de Antropolgía, San Luis Potosi, Mexico.

Looper, Matthew G.

1995a   The Sculpture Programs of Butz'-Tiliw, an Eighth-Century Maya King of Quiriguá, Guatemala. Ph.D. dissertation, University of Texas at Austin, Austin.

1995b   The Three Stones of Maya Creation Mythology at Quiriguá. *Mexicon* 17(2):24–30.

1995c   Action, Not Words: Changing Narrative Media in the Terminal Classic at Quiriguá, Guatemala. Paper presented at the 94th Annual Meeting of the American Anthropological Association, November 15–19, Washington, D.C.

2001   Dance Performances at Quirigua. In *Landscape and Power in Ancient Mesoamerica,* edited by Rex Koontz, Kathryn Reese-Taylor, and Annabeth Headrick, pp. 113–135. Westview Press, Boulder, Colorado.

Looper, Matthew G., and Julia Guernsey Kappelman

2000   The Cosmic Umbilicus in Mesoamerica: A Floral Metaphor for the Source of Life. *Journal of Latin American Lore* 21(1):3–54.

López Raquec, Margarita

1989   *Acerca de los alfabetos para escribir los idiomas mayas de Guatemala.* Colección Literatura Guatemalteca Siglo XX, No. 2. Ministerio de Cultura y Deportes, Guatemala City.

Lounsbury, Floyd G.

1982   Astronomical Knowledge and Its Uses at Bonampak. In *Archaeoastronomy in the New World,* edited by Anthony F. Aveni, pp. 143–168. Cambridge University Press, Cambridge.

1983 The Base of the Venus Tables of the Dresden Codex, and Its Significance for the Calendar-Correlation Problem. In *Calendars in Mesoamerica and Peru: Native American Computations of Time,* edited by Anthony F. Aveni and Gordon Brotherston, pp. 1–26. BAR International Series 174. British Archaeological Reports, Oxford.

1989 A Palenque King and the Planet Jupiter. In *World Archaeoastronomy: Selected Papers from the Second Oxford International Conference on Archaeoastronomy,* edited by Anthony F. Aveni, pp. 246–259. Cambridge University Press, Cambridge.

Lowe, Gareth W., Thomas A. Lee Jr., and Eduardo Martínez Espinosa

1982 *Izapa: An Introduction to the Ruins and Monuments.* Papers of the New World Archaeological Foundation 31. New World Archaeological Foundation, Provo, Utah.

Maca, Allan

1999 Ritual Circuits at Copan, Honduras. Paper presented at the 64th Annual Meeting of the Society for American Archaeology, March 24–28, Chicago.

MacLeod, Barbara

1991 Maya Genesis: The First Steps. *North Austin Hieroglyphic Hunches 5.*

1992 Maker, Modeler, Bearer, Begetter: The Paddlers as Chan Its'at. Reprinted in *Notebook for the 16th Maya Hieroglyphic Workshop at Texas. The Group of the Cross at Palenque: A Commentary on Creation.* Department of Art and Art History, College of Fine Arts, and the Institute of Latin American Studies, University of Texas at Austin, Austin.

MacLeod, Barbara, and Dennis E. Puleston

1979 Pathways into Darkness: The Search for the Road to Xibalba. In *Tercera Mesa Redonda de Palenque,* vol. 4, edited by Merle Greene Robertson and Donnan Call Jeffers, pp. 71–77. Pre-Columbian Art Research, Herald Printers, Monterey, California, and Palenque, Chiapas.

Marcus, Joyce

1992 *Mesoamerican Writing Systems: Propaganda, Myth, and History in Four Ancient Civilizations.* Princeton University Press, Princeton.

Martin, Simon, and Nikolai Grube

1995 Maya Superstates. *Archaeology* 48(6):41–46.

Mason, J. Alden

1937 Thrones at Piedras Negras. *Bulletin* 7:18–23. University Museum, University of Pennsylvania.

Masson, Marilyn, and Heather Orr

1998 Writing on the Wall: Political Representation and Sacred Geography at Monte Alban in Programs of Building Dedication, Nahual Transformation, and Captive Sacrifice. In *The Sowing and the Dawning: Termination, Dedication, and Transformation in the Archaeological and Ethnographic Record of*

Mesoamerica, edited by Shirley Boteler Mock, pp. 165–175. University of New Mexico Press, Albuquerque.

Master Study Bible

1981 *New American Standard.* Holman Bible Publishers, Nashville, Tennessee.

Matheny, Ray T.

1989 Early States in the Maya Lowlands during the Late Preclassic Period: Edzna and El Mirador. In *City States of the Maya: Art and Architecture,* edited by Elizabeth P. Benson, pp. 1–44. Rocky Mountain Institute for Pre-Columbian Studies, Denver.

Mathews, Peter

1980 Notes on the Dynastic Sequence of Bonampak, Part I. In *Third Palenque Round Table, 1978,* vol. 4, pt. 2, edited by Merle Greene Robertson, pp. 60–73. University of Texas Press, Austin.

1988 The Sculpture of Yaxchilan. Ph.D. dissertation, Yale University, New Haven.

1991 Classic Maya Emblem Glyphs. In *Classic Maya Political History: Hieroglyphic and Archaeological Evidence,* edited by T. Patrick Culbert, pp. 19–29. Cambridge University Press, Cambridge.

1993 An Introduction to Piedras Negras, Guatemala. In *Proceedings of the Maya Hieroglyphic Weekend.* Cleveland State University, Cleveland.

Mathews, Peter, and Linda Schele

1974 Lords of Palenque: The Glyphic Evidence. In *Primera Mesa Redonda de Palenque,* pt. 1, edited by Merle Greene Robertson, pp. 63–75. Robert Louis Stevenson School, Pebble Beach, California.

Mayer, Branz

1844 *Mexico as It Was and as It Is.* J. Winchester, New World Press, New York.

Mayer, Karl Herbert

1991 *Maya Monuments: Sculptures of Unknown Provenance,* supp. 3. Verlag von Flemming, Berlin.

McAnany, Patricia A.

1995 *Living with the Ancestors: Kinship and Kingship in Ancient Maya Society.* University of Texas Press, Austin.

McCafferty, Sharisse D., and Geoffrey G. McCafferty

1993 Engendering Tomb 7 at Monte Albán. *Current Anthropology* 35(2):143–166.

McDougal, Steven R.

1997 Archaeological Investigations at Ballcourt 2, Dos Hombres, Belize. Master's thesis, Department of Anthropology, University of Cincinnati, Cincinnati.

McGee, R. Jon, and F. Kent Reilly III

1997 Ancient Maya Astronomy and Cosmology in Lacandon Life. *Journal of Latin American Lore* 20(1):125–142.

Meeus, Jean

1997 Stations of Jupiter, Saturn, Venus, and Mars. Unpublished manuscript in the possession of the author.

Milbrath, Susan

1979   *A Study of Olmec Sculptural Chronology.* Studies in Pre-Columbian Art and Archaeology, 23. Dumbarton Oaks, Washington, D.C.

1997   Cross Constellations and Celestial Trees in Classic Maya Iconography. *Pre-columbian Art Research Institute Newsletter* May:3–5.

1999   *Star Gods of the Maya: Astronomy in Art, Folklore, and Calendars.* University of Texas Press, Austin.

Miller, Arthur G.

1974   The Iconography of the Painting in the Temple of the Diving God, Tulum, Quintana Roo, Mexico: The Twisted Cords. In *Mesoamerican Archaeology: New Approaches,* edited by Norman Hammond, pp. 167–186. Duckworth, London.

1986   *Maya Rulers of Time: A Study of Architectural Sculpture at Tikal, Guatemala.* University Museum, University of Pennsylvania, Philadelphia.

Miller, Mary Ellen

1986   *The Murals of Bonampak.* Princeton University Press, Princeton.

Miller, Virginia

1989   Star Warriors at Chichén Itzá. In *Word and Image in Maya Culture: Explorations in Language, Writing, and Representation,* edited by William Hanks and Donald Rice, pp. 287–305. University of Utah Press, Salt Lake City.

Montgomery, John

1994   Sculptors of the Realm: Hieroglyphic Inscriptions and Monumental Art of Piedras Negras Ruler 7. Ph.D. dissertation, University of Texas at Austin, Austin.

1998   The Monuments of Piedras Negras, Guatemala: Stelae. Unpublished manuscript in the possession of the author.

Morley, Sylvanus G.

1920   *The Inscriptions at Copán.* Carnegie Institution of Washington, Washington D.C.

1935   *Guide Book to the Ruins of Quiriguá.* Supplementary Publication 16. Carnegie Institution of Washington, Washington, D.C.

1937–   *The Inscriptions of Peten.* 5 vols. Publication 437. Carnegie Institution of
1938   Washington, Washington, D.C.

1943   Archaeological Investigations of the Carnegie Institution of Washington in the Maya Area of Middle America during the Past Twenty-eight Years. *Proceedings of the American Philosophical Society* 86:208–219. Philadelphia.

1946   *The Ancient Maya.* Stanford University Press, Stanford, California.

Morley, Sylvanus G., George W. Brainerd, and Robert J. Sharer

1983   *The Ancient Maya.* 4th ed. Stanford University Press, Stanford, California.

1997   *Understanding Maya Inscriptions: A Hieroglyph Handbook* 2nd rev. ed. University Museum, University of Pennsylvania, Philadelphia.

Morley, Sylvanus G., and Ralph Roys

1941   *The Xiu Chronicle.* Xiu probanzas and family records (Crónica de Oxkutzcab). Appendix A: Mani land treaty (1557). Appendix B: Family Studies in

Yucatan XIX—XX century names of Xiu descendants. Manuscript on file at Tozzer Library, Harvard University, Cambridge.

Neumann, Franke J.

1988   The Otomí Otontecuhtli and the Mummy Bundle. In *Smoke and Mist: Mesoamerican Studies in Memory of Thelma D. Sullivan,* edited by J. Kathryn Josserand and Karen Dakin, pp. 279–288. BAR International Series 402, pt. 1. British Archaeological Reports, Oxford.

Newsome, Elizabeth

1991   The Trees of Paradise and Pillars of the World: Vision Quest and Creation in the Stelae Cycle of 18-Rabbit-God K, Copan, Honduras. Ph.D. dissertation, University of Texas at Austin, Austin.

1999   Letting the Fire Run: An Observation on Radial Pyramids and Spacio-Temporal Circuits in Maya Katun-ending Rites. Paper presented at the 6th Annual Maya Weekend, October 16–17, University of California at Los Angeles, Los Angeles.

Nicholson, H. B.

1971   Religion in Pre-Hispanic Central Mexico. In *Handbook of Middle American Indians,* vol. 10, edited by Gordon F. Ekholm and Ignacio Bernal, pp. 395–446. University of Texas Press, Austin.

Norman, V. Garth

1973   *Izapa Sculpture.* Papers of the New World Archaeological Foundation No. 30, pt. 1. New World Archaeological Foundation, Provo, Utah.

1976   *Izapa Sculpture.* Papers of the New World Archaeological Foundation No. 30, pt. 2. New World Archaeological Foundation, Provo, Utah.

Nuttall, Zelia

1903   *The Book of the Life of the Ancient Mexicans.* University of California Press, Berkeley.

Oliver, Paul (editor)

1999   *Lifelong and Continuing Education: What Is a Learning Society?* Ashgate Publishers, Aldershot, U.K.

Orr, Heather

1997   Power Games in the Late Formative Valley of Oaxaca: The Ballplayer Carvings at Dainzu. Ph.D. dissertation, Department of Art History, University of Texas at Austin, Austin.

2001   Procession Rituals and Shrine Sites: The Politics of Sacred Space in the Late Formative Valley of Oaxaca. In *Landscape and Power in Ancient Mesoamerica,* edited by Rex Koontz, Kathryn Reese-Taylor, and Annabeth Headrick, pp. 55–79. Westview Press, Boulder, Colorado.

Orrego Corzo, Miguel

1990   *Investigaciones arqueológicas en Abaj Takalik.* Proyecto nacional Abaj Takalik reporte no. 1. Instituto de Antropología e Historia de Guatemala, Ministerio de Cultura y Deportes, Guatemala City.

Palaima, Thomas G., Elizabeth I. Pope, and F. Kent Reilly III

2000 *Unlocking the Secrets of Ancient Writing: The Parallel Lives of Michael Ventris and Linda Schele and the Decipherment of Mycenaean and Mayan Writing.* Thomas G. Palaima for the Program in Aegean Scripts and Prehistory, Austin, Texas.

Paredes Maury, Sofía, María José Gonzáles, and Jorge Cardona

1996 *Vida silvestre en el arte maya de Tikal; Maya Art of Tikal: Flora and Fauna.* Ediciones "Don Quijote," Guatemala City.

Parsons, Lee Allen

1986 *The Origins of Maya Art: Monumental Stone Sculpture of Kaminaljuyu, Guatemala, and the Southern Pacific Coast.* Dumbarton Oaks, Washington, D.C.

Pascual Soto, Arturo

1990 *Iconografía arqueológica de El Tajín.* Universidad Nacional Autónoma de México, Mexico City.

Pasztory, Esther

1972 The Gods of Teotihuacan: A Synthetic Approach in Teotihuacan Iconography. In *Atti del XL Congresso Internazionale degli Americanisti,* vol. 1, pp. 147–159. Rome.

1974 *The Iconography of the Teotihuacan Tlaloc.* Studies in Pre-Columbian Art and Archaeology No. 15. Studies in Pre-Columbian Art and Archaeology No. 28. Dumbarton Oaks, Washington, D.C.

1976 *The Murals of Tepantitla, Teotihuacan.* Garland Publishing, New York.

1983 *Aztec Art.* Harry N. Abrams, New York.

1988 A Reinterpretation of Teotihuacan and Its Mural Painting Tradition. In *Feathered Serpents and Flowering Trees: Reconstructing the Murals of Teotihuacan,* edited by Kathleen Berrin, pp. 45–77. Fine Arts Museums of San Francisco, San Francisco.

1997 *Teotihuacan: An Experiment in Living.* University of Oklahoma Press, Norman.

Peregrine, Peter N., and Gary M. Feinman (editors)

1996 *Pre-Columbian World Systems.* Monographs in World Archaeology No. 26. Prehistory Press, Madison, Wisconsin.

Pohl, Mary

1981 Ritual Continuity and Transformation in Mesoamerica: Reconstructing the Ancient Maya *Cuch* Ceremony. *American Antiquity* 46(3):513–529.

1988 Maya Ritual Faunas: Vertebrate Remains from Burials, Caches, Caves, and Cenotes in the Maya Lowlands. In *Civilizations in the Ancient Americas: Essays in Honor of Gordon Willey,* edited by Richard M. Levanthal and Alan L. Kolata, pp. 55–103. University of New Mexico, Albuquerque, and Peabody Museum of Archaeology and Ethnology, Harvard University, Cambridge.

Porter, James B.

1989 Olmec Colossal Heads as Recarved Thrones: Mutilation, Revolution, and Recarving. *Res: Anthropology and Aesthetics* 17/18:23–30.

1996   A New Olmec Sculpture Type and Its Implication for Epigraphers. In *Beyond Indigenous Voices,* LAILA/ALILA 11th International Symposium on Latin American Indian Literatures (1994), edited by Mary H. Preuss, pp. 65–72. Labyrinthos Press, Culver City, California.

Prater, Ariadne

1989   Kaminaljuyu and Izapan Style Art. In *New Frontiers in the Archaeology of the Pacific Coast of Southern Mesoamerica,* edited by Frederick Bove and Lynette Heller, pp. 125–133. Arizona State University Anthropological Research Papers No. 39. Arizona State University, Tempe.

Proskouriakoff, Tatiana

1946   *An Album of Maya Architecture.* University of Oklahoma Press, Norman.

1950   *A Study of Classic Maya Sculpture.* Publication 593. Carnegie Institution of Washington, Washington, D.C.

1960   Historical Implications of a Pattern of Dates at Piedras Negras, Guatemala. *American Antiquity* 25(4):454–475.

1963   Historical Data in the Inscriptions of Yaxchilan, Part I. *Estudios de Cultura Maya* 3:149–167.

Puleston, Dennis

1983   *The Settlement Survey of Tikal.* Tikal Reports No. 13. University Museum, University of Pennsylvania, Philadelphia.

Pyburn, K. Anne

1998   Consuming the Maya. *Dialectical Anthropology* 23:111–129.

1999   Repudiating Witchcraft. In *Manifesting Power: Gender and the Interpretation of Power in Archaeology,* edited by Tracy L. Sweely, pp. 190–197. Routledge, London.

Quenon, Michel, and Geneviève Le Fort

1997   Rebirth and Resurrection in Maize God Iconography. In *The Maya Vase Book,* vol. 5, edited by Justin Kerr. Kerr Associates, New York.

Quirarte, Jacinto

1973   *Izapan-Style Art: A Study of Its Form and Meaning.* Studies in Pre-Columbian Art and Archaeology No. 10. Dumbarton Oaks, Washington, D.C.

1976   The Relationship of Izapan-Style Art to Olmec and Mayan Art: A Review. In *The Origins of Religious Art and Iconography in Preclassic Mesoamerica,* edited by Henry B. Nicholson, pp. 74–86. UCLA Latin American Center Publications, Los Angeles.

1977   Early Art Styles in Mesoamerica and Early Classic Maya Art. In *Origins of Maya Civilization,* edited by Richard E. W. Adams, pp. 249–283. University of New Mexico Press, Albuquerque.

Reents-Budet, Dorie

1994   *Painting the Maya Universe.* Duke University Press, Durham, North Carolina.

Reese, Kathryn V.

1996   Narrative and Sacred Landscape: Late Formative Civic Center Design at
        Cerros, Belize. Ph.D. dissertation, Department of Anthropology, Univer-
        sity of Texas at Austin, Austin.

Reese-Taylor, Kathryn

1999   Ritual Circuits as Key Factors in the Design of Maya Civic Centers. Paper
        presented at the 64th Annual Meeting of the Society for American Archae-
        ology, March 24–28, Chicago.

Reilly, F. Kent, III

1989   The Shaman in Transformation Pose: A Study of the Theme of Rulership
        in Olmec Art. In *Record of the Art Museum, Princeton University* 48(2):4–21.

1991   Olmec Iconographic Influences on the Symbols of Maya Rulership: An
        Examination of Possible Sources. In *Sixth Palenque Round Table, 1986,* ed-
        ited by Virginia M. Fields, pp. 151–174. University of Oklahoma Press,
        Norman.

1994a   Visions to Another World: Art, Shamanism, and Political Power in Middle
        Formative Mesoamerica. Ph.D. dissertation, Institute of Latin American
        Studies, University of Texas at Austin, Austin.

1994b   Enclosed Ritual Spaces and the Watery Underworld in Formative Period
        Architecture: New Observations on the Function of La Venta Complex A.
        In *Seventh Palenque Round Table, 1989,* vol. 9, volume editor Virginia Fields,
        general editor Merle Greene Robertson, pp. 125–135. Pre-Columbian Art
        Research Institute, San Francisco.

1995   Art, Ritual, and Rulership in the Olmec World. In *The Olmec World: Ritual
        and Rulership,* edited by Jill Guthrie, pp. 26–45. The Art Museum, Prince-
        ton University, Princeton.

1996   The Ritual Function of La Venta: Architecture and Ritual Space as Sacred
        Landscape. Paper presented at the 61st Annual Meeting of the Society for
        American Archaeology, April 11, New Orleans.

1998   Cosmos and Rulership: The Ritual Function of Architecture at the Olmec
        Site of La Venta. Paper presented at the 97th Annual Meeting of the Ameri-
        can Anthropological Association, December 4, Philadelphia.

1999   Mountains of Creation and Underworld Portals: The Ritual Function of
        Olmec Architecture at La Venta, Tabasco. In *Mesoamerican Architecture as a
        Cultural Symbol,* edited by Jeff Karl Kowalski, pp. 14–39. Oxford University
        Press, New York.

Reilly, F. Kent, III, and Linda D. Henderson

1998   Linda Schele (1942–1998). *Art History Newsletter* 5:2–3. Department of Art
        and Art History, University of Texas at Austin, Austin.

RGY

1983   *Relaciones histórico-geográficas de la gobernación de Yucatán* (Mérida, Valladolid y Tabasco). 2 vols. Universidad Nacional Autónoma de México, Mexico City.

Robertson, Merle Greene

1985a   *The Sculpture of Palenque: 2. The Early Buildings of the Palace.* Princeton University Press, Princeton.

1985b   *The Sculpture of Palenque: 3. The Late Buildings of the Palace.* Princeton University Press, Princeton.

1991   *The Sculpture of Palenque: 4. The Cross Group, the North Group, the Olvi-dado, and Other Pieces.* Princeton University Press, Princeton.

Robicsek, Francis

1979   The Mythical Identity of God K. In *Tercera Mesa Redonda de Palenque,* vol. 4, edited by Merle Greene Robertson and Donnan Call Jeffers, pp. 111–128. Pre-Columbian Art Research. Herald Printers, Monterey, California.

Roys, Ralph L.

1933   *The Book of Chilam Balam of Chumayel.* Publication 438. Carnegie Institution of Washington, Washington, D.C.

1965   *Ritual of the Bacabs.* University of Oklahoma Press, Norman.

Roys, Ralph L., and Margaret W. Harrison

1949   Sylvanus Griswold Morley, 1883–1948. *American Antiquity* 3:215–19.

Rust, William F., III

1992   New Ceremonial and Settlement Evidence at La Venta, and Its Relation to Preclassic Maya Culture. In *New Theories on the Ancient Maya,* edited by Elin C. Danien and Robert J. Sharer, pp. 123–130. University Museum, University of Pennsylvania, Philadelphia.

Sahagún, Bernardino de

1950–   *Florentine Codex: General History of the Things of New Spain.* 12 vols. in 13
1982   parts. Translated and edited by Arthur J. O. Anderson and Charles E. Dibble. School of American Research, Sante Fe, and the University of Utah, Salt Lake City.

1993   *Primeros Memoriales: Facsimile Edition.* University of Oklahoma Press,
[1558]   Norman.

1997   *Primeros Memoriales.* Translated by Thelma D. Sullivan. University of Ok-
[1558]   lahoma Press, Norman.

Scarborough, Vernon L.

1980   The Settlement System at a Late Preclassic Maya Community: Cerros, Northern Belize. Ph.D. dissertation, Department of Anthropology, Southern Methodist University, Dallas.

1983a   Raised Field Detection at Cerros, Northern Belize. In *Drained Field Agriculture in Central and South America,* edited by J. P. Darch, pp. 123–136. BAR International Series 189. British Archaeological Reports, Oxford.

1983b   A Preclassic Maya Water System. *American Antiquity* 48:720–744.

1985a   Resourceful Landscaping: A Maya Lesson. *Archaeology* 38:58–59, 72.

1985b Late Preclassic Northern Belize. In *Status, Structure, and Stratification: Current Archaeological Reconstructions,* edited by Marc Thompson, Maria Teresa Garcia, and Francois J. Kense, pp. 331–344. Proceedings of the 16th Annual Chacmool Conference, Archaeological Association, University of Calgary, Calgary.

1991 *Archaeology at Cerros, Belize, Central America. Volume 3: The Settlement System in a Late Preclassic Maya Community.* Southern Methodist University Press, Dallas.

Schele, Linda

1974 Observations on the Cross Motif at Palenque. In *Primera Mesa Redonda de Palenque, Part I,* edited by Merle Greene Robertson. Pre-Columbian Art Research Institute, Robert Louis Stevenson School, Pebble Beach, California.

1976 Accession Iconography of Chan-Bahlum in the Group of the Cross at Palenque. In *The Art, Iconography, and Dynastic History of Palenque, Part III,* edited by Merle Greene Robertson, pp. 9–34. Proceedings of the Segunda Mesa Redonda de Palenque. Robert Louis Stevenson School, Pebble Beach, California.

1977 Palenque: The House of the Dying Sun. In *Native American Astronomy,* edited by Anthony Aveni, pp. 42–56. University of Texas Press, Austin.

1979a The Palenque Triad: A Visual and Glyphic Approach. *Actes du XLIIe Congrès International des Americanistes, 1976,* vol. 7, pp. 407–423. Musée de l'Homme, Paris.

1979b The Puleston Hypothesis: The Water-Lily Complex in Classic Maya Art and Writing. Unpublished manuscript in the possession of the author.

1982 *Maya Glyphs: The Verbs.* University of Texas Press, Austin.

1984a Some Suggested Readings of the Event and Office of Heir-Designate at Palenque. In *Phoneticism in Mayan Hieroglyphic Writing,* edited by John S. Justeson and Lyle Campbell, pp. 287–305. Institute for Mesoamerican Studies Publication No. 9. State University of New York at Albany, Albany.

1984b Human Sacrifice among the Classic Maya. In *Ritual Human Sacrifice in Mesoamerica,* edited by Elizabeth Benson, pp. 7–48. Dumbarton Oaks, Washington, D.C.

1985 Balan-Ahau: A Possible Reading of the Tikal Emblem Glyph and a Title at Palenque. In *Fourth Palenque Round Table, 1980,* vol. 6, volume editor Elizabeth Benson, general editor Merle Greene Robertson, pp. 59–65. Pre-Columbian Art Research Institute, San Francisco.

1986 The Tlaloc Heresy: Cultural Interaction and Social History. Paper presented at Maya Art and Civilization: The New Dynamics, a symposium sponsored by the Kimbell Art Museum, Fort Worth, Texas.

1992 *Notebook for the 16th Maya Hieroglyphic Workshop at Texas. The Group of the*

        Cross at Palenque: A Commentary on Creation. Department of Art and Art History, College of Fine Arts, and the Institute of Latin American Studies, University of Texas at Austin, Austin.

1993   Creation and the Ritual of the Bakabs. *Texas Notes on Precolumbian Art, Writing, and Culture No. 57.* Center for the History of Art of Ancient American Cultures, Art Department, University of Texas at Austin, Austin.

1995a   The Olmec Mountain and Tree of Creation in Mesoamerican Cosmology. In *The Olmec World: Ritual and Rulership,* edited by Jill Guthrie, pp. 105–117. The Art Museum, Princeton University, Princeton.

1995b   The Wars of Hanab-Pakal. Paper presented at the 1995 Mesa Redonda de Palenque, Palenque, Mexico.

1996   History, Writing, and Image in Maya Art. *Art Bulletin* 78(3):412–416.

Schele, Linda, and David Freidel

1990   *A Forest of Kings: The Untold Story of the Ancient Maya.* William Morrow and Company, New York.

Schele, Linda, and Nikolai Grube

1990   The Glyph for Plaza or Court. *Copán Note 86.* Copán Mosaics Project and the Instituto Hondureño de Antropología e Historia, Honduras.

1994a   *Notebook for the 18th Maya Hieroglyphic Workshop at Texas. Tlaloc-Venus Warfare: The Peten Wars 8.17.0.0.0–9.15.13.0.0.* Edited by Timothy Albright. Department of Art and Art History, College of Fine Arts, and the Institute of Latin American Studies, University of Texas at Austin, Austin.

1994b   Notes on the Chronology of Piedras Negras Stela 12. *Texas Notes on Precolumbian Art, Writing, and Culture No. 70.* Center for the History of Art of Ancient American Cultures, Art Department, University of Texas at Austin, Austin.

1995   *Notebook for the 19th Maya Hieroglyphic Workshop at Texas. The Last Two Hundred Years of Classic Maya History: Transmission, Termination, Transformation Post-9.15.0.0.0.* Department of Art and Art History, College of Fine Arts, and the Institute of Latin American Studies, University of Texas at Austin, Austin.

1996   The Workshop for Maya on Hieroglyphic Writing. In *Maya Cultural Activism in Guatemala,* edited by Edward Fischer and R. McKenna Brown, pp. 131–140. University of Texas Press, Austin.

1997   *Notebook for the 21st Maya Hieroglyphic Workshop. The Dresden Codex.* Department of Art and Art History, College of Fine Arts, and the Institute of Latin American Studies, University of Texas at Austin, Austin.

Schele, Linda, and Julia Guernsey Kappelman

2001   What the Heck's Coatepec? In *Landscape and Power in Ancient Mesoamerica,* edited by Rex Koontz, Kathryn Reese-Taylor, and Annabeth Headrick, pp. 29–53. Westview Press, Boulder, Colorado.

Schele, Linda, and Matthew Looper

1996   *Notebook for the 20th Maya Hieroglyphic Forum at Texas. The Inscriptions of Quirigua and Copan.* Department of Art and Art History, College of Fine Arts, and the Institute of Latin American Studies, University of Texas at Austin, Austin.

Schele, Linda, and Peter Mathews

1979   *The Bodega of Palenque, Chiapas, Mexico.* Dumbarton Oaks, Washington, D.C.

1993   *Notebook for the 17th Maya Hieroglyphic Workshop at Texas. The Dynastic History of Palenque.* Department of Art and Art History, College of Fine Arts, and the Institute of Latin American Studies, University of Texas at Austin, Austin.

1998   *The Code of Kings: The Language of Seven Sacred Maya Temples and Tombs.* Scribner, New York.

Schele, Linda, and Jeffrey H. Miller

1983   *The Mirror, the Rabbit, and the Bundle: Accession Expressions from the Classic Maya Inscriptions.* Studies in Pre-Columbian Art and Archaeology No. 25. Dumbarton Oaks, Washington, D.C.

Schele, Linda, and Mary Ellen Miller

1986   *The Blood of Kings: Dynasty and Ritual in Maya Art.* George Braziller, New York.

Schele, Linda, and Khristaan Villela

1996   Creation, Cosmos, and the Imagery of Palenque and Copán. In *Eighth Palenque Round Table, 1993*, vol. 10, volume editors Martha Macri and Jan McHargue, general editor Merle Greene Robertson, pp. 15–30. Pre-Columbian Art Research Institute, San Francisco.

Schellhas, Paul

1904   *Representation of Deities of the Maya Manuscripts.* Papers of the Peabody Museum of Archaeology and Ethnology Vol. 4, No. 1. Peabody Museum of Archaeology and Ethnology, Harvard University, Cambridge.

Schiller, Gertrude

1972   *Iconography of Christian Art.* 2 vols. Translated by Janet Seligman. Lund Humphries, London.

Schmidt, Peter

1999   Chichén Itzá: Resultados y proyectos nuevos (1992–1999). *Arqueología Mexicana* 7(37):32–39.

Seler, Eduard

1960–   *Gesammelte Abhandlungen zur Amerikanischen Sprach- und Altertumskunde.*
1961   5 vols. Akademische Druck-ü. Verlagsanstalt, Graz, Austria.

1963   *Comentarios al Códice Borgia.* 2 vols and facsimile. Fondo de Cultura Económica, Mexico City.

1990– *Collected Works in Mesoamerican Linguistics and Archaeology.* Translation un-
1998 der the supervision of Charles P. Bowditch, vols 1–6, Frank E. Comparato,
general editor. Labyrinthos Press, Lancaster, California.

Sharer, Robert J.

1994 *The Ancient Maya.* 5th edition. Stanford University Press, Stanford, California.

Shook, Edwin M.

1965 Archaeological Survey of the Pacific Coast of Guatemala. In *Handbook of
Middle American Indians,* vol. 2, edited by Gordon R. Willey, pp. 180–194.
University of Texas Press, Austin.

Smith, Virginia G.

1984 *Izapa Relief Carving: Form, Content, Rules for Design, and Role in Mesoamerican Art History and Archaeology.* Studies in Pre-Columbian Art and
Archaeology No. 27. Dumbarton Oaks, Washington, D.C.

Smithe, Frank B., and H. Wayne Trimm

1966 *The Birds of Tikal.* Natural History Press, Garden City, New York.

Son Chonay, Obdulio, Pakal Balam, and José Obispo Rodríguez

1994 *Maya' tz'ib': Introducción a la escritura maya.* Editorial Cholsamaj, Guatemala City.

Spinden, Ellen

1933 The Place of Tajín in Totonac Archaeology. *American Anthropologist* 35:
225–270.

Spinden, Herbert J.

1913 *A Study of Maya Art: Its Subject Matter and Historical Development.* Memoir
No. 6. Peabody Museum of American Archaeology and Ethnology, Harvard University, Cambridge.

Stephens, John Lloyd

1841 *Incidents of Travel in Central America, Chiapas and Yucatan.* 2 vols. Harper
and Brothers, New York.

1843 *Incidents of Travel in Yucatan.* 2 vols. Harper and Brothers, New York.

Stirling, Matthew W.

1943 *Stone Monuments of Southern Mexico.* Smithsonian Institution, Bureau of
American Ethnology Bulletin 138. U.S. Government Printing Office, Washington, D.C.

Stomper, Jeffrey A.

2001 A Model for Late Classic Community Structure at Copán, Honduras.
In *Landscape and Power in Ancient Mesoamerica,* edited by Rex Koontz,
Kathryn Reese-Taylor, and Annabeth Headrick, pp. 197–229. Westview
Press, Boulder, Colorado.

Stone, Andrea

1983 The Zoomorphs of Quirigua, Guatemala. Ph.D. dissertation, University of
Texas at Austin, Austin.

1985   Variety and Transformation in the Cosmic Monster Theme at Quirigua, Guatemala. In *Fifth Palenque Round Table, 1983,* Palenque Round Table Series No. 7, volume editor Virginia Fields, general editor Merle Greene Robertson, pp. 39–48. Pre-Columbian Art Research Institute, San Francisco.

1995a   *Images from the Underworld: Naj Tunich and the Tradition of Maya Cave Painting.* University of Texas Press, Austin.

1995b   The *Nik* Name of the Codical God H. Paper presented at the 94th Annual Meeting of the American Anthropological Association, Washington, D.C.

Stuart, David

1978   Some Thoughts on Certain Occurrences of the T565 Glyph Element at Palenque. In *Tercera Mesa Redonda de Palenque,* vol. 4, edited by Merle Greene Robertson and Donnan Call Jeffers, pp. 167–172. Pre-Columbian Art Research Institute, San Francisco.

1984   Royal Auto-Sacrifice among the Maya. *Res: Anthropology and Aesthetics* 7/8:7–20.

1985   The Inscriptions on Four Shell Plaques from Piedras Negras, Guatemala. In *Fourth Palenque Round Table, 1980,* volume editor Elizabeth P. Benson, general editor Merle Greene Robertson, pp. 175–183. Pre-Columbian Art Research Institute, San Francisco.

1987   *Ten Phonetic Syllables.* Research Reports on Ancient Maya Writing No. 14. Center for Maya Research. Washington, D.C.

1992   The Iconography of Flowers in Maya Art. Paper presented at the 8th Texas Symposium on Maya Hieroglyphic Writing, University of Texas at Austin, Austin.

1996   Kings of Stone: A Consideration of Stelae in Ancient Maya Ritual and Representation. *Res: Anthropology and Aesthetics* 29/30:148–171.

2000   Ritual and History in the Stucco Inscription from Temple XIX at Palenque. *PARI Journal* 1(1):13–19.

Stuart, David, and Stephen Houston

1994   *Classic Maya Place Names.* Studies in Pre-Columbian Art and Archaeology No. 33. Dumbarton Oaks, Washington, D.C.

Stuart, David, Stephen Houston, and John Robertson

1999   Recovering the Past: Classic Maya Language and Classic Maya Gods. In *Notebook for the 23rd Maya Hieroglyphic Forum at Texas,* pp. II-1–96. Department of Art and Art History, College of Fine Arts, and the Institute of Latin American Studies, University of Texas at Austin, Austin.

Stuart, George E.

1992   Quest for Decipherment: A Historical and Bi[bli]ographical Survey of Maya Hieroglyphic Investigation. In *New Theories on the Ancient Maya,* edited by Elin C. Danien and Robert J. Sharer, pp. 1–63. University Museum, University of Pennsylvania, Philadelphia.

Sturm, Circe

1996   Old Writing and New Messages: The Role of Hieroglyphic Literacy in
        Maya Cultural Activism. In *Maya Cultural Activism in Guatemala,* edited
        by Edward Fischer and R. McKenna Brown, pp. 114–130. University of
        Texas Press, Austin.

Sugiyama, Saburo

1993   Worldview Materialized in Teotihuacan, Mexico. *Latin American Antiquity*
        4(2):103–129.

Tate, Carolyn E.

1992   *Yaxchilan: The Design of a Maya Ceremonial City.* University of Texas Press,
        Austin.

1999   Patrons of Shamanic Power: La Venta's Supernatural Entities in Light of
        Mixe Beliefs. *Ancient Mesoamerica* 10(2):169–188.

Taube, Karl A.

1983   The Teotihuacan Spider Woman. *Journal of Latin American Lore* 9(2):
        107–190.

1985   The Classic Maya Maize God: A Reappraisal. In *Fifth Palenque Round
        Table, 1983,* vol. 7, volume editor Virginia Fields, general editor Merle
        Greene Robertson, pp. 171–181. Pre-Columbian Art Research Institute, San
        Francisco.

1986   The Teotihuacan Cave of Origin: The Iconography and Architecture of
        Emergence Mythology in Mesoamerica and the American Southwest. *Res:
        Anthropology and Aesthetics* 12:51–82.

1992   *The Major Gods of Ancient Yucatan.* Studies in Pre-Columbian Art and Ar-
        chaeology No. 32. Dumbarton Oaks, Washington, D.C.

1994   The Birth Vase: Natal Imagery in Ancient Maya Myth and Ritual. In *The
        Maya Vase Book,* vol. 4, edited by Justin Kerr, pp. 652–685. Kerr Associates,
        New York.

1995   The Rainmakers: The Olmec and Their Contribution to Mesoamerican Be-
        lief and Ritual. In *The Olmec World: Ritual and Rulership,* edited by Jill
        Guthrie, pp. 83–104. The Art Museum, Princeton University, Princeton.

1996   The Olmec Maize God: The Face of Corn in Formative Mesoamerica. *Res:
        Anthropology and Aesthetics* 29/30:39–81.

1998   The Jade Hearth: Centrality, Rulership, and the Classic Maya Temple. In
        Function and Meaning in Classic Maya Architecture, edited by Stephen D.
        Houston, pp. 427–478. Dumbarton Oaks, Washington, D.C.

Tedlock, Barbara

1982   *Time and the Highland Maya.* University of New Mexico Press, Albu-
        querque.

Tedlock, Dennis

1985   *Popol Vuh: The Definitive Edition of the Maya Book of the Dawn of Life and
        the Glories of Gods and Kings.* Simon and Schuster, New York.

1992   Myth, Math, and the Problem of Correlation in Mayan Books. In *The Sky in Mayan Literature,* edited by Anthony F. Aveni, pp. 247–273. Oxford University Press, Oxford.

Tezozómoc, Fernando Alvarado

1878   *Crónica mexicana.* Impr. y. litog. de I. Paz, Mexico.

1992   *Crónica mexicáyotl.* Translated by Adrián León. Universidad Nacional Autónoma de México, Mexico City.

Thompson, J. Eric S.

1930   *Ethnology of the Mayas of Southern and Central British Honduras.* Anthropological Series 2. Field Museum of Natural History, Chicago.

1954   *The Rise and Fall of Maya Civilization,* University Oklahoma Press, Norman.

1960   *Maya Hieroglyphic Writing: An Introduction.* 3rd ed. University of Oklahoma Press, Norman.

1962   *A Catalog of Maya Hieroglyphs.* University of Oklahoma Press, Norman.

1970   *Maya History and Religion.* University of Oklahoma Press, Norman.

1972   *A Commentary on the Dresden Codex.* Memoirs Vol. 93. American Philosophical Society, Philadelphia.

Toor, Frances

1947   *A Treasury of Mexican Folkways.* Crown, New York.

Townsend, Richard F.

1992   *The Aztecs.* Thames and Hudson, London.

Tozzer, Alfred M.

1907   *A Comparative Study of the Mayas and the Lacandones.* Archaeological Institute of America, Macmillan, London.

1941   *Landa's Relación de las Cosas de Yucatán: A Translation.* Papers of the Peabody Museum of Archaeology and Ethnology Vol. 18. Peabody Museum of Archaeology and Ethnology, Harvard University, Cambridge.

1957   *Chichen Itza and Its Cenote of Sacrifice.* Memoirs of the Peabody Museum, vols. 11 and 12. Peabody Museum of Archaeology and Ethnology, Harvard University, Cambridge.

Underwood, Paul A.

1950   The Fountain of Life in Manuscripts of the Gospels. *Dumbarton Oaks Papers* 5:80. Washington, D.C.

Usher, Robin, and Ian Bryant (editors)

1989   *Adult Education as Theory, Practice, and Research: The Captive Triangle.* Routledge, London.

Villacorta, J. Antonio, and Carlos A. Villacorta

1977   *Códices mayas.* 2nd ed. Tipografía Nacional, Guatemala City.

Villa Rojas, Alfonso

1934   *The Yaxuna-Coba Causeway.* Carnegie Institution of Washington Publication 436, Contribution to American Archaeology No. 9. Carnegie Institution, Washington, D.C.

Vogt, Evon Z.

1968   Some Aspects of Zinacantan Settlement Patterns and Ceremonial Organization. In *Settlement Archaeology,* edited by K. C. Chang, pp. 154–175. National Press Books, Palo Alto, California.

1969   *Zinacantan: A Maya Community in the Highlands of Chiapas.* Belknap Press of Harvard University, Cambridge.

1988   Indian Crosses and Scepters: The Results of Circumscribed Spanish-Indian Interactions in Mesoamerica. Paper prepared for the symposium "Word and Deed: Interethnic Images and Responses in the New World," December 12–16, Trujillo, Spain.

1994   *Fieldwork among the Maya: Reflection on the Harvard University Chiapas Project.* University of New Mexico Press, Albuquerque.

von Winning, Hasso

1987   *La iconografía de Teotihuacán: los dioses y los signos.* 2 vols. Universidad Nacional Autónoma de México, Mexico City.

Wald, Robert

1993   The Names and Times of Ruler 3, His Wife and His Father: Selected Texts from Piedras Negras. Unpublished manuscript in the possession of the author.

1997   The Politics of Art and History at Palenque: Interplay of Text and Iconography on the Tablet of the Slaves. *Texas Notes on Precolumbian Art, Writing, and Culture No. 80.* Center for the History of Art of Ancient American Cultures, Art Department, University of Texas at Austin, Austin.

Waldeck, J. F.

1838   *Voyage pittoresque et archéologique dans la province d'Yucatan (Amerique Centrale), pendant les années 1834 et 1836.* Bellizard Dufour et Cie, Paris.

Walker, Debra S.

1990   Cerros Revisited: Ceramic Indicators of Terminal Classic and Postclassic Settlement and Pilgrimage in Northern Belize. Ph.D. dissertation, Department of Anthropology, Southern Methodist University, Dallas.

1996   Religion and Trade in Postclassic Yukatan: The Material Evidence from Chetumal Province. Paper presented at the 61st Annual Meeting of the Society for American Archaeology, April 10–14, New Orleans.

Wallace, Anthony F. C.

1956   Revitalization Movements. *American Anthropologist* 58:264–281.

Warren, Kay B.

1998   *Indigenous Movements and Their Critics: Pan-Maya Activism in Guatemala.* Princeton University Press, Princeton.

Watson, Arthur

1934   *The Early Iconography of the Tree of Jesse.* Oxford University Press, London.

Wedel, Waldo R.

1952   *Structural Investigations in 1943 in La Venta, Tabasco: A Study of Olmec Ce-*

ramics and Art. Smithsonian Institution, Bureau of American Ethnology Bulletin No. 153. U.S. Government Printing Office, Washington, D.C.

Weiss, Pamela

1995   Structure 4 Excavations. In *Archaeological Research at Blue Creek, Belize: Progress Report of the Third (1994) Field Season,* edited by Thomas H. Guderjan and W. David Driver, pp. 46–61. St. Mary's University, San Antonio, Texas.

1996   The Continuation of Excavations at Structure 4. In *Archaeological Research at Blue Creek, Belize: Progress Report of the Fourth (1995) Field Season,* edited by Thomas H. Guderjan, W. David Driver, and Helen Haines, pp. 35–42. St. Mary's University, San Antonio, Texas.

Wheatley, Paul

1971   *The Pivot of the Four Corners.* Aldine, Chicago.

Wilk, Richard

1985   The Ancient Maya and the Political Present. *Journal of Anthropological Research* 41(3):307–326.

Wilkerson, S. Jeffrey K.

1984   In Search of the Mountain of Foam: Human Sacrifice in Eastern Mesoamerica. In *Ritual Human Sacrifice in Mesoamerica,* edited by Elizabeth H. Boone, pp. 101–132. Dumbarton Oaks, Washington, D.C.

1990   El Tajín: Great Center of the Northeast. In *Mexico: Splendors of Thirty Centuries,* pp. 155–185. Metropolitan Museum of Art, New York.

Willey, Gordon, and Jeremy Sabloff

1993   *A History of American Archaeology.* 3rd ed. Thames and Hudson, London.

Wisdom, Charles

1950   Materials on the Chorti Language. Microfilm Collection of Manuscript Materials on Middle American Cultural Anthropology, Fifth Series, No. 28. University of Chicago, Chicago.

Wren, Linnea, and Lynn Foster

1995   Ritual Space and Ritual Dance at Chichén Itzá, Yucatan, Mexico. Paper presented at the 94th Annual Meeting of the American Anthropological Society, November 15–19, Washington, D.C.

Yasugi, Yoshiho, and Kenji Saito

1991   *Glyph Y of the Maya Supplemental Series.* Research Reports on Ancient Maya Writing No. 34. Center for Maya Research, Washington, D.C.

Zender, Marc

1998   Sak-Tz'i': Lost City of the Ancient Maya (Found?). Paper delivered at the Vernon Museum, April 4, Vernon, British Columbia, Canada.

1999   Diacritical Markers and Underspelling in the Classic Maya Script: Implications for Decipherment. Master's thesis, Department of Archaeology, University of Calgary, Calgary.

Contributors

Anthony F. Aveni is Russell B. Colgate Professor of Astronomy and Anthropology at Colgate University. He works primarily in the history of astronomy and the study of calendars of the world, especially those in Mesoamerica and is, most recently, the author of *Skywatchers* (University of Texas Press, 2000), a revised and updated version of *Skywatchers of Ancient Mexico*.

Elizabeth P. Benson, a research associate of the Institute of Andean Studies, Berkeley, California, is now writing a book on the Moche culture of the north coast of Peru. Her most recent published book is *Birds and Beasts of Ancient Latin America* (University Press of Florida, 1997). She is coeditor of *Ritual Sacrifice in Ancient Peru* (University of Texas Press, 2001).

Michael D. Coe is Charles J. MacCurdy Professor of Anthropology Emeritus, Yale University. The author of many books on the Olmec and Maya civilizations, he is currently writing a general culture history of the Khmer empire of Cambodia.

Constance Cortez is assistant professor of art history at Santa Clara University in California. She studies and writes about the Precolumbian and Colonial visual culture of Mesoamerica as well as about contemporary Chicano/Chicana art.

As the public programs coordinator of the University of Pennsylvania Museum of Archaeology and Anthropology, **Elin Danien** created their annual Maya Weekends. On several occasions Linda followed her Texas Meetings with appearances in Philadelphia. Danien is now a research associate in the American Section of the Penn Museum and is writing a biography of Robert Burkitt.

Duncan Earle is associate professor of anthropology, sociology, and Chicano studies at the University of Texas at El Paso. He has spent more than a quarter century studying the contemporary Maya of highland Guatemala and Chiapas,

Mexico. Currently, he is carrying out community dynamics and development research in the borderlands region of Chiapas and finishing a book on the U.S.-Mexico border, where he resides.

Federico Fahsen is currently the epigrapher for the Cancuen archaeological project with support from Vanderbilt and Del Valle Universities. His most recent publications deal with the dynastic sequence of Uaxactun written in collaboration with Juan Antonio Valdés and "The Origin of Highland Maya States" in *Maya Kingdoms in the Jungle* edited by Nikolai Grube (Könemann Verlag, 2000).

David Freidel is professor of anthropology at Southern Methodist University. He is coauthor of two books with Linda Schele, *A Forest of Kings* (William Morrow, 1990) and *Maya Cosmos* (William Morrow, 1993). He has carried out research on the ancient Maya in Belize and Mexico and is planning research in Guatemala.

Gillett Griffin is faculty curator of Precolumbian art at the Art Museum, Princeton University, and also serves as lecturer in the Department of Art and Archaeology. His primary field of research is Preclassic Mesoamerica, with an emphasis on highland Olmec. Since the early 1970s, he shared a close friendship with Linda Schele.

Nikolai Grube is Linda and David Schele Chair for the Art and Writing of Mesoamerica at the University of Texas at Austin. His research and publications focus on Maya hieroglyphic writing and history as well as on contemporary Maya ethnography and ethnolinguistics. Grube collaborated with Schele at Copan and other archaeological sites in Mesoamerica and taught workshops with her in Mexico and Guatemala.

Annabeth Headrick is an assistant professor of art history at Vanderbilt University and was a student of Linda Schele's at the University of Texas at Austin. She is currently writing a book about the sociopolitical structure of Teotihuacan.

Julia Guernsey Kappelman is assistant professor in Precolumbian art in the Department of Art and Art History at the University of Texas at Austin and is currently writing a book on Late Preclassic Izapan sculpture. She was one of Linda Schele's last doctoral students to complete her degree and had the privilege of team-teaching with her after Schele became ill.

David Kelley is professor emeritus of archaeology at the University of Calgary, Alberta. He worked with Linda on the Palenque inscriptions. He wrote *Decipher-*

ing the Maya Script (University of Texas Press, 1976) and is preparing *Exploring Ancient Skies,* with Gene Milone, for publication.

Rex Koontz is assistant professor in the Department of Art at the University of Houston. His most recent publication is the volume *Landscape and Power in Ancient Mesoamerica* (Westview Press, 2001), edited with Kathryn Reese-Taylor and Annabeth Headrick.

Matthew G. Looper is assistant professor in the Department of Art and Art History at California State University at Chico. He is the author of *Gifts of the Moon: Huipil Designs of the Ancient Maya* (San Diego Museum of Man, 2000).

Barbara MacLeod is an independent scholar in Austin, Texas, who specializes in linguistic approaches to Maya hieroglyphic decipherment. When not engaged in epigraphic research, she manages a flight school and teaches aerobatics in Austin.

Susan Milbrath is curator of Latin American art and archaeology at the Florida Museum of Natural History and affiliate professor of anthropology at the University of Florida. Her research focuses on Mesoamerican archaeoastronomy, especially the visual images relating to astronomy. She also is conducting research on Postclassic Maya art and archeology. Her most recent book is *Star Gods of the Maya: Astronomy in Art, Folklore, and Calendars* (University of Texas Press, 1999).

Mary Ellen Miller is the Vincent Scully Professor of the History of Art at Yale University and master of Saybrook College. She and Linda Schele wrote *The Blood of Kings* together in 1985. Her most recent book is *Maya Art and Architecture* (Thames and Hudson, 1999).

Dorie Reents-Budet is a research associate at the Smithsonian Center for Materials Research and Education, Museum Support Center, Smithsonian Institution. She is a specialist in ancient Maya culture, and her book *Painting the Maya Universe* (Duke University Press, 1994) has become a prime text on Maya painted ceramics. She is the second student to receive a Ph.D. under the supervision of Linda Schele at the University of Texas at Austin.

Kathryn Reese-Taylor is an assistant professor of Maya archaeology at the University of Calgary, Alberta. She was graduated from the University of Texas at Austin in 1996 and was one of the few archaeology students who trained extensively with Linda Schele. She specializes in landscape studies and the ideology of power among the ancient Maya. She is coeditor of *Landscape and Power in Ancient Mesoamerica* (Westview Press, 2001).

F. Kent Reilly III is an associate professor of anthropology at the University of Memphis and director of the Chucalissa Archaeological Museum. He works primarily on the iconographic systems of Mesoamerica, in particular the Olmec symbol system. He was a guest curator for Princeton University's exhibition *Olmec: Ritual and Rulership* and is the coauthor (with Julia Kappelman) of "Paths to Heaven, Ropes to Earth: Birds, Jaguars, and Cosmic Cords in Formative Period Mesoamerica," *Ancient America* 1, no. 2 (January 2001).

Merle Greene Robertson is the chairman of the board of the Pre-Columbian Art Research Institute in San Francisco. She is author of the four-volume set *The Sculpture of Palenque* (Princeton University Press, 1983–1991). She is currently director of the Proyecto Grupo de las Cruces, investigating the archaeology of Palenque, Mexico.

David Schele is a registered architect practicing in Austin, Texas, and the husband of Linda Schele. In his spare time he is helping the Foundation for the Advancement of Mesoamerican Studies, Inc., to make Linda's drawings and slide collection available on the FAMSI web site.

Andrea Stone is professor of art history at the University of Wisconsin–Milwaukee. In 1983 she became the first student to receive a doctoral degree under Linda Schele's supervision. Specializing in Central American rock art and Maya iconography, she is author of *Images from the Underworld: Naj Tunich and the Tradition of Maya Cave Painting* (University of Texas Press, 1995).

Marc Zender is a doctoral candidate in the Department of Archaeology at the University of Calgary, Alberta. He is the author of several articles on Maya archaeology, epigraphy, and linguistics and is coauthor (with Peter Mathews and Stan Guenter) of *The History and Archaeology of Palenque,* a book forthcoming from the Pre-Columbian Art Research Institute.

Index